A History of
Women's Boxing

A History of
Women's Boxing

Malissa Smith

ROWMAN & LITTLEFIELD
Lanham • Boulder • New York • Toronto • Plymouth, UK

Published by Rowman & Littlefield
4501 Forbes Boulevard, Suite 200, Lanham, Maryland 20706
www.rowman.com

10 Thornbury Road, Plymouth PL6 7PP, United Kingdom

British Library Cataloguing in Publication Information Available

Library of Congress Cataloging-in-Publication Data

Smith, Malissa.
A history of women's boxing / Malissa Smith.
pages cm
Includes bibliographical references and index.
ISBN 978-1-4422-2994-5 (cloth : alk. paper) — ISBN 978-1-4422-2995-2 (ebook)
1. Women boxers. 2. Boxing—History. I. Title.
GV1136.3.S55 2014
796.83—dc23
2014001827

Printed in the United States of America

For Jed and Izzi, with my love.

Contents

Acknowledgments

The genesis for writing *A History of Women's Boxing* came out of my love for the sport and the women I have come to know who perfect their craft, boxing, from the wee hours of the morning before work, till late at night after their obligations for the day are done.

A few years ago, I applied to graduate school to pursue a master's degree in liberal studies at the State University of New York's Empire State College (ESC). The beauty of the program was it allowed me to "tickle" my academic fancy. I'd also started a blog called *Girlboxing* by then with stories about women's boxing and personal experiences related to the sport.

In my second year at ESC, I began to hone in on my thesis topic with my mentor, Dr. Elana Michelson. After a lot of soul searching, I had one of those eureka moments and decided to write about women's boxing. There was some wonderful scholarship that had already been published by Jennifer Hargreaves, Carlo Rotella, and others, but the topic was ripe for exploration. With encouragement, assistance, and insights from my thesis advisor, Dr. Peggy Quinn, and the continued mentoring and intellectual challenges offered by Elana, I was able to successfully complete my master's thesis, entitled *Boundaries in Motion: Women's Boxing*.

Doing the research for the thesis, I discovered that there was no one source that had even attempted to explore the history of women's boxing—a rich, textured, and multilayered chronicle that began in the 1720s in England and continues to unfold to this day all around the world.

Writing this work has been fraught with the kinds of dilemmas all historians face when it comes to choosing what constitutes history. All I can do is issue an apology for any aspects of the sport I may have missed that other scholars and enthusiasts of women's boxing feel I was an idiot to not have included in this work. I am particularly sensitive to those athletes who practiced the sport beginning in the 1950s on through today's athletes who may feel slighted by my lack of inclusion, or for perhaps giving too little to their place in the history, or for perhaps presenting facts they feel should have been expanded upon or been more nuanced in their presentation.

While I tried my hardest to fact-check each instance through meticulous research and confirmation of information, the written record has been difficult if not impossible to obtain in many cases. Still, I shall be chagrined if an inaccuracy has found its way onto the printed page that was not couched in language that called into question the complete veracity of the account.

In this endeavor I have also had the invaluable assistance of many people. Foremost has been Bruce Silverglade, owner of Gleason's Gym. His generosity, which has extended to providing me a place to write portions of this book, has been nothing short of incredible. He has also been giving with his time, allowing me to interview him extensively on the topic of contemporary women's boxing, as well as giving me several of the files he maintained on the sport that included original notes, photographs, and other documentation. I shall forever be in his debt for his assistance.

No book on women's boxing could ever be written without the assistance and acknowledgment of Sue TL Fox and her remarkable website, Women Archive Boxing Network (WBAN). Sue's website is a treasure trove of information and documentation on women's boxing from the 1970s on, with additional information on women's boxing that stretches as far back as the 1720s. She has also been an inspiration to the fighters she so lovingly chronicles, providing a nexus point for communication and information about the sport.

Photographers Mary Ann Owen and Sue Jaye Johnson have also been remarkably generous in their support of this work. Both have allowed me to troll through their remarkable photographs of contemporary practitioners of the sport, some of which have been included in the book.

Mary Ann has been photographing athletes since the late 1990s as a photographer for *Lady Boxer* magazine and continues to this day as one of boxing's premier photographers. Sue's contributions to the sport have been in her chronicling of the United States' first Olympic women's boxing trials and, in particular, Claressa Shields, who brought home the first gold medal to have ever been awarded to a female middleweight.

Professional and amateur female boxers Alicia Ashley, Bonnie Canino, Jill Emory, Gina M. Giudi, Deirdre Gogarty, Jen Hamann, Chevelle Hallback, Dee Hamaguchi, Heather Hardy, Melissa Hernandez, Ana Julaton, Sonya Lamonakis, Keisha McLeod-Wells, Michel Perlstein, Asa Sandell, Claressa Shields, Queen Underwood, Tricia Arcaro Turton, Shelito Vincent, and Kaliesha West have provided me with invaluable insight into their lives as fighters and the challenges they have faced in the sport. I am also indebted to my trainer, Lennox Blackmoore, for his perspectives on training women to box whether as amateurs or professionals.

Boxing writers (and in some instances former fighters themselves) Sarah Deming, Cory Erdman, Mark A. Jones, Binnie Klien, Mischa Merz, Jill Morley, Michael O'Neill, Marq Piocos, Rachel Ruiz, Kate Sekules, and Michael Rivest have all been overly generous with the time they have given me—including endless hours of conversation, Twitter messages, and Facebook posts on the sport that may have bordered on tedium. Michael O'Neill in particular provided invaluable assistance when researching the Olympics.

I am particularly grateful to Dr. Cathy Van Ingen, Dr. Benita Heiskanen, and Dr. Anju Reejhsinghani, who put in the painstaking work to host Fighting Women: A Symposium on Women's Boxing, the first scholarly conference on the sport, held in Toronto, Canada, on June 21–22, 2012. Their forum gave me the opportunity to present some of my work on the topic—and their gracious support of the project and helpful insights were greatly appreciated.

Research on the topic proved particularly challenging. Thankfully, I was given access to the Brooklyn College Library Archives and the Hank Kaplan Boxing Archive, and in particular I want to thank Jahongir Usmanov and Edythe Rosenblatt for their resourcefulness and assistance, especially making hundreds of Xerox copies.

My editors at Rowman & Littlefield have also afforded me invaluable support. Christen Karniski guided me through the preparation of the book for publication, including huge assistance editing an overly long manuscript. Kellie Hagan, my production editor, also provided invaluable assistance—and I could not possibly have written the book without her expert guidance and editorial expertise.

My friend Myles Ashby also took on the task of searching through digital photo libraries to assist me in locating images to add to the book and spent many hours helping me negotiate the ins and outs of photo licensing. I truly could not have done it without him.

This work also could not have been completed without the incalculable assistance of my husband, Jed Stevenson, whose brilliant, patient, and painstaking editing of the manuscript (while maintaining our marriage and keeping our household going) has been a testament to his skill, his fortitude, and his love. As a white-collar boxer and boxing aficionado himself, he also brought insights from the male perspective that proved very helpful.

My daughter, Izzi Stevenson's, enthusiasm, perceptive commentary, and warm embraces have also been of immense help as I labored on this book—particularly when she shepherded her friends in and around the living room where "Mom" was working.

My friends Patti and Pren Claflin have been wonderful boosters of the writing process—and provided me with my own personal writer's retreat at their lovely home in Vermont. Barry Greenspan was also very understanding of the time I needed to write when he approved my last-minute vacation days at the end of the project. At the end of the project, Nadia Jaber was a whiz at solving the problems of indexing.

Most of all, I am indebted to the thousands of women who have lifted up their fists to practice the sweet science. Their strength, dedication, and fortitude in the face of tremendous odds has been a source of continued inspiration—and it is for them that I have worked to assiduously and accurately depict their history.

Acronyms and Abbreviations

AAU	American Amateur Association
AIBA	International Amateur Boxing Association
BBBC	British Boxing Board of Control
GBU	Global Boxing Union
IBA	International Boxing Association
IBC	International Boxing Council
IBHOF	International Boxing Hall of Fame
IBU	Irish Boxing Union
IFBA	International Female Boxing Association
IWBA	International Women's Boxing Association
IWBF	International Women's Boxing Federation
IWPBA	International Women's Professional Boxing Association
LCC	London County Council
MMA	Mixed Martial Arts
NAC	Nevada Athletic Commission
NBA	National Boxing Association
NWA	National Wrestling Association
NYSAC	New York State Athletic Commission
PAL	Police Athletic League
PNABA	Pacific Northwest Amateur Boxing Association

SAC	California State Athletic Commission
TKO	Technical Knock Out
UFC	Ultimate Fighting Championship
USABA	USA Boxing Association
VFA	Variety Artists' Federation
WBAN	Women Boxing Archive Network
WBB	Women's Boxing Board
WBC	World Boxing Council
WBF	Women's Boxing Federation
WBO	World Boxing Organization
WIBA	Women's International Boxing Association
WIBF	Women's International Boxing Federation
WIBO	Women's International Boxing Organization
WWBA	Women's World Boxing Association

Introduction

I am proud to be part of the movement that opened up women's boxing at the amateur and professional level. [1]
—Sonya Lamonakis, heavyweight pro boxer, Golden Gloves champion

As an eleven-year-old growing up in Flint, Michigan, Claressa Shields didn't really dare to dream about boxing in the Olympics. That was in 1995. Women had won the right to box as amateurs only two years before, and Olympic competition seemed a world away. When her trainer asked her why she wanted to take up boxing, she said simply, "I'm just tired of losing." [2]

Over the years she gained confidence and the skills that culminated in her winning the 2011 National PAL Middleweight Championship. Her triumph led to a berth in the first-ever women's USA Boxing Olympic Trials Championships, where the then sixteen-year-old defeated all comers to become the first women's USA Boxing Olympic Trials champion in the history of her division.

What was even more remarkable was that the then seventeen-year-old became the first American woman in history to win a gold medal at the Olympics for boxing in one of the three weight categories open to women at the 2012 London Games.

Claressa Shields's teammate, the Texas-born Marlen Esparza, began boxing at eleven, too, picking up the gloves as a troubled young girl and eventually winning her first USA Boxing National Championship at barely sixteen years of age—all while earning straight As in school.

Continuing to both box and excel in her schooling, Marlen Esparza became the reigning 2012 USA Boxing Women's Flyweight champion at the age of twenty-two. She went on to capture the first USA Boxing Olympic Trials title in her division and holds a record-breaking six consecutive national championships—but her accolades do not stop there.

Her most important accomplishment has been to make history as the first female USA boxing team member to qualify for the Olympic Games, an honor she says is "a big step—not really just for boxing, but for women in general."[3]

More amazingly, she walked away with the first-ever bronze medal in boxing for women by an American. In early 2014, she also captured her record-breaking eighth national title.

The third woman to represent the United States at the London 2012 Games was Queen Underwood, a lightweight boxer from Seattle, Washington, who overcame adversity to reach the pinnacle of amateur sports. While she did not medal, she proudly won the right to represent the United States when she won the lightweight championship at the Olympic trials. She had also been a USA boxing national champion with a superb record of accomplishment inside the squared circle.

The road to the pantheon of amateur sports—the Olympics—has been paved by the hard work, dedication, and passion of countless women over the centuries who have each made a contribution to the sport they love whether as practitioners, spectators, trainers, managers, referees, judges, or writers.

Much is owed to these women, and while Claressa Shields, Marlen Esparza, and Queen Underwood each shared in the glory of the 2012 Summer Games, they are the living continuum of a dream of Olympic greatness first begun in St. Louis in the 1904 Games when a handful of women put on a demonstration of their fistic prowess in accordance with the prevailing Marquis of Queensbury rules.

One more recent heroine of the boxing world is Christy "The Coal Miner's Daughter" Martin, whose legendary battle against Deirdre "Dangerous" Gogarty in 1996 landed Christy on the cover of *Sports Illustrated* and put women's boxing on the map—having already been the first woman signed by the notorious boxing promoter Don King.

Other recent pioneers in the sport, such as Barbara "The Mighty Atom of the Ring" Buttrick, who began her career fighting in carnival boxing shows in the late 1940s and 1950s, are less well-known but part of a long line of pugilist females who have plied their trade since the first documented women's boxing encounter in 1722. An advertisement that year placed in the *London Journal* read:

Challenge

I, Elizabeth Wilkinson, of Clerkenwell, having had some words with Hannah Hayfield and requiring satisfaction, do invite her to meet me on the Stage, and box with me for three guineas, each woman holding half a crown in each hand, and the first woman that drops her money to lose the battle.

Answer

> I, Hannah Hayfield, of Newgate Market, hearing of the resoluteness of Eliza-
> beth Wilkinson, will not fail, *God willing*, to give her more blows than
> words—desiring home blows, and from her, no favor; She may expect a good
> thumping.[4]

Women of the ring have fought for gold guineas, butter dishes, a percentage
of the ticket sales, and championship titles, but have mostly come into the
game for nothing more than their love of boxing—a sport that tests their will,
their courage, and even their right to cross the velvet ropes into what has
historically been considered a male-only domain.

What is surprising to many is the rich and grand tradition of earlier
martial women rooted in the writings of Homer, Plutarch, and Herodotus,
who gave us wonderful mythological tales and historical interpretations of
Greek goddesses and Amazons. Herodotus famously wrote:

> When the Greeks were at war with the Amazons (whom the Scythians call
> Oiorpata, a name signifying in our tongue killers of men, for in Scythian a man
> is "oior" and to kill is "pata"), the story runs that after their victory on
> the Thermodon they sailed away carrying in three ships as many Amazons as
> they had been able to take alive; and out at sea the Amazons attacked the crews
> and killed them.[5]

Whether as young Spartan girls who wrestled and boxed for exercise against
boys or the mythic character Atalanta who famously wrestled Peleus at King
Pelius's funeral games, on through the exploits of the goddesses Athena and
Artemis—not to mention the Amazon "race"—these classical images dem-
onstrate that women have been imagined as warriors throughout history.

Since antiquity there have been frequent flurries of female participation in
the martial arts—instances that are often at the margins of history and yet can
be found by teasing out the little bits of evidence that lie in old manuscripts,
works of art, newspaper clippings, and the overstuffed file cabinets of collections of boxing memorabilia that reveal handbills and dusty photographs of
female fighters from bygone eras. These documents include the late 13th- or
early 14th-century folio page from the famed Tower manuscript of women
learning to sword fight.

English ballads beginning in the mid-17th century spoke of female sailors
and soldiers who, donning the clothes of young men, sought their fortunes
for adventure, fealty, or in pursuit of their sweethearts.

While a lot of the history of female martial efforts has yet to be uncovered, as far back as the early 18th century, women such as Elizabeth Wilkinson and Hannah Hyfield have plied their trade as professional and amateur
boxers. Sporting names such as "The Ass-Driver from Stoke Newington" or
"The Market Woman," what comes down to us is not only the flavor of the
times, but also the sense of these oft-referred to viragos and Amazons as

working women, with ring aliases not so different from modern ones such as "The Coal Miner's Daughter" or "The Preacher's Daughter."

Conveying the poetic musings of the ring, they add a statement of implicit pedigree, whether as a denizen of a trade or, in the case of more contemporary fighters, as part of a long line of proud working people exhibiting profound familial pride.

Women who box intuit that donning the gloves—whether as regulars of amateur fight nights in the local gym, tacky Vegas-style casinos, or fighting off the recently defeated call for amateur boxers to wear skirts in competition—means they are free to create their own identities. These self-made monikers have less to do with whether it's "okay" to fight if you're a "girl" and more to do with finding their own reserves of courage and strength as they engage in what is lovingly referred to by practitioners and fans as the "sweet science."

Boxing by its very nature is a pas de deux of defensive and offensive posturing played out with all of the improvisational skills of a jazz musician. To find oneself in the ring at all, as on the stage of a music hall, is a testament to years of repetitive labor for the opportunity to perform for an audience. And just as musicians will riff and trill off the lines of a melody, so will a boxer begin with a jab and a straight right before finding the best angles of offense and defense to overcome an opponent.

As with music, such actions can come in great spurts of creative, aggressive posturing or quiet, defensive moments. Aggression, however, is clearly harnessed to the repertoire of movements available to a skilled fighter who seeks out all opportunity and advantage in the ring in order to win.

The harnessing of such skill and power for women who box today is not so much a new arena as an old one rediscovered, given that women have labored at boxing regularly since the 18th century. These noteworthy fighters have weighed the balance sheet of boxing as one of physical capital against the potential loss and have continued to box. They have also balanced the social costs and nonetheless still push at the ropes of the ring for a place inside its vaulted canvas.

In describing the boxing gym, writer and amateur women's boxing champion Mischa Merz wrote about seeing the women fighters at Gleason's Gym for the first time. Her perspective perhaps shines a light on what it means for women when they pick up the gloves.

> And here they were, neither subverting nor perverting masculinity or femininity, nor bringing the sport into disrepute. The women inhabited Gleason's as if they'd always been there. And any questions about their right to be there would be met with bewildered silence from the men I asked, as if the suggestion were weird, like asking if women should be allowed to wear trousers.[6]

The complex history of female boxing has many starting points. In the United States one such beginning is on March 17, 1876. As reported in no less a newspaper than the *New York Times*, a match was set between two variety dancers—Miss Nell Saunders and Miss Rose Harland—for the tidy sum of $200 and a piece of silver-plate that was purportedly a butter dish. The match was set at the world-famous Henry Hill's concert saloon, a veritable institution of the "swell set" on Houston Street in lower Manhattan with the *New York Times* reporting both women "at once went into training—Miss Saunders under the tuition of her husband, while James Kelly gave Miss Harland lessons in the pugilistic art."[7]

Over the next thirty years, women's boxing took hold with more and more women appearing in matches at Henry Hill's where world championship titles were bestowed under the auspices of Richard K. Fox's *National Police Gazette* newspaper. The action branched out across the country onto early vaudeville stages and became a feature of variety shows in places stretching from Kansas City to San Francisco.

Women's boxing even appeared in one of Thomas A. Edison's early film reels. That short showed a brief sequence from the Gordon Sisters famed vaudeville act (starring Bessie, sometimes known as Belle, and Minnie)—the sisters were astonishingly one of two pairs of Gordon Sisters (unrelated) performing in boxing shows on the circuit.

Women spectators in the late 19th century were also beginning to be featured at the fights in special seats set aside for them, and the writers Nellie Bly and Annie Laurie were among the first to author newspaper articles about the sport from the perspective of the "gentler sex."

Bly quoted the famed world champion fighter John L. Sullivan as saying, "You are the first woman who ever interviewed me. And I have given you more than I ever gave any reporter in my life."[8] A woman was also famously depicted as a boxer in William H. Bishop's utopian novel *The Garden of Eden*, published in 1895, mirroring changing ideals of womanhood and the embrace of athleticism as a welcomed attribute of the New Woman.

With the coming of World War I and its aftermath, female boxing was becoming more visible in the United Kingdom, France, Germany, and the United States, both in the ring and as a form of exercise. Women's attendance at sanctioned prizefights was promoted to show that prize fighting was an acceptable entertainment—even for the ladies.

The most blatant attempt at drawing in female paying customers was when the Don King of his era, Tex Richard, came up with the idea of a "Jenny Wren" section to help promote female attendance at a Jack Dempsey contest, rightly figuring that if he could fill his seats with bona fide ladies, gentlemen would surely follow.

A new generation of women reported on boxing from Djuna Barnes in *Vanity Fair* to Katherine Fullerton Gerould in *Harper's*. Pockets of women's boxing subcultures began to sprout up as well, including the Busters Club in Flint, Michigan—according to Kate Sekules in her book about her own experiences as a professional boxer in the late 1990s.

Boxing exercises became a craze every bit as potent as "contemporary boxercise." In Weimar Germany boxing for women became so mainstream it was featured as a fitness option aboard German luxury liners, while in England female fighters began to make the rounds as carnival sideshow attractions.

After her success in carnival shows in the early 1950s both in Britain and France, England's Barbara "The Mighty Atom of the Ring" Buttrick came to the United States. Once there, she pushed her way into the ring by finding other women boxers who were following the same path. She also fought men and throughout her career in the sport stayed one step ahead of the boxing commissioners who continued to refuse to legalize women's participation. Buttrick was never daunted. She was able to draw large crowds and had the first female bout called live on the radio in 1954. Buttrick's tenaciousness in the ring set the stage for wider acceptance of a steady stream of professional female fighters who plied the canvas in the 1960s, 1970s, and 1980s.

This roster of these fighters included Sue "Tiger Lily" Fox, a true trailblazer for the sport of women's boxing, and such boxers as Caroline Svendsen, the first woman fighter to be licensed by the Nevada State Athletic Commission in 1975, and Pat Pineda, the first woman fighter to be licensed in California in 1976.

No mention of these 1970s pioneers would be complete without making note of the incredible contributions of Jackie "The Female Ali" Tonawanda. In 1975 she sued New York State for the right to fight legally, but not satisfied to wait, she became the first woman to fight in Madison Square Garden as part of the Aaron Bank's Oriental World of Self Defense show, knocking out her male opponent, kickboxer Larry Rodania, in the second round. Tonawanda continued her battle against the New York State Athletic Commission, finally in 1978 gaining one of the first boxing licenses issued to a female boxer, along with Cathy "Cat" Davis and Marian "Lady Tyger" Trimiar.

The biggest rise in the sport in the United States began in the early 1990s when the parallel tracks of Christy Martin's rise to fame and the recognition of women's boxing as an amateur sport led to exponential participation. No longer a strange novelty, women's boxing began to be featured on the undercard of major pay-per-view championship fights, while winning an audience of loyal fans along the way.

The next big star in women's boxing was none other than Muhammad Ali's daughter Laila "She Bee Stingin'" Ali. Her natural charisma, striking beauty, and surprisingly high level of boxing skills further galvanized the sport and piqued the interest of a growing fan base. What followed, however, was a huge crash as women without the skills of Christy and Laila were pushed into the ring, leading promoters to start shying away from adding women's bouts to their fight cards, claiming they were not "ready."

Women's boxing, however, had made an impact and a big one. Hilary Swank's character, Maggie, in the Clint Eastwood 2005 Oscar-winning movie *Million Dollar Baby* (based on the boxing writer F. X. Toole's short story in his book *Rope Burns*) was reflective of the highs and lows of the women's game and added a new iconic figure to the lexicon of the boxing genre film— only this time, as a female character. The images of Maggie resonated with many women in boxing who have had to persevere against tremendous odds to rise—and perhaps fall—only to find redemption and a state of grace along the way.

In the realm of women's boxing, however, boxing was and still is more often than not relegated to the backwaters of boxing gyms, VFW halls, restaurants, and the like. Televised fights, while plentiful in the heady days of Don King's early promotion of Christy Martin in the mid-1990s, have all but dried up for women in the United States attempting to make careers as professional fighters—while newer sports, such as MMA, have begun to replace the public's appetite for boxing.

That does not deter women from continuing to climb through the ropes on their own terms. They push their bodies, garnering the muscles and sinews of exquisite health, on through the triumphs and trophies of the amateur world to the opportunity to win professional championship titles and even some modicum of celebrity in the realm of the larger boxing world.

These remarkable women ultimately inhabit an understanding of themselves and their place as self-invented and self-actualized. When asked about life without boxing, professional champion fighter-turned-trainer Bonnie "The Cobra" Canino "drew a blank" as if such a life were unfathomable.

For the women of the ring the invention of a boxing identity comes with a complex set of emotions: on the one hand celebratory at having mastered the skills necessary to comport themselves like a *boxer*, while on the other a deep sense of frustration at not being taken seriously.

In a recent interview WBO welterweight champion Kaliesha "Wild Wild" West exemplified these feelings. West said, "The whole idea of women's boxing has been frustrating for me because it is nothing that I expected or looked into when I was little even being number one—it's not how it should be for us."

What she expected was to be treated like a champion, feted and sought after for opportunities in the ring and the recipient of lucrative financial deals as a spokesperson. What she's gotten is the real-world experience of "telling promoters, 'Hey, we'll sell this many tickets and we'll be able to fill this many seats if you put us on your card for this budget and it will only cost you this much.'"[9]

West is not unique in feeling let down by the business side of boxing. She has sacrificed years of her life to excel, and yet despite the disappointments, she continues to organize everything around boxing, making her way to the gym seven days a week to train, not unlike countless other women—professionals and amateurs, fitness nuts and boxercisers, each of whom has grown to love the sport.

As noted earlier, women have had a long tradition as pugilists plying the canvas of the ring. Through enormous effort and fortitude these women are finally being honored as Olympians. In the ephemera of opportunities lost and gained, this ultimate test does have meaning and that legitimacy will provide an entirely new generation of female boxers a chance to dream.

Chapter One

She-Devils and Amazonian Tigresses

Women Enter the Boxing Ring

Boxing as we know it today dates back to the early 1700s in London, England. Almost from the start, women participated in bouts, which were both well publicized and rousing crowd-pleasers. The earliest female fighters—women like Elizabeth Wilkinson Stokes, known as "The City Championess"—advertised their battles in the London newspapers of the day. Wilkinson, along with Hannah Hyfield, "The Newgate Market Basket-Woman," fought with great pugilistic prowess and gained prominence in the 1720s using the bare-knuckle boxing style of James Figg.

The popularity of these female contests began to wane as the century wore on due to changing ideals of acceptable female behavior. At the same time boxing not only became identified as a "manly art," but also as an important virtue of Britishness in the Regency era. The role of women changed from participant to spectator by the close of the 18th century. Hence, though women's bare-knuckle boxing bouts are shown to have persisted, the identification of boxing with masculinity came to mean that women's boxing was less visible to the public—but it was neither forgotten nor unattended.

FEMALE PRIZEFIGHTERS ENTER THE RING

From Figg's Theatre he will not miss a night.
Though cocks, and bulls and Irish women fight.
—James Bramston, *The Art of Politicks* [1]

Elizabeth Wilkinson first came to prominence on the boxing stage in 1722. Little is known about where she came from, but she has been linked to a boxer and sword fighter named Robert Wilkinson who performed at the Hockley in the Hole theater, where she first appeared. (Robert Wilkinson was a renowned rogue who was executed at Newgate Prison for an infamous murder.) How Elizabeth came to be such a skilled fighter has also not been established—but what is known is that she certainly did participate in prize-fights.

Her advertisement in the *London Journal* challenging Hannah Hyfield may well have resulted in the first female prizefight in London. Mention of a fight in 1722 does come to us from a notice published on June 23, 1722, in the *London Journal*:

> Boxing in publick at the Bear Garden is what has lately obtained very much amongst the Men, but till last Week we never heard of Women being engaged that Way, when two of the Feminine Gender appeared for the first Time on the Theatre of War at Hockley in the Hole. [2]

There is some question as to whether the Wilkinson v. Hyfield bout ever actually occurred or, if it did, whether it was fought at the time and place appointed or if it was the fight noted in the *London Journal* article. (Wilkinson's opponent in that fight may well have been Martha Jones, whom sources claim she fought for twenty-two minutes—although the exact date of the fight is in question.) What we do know is that there already was a published account describing a likely match between two women in a book by the German Zacharias Conrad von Uffenbach who, traveling through England in 1710, wrote about his impressions of a prizefight.

Uffenbach marveled at the boisterous crowds and learned, while speaking with a highly "vociferous" female spectator, "that two years ago she had fought another female in this place without stays and in nothing but a shift. They had fought stoutly and drawn blood, which was apparently no new sight in England."[3]

The French writer Martin Nogue also wrote of his experiences, observing women fighting in his book entitled *Voyages et Aventures*, published in 1728, stating, "Des femmes & des filles même combattent de la même forte, dépouillées jusqu'a la ceinture,"[4] roughly translated as his having viewed women and girls fighting with the same strength (as men) whilst stripped down to their belts. Whether they were actually bare breasted or clothed in undergarments is not stated, although other writers have indicated that women fought topless, certainly adding to the prurient interest.

Elizabeth Wilkinson Stokes's popularity, however, was evident from 1722 onwards, drawing crowds to both her single-combat fights and to mixed bouts with her partner and eventual husband, John Stokes. The popularity of these bouts was very likely confined to the "low haunts" of boxing amphitheaters and the like, with their crowds of rowdy regulars plus a large helping of assorted male "gentry" from the higher classes who delighted in rubbing shoulders with the wild assortment of working men and women at the fights—scenes captured in the drawings of the noted 18th century artist William Hogarth.

The allure of women's contests at places like Hockley in the Hole can be surmised from this snippet in the *London Journal* from August 31, 1723, which stated, "Scarce a Week passes but we have a Boxing-Match at the Bear-Garden between Women."[5]

Another example was Elizabeth Wilkinson's bout on August 8th, 1723, at the Boarded House in Marybourne where she faced a basket-woman at Newgate Market known as Joanna Heyfield. Given how close Joanna Heyfield's name was to Hannah Hyfield, whom she was to have fought in 1722, it is likely the same person, but it is unknown which was her actual name. Also on the "card" was no less a boxing figure than James Figg fighting James Stokes—although their fight was for only three guineas.

The draw of women's boxing continued as shown by this advertisement in the *Weekly Journal* from October 1, 1726:

> In Islington Road, near Sadler's Wells, on Monday next, being the 3d of October, will be perform'd a trial of skill by the following Championesses. Whereas I Mary Welch, from the Kingdom of Ireland, being taught, and knowing the noble science of defence, and thought to be the only female of this kind in Europe, understanding there is one in this Kingdom, who has exercised on the publick stage several times, which is Mrs. Stokes, who is stiled the famous Championess of England; I do hereby invite her to meet me, and exercise the usual weapons practis'd on the stage, at her own amphitheatre, doubting not, but to let her and the worthy spectators see, that my judgment and courage is beyond hers.
>
> I Elizabeth Stokes, of the famous City of London, being well known by the name of the Invincible City Championess for my abilities and judgment in the abovesaid science; having never engaged with any of my own sex but I always came off with victory and applause, shall make no apology for accepting the challenge of this Irish Heroine, not doubting but to maintain the reputation I have hitherto establish'd, and shew my country, that the contest of its honour, is not ill entrusted in the present battle with their Championess, Elizabeth Stokes.
>
> Note, The doors will be open'd at two, and the Championesses mount at four.
>
> N.B. They fight in close jackets, short petticoats, coming just below the knee, Holland drawers, white stockings, and pumps.[6]

As can be seen, boxing at this time not only consisted of fighting with fists, but also with short swords called cudgels. The idea of women practicing scientific prizefighting was also introduced, and was in keeping with the growth of boxing as a highly technical sport under the tutelage of James Figg.

The following year, Elizabeth Wilkinson Stokes and her husband James Stokes also competed in "mixed-double" pairs. In one such instance the couple fought Robert Barker and Mary Webb. The advertisement for that engagement read in part:

> In Islington road, on Monday, being the 17th of July, 1727, will be performed a trial of skill by the following combatants. We Robert Barker and Mary Welsh, from Ireland, having often *contaminated* out swords in the *abdominous coporations* of such antagonists as have had the insolence to dispute our skill, do find ourselves once more necessitated to challenge, defy, and invite Mr. Stokes and his bold Amazonian *virago* to meet us on the state, where we hope to give satisfaction to the *honourable Lord* of our nation who has laid a wager of twenty guineas on our heads. They that give the most cuts to have the whole money."[7]

The battle, with its potential for a brutal outcome given that the losing pair would be marked by cuts and gashes from their opponents, was purported to be Elizabeth Wilkinson Stokes's last prizefight.

If the advertisements were any indication, she did not retire after her 1727 bout, but fought in at least one more for the tidy sum of ten pounds at her husband's amphitheater:

> This present Monday, being the 7th of October, will be a complete Boxing Match, by the two following Championesses: Whereas I, Ann Field, of Stoke Newington, ass driver, well-known for my abilities in my own defence, whenever it happened in my way, having been affronted by Mrs Stokes, styled the European Championess, do fairly invite her to a trial of her best skill in Boxing, for 10 pounds; fair rise and fall: and question not but to give her such proofs of my judgment that shall oblige her to acknowledge me Championess of the Stage, to the entire satisfaction of all my friends.
>
> I, Elizabeth Stokes, of the City of London, have not fought this way since I fought the famous Boxing Woman of Billingsgate 29 minutes and gained a complete victory (which is six years ago); but as the famous ass-woman of Stoke Newington dares me to fight her for the ten pounds, I do assure her I shall not tail meeting her for the said sum, and doubt not that the blows I shall present her with will be more difficult to digest than any she ever gave her asses.
>
> N.B Attendance will be given at one, and the encounter is to begin at four precisely. There will be the diversion of cudgel playing as usual.[8]

After this fight, there is nothing more on the record that can be found about Elizabeth Wilkinson Stokes, so it is highly likely that she retired from the ring after having fought for six years.

This popularity of boxing aside, the "middle class" attitude toward female pugilists in the 1720s can likely be gleaned from the English actress and writer Eliza Haywood's reference to it in her play entitled *A Wife to Be Let,* first performed in 1723. In her comedy of manners, a male footman pretends to be a member of the gentry in the guise of Sir Tristam and marries the wealthy Widow Stately. Learning that she has been hoodwinked, she yells, "Villain! Rogue! I'll tear you to pieces." In response to her outburst, a character named Gaylove admonishes her with the words, "Patience, madam, patience! Boxing does not become a woman of quality."[9]

During this period, training at Figg's Academy was becoming almost de rigueur for young gentlemen. By the 1730s they were taking to heart Figg's calls to masculinity and were learning the "noble art of self-defense" in greater and greater numbers. It didn't hurt that no less a person than George II had been in attendance at a Figg fight. Yet, heedless of the fact that female prizefighters were not trained at the popular boxing school, women's bouts remained popular in the 1720s and 1730s, and these fighters were skilled enough to fill seats and spur on robust betting.

In what was a decided testament to the working-class roots of the boxing women of this period, early female pugilists wore their affiliations with names such as "A Female Boxing Blacksmith," "The Market Woman," and the renowned "Fighting Ass-Driver" from Stoke Newington (a district in London). Their names spoke of the rough world of work demanded of 18th century women that not only required inordinate physical strength, but also a fierce independent pluckiness that would have them risk injury or maiming as part of their work-a-day world. Entering the prizefighting ring also required an inner fortitude that spurred them on to pick up the cudgel, the sword, and their bare fists to fight until one or the other of the two opponents dropped to the floor in a bloody heap.

This prizefighting world of the Figg era, to which women added their weight, was rough-and-tumble at best. There was no concept of such things as boxing rounds, low blows, or the standing eight count that became the mainstays of a fair fight in later eras. Each participant fought until he or she was no longer able to fight.

Much as with the animal-on-animal fighting or animal baiting that were the precursors to the prizefighting contests between armed human combatants, the rowdy crowds yelled for blood, which was assuredly in abundance with fighters willingly obliging to spill. The crowd also intently followed the action, exchanging shillings throughout and placing bets on one or another of the fighters as the bout pressed on with the hope that they had backed the winner. The effect was a maelstrom of crowd noise, the shouts from each of the fighter's camps, the clinking of tankards, and the general din of an overcrowded space intermingled with the grunts and groans of the combatants. So loud were these events that Pepys writing in 1663 said it made his "head ake all the evening."[10]

Thomas Brown, writing about a prizefight in 1705 at a beer garden, offered a more elaborate description.

> Seats fill'd and crowded by Two: Drums beat, Dogs yelp, Butchers and Foot-soldiers clatter their Sticks: At last the two Heroes in their fine borrow'd Holland shirts, mount the Stage about Three; Cut large Collops out of one another to divert the Mob, and make Work for the Suregeons: Smoaking, Swearing, Drinking, Thrusting, Justling, Elbowing, Sweating, Kicking, Cuffing, Stinking, all the while the Company stays.[11]

The carnival spectacle of such fights also lent itself to the notion of having females in the ring. Not unlike the animals that still fought in some of the same venues, whether anthropomorphizing animals with human characteristics, or females with masculine-gender attributes, the fights were irresistible within a milieu where gender views, while quite clearly delineated through custom and dress, held a fascination for the possibilities of what happened when genders were mixed up.

Certainly this is an interesting consideration given the robust sales of female warrior ballads during the period. The very fact that women worked as ass drivers or blacksmiths attests to the permeability of gender connotations in the world of work among these classes. It must also not be forgotten that many of the women who boxed were true professionals when they were in the ring. They risked life and limb for hard-earned cash (or goods) for their labors as prizefighters—which given the purse sizes was not insignificant for its time and place. As with their male counterparts, there was an honor of place to their positions and consideration given for their evident bravery in entering the fray.

The use of cudgels, swords, and fists in this early period must have both thrilled and terrified the throngs, with each spurt of blood a death-defying moment. That women also willingly took up these instruments must have driven the crowds into a wild frenzy of emotion as they watched such characters as the "Ass Driver" of Stoke Newington risking all for the joy of the crowd and the guineas that lined the purses of the winners.

SHE-DEVILS AND THE FIGHTING OF BRUISING PEG

The famed 18th-century rake and memoirist William Hickey, born to wealth in 1749, made a detailed description of a female bout he witnessed in 1768 at a bar called Wetherby's just off Drury Lane. He describes himself as somewhat intoxicated and in the company of an older brother and other friends who wanted to hobnob with the lower classes in what the book describes as a "den." Upon his arrival he made note of his impressions of two women in the midst of a fight:

> Two she-devils, for they scarce had human appearance, engaged in a scratching and boxing match, their faces entirely covered with blood, bosoms bare, and the clothes nearly torn from their bodies. For several minutes not a creature interfered between them, or seemed to care a straw what mischief they might do each other, and the contest went with unabated fury. [12]

Hickey's discomfort with the experience was clear, especially when he turned to observe a fight in progress between an "uncommonly athletic man of about twenty-five" and "no less than three Amazonian tigresses [who] were pummeling him with all their might." [13] The scene provoked him to "an immediate restoration of my senses the effect of which was an eager wish to get away." [14]

In a later reference to the "riot" he had endured at Wetherby's, he was enticed by his brother and a friend to return. Once there, he recognized one of the two "she-devils" from his previous visit, a singer named Burgess whom he observed for some time before getting the courage to speak with her:

> Burgess and I became very sociable, and I asked her how it happened that she could have been principal in such a horrid broil as I had witnessed; to which she replied that both herself and her antagonist were exceedingly intoxicated, having drank an unusual quantity of spirits, and in their cups had quarreled; that the other battle royal, of which I was also a spectator arose from the man (who was a notorious women's bully) having basely robbed the two who attacked him, that the rest concerned the friends of one party or other and acted accordingly. [15]

Hickey seemed satisfied by the explanation, and while still acutely aware of his own discomfort became at ease with the idea that the "fight" was not so much a boxing match per se as the actions of drunks in a low-haunt bar, fermented by a combination of liquor and "questionable" morals.

The same year as Hickey's "remembrances," an article appeared in London's *Daily Advertiser* on June 22, 1768, that read in part:

> On Wednesday last, two women fought for a new shift, valued at half-a-guinea, in the Spaw Fields near Islington. The battle was won by a woman called "Bruising Peg," who beat her antagonist in a terrible manner. [16]

Spaw Fields, in Clerkenwell, was also known as Spa Fields and London Spa. It was a well-known haunt for such sports as bull-baiting, duck-hunting, and wrestling, beginning in the 17th century, and for prizefighting in the 18th century.

Whether Bruising Peg's defeat of her unnamed opponent "in a terrible manner" was in line with her other appearances at Spaw Fields as a professional pugilist is unknown, as is the reason for the fight. Its appearance as a line item in the *Daily Advertiser*, a London paper founded in 1703, which featured political, social, and business news, as well as a large classified section, leads to the strong probability that the fight had been advertised and might well have been part of a larger fight card. It is also likely that the bout saw heavy betting and that Bruising Peg was a known quantity before the epic battle.

Despite what seems like a paucity of information in the written record about Bruising Peg, her renown, and her association with any later boxing shows at Spaw Fields, she became a symbol of female pugilism more than one hundred years later with the publication of Paul Creswick's 1898 book entitled *Bruising Peg: Pages from the Journal of Margaret Malloy, 1768–9*. Reference is also made to her in books about London in the 1700s and Spa Fields in particular, published during roughly the same period as Creswick's book. That she should become an object of such fascination in the late Victorian era, at a time when women's boxing was undergoing a renaissance, is fascinating in and of itself. As an 18th-century heroine, however, she remains an interesting figure in the transition of gender meaning and a significant figure in the history of women's boxing.

Another fight of renown in the late 1700s found in the written record was the June 5, 1795, bout between Mrs. Mary Ann Fielding and the "Jewess of Wentworth Street." The bout was reported as seconded by two legendary boxing figures, "Gentleman" John Jackson and the Jewish champion, Daniel Mendoza. The bout even had bottle holders in accordance with the standard rules of the day—though they were also said to be women.

As described in *Pancratia or, A History of Pugilism*, published in 1812, the fight had an air of legitimacy from the beginning:

> Every thing having been properly arranged, the combatants set to, and for some time each displayed great intrepidity and astonishingly well-concerted maneuvers in the art of boxing. Fielding fought with great coolness and singularity of temper, and by well-directed hits knocked down her adversary upwards of 70 times. After the battle had lasted one hour and 20 minutes, with much alternate dexterity, Fielding was declared the conqueror. [17]

Pancratia also describes another fight from the same general time period. The bout occurred in August 1793 at "Elmstead near Chelmsford, Essex," between "two LADIES of pugilistic spirit." In this description, however, the author writes:

> They set to, and for 45 minutes supported a most desperate conflict; when, although one of them was so dreadfully beat as to excite apprehension for her

life, her husband possessed brutality enough still to prompt her to fight; but, through the interference of the spectators they were separated.[18]

In discussing the fight, the author opines that though he "strongly advocates the cause of pugilism, he by no means feels desirous to see such conflicts displayed by the *softer sex*" [italics added].[19]

The glaring contradiction of the two descriptions represents the evident changes in how women were viewed in relation to the shifting signifiers of gender between the time women first entered the ring and the late 1700s. On the one hand, the author shows us that the women in the fight, seconded by two legitimate boxing champions, demonstrated "astonishingly well-concerted maneuvers in the art of boxing," perhaps influenced by the evident legitimacy of having two well-respected champions sponsoring Fielding and the unnamed Jewess of Wentworth. The two female fighters showed skill, adhered to the rules, and acquitted themselves well in the ring, attributes that can be worthy of praise, even though they are women, because they were supervised by men.

As for the "two LADIES of pugilistic spirit," they were unsponsored and clearly unskilled, leading the author to view them as *softer*, a state he further explained when he wrote, "It is the gentleness of their manners, and their acknowledged inability of defending themselves, that frequently excite us to acts of the greatest bravery and gallantry!"[20]

THE GOLDEN AGE OF BRITISH BOXING: MEN AND WOMEN AT THE FIGHTS

In the 1780s, boxing began another remarkable transformation in England—entering what many scholars call the "Golden Age." It had come a long way from the rough and tumble beginnings of prizefighting in the fair booths and Bear Gardens of the 1720s, and despite its illegal status, the sport had begun a climb to a level of respectability that saw such patrons as the Prince of Wales extol the virtues of British boxing.

One thing was apparent: Boxing had become inextricably linked to British manhood—an important consideration given the political realities of the period.

England was engaged in a series of wars, not the least of which was the Revolutionary War, won by the United States in 1783. War with France was again also in the offing, and the characterization of boxing as a uniquely British form of courage seemed irresistible: No need for fighting at a distance with swords; the British were willing (and able) to fight man-to-man with their fists if necessary. Boxing also connoted the idea of fair play, another British virtue that meant playing by the rules—an attribute of boxing since

Jack Broughton first promulgated fairness in the ring in 1843 (Broughton's Rules).

The sport of boxing was also evolving. No longer just a contest of brute force, fighters such as Daniel Mendoza combined quick hands, defensive posturing, and movement around the ring to expand the pugilist's repertoire of boxing moves, exciting the crowd with a new elegance and level of sophistication that was viewed as scientific. Mendoza himself published a how-to book in 1787 entitled *The Art of Boxing*. Schools of boxing sprang up again as did numerous pamphlets.

Another feature of this period, alternatively referred to as the Fancy, was the shift in the audiences for contests. No longer just the sport for lower-class men and women with a smattering of men from the upper classes, this period saw the development of venues where even respectable women could watch a display of the manly art of boxing and a sparring contest—if not an actual prizefight. Pierce Egan, the author of the 1820 work *Boxiana*, discussed this change by describing Daniel Mendoza's new venue as:

> In the Strand for the express purpose of public exhibitions of sparring . . . [wherein] the manly art of boxing would be displayed . . . with the utmost decorum, that the female part of the creation might attend.[21]

The fact was women had been attending the prizefights since boxing's inception. Egan's sentiment that the "female part of the creation might attend," however, had clear implications as to the class of women who would be in attendance. Boxing, because it had become elevated enough for even the most refined feminine sensibilities, had, in short, arrived.

What this meant for the female practitioners of the sport though was unclear. There continued to be women's boxing contests—with some bouts fought with evident skill and adherence to the boxing rules of the day, and others featuring fighters with few boxing abilities—but as with earlier eras there was no particular place for women's boxing. It remained an afterthought at best, acknowledged through the continued reportage in newspapers of the day and as reference points in books about boxing—but it was not quite legitimate either. Without any clear sponsorship or system of promotion, female pugilism as a sport remained precarious at best. Taken all together, the popular female contests that had helped launch boxing at its inception seem to have all but disappeared from the landscape of British boxing by the century's end. Boxing had by this time become associated with British notions of manliness and even Britishness itself. As for the role of women in the sport—the female pugilist had been transformed to that of a dainty spectator, marveling in support of British might.

Chapter Two

Victorian Ladies Boxing

"Oh, I can swing clubs, and box and fence," she cried, successively striking
the typical postures; "and swim, and make high dives, chin a bar twenty times,
and—walk on my hands. There!"[1]
—Jack London, *A Daughter of the Snows*

With the advent of the early 1800s, women's boxing began to wane in Britain. By the 1830s displays of women's boxing became invisible, if not extinct, save for reports of street brawls and related battles amongst women of the lower classes. The earlier freedoms to attend boxing matches or sparring exhibitions were also no longer available to women.

Boxing itself lost its luster in England through the 1830s, and by the 1850s the hub of boxing had switched to the United States. Boxing was barely known among women in America in the early part of the century except for fistic contests reported in newspapers of the day and occasional street brawls. Beginning in the 1870s, and coinciding with the expanding popularity of men's boxing, women in the United States took up the gloves alongside their male counterparts. These forays included legitimate boxing contests with winners crowned "world champions," as well as playful sparring exhibitions and more serious ones labeled as pugilistic contests.

As the century came to a close, vaudeville and burlesque shows popularized both male and female pugilism around the United States. Women's boxing and wrestling contests also drew in customers in France and Germany and eventually found their way to the music halls of Britain beginning in the 1880s. This resurgence of women's participation in boxing was one aspect of the changing conversation about a women's place in the world and gender relations in general.

Not to be underestimated was the belief that contact sports were physically and mentally dangerous to feminine health, a view promulgated by the medical "experts" of the day. Based on these beliefs, women were pushed to practice more "genteel" sports such as tennis and croquet. Conversely, pugilism, wrestling, field hockey, and swimming were considered too rigorous—even for the New Woman of the 1880s and 1890s.

It was hard for a woman to be immune to such efforts of continued control over their bodies and while some boxed, ran track, and lifted weights, most who participated in sports of any kind chose to exercise by riding bicycles, taking long walks, roller skating, playing tennis, or swimming. Still, such participation presaged a new era of freedom for women—and a boon for women's boxing.

WINDS OF CHANGE: AN OUTRAGE ON DECENCY

The early 1800s saw a continued upswing in British boxing. A plethora of books were published recounting the history of the sport, training methods, and even diet. The virtues of boxing were extolled and publications such as the *Sporting Magazine* regularly reported on bouts, boxers, and the spirit of the sport. The practice of holding sparring exhibitions in upmarket venues also continued. The Royal Amphitheatre at Westminster Bridge, where pugilists donned boxing gloves as they showed off their fistic prowess, was particularly popular in the early 1820s. A good percentage of the audience at these exhibitions were women—so many that despite the efforts to "elevate" the sport by hosting sparring contests even the "gentler sex" could watch, with men on stage stripped to their waists, it might well have been a little risqué.

A ready acceptance of female audience members at sparring contests did not necessarily extend the license for their further participation in the sport. Still, there were instances of female bouts reported in the popular press. Typical of the reporting of women's boxing at the time was this article from the *Sporting Magazine* in December 1811:

> Amazonian Boxing.—A pitched battle, for a pint of gin and a new shawl, took place . . . between Molly Flower and Nanny Gent. The set-to was contested for twenty minutes, with some skill and determined courage. Both were good hitters, and they were worse hit about the head than is witness amongst many second-rate pugilists. Nanny *jibbed a bit* in the twelfth round, and "gave in from a dexterous hit down in the following round."[2]

Women's bouts—as infrequently held as they seem to have been—also continued to have a modicum of acceptance, if not the apparatus of support that pugilism, in general, enjoyed in this period. There were, after all, no schools for female fighters, just as there were few if any promoters and trainers. Pugilism as the tool for settling perceived wrongs did remain a viable option for women, and while most of their bouts were likely ad hoc at best, the crowds enjoyed them, and the women who fought received a guarded recognition in the press.

These bouts were held in the period of the Fancy, stretching from the 1780s through the early 1820s, a time of growth and popularity for bare-knuckle boxing encompassing the late Georgian and Regency eras in Britain. Its last true "hurrah" centered on the fights in the 1810s (which corresponded with Britain's wars with France and the United States), the popularity of the writings of Pierce Egan and other followers of the Fancy, and the seeming respectability of the sport that even allowed the continued appearance of genteel female spectatorship.

Still, there were forces from the British evangelical Christian movement and within Parliament who were genuinely outraged by the sport. They advocated for boxing's demise by giving teeth to the legal constraints against pugilism already in place (with women's participation viewed as something even lower than an abomination). The evangelical perspective argued that pugilism was a pleasure of the flesh to be rooted out in the search for salvation and the revocation of sin through acts of free will. As for women, their association with the sport was nothing if not unnatural.

Other social and political considerations touched upon boxing as well. The Fancy was considered a mixture of the rabble, the worst of the layabout swells, and the British aristocracy, who in effect became aligned against the newer voices of the burgeoning middle classes who saw pugilism as profligacy of the worst sort. Even some trade unionists, looking for empowerment in the new economic reality of the nascent revolution that was changing the face of British industry, allied themselves with the reformers in response to the downturns that accompanied the end of Britain's Napoleonic adventures in 1815.

As the public perception turned negative, the aristocratic support—once so bountiful—began to disappear along with the monies that kept the pugilistic clubs open for business. Even gambling, the mainstay of pugilism since its inception one hundred years earlier, could no longer be trusted due to scandals involving fixed fights—serving to heighten the message of the evangelicals that such profligacy would only lead to perdition.

No less affected were female denizens of the fight game. On October 15, 1824, the *Stamford Mercury*, a well-respected newspaper in Britain published since 1695, reported on a bout at the Five Fields in Chelsea. Attended by a crowd of two thousand or more people, the article, under the heading *Female Pugilism*, began with the words "A most abominable exhibition was presented on Thursday the 7th . . ."

> The disgust to a spectator wants not description. . . . They fought with considerable skill and nothing but earnest right and left was given and received; they

bled profusely, and nothing more horrific can be imagined than their appearance. The seconds endeavoured as much as possible to keep them to something
like the ring; but owing to the slippery state of the weather, and the ring being
repeatedly broken into, it was found impracticable; and so great was the fury
of the antagonists, that although drenched in blood and covered with filth, they
disputed every inch of ground, and actually fought with Amazonian valour for
two hours and a half.[3]

Had the bout been fought even five years earlier, the "considerable skill" and
"Amazonian valour" on display may have been more positively viewed as
being in the scientific tradition of pugilism as can be surmised in a brief
notice of a women's bout from 1819 reported in the *Chester Chronicle*:

On Monday night last, two Amazonians, named Weaver, and Scully, gratified
the female lovers of pugilism with a pitched battle in Hoole-lane-field, near the
Bridge, in [Chester, northwest of London]. They fought some time, when
victory settled her wreath on the brows of the former lady—This is a spirited
age![4]

The author of the article from 1824, however, chose to dwell on the female
pugilists "most abominable exhibition," their "horrific" appearance
"drenched in blood and covered with filth," and the intractability of the
crowd that "repeatedly" broke into the ring.

The behavior of the crowd, as described further, can also be an instructive
indicator of the place of pugilism and the feminine practice of it beginning in
this period.

At length the sight aroused the feelings of a satiated mob; the ring was broken
in, and the parties were assisted away in a mutilated state, having scarcely a
rag to cover them, thereby making it a drawn battle, which it is understood, is
to be renewed at a future day. We trust, however, that the then interference of
the magistrates will prevent a repetition of so gross an outrage on public
decency.[5]

The abomination described is not only against the "nature" of renewed gen-
tility in female-kind, but indicative of the rising fear of crowds. Not for
nothing was there already a law on the books that limited assembly to no
more than fifty persons; here was a crowd that repeatedly broke the sacro-
sanct area of the ring, into what one can only imagine was a sludge of mud,
blood, sweat, saliva, and goodness knows what other impurities that became
the "filth" that clung to the two unnamed fighters' near-naked bodies.

The *Westmorland Gazette* reporting on the fight the following day did
point out that "They fought with considerable science." The emphasis, however, was tilted toward a decidedly negative view of female pugilism, while
choosing not to highlight the machinations of the unruly crowd.

They bled profusely; and in their rallies, when, in addition to the loathsome appearance of their persons, their hair became loose, hanging in clotted disorder over their shriveled bosoms, nothing more horrific can be imagined.[6]

The negative views of female boxing in particular that coincided with the downturn of the Fancy were not, however, exclusive to the 1820s. There were many voices against pugilism in general, with an added bit of choice invective for the specter of two women waling on each other when the occasion arose. A short article in the *Hampshire Chronicle and Courier* from 1817 makes the point:

It is no wonder that foreigners should form a very unfavourable opinion of us, when they see with what care the account of a pugilistic contest is circulated in the public prints. But these scenes disgraceful as they are to a nation professedly composed of civilized beings, and which aims at bearing the palm in moral, fall far short in depravity to what we are now about to relate: . . . A dreadful battle . . . between two amazons.[7]

The *London Times*, as early as 1807, was no particular fan of pugilism—female pugilism in particular—noting the two "Amazon" protagonists were "hideously disfigured by hard blows," which "afforded the most disgust."[8]

Given the spirited debate in and around the publication of the *London Times* piece, including William Cobbett's *Defence of Pugilism* article published two years earlier, the forces for and against pugilism were clearly in two camps, with a special emphasis placed on eliminating female fisticuffs by the antipugilism group.

Even as boxing was beginning to lose popularity, writers such at Pierce Egan, whose 1812 *Boxiana* was considered canon a mere ten years after publication, were continuing to write with much success. Newspapers also continued, in the main, to report favorably on men's pugilistic encounters. The *Westmorland Gazette*, publisher of the scathing piece on fight fixing, stated, "Two braver men never enter a ring,"[9] when describing the October 1824 encounter between Bob Baldwin and Ned O'Neal.

Regardless of the number of actual fights, it was clear the glory days of the Fancy were waning. Voices outside of the boxing world were calling for its immediate stoppage and even elements within the boxing world recognized that the sport needed to be cleaned up. When it came to women as denizens of the Fancy, participants, even skilled ones, were no longer welcome in the prize ring—nor were the female boxing fans that had once been so sought after as spectators.

The symbolic end of the era, however, was heralded when the huge Fives Court boxing complex, site of famous battles and sparring exhibitions during the heyday of the Fancy, was torn down in 1826 making way for Trafalgar Square and Britain's reinvention of itself as an imperial and economic power.

BOXING OVER THE POND: THE UNITED STATES BEGINS TO TAKE UP THE GLOVES

American boxing began inauspiciously in the 1700s on the Colonial planta-tions of the South when slaves purportedly fought against one another other in boxing and wrestling contests. Frederick Douglass mentions boxing and wrestling in his slave narrative. His recollections from the 1830s show that during the Christmas-to-New Year period slaves were encouraged to "engage in sports." Douglass, however, was engaged in teaching his "loved fellow-slaves how to read," but it had to be kept secret. He wrote, "It was necessary to keep our religious masters . . . unacquainted with the fact, that, instead of spending the Sabbath wrestling, boxing, and drinking whisky, we were to learn how to read the will of God."[10]

Despite such recollections, the historical record is sketchy on how preva-lent the practice was in the late 1700s, and while the British boxing author Pierce Egan noted that Tom Molineaux said that he had learned to fight under his father's tutelage while still in bondage, the evidence is scant. What *is* evident is the popularity of British sports and sports betting among the slave-owning classes in the Colonial South and the rise of horse racing and cockfighting (even though it was illegal from 1740 on) as important events on the social calendar.

Formal boxing of a sort does appear in the writings of Moreau de St. Mery, a Frenchman who took up residence in Philadelphia in the early 1790s. He wrote an account of pugilism in a book about his experiences in America. "Boxing has its rules and regulations," he wrote. "Athletes settle on a site for the fight . . . strip to their shirts, and roll up their sleeves."

The fights he described, however, had none of the formalities of the boxing rules followed in England and the ring itself was reminiscent of the early fights of the Figg era—a circle of fans where "the spectators urge on their favorites"—rather than the more formal cordoned square with posts and ropes to hold the crowds at bay.

The first "recognized" boxing contest in America was in New York City in 1816 between Jacob Hyer and Tom Beasley. As noted in *American Fistia-na*, published in 1849:

> This fight . . . proceeded from a personal quarrel between the men . . . both of whom were very large and powerful first class men. [The fight] lasted through severe rounds, but was at length decided in favor of the latter [Beasley] by an accident and Hyer retired from the ring with a broken arm.[11]

There were other periodic accounts of boxing matches in the 1820s in New York and its environs and even a smattering of gentlemanly fisticuffs at the

New York Gymnasium, opened in 1826 by the British pugilist William Fuller.

By the 1830s a steady stream of British and Irish boxers were making their way to America to seek out opportunities, again, mostly in and around New York City. The practice of boxing itself was illegal for the most part, but it didn't stop newspapers from giving accounts.

Boxing had reached sufficient renown in the United States by 1843 to warrant inclusion in the "The Sporting Chronicle, a weekly paper devoted to amusements." The addition was not without controversy, as the Whig newspaper the *New York Daily Tribune* reported with "regret" that the sporting newsweekly would carry stories about "Pugilism."[12]

Prizefighting in this period had not yet arrived as an outlet for women, and although female boxing was not yet sufficiently recognized to be part of the public story, it was in the public realm. An article about a prizefight between two women in Great Britain that ran in the *London Times* provides a ready example. Republished in the *Brooklyn Eagle* on September 24, 1852, and no doubt picked up by other American newspapers, the piece described a first-person account:

> About a month ago . . . I perceived a number of persons passing through the field adjoining my house. The stream of men and women had come from Paddington to a prize-fight between two—no, not men—women! One of my family, being incredulous, contrived to look across the fields, and there saw the combatants stripped to the waist, and fighting. Men took them there, men backed them, men were bottle-holders and time keepers. They fought for about half an hour, some say for five shillings, some say for five pounds, and say they will do it again. I saw the winner led back in triumph by men."[13]

A small notice in the *Brooklyn Eagle*, in 1847, also took the leap to associate a woman with pugilism. The piece was about a mother who, while seated in a box in the upper level of a theater in Pittsburg, observed her son fighting below whereupon she "leaped from the boxes into the pit." Having landed chest first onto a bench, she

> immediately sprung up again, notwithstanding she must have been badly hurt, and rushed like a tigress on the boy's antagonist. By this time the police had reached the place, and in a moment cleared the pugilists out of the theatre.[14]

While not exactly a "prizefight," the association of fighting with pugilism—whether male or female—reveals the place of boxing in the popular culture of the time. The fact that boxing was in the main negative in the early history of the sport in America did not deter the images of fighting, whether in the ring or in a street altercation, to be seen as pugilism, nor for the rudimentary rules of boxing to be followed in many sorts of fights.

The following, published in 1856, precisely associates a brawl between two women in Chicago with prizefighting, under the heading "Women's rights must be progressing in Chicago, if we may judge by the following:"

> A *prize fight* took place on the lake shore between a couple of whiskey-bloated female denizens of that locality, in presence of an audience of fifty or sixty people of both sexes. A ring was made, seconds were chosen, and stripping themselves to the waist the two degraded creatures went at it. The fight lasted some twenty minutes and the yells and curses of the combatant might have been heard a full quarter of a mile. [15]

The language is certainly pejorative, echoing the disgust and dismay of stories written in the British press in the 1820s, the more so perhaps because of the association of the two women with alcohol. We are also not privy as to the cause of the fight—though attendance by a sizable crowd and some modicum of attention to rules does give us the idea that all involved had some basic understanding of pugilism. Not to be lost is the added editorial commentary equating women's rights with prizefighting. Certainly it is meant to be sardonic at best. However, the commentary is not only illustrative of how much the women's rights movement had become part of the national conversation in the period, but also placed pugilism on a national footing.

By 1860 a story entitled "Female Prize Fight" about a bout near Concord, New Hampshire, was of sufficient interest to have been picked up by a local paper in Ohio, the *Holmes County Farmer*. While the cause of the fight is unknown, as is whether any prize money was offered, the fight had a modicum of legitimacy in that "both parties" trained "for several weeks" prior to the match. Even so, the article describes the fight as "disgraceful," and while it was an eighteen-round contest "lasting twenty minutes, in the presence of a large number of the roughs who reside in that section of the city," the tone was decidedly negative, with one of the fighters described as the "notorious Mrs. Storin" who was "knocked completely off her pins in nearly every round." [16]

Female pugilism may not yet have risen above the occasional negative account in an American newspaper, but the last years of the antebellum period did see a huge boom in the popularity of the sport in general. The successful marketing of boxing contests also led to the rise of boxing as a leisure activity for gentlemen and eventually gentlewomen.

POST–CIVIL WAR BOXING: THE FIRST FEMALE FIGHT AT HARRY HILL'S

Under the heading "A Female Boxing Match. A Novel and Nonsensical Exhibition at Henry Hill's," the *New York Times* published an article on March 17, 1876, about two female pugilists, marking the beginning of the era of Victorian women's boxing:

> Some weeks ago Prof. James Campbell, the manager of Harry Hill's establishment in Houston Street, conceived the idea of having as a feature of its benefit, which took place yesterday, a sparring match with boxing-gloves between two women, and offered as a prize $200 and a piece of silver-plate. The opportunity offered by Mr. Campbell was embraced by two variety dancers, Miss Nell Saunders and Miss Rose Harland. [17]

The *New York Times* piece made note of the fact that neither woman had any boxing experience prior to the announcement of the contest. Both women did, however, receive some modicum of training for the fight: Nell Saunders from her pugilist husband and Rose Harland under the tutelage of boxer James Kelly. This training gave Saunders "science," adding to the air of "legitimacy" of the bout, whereas Harland, not to be outdone, though "overmatched in science, presumed on her superior strength, and 'sailed in' for punishment."

The *New York Herald* also reported on the event under the less editorialized heading "Female Boxers." It noted:

> Rose is decidedly the heavier of the two, weighing yesterday 150 pounds, while Nell tipped the scale at less than 120 pounds. Both were attractively dressed. Rose wore a white shirt, blue silk trunks, white tights, red and gray stripped hose and neat morocco slippers surmounted by silver buckles. Nell was attired in white shirt, red plus knee breeches, red hose and light boots. [18]

Both fighters were shown to have had a "mutual respect for each other" with Nell breaking "ground and in a little rally did slightly more effective work than her antagonist." The article went on to note that in their second-round work they both "displayed considerably more science than some of the male novices that infrequently box before the public."

At the end of the third round the bout was called a draw with the score, according to the *New York Times*, 20-20. Nell Saunders was viewed as the better of the two and was given the prize. In the spirit of fairness, "Some gentleman handed Miss Harland a ten-dollar bill, and the two female boxers left the stage arm in arm." The *New York Herald* reported it slightly differently, noting:

A lively rally was in progress when Hill stopped the girls, and shaking hands they awaited the decision which came from Harry and was "that the counter hits were equal, but Saunders had landed one more straight blow than Harland." Thereupon he presented Nell with the butter dish, and thus the first public female boxing match ever seen in New York was over.

The show, quite obviously well received, was widely reported outside of New York with an article about the fight appearing in Scotland's *Edinburgh Evening News* a few weeks later with a repeat of the story from the *New York Herald*.

Harry Hill's Variety Theatre was a notorious nightclub in the tradition of Bowery taverns from the 1840s and 1850s. With its dance-hall girls, variety entertainments including minstrel shows with African American performers, and sparring matches, Harry Hill's was lively at all hours of the day and night. It also counted a cross section of New York types as customers from the well-heeled to workingmen, and on any given day one could count on seeing one or another society swell, politician, or even the likes of P. T. Barnum.

Viewing pugilism as entertainment, Harry Hill's sparring shows not only brought in fans but also provided the setting for brokering prizefights, some of which were held at Hill's place with such boxing luminaries as John L. Sullivan counted among his coterie of fighters. It was Harry Hill's showman's eye, however, that saw him putting on the first "acknowledged" female prizefight in America. Well attended by the usual array of sporting men whom he counted as his loyal customers, Hill's instincts had proven themselves to be correct—and thus began the era of female boxing shows, championships, and other related entertainments that spread from Hill's establishment on across the country.

Hill also quickly built on the momentum of his first show. A week and a half later, the *New York Herald*, writing about Harland's and Saunders's appearance in a boxing show at Hill's, noted that:

> Both girls have improved since their first appearance, and if their progress in acquiring the "points" and "tricks" in the art of self-defence is as rapid in the future as it has been in the past it will not be long before they will show to great advantage. [19]

Harry Hill's also continued making announcements of other upcoming female boxing entertainments such as the one listed in the *New York Herald* on June 8, 1876:

> A unique exhibition of boxing may be witnessed at Harry Hill's Variety Theatre this afternoon. It is proposed to give a benefit to the "Pioneer Female Boxers." As Misses Rose Harland and Nellie Saunders are called in the

bills. . . . The entertainment is to finish with a set-to in "full ring costume" between the "fair beneficiaries."[20]

In all likelihood, the popularity of the risqué establishment meant that it had license to push the boundaries of what was and was not acceptable without going so far as to lose its well-heeled patrons. This attitude toward Hill's, and the money he paid "under the table" to police authorities, gave him the further impetus to put on new forms of entertainment. Also helping were the press outlets such as the *New York Herald,* which were quite receptive to Hill's promotion of female pugilism.

While the fight in 1876 at Harry Hill's is considered the first fight between two women in the United States, there are tantalizing clues of a major prizefight held in the spring of 1872 in Canada. The fighters were likely from New York City and were brought to a training camp near Akron, Ohio. The story publicizing the bout was reported in an Ohio paper and republished in several newspapers across the country and even as far afield as Australia.

The article noted that a party of "sports" from New York City were "engaged in training two young ladies for a genuine prize fight for $1,000 a side." Both women were said to have "thrashed everything in their immediate neighborhoods" and had "agreed to meet in the prize ring and be governed by the rule that has made that time-honored institution, so famous."

The article continued:

> The ladies are in the hands of experienced trainers and the following is the order of their exercises: In the morning at 6 o'clock they get up and drink a cup of tea and eat a piece of brown bread; they get on their bloomer costumes, heavy soled shoes and dog-trot with the trainer for five miles. They then bathe, and are rubbed down in the most approved style, and permitted to rest in bed an hour. At 9 o'clock they breakfast. . . . At 11 they go to sparring or striking the sand bags. This exercise lasts about thirty minutes, when the trainer steps up and they have two hours of boxing. Then a bath and the usual rubbing down, and then their dinner. . . . Then a rest of thirty minutes and a walk or dog-trot with their trainers of a mile. . . . Then a half-hour's exercise with sand-bags—that is, striking from the shoulder a bag of sand suspended about the height of their breasts and weight 175 pounds.[21]

These unnamed female boxers were provided a training regimen in the time-honored tradition of the classic boxing camp—and it was obvious that no expense was spared in the run-up to the fight.

The popularity of the first boxing show at Harry Hill's led him to promote nightly female boxing events. Hill's bold inclusion of female pugilists at this theater led other impresarios to add women's fighting events to their roster of entertainers. A notice in a Virginia newspaper in 1877 of an upcoming show, including "Miss Rose Harland, the champion female boxer" as part of a card considered to be "monster entertainment," was a case in point.[22]

By the early 1880s Hill's nightly shows featured a stable of female fighters including regular African American women's bouts. Hill's also became the model for others of what were called concert saloons that greeted customers from all classes to a night of entertainment as far afield as California and in towns that crisscrossed the "wild" West. His inclusion of female boxers as part of his set of theatrical offerings also acted to legitimize women's prizefighting as a form of entertainment, as well as to give credence to the idea of female pugilists as champions in their own right.

Hill also banded together with the *National Police Gazette* to promote female pugilism. Founded in 1845 as a police organ to help capture criminals, under the ownership of Richard K. Fox, beginning in 1876 the *Police Gazette*, as it was popularly known, became renowned for its lurid headlines and a growing association with professional boxing. Its covers often featured scantily clad young women as victims of crimes or as exhibiting risqué behaviors.

Newspapers such as the *Police Gazette* also became part of the conversation about what was and was not lurid and respectable—and, in particular, helped frame women's participation in sports. Whether boxing in a saloon or bicycling at the forefront of a race in a prominent park, the *Police Gazette* featured stories and an illustration—often on the cover—that helped expose the outer reaches of Victorian decorum and the changing boundaries for those mores.

Hill's penchant for publicity and boxing promotion made his association with the *Police Gazette*—which began billing itself as "The Leading Illustrated Sporting Journal in America"—a natural. When it came to female boxing, Hill's association with the newsweekly included the publication of a woodcut drawing entitled *Honoring Nell Saunders*, as well as other advertisements and coverage of Hill's female bouts.

As an example of the *Police Gazette's* coverage of Hill's promotions as early as 1880, it announced that Miss Libbie Ross was crowned a female boxing champion in her win over Carrie Edwards at Henry Hill's. Ross went on to a career as a leading female pugilist, appearing on the stage and touring the country in concert saloons and theaters not unlike Harry Hill's. She ended up as a featured player at the City Hall Theater in Leadville, Colorado, in the early 1890s. In yet another illustration from Harry Hill's published in the *Police Gazette*, the world-title bare-knuckle boxing match between Hattie Stewart and Anne Lewis was displayed—though as the women were fully clothed in the tight-bodiced dresses of the day, it is fair to say that it was not a "literal" depiction of the event, which actually took place in Houston, Texas, as will be discussed.

VICTORIAN WOMAN OF THE RING: HATTIE STEWART

Hattie Stewart likely came to New York in 1884 and began promoting herself as "The Female 'John L. Sullivan' and Champion Woman Heavyweight Boxer." In a typewritten description of her exploits, neatly attached to an undated copy of a photograph of her from the early 1880s dated 1-5-1925, she is described as having "proved her right to the title . . . and on many occasions asserted her pugilistic superiority over some men opponents."[23] An etched copy of the same photograph is displayed in the May 17, 1884, edition of the *National Police Gazette:*

> In this issue we publish a portrait of Hattie Stewart, the female champion boxer, who is eager to box any of the many female champions of America. . . . She has boxed at all the leading variety theatres, and she is ready to meet all challengers who will put up a deposit with the Police Gazette.[24]

Speaking about her love of fighting to a reporter in Buffalo, New York, during a run of a boxing exhibition show in December 1887, she said:

> I love to fight. . . . As a girl at school in Philadelphia I was always fighting with boys. I was born [on October 27, 1858] and brought up in Philadelphia. I learned boxing and club-swinging in 1876 when I was 17 years old. For three years I taught boxing to ladies in the Norfolk, Va. Gymnasium. The southern women are pretty rough too. They can put on the gloves with any man. All they care for is horse racing and sport.[25]

She also told the reporter she was "married to Richard Stewart at Norfolk," where he "was master-of-the-sword at the gymnasium, where I taught boxing to women."

There is no mention of how she came to fight at Harry Hill's in New York City, though it can be surmised that, since she had already been on the theater circuit as a female pugilist, she was either invited to participate in a match at Hill's or made inquiries on her own. She was known to have boxed at Harry Hill's in April of 1884, including a three-round bout with Miss Millie Aleta, about whom the *New York Herald* noted that she "show[ed] that she understood how to hit, stop and get away in good style."[26]

A later notice in the *Police Gazette* from January 1885 said that Stewart's husband, Dick, was himself the "lightweight champion pugilist of East Virginia," and added that he would be "boxing with his wife, Hattie Stewart, at Apollo Hall, Troy, N.Y."[27] In fact, the Stewarts spent some time giving boxing exhibitions in and around Schenectady and Troy, New York, during the winter of 1885.

Through the pages of the *Police Gazette*, a Miss A. [Anne] Lewis and Hattie Stewart challenged each other to a boxing match. The terms of the

challenge were discussed in a letter from Anne Lewis to the sporting editor
about boxing Hattie Stewart in the December 27, 1885, edition of the paper:

> In her challenge she offers to box me four, six or eight rounds for from $250 to
> $600 and the entire gate receipts, or the winner to take sixty-five per cent
> thereof. I wish to state through your paper that I will box Miss Stewart eight
> rounds for $500 and the entire gate receipts after all expenses are paid, or the
> winner to take seventy-five and the loser twenty-five percent. [28]

Further arrangements were offered, including the place of the match, "New
York, Boston, Philadelphia or Chicago," an agreement to use "Queensbury
rules" and the further agreement to allow "Richard K. Fox to appoint the
referee," and signed, "Madame A. Lewis, Champion all-round female athlete
of America." The letter ended with the challenge to any and all women
interested in a wrestling match.

The *Police Gazette* published additional news stories about the fight as
they became available. In the February 14, 1885, edition, the rules of agreement for the fight were published. The following week, the newsweekly
published that the contest would be fought in New Orleans on "Sunday,
February 22," and that the bout had "created quite a breeze in sporting circles
in that vicinity." The fight itself would consist of "eight 3-minute rounds
according to 'Police Gazette' Revised Queensberry rules."[29]

Speaking of her fight against Lewis in 1887, Stewart said:

> Here's a picture of Anne Lewis. I licked her at Houston, Tex. on February 27,
> 1885. A match was made for us at New Orleans, for $200 a side, but the
> Sheriff intervened and we had to quit. She was the hardest woman I ever
> defeated, but I did it in less than two minutes. That's the great trouble in my
> business—the Sheriff. Whenever I get a chance to fight, even if its advertised
> as 'only a friendly set-to' the authorities get onto it and stop the mill. All the
> 'work' I do now has to be private. [30]

Whether the particulars of the fight were ever reported in the local press in
Louisiana and Texas is unknown; however, the fight remained an important
one for Stewart and Lewis.

After defeating Lewis, Hattie toured on and off with her husband, Dick,
winding up in Denver and other parts of Colorado giving boxing exhibitions
in the autumn of 1885.

By 1886 Stewart was appearing in variety shows in St. Paul, Minnesota,
both with her husband and in a separate exhibition consisting of female
athletes. The shows and the reportage about them provide a glimpse into the
public perception of women's boxing a mere ten years after the first fight at
Harry Hill's. They also give a hint of the progressive development of the
sport as an entertainment from one venue in New York City to a variety of

venues across the country, not to mention the interferences from local authorities from what Stewart called "the Sheriff."

Billed as part of "The Stewarts' All Star Specialty company," an item
appeared in the October 3, 1886, edition of the *St. Paul Daily Globe*, noting
that Hattie Stewart was "the champion female pugilist of America" and that
she, along with her husband, Dick, were said to be "novelty sketch people."
Their show was put on at the Olympic Theater and included not only her
pugilistic prowess but also song-and-dance men, clog dancing, flying trapeze
artists, Minnie Lamont enacting seriocomic roles, and a pair of sketch artists.[31]

A favorable notice was published about the night's entertainment, judging
them "a good company" that had "played to a more than average audience
last night" with "several unusually clever members."[32] One can presume that
this included Hattie Stewart's pugilism act, which was certainly a decided
novelty. A week later the company was said to have given a "creditable
variety performance," so much so that they were booked at the Theater
Comique in Minneapolis for a second week.[33]

Hattie Stewart also performed in December of that year as part of Col.
Joseph H. Wood's female athletic exhibition. The production was originally
booked for a one-week stand at the Exposition Rink in St. Paul, Minnesota.
An article appearing in the paper, however, noted that the "chief of police
was informed . . . by the mayor that the proposed 'female athletic and gymnastic entertainment' . . . would not be allowed." The show was to feature "'a
female John L. Sullivan,' . . . wrestling bouts by female athletes, and other
athletic sports by a troupe of female gymnasts."[34]

The following day a note appeared providing tantalizing clues as to why
the show had been stopped—particularly given that Hattie Stewart, the "female John L. Sullivan," had successfully played in St. Paul to good notices
two months prior to the December engagement. In the article, the journalist
wrote "The edict . . . will have a demoralizing effect on this class of sport in
St. Paul in the future"; however, he further wrote that "While the suspicion is
probably unjust, there is a rumor current that Ald. Pat Conley had something
to do with the freezing out—solely in the interest of legitimate amusements."[35] In other words the fix was in—perhaps because entertainments
featuring female athletes were proving popular to the detriment of other more
standard programs.

Whatever the actual reason, Col. Wood was able to rebook the show at
the Theater Comique in neighboring Minneapolis without incident for a one-
week stand. Thus the show—featuring not only Hattie Stewart but also an
assortment of wrestlers and boxers including Nellie Gorman, Belle Leslie,
Laura Henderson, Agnes Fleming, and Ellen Marr—was able to go on.

In the follow-up article that appeared in the press touting the show, it was
noted, "that there is nothing in [Col. Wood's] show which violates any law or

ordinance. It being simply an exposition of the possibilities of the female sex in the development of physical strength."[36]

The show's promoter, Col. Wood, was renowned as the P. T. Barnum of the Midwest. He was primarily known as a theatrical producer and showman who had built Wood's Museum, first in Cleveland and later in Chicago. The Chicago venue proved to be a highly popular circus-like site for "curiosities" and other theatrical entertainments, and even housed Egyptian mummies, until it burned down in the Great Chicago Fire of 1871.

The show consisted of various athletic exhibitions including club swinging, a Greco-Roman wrestling match followed by a catch-as-catch-can wrestling match between two champions: Miss Laura Henderson (Greco-Roman) and Miss Agnes Fleming (catch-as-catch-can). Once those were completed, the main event of the evening was introduced, a four-round bout between Hattie Stewart (noted as the female John L. Sullivan) and Leslie Remington, a female middleweight champion. The author felt that Stewart "out-classed" her opponent in the "science" of boxing and that "she presented a strong guard and struck straight from the shoulder, man-like." Remington's blows by contrast were noted as "bias swipes, as she looked one way and struck another."

Given that Stewart outweighed her opponent by some thirty pounds and had far superior skills, the author ended his piece dolefully opining, "It is doubtful as to whether the deed of 'noble women in a noble art' were particularly edifying."

Other than the attention given to the appearance of the women and some blow-by-blow descriptions, the review did not at all discuss the right of women to perform athletic feats or to object to the show—except perhaps to complain at the relative quality of their efforts save for Stewart's.

As an interesting side note to the story, appearing not three months later, in March 1887, "A boxing match between female pugilists [was] arranged to take place at the Olympic Theater, St. Paul." The two fighters were said to be Marcia Meade and Eugenia Meade who were to compete in a ten-round bout. The brief item closed with the sentiment "a novel and interesting match is looked for."[37] No other articles related to the fight could be found.

Hattie herself returned to St. Paul with her husband, Dick, to play at the Olympic Theater in February 1888, where they are said to have put on "one of the best boxing matches one would care to witness." Coincidently, her old boxing teacher, Prof. Johnnie Clark, was in the audience, which only added to hilarity, when following the instructions in his note to her that read, "Please know the old man silly for me," Hattie did just that, actually bringing out "the claret" with "a terrific right hander."[38]

Her career as a boxer continued, doing shows with her husband or taking on all comers when afforded the opportunity. Asked in 1887 if she ever fought men, she said, "Oh yes, many times. My husband don't like to have me fight men, because it's no credit to them if they knock me out, and if the men are defeated the crowed always says it was a 'hippodrome.'"

Her opinion of her female opponents was not all that great either. "Most of the women I meet in the ring are no good. They won't stand up and give the people the worth of their money."[39]

Hattie did, however, continue to offer challenges for fights. One such challenge in 1890 was to Hattie Leslie (born Libbie Sporn), who had a controversial win over Alice Leary (born Barbara Dillon) for the title of female world champion in 1888, as shall be discussed. Stewart, then performing in Seattle, Washington, offered a fight for $500 a side. Leslie responded, noting "she would meet in a glove contest for $250 a side . . . [with] *Police Gazette* rules to govern with gloves weighing not over two ounces, bare hand preferred." Leslie signed the challenge, "Hattie Leslie, Champion Female Pugilist Boxer of the World."[40] The fight, however, was never held.

At some point in the early 1890s, Hattie Stewart remarried, to a man named Thomas Gillen, a former lightweight pugilist and actor. It is unknown if she and Dick Stewart divorced or if he died. Hattie was still billed as the "Female John L. Sullivan" and she and her new husband continued to give boxing exhibition shows across the United States well into the turn of the century, eventually settling down to live in the Bronx, New York.

THE FIRST FEMALE WORLD BOXING CHAMPIONSHIP

In early July of 1888, "Two well dressed young women and several men met . . . at the restaurant Napoleon, on Main Street [in Buffalo, New York] to make arrangements for a prize fight."

The fighters were noted to be "Hattie Leslie, who is doing a club swinging act in a variety theater, and Alice Leary a serio comic."

Of the two women, Hattie Leslie was stated to be the more experienced. She was described as "twenty years old, 5 feet 7 inches tall, weighs 180 pounds and is muscular and well developed. She is a boxer of unusual ability and has knocked out pretty fair fighters in practicing with them."

Alice Leary by contrast was "six feet tall, twenty-four years old, weighs 180 pounds, and is also a brunette. She has not as much science as her opponent, but is more of a slugger."

Training was set to commence immediately for Alice, while Hattie's would not as "her club swinging requires she keep in good physical condition."

Having agreed upon the rules, both fighters signed the articles of agreement, which read in part:

> We hereby agree to fight a fair stand up prize fight with skin tight gloves according to the new rule of the London prize fight to take place between

August 23 and 27 place to be agreed on August 20, the fight to be for $500 a
side and the championship of the world. The fight is to take place within one
hundred miles of Buffalo. [41]

One unusual aspect of the rules of engagement was the agreement to use
skintight gloves rather than the six-ounce gloves typically used in prizefights
at that time. Unfortunately, there is no understanding as to why the combatants did not insist upon padded gloves, which provided much more safety to
the fighters. Another aspect of the promotion for the fight was the absence of
the *Police Gazette* imprimatur, which may well have insisted upon the use of
some padding even if it were only two ounces.

The date of the fight was also delayed until September 16, 1888. The
locale eventually chosen was Navy Island, Ontario, Canada—a tiny island
originally colonized by the French on the Niagara River just south of Niagara
Falls and the site of the small but popular Queens Hotel resort along with a
few farmsteads. It was also the site of "three" of local pugilist "Billy Baker's
fights," who was also acting as one of the promoters of the bout. [42]

The fight group putting on the contest had been anticipating heavy betting
on the outcome of the bout—and due to their publicity efforts, the press was
to be well represented by reporters at the scene from some of the New York
papers who would file their stories by telegraph after the contest.

True to their word, the press was in attendance and reported that some
fifty "toughs" or "sports" viewed the fight, depending upon which account of
the fight was read. Others in attendance included the promoters, four well-
known male pugilists who acted as seconds and referees, and Hattie's pugilist husband, John Lewis, who allegedly taught her to box and worked alongside her in a variety act that included sparring and club swinging. He also
helped train her for the bout against Leary. One thing none of them had
considered was that the day they'd chosen for the fight was a Sunday.

In the predawn hours of the day of the match, in a heavy rain, the fighters
and their entourage along with some fifty attendees and reporters boarded a
"steamer towing a barge filled with liquids and solids" [43] for the three-hour
trip up the Niagara River to Navy Island. Upon arrival, and with the rain
coming down around them, it was evident that the ground they intended to
use for the fight was too wet. The group scouted out an old empty farmhouse
as an alternative, but it was found to be unsuitable and eventually they settled
upon a barn.

The barn itself was smaller than the usual square ring of twenty or twenty-four feet. Measuring only ten feet by twenty feet, there was no place for
the usual ropes, and the people in attendance had to either stand flat against
the hay and oat bales lining the walls of the barn or sit in the rafters above.

Along with finding a locale for their set-to, the fighters switched from
using the London prizefighting rules to the newer Queensbury rules—though

no explanation was given for the change. Seconds were chosen as well. George "The Marine" LeBlanche, a well-known fighter from New York City, agreed to act as Hattie Leslie's second, and the local fighter Billy Baker did the honors for Alice Leary. The referee chosen for the bout was "local sport" Jack Leonard, along with "Fistic" Carroll,[44] who was chosen as the timekeeper.

Weighing in at 160 lbs., Leslie was the tauter of the two fighters and seemed in better condition. Leary, weighing in at 148 lbs., was in the opinion of the reporter from the *Sun*, "not trained down fine enough,"[45] even though she wore her weight on her six-foot frame. Both women readied for the fight out of sight of the barn, stripping down to their fighting costumes, which consisted of tights (black for Leslie, white for Leary), sleeveless wrappers (white for both), trunks (wine colored for Leslie, blue for Leary), and "regulation buff fighting shoes without spikes,"[46] with each woman covered by a white skirt and towels, to be removed at the time of the fight.

Both women were also given their gloves. As described by the *New York Herald*, they were "driving kids, lined with a thin flannel [with] the ends of the fingers and thumbs . . . clipped off and the cording taken out of the backs to avoid cutting the pretty faces of the fighters."[47] While not a bare-knuckle fight, the use of the gloves added protection for the boxers' hands, but otherwise did little to protect the fighters, and if anything the use of such gloves was thought to have the potential to cause more damage as the fighters would feel more license to hit the bones of the face.

All in readiness, the two women entered the barn to the excited hoots and howls of the crowd before making their way to their respective corners and their seats on inverted peach baskets. Within minutes, both fighters were stripped down and, after shaking hands in the center of the "ring," commenced their battle at 8:14 in the morning.

The fight itself lasted seven rounds. It was agreed upon by everyone in attendance that Leary had drawn first blood in the fourth round and drew blood again in the fifth round. Leslie, though, was the harder puncher and the better fighter with the fifth round proving to be a tough slog for both fighters. In the sixth round, in the opinion of the *New York Herald* reporter, "Leary's heart was broken," though Leslie did not take advantage of that and rather than aim for the knockout she continued to spar with Leary. By the seventh round, with Leary clearly wilting to the consternation of the crowd, Leslie's second, George LeBlanche "warned her if she didn't knock Leary out to the best of her ability he would quit." This got Leslie to attack with renewed vigor as she let loose a barrage of "vicious pegs at pretty nearly every part of her opponent's anatomy," to the continued shouts of LeBlanche. With time called, Leary, "held out her hands for the gloves to be pulled off," and Leslie was declared the winner with the time at 8:38 a.m.

Both fighters were clearly spent at the end. According to the *New York Herald*, Leslie sported "two black eyes" and Leary "one," with both their "faces and hands . . . badly swollen." One paper also reported: "The sum of money the winner is to receive is rather speculative, but the loser had a $10 purse made up among the spectators after the close of the fight."[48]

By 12:30 that afternoon, they had all arrived back in Buffalo.[49] The aftermath of the fight, however, had barely begun.

Perhaps because the fighters were women who were both evidently so beaten, or perhaps because as the *New York Herald* noted it occurred "in the presence of fifty as tough, bad men as divine Providence ever allowed to congregate on a Sabbath morning," the fight was immediately condemned by the press and by the authorities in Buffalo and the surrounding Erie County.

While the coverage by the *Sun* newspaper was neutral, the story in the *New York Herald*, which was picked up and carried across the country, was decidedly aghast. In hyperbolic prose, including the remark that the bout was "one of the most remarkable exhibitions ever presented in a civilized country," it clearly sensationalized what it called the "fistic encounter" that would have been "a rather common place affair," but for the fact that the "fight was between two women."

The sub-headlines also cast a negative light. The round-by-round descriptions were sub-headlined "The Disgraceful Exhibition" followed by "Blood and Staggering Blows" for the third and fourth rounds, and just a one-word heading—"Brutal!"—for the fifth, sixth, and seventh, all of which further sensationalized the encounter.

The contrast to the *Sun's* descriptions, which were matter of fact and devoid of any particular editorial content to guide the readers' interpretation of the fight, was also interesting, especially since both papers routinely reported on female pugilism in New York, and the *New York Herald*, in particular, had a history of publishing positive stories about Harry Hill's women's boxing entertainments.

Other newspapers both local and regional also published stories about the fight. New York City's *New York World* had sub-headlines that read: "A Disgraceful Match Between Amazons Near Buffalo. Alice Leary and Hattie Leslie Pound Each Other Like Real Pugilists—An Exciting Affair in Which Blood Was Drawn—Alice's Second Threw up the Sponge for Her After the Seventh Round."[50]

The *Troy Daily Times* wrote:

> One gets a square look of barbarism in the face when he reads how Mrs. Hattie Leslie and Miss Alice Leary . . . fought for $500 and the female championship of the world. . . . The principals pounded each other for seven rounds, the reported incidents having all the savagery and loathsomeness of a regular mill

between brutes of the other sex. Civilization has a great deal of work to do yet.[51]

The Washington *Evening Star* published edited portions of the *New York Herald* story with a sub-headline that read: "A Brutal and Disgusting Encounter on an Island in Niagara River."[52]

By the following day, the *New York Herald* published a piece under the heading "Divine Woman!" that began: "Women's rights, indeed! Why, if things go on in this way much longer, the men of the community will have to organize for mutual protection." The piece continued:

> When ladies take to prize fighting our home life has touched its zenith of glory and refinement. There is no sight under heaven so inspiring, so ennobling, so soul entrancing, so full of all that goes to make poor human nature angelic and god-like, as that of two women in a country barn, with fifty roughs and toughs for spectators, stripping themselves to their tights and preceding to maul, smash, mash, gash, knock each other's teeth out and pound each other's faces until they are black and blue."[53]

Within two days, on September 20, Hattie Leslie and her husband, John (Spond) Leslie (she was also known as Mrs. Lizzie Spond), were arrested at their home in Buffalo, New York. At police headquarters they "were examined by Police Superintendent Morin," before Hattie was brought "before the grand jury" for more questioning. Also arrested for "aiding and abetting a prize fight" was Bill Baker, Alice Leary's second. Alice herself was not indicted at that time, but had otherwise disappeared, some said across the border to Canada. According to the newspaper account in the *Daily Leader*, the police were willing to go so far as to haul in every "spectator, including the newspaper men," if necessary.[54]

The next arrest came on September 24. George "The Marine" LeBlanche, who had been indicted by the Erie County Grand Jury on the same charges of aiding and abetting a prizefight, was taken into custody in New York City at the behest of the Buffalo police superintendent. The first assistant district attorney in Erie County, William D. Mossey, had issued the bench warrant and LeBlanche was to be brought to Buffalo for trial. John Floss, who had helped promote the bout, was also arrested along with a man name Curley Hughes who was described as "a dead game" (a colloquial expression for what we would call a "straight shooter.")

The case was brought to trial two weeks later, on October 4. Hattie Leslie provided testimony for the prosecution, stating that she had been approached by Billy Baker and had agreed to a prizefight for money. She also testified that she'd been taken to Navy Island by boat to fight, and that John Floss had only given her $15 for her part rather than the $250 she had been promised.

The defense took the position that it was not a real prizefight, but a publicity stunt for Hattie Leslie's growing career as a club swinger and boxer. They further contended that signing the article of agreement was a way of making the fight seem legitimate and of enticing the newspapers to cover it.

The district attorney, however, clearly laid out the plot as one of malfeasance at best and saved his strongest condemnation for his closing argument:

> The women . . . were to share the proceeds of this most brutal, most outrageous affair. The price was $6 to be entertained on the Sabbath by women fighting. If this is not disgusting, I have nothing to say. I don't blame the women so much, though they are indicted. It is these men, these creatures, who are at fault. It is a disgrace to you and a disgrace to me—a shame to a city known for its law-abiding character, to think that men so brutal, so lost to every instinct in manhood should engage in such an enterprise.[55]

At eight o'clock that evening, after the jury had deliberated for two hours, the verdict came back with convictions for four of the five male defendants in the case. George LeBlanche and John Floss were each eventually sentenced to three months, while Billy Baker and John Spann [Leslie] were both sentenced to six months in the penitentiary. Hattie Leslie, who was to have been tried separately, was discharged and all pending charges were dropped against Alice Leary. John Floss also had his conviction overturned on appeal November 19, 1889.

The uproar about the fight, however, didn't stop with newspaper accounts or even in the courts of Erie County, New York. No less a personage than Dr. Thomas De Will Talmage, the pastor of the famed Brooklyn Tabernacle Church, took up the matter of the fight from the pulpit, having received a letter of complaint because an article about the bout was carried in a newspaper on the same page as one of his sermons. In addressing the issue, Dr. Talmage said in part:

> My reply is, that a newspaper which professes to be a picture of everyday life must give all of it. . . . Beside that, in an age when pugilism is so popular . . . and we are daily informed . . . of the different stage of illness in the case of [John L.] Sullivan, the celebrated bruiser, it is no wonder that women aspire to the honors being won by our sex. I do not know why women may not as well fight as men. Will you not deny them all privileges? You will not let them vote, and you will not let them preach, and now you would put limitation on the swing of their fists. . . . But, to take a more sedate tone, there may come some good from that encounter at Buffalo. It demonstrates to men as hardly anything else could what a mean, absurd, brutal, loathsome and disgusting thing is pugilism and that there may be a recoil most healthful and fighting matches [will end] . . . which have been the disgrace of our cities . . . on the

same level with dog fights in which a Sullivan bloodhound or a Kilrain New-foundland leave each other mauled and bleeding in the sawdust of the pit. [56]

As in England before, the issue of the brutality of the ring was a vexing one that was only exacerbated by the presence of women. Boxing remained illegal in most locales across the country, and while the vehemence with which the prosecutors in Erie County pursued the promoters in the Leslie-Leary fight was based on the contest having been between two women, it was by no means the first or the last of such prosecutions for prizefighting.

Reports of brutal prizefights were also not limited to women in the ring. Within days of the verdict, a "Brutal Prize-Ring Fight" made page one headlines in the *New York World*. The fight held in Canarsie, Brooklyn, was between "Johnnie Maher, of Fort Hamilton" and "Eddie Hart, of Flushing" and was noted as "eleven rounds, in which Hart was terribly punished" and "frightfully battered." [57]

The *Police Gazette,* which had championed women's boxing since its early associations with Harry Hill in the 1870s, also seemed to put a tentative foot toward questioning women's participation in the sport when it published a series of quotes from London's *Lancet* that also spoke to this issue in October 1890:

> We noticed with some degree of alarm in the columns of a contemporary recently that "another step is to be noted in the progress of women. Henceforth the noble art of self-defence is to be included in the list of her many accomplishments." It is satisfactory to find that this statement is merely alleged in regard to our fair American cousins.

In the same edition, a piece about the proposed fight between Hattie Stewart and Hattie Leslie, obviously penned by the paper's owner, Richard K. Fox, was published. He offered that while "both champions . . . are clever with the mufflers . . . it is a game that they should allow the men to figure in." Continuing, Fox wrote, "Boxing between females is a very dangerous sport, and those who have followed it have never created a sensation, neither will they."

Had the tide turned? Was the outrage against boxing due in some small measure to the popularity of the gloved sport among women? Other articles in the *Police Gazette* about female pugilists tended toward short-paragraph pieces of boxing news relating information on upcoming bouts or the results of completed ones. Why, at that time, Richard Fox should have voiced disapproval for women's participation is an unknown, as other pieces after the 1890 article did not follow suit. The *Police Gazette's* reportage of the Leslie-Leary fight and the subsequent court case two years earlier were also absent of any editorial commentary. It is possible that something more personal regarding Stewart and Leslie was at work, or perhaps Fox was voicing the frustration of the diminishing financial returns on female bouts. As it is, without further clarity, the reasons for Fox's change of heart remain an unknown.

All of the complexities of the fight game were certainly at play in the Leslie-Leary fight, magnified by the gender of the two contestants. The court case and associated press, however, did not stop women's participation in the sport, and Leslie was to enjoy much greater success and recognition for her skills after the fight. Neither did it resolve the place of women in the frame of boxing's masculine domain. If anything, the question became even more complex, as the evident skill of Leslie as a boxer contradicted the prevailing view of women as incapable of such athletic feats. That she had to be "egged" on for the kill by her second, gave credence to the prevailing view that women were ill-suited by temperament for a blood sport. The fact remains, however, that Leslie executed the commands and finished her job in the ring in the tradition of the game, much as the men, routinely pushed by their corners, gave their all to the sport in the same situation.

OTHER BOXING WOMEN 1870S–1892

Until the past two decades athletic sport in all its branches was confined to the male division of the human race. But during the past twenty years many females have tried to emulate and follow in the path of the various athletic champions by attempting to become proficient with the oar, the boxing glove, as well as shoot, run, wrestle and walk.
—*National Police Gazette*[58]

In 1892 the *Police Gazette,* having overcome its briefly stated reticence about female boxers from two years before, published an article entitled "Women in the Prize Ring." The write-up made reference to the women who "decades ago in England" had boxed and "posed as clever exponents of the art of self defence," before touting what it saw as the true pioneers of American female pugilism.

One such person was Libby Kelly (Ross). Born in Jacksonville, Florida, Kelly "was a tall, athletic looking girl, possessed a long reach, understood how to hit, stop and counter to perfection," and beginning in 1878 "appeared at Harry Hill's . . . [making] her name famous by the science she displayed."[59] Kelly was trained by the Harry Hill denizen Jimmy Kelly, and in the opinion of the *Police Gazette* "was at the time she made her *debut* the most scientific of her day."[60]

Libby and Carry (Carrie) Edwards, another one of the original group of female pugilists who started boxing in the late 1870s, often performed together in a boxing act around the country, billing themselves as the "Original Champion Female Sparrers."[61] One such appearance in November 1880 at

Thompson's Theater in Dallas, Texas, listed them as "rare attractions" of "renowned athletes who, in their role, have no superiors."[62]

The *Police Gazette* also ran an item on the pair noting "the champion female boxers of New York have created quite a sensation at St. Antonio, Texas.[63]

Libby Kelly, considered by the *Police Gazette* to be "the first female champion boxer" of the United States, continued to box until 1882, when on "a boxing tour . . . [in] Pensacola . . . she knocked against an admirer with such force that he fell in love with her, and a wedding was the result." The story continued, noting that "poverty finally came in at the door and love flew out the window, which accounts for the female champion's return to [New York]."[64] Boxing under her married name, Libby Ross, she put in appearances at Harry Hill's and resumed touring with her sparring partner, Carry Edwards.

The honors for the original and foremost female pugilist on the stage, however, belonged to Mlle. (or Madame) D'Omer. Said to have come to the United States from France with her husband, Mons. D'Omer (who was very likely Irish or English), and performing for the first time in New York in October 1874, the two put on a death-defying sword act to enthusiastic crowds, followed by other athletic exhibitions and a boxing finale that included a boxing match between them. For the show at New York's Theatre Comique, Mlle. D'Omer was listed as "the champion female athlete."[65]

In describing their act, the *New York Clipper* noted that "Mons. D'Omer, aided by Mlle. D'Omer, performed a number of feats, evincing his skill and dexterity with the sword," including cutting a lemon in half that rested on the nape of Mlle. D'Omer's neck "without leaving a mark upon the lady's neck."

His next feat was to shoot "an arrow through an apple placed upon Mlle. D'Omer's head" with a blowgun, after which:

> Their performance concluded with an exhibition of the manly art of self-defence, boxing-gloves being need[ed]. Mlle. D'Omer proved to be a skillful boxer, and got in some very telling blows upon the head and face of her opponent, while she parried with grace and agility those aimed at herself. Both were loudly applauded during their various rounds, and recalled at the close of their feats. This portion of their entertainment has no objectionable features, and enables ladies to gain an insight into the manner in which professional "mills" are conducted, without having their sensibilities shocked.[66]

The popularity of the boxing portion of the show and the review noting that even women could watch had an impact on the future of this kind of entertainment. For one, it legitimized the presence of women in the theater while giving credence to the popularity that pugilism had obtained in mainstream culture. Secondly, it gave the D'Omers license to begin touting Mlle. D'Omer's boxing prowess more openly as a marketable aspect of their show.

This is precisely what happened in early 1875 when the two booked in at Brooklyn's Novelty Theater and for another week at the Park Theater. Mlle. D'Omer's billings for the shows listed her as "The accomplished Athlete and Amazonian Scientist" and noted that the two would "appear in a pleasing Scientific Display of Valor!" in addition to their sword act—in other words they would box.[67]

The following November 1875 saw the two in a return engagement at the Park Theater. For that series of shows, Mlle. D'Omer openly touted her boxing abilities with an ad that billed her as "The Lady Athlete and Only Female Boxer in the World."

Building on that success, the D'Omers played to packed houses in St. Louis in December 1875, while the duo of "Fayette Welch and Jennie Satterlee gave an excellent burlesque on the D'Omer [act] . . . at a rival establishment."[68]

If one considers mimicry as the best form of flattery, the "burlesque" of the D'Omer show, and particularly of Mlle. D'Omer's athletic prowess, likely meant that she had tapped into something that resonated with both the audiences and thereby the financial potential that other performers could capitalize upon. It is also telling that she had chosen to label herself a "female boxer" in her advertisements as she not only furthered the legitimation of boxing as a female performance art, but also provided a strong indication of the acceptance she was receiving for her display of boxing's highest accolade: good science.

A review of their act the following February, in 1876, appearing on page one of the *New York Sun*, gives credence to that assessment and also shows that she had not only staying power on the stage but also a solidly positive appeal, even though she was performing male physical feats:

> Her position in sparring is graceful, and every blow is given with judgment. When apparently exhausted, after a lively bout, she walks around her antagonist, and, watching a favorable opportunity, strikes out, always keeping her face well guarded. She is possessed with an excellent temper and laughs as heartily when worsted as when holding the vantage ground. In her contest . . . she pummeled the Monsieur so scientifically and effectually that he, panting for breath bowed to the audience saying: "That's my first defeat in a long while!" Madame D'Omer went from the stage, her face crimson from the hard blows. The Madame has in her possession a costly silver belt, studded with precious stones, which was presented to her as the champion woman boxer in England. She has walked a mile inside of eight minutes.[69]

Given the success of her pugilism show on the so-called "legitimate" stage, it is clear why Harry Hill thought to bring female pugilism into his more decidedly "low brow" entertainments so closely following the review of the D'Omer show in the *New York Sun*. And while there is no definitive understanding on why he chose to add female boxing to the acts he already presented, he would certainly have been aware of the popularity of her show.

Over the next few years, several women successfully performed sparring and boxing acts in theaters across the country. Rose Harland of Harry Hill's fame even found herself on the same bill as the D'Omers in 1878 at the Olympic Theater in New York. The *New York Clipper* often carried advertisements for female pugilists seeking opportunities for shows, such as Nettie Burt and Alice Livingston, who advertised themselves as "The Original Female Boxers, in their act The Art of Self-Defence." Nettie in particular claimed that she had "held the Champion Medal for over a year" and was the "Champion Female Boxer of America"—offered as part of Harry Hill's boxing shows at that time.[70]

Nettie had gotten her start boxing at Harry Hill's in or around 1878 in a "set-to" with Carrie Wells. The *New York Herald* wrote:

> For three rounds they showed considerable science, and though the claret was not drawn, still they managed to disarrange one another's headgear and to deliver some very telling blows on each other's frontispiece. Nettie Burt, who is the taller and also longer in reach, seemed to have slightly the best of it in the wind up, but the majority of the audience was enthusiastic over the smaller antagonist, Carrie Wells.[71]

Alice Jennings, another fighter out of Harry Hill's, was deemed to "display" good "science" in a bout against Libby Kelly's sparring partner, "Carrie Edwards," in 1882, and though she lost the fight, she offered to meet any fighter for $500 and gold medal awards.[72] Professor John R. (Johnny) Clark, Hattie Stewart's old boxing teacher, gave Jennings "a diamond ring" at a "benefit" held in her honor "in Philadelphia at the Olympic Garden" in 1883.[73] Jennings also published "a standing challenge to any female boxer in the world" for the extraordinary amount of "$2,500, at either 110 or 125 pounds."[74] Whether she ever realized that sum is unknown, but the offering gives a sense of her popularity in the ring at that time.

Anne Lewis, known as the "Cleveland Wonder," and who famously lost a bout to Hattie Stewart, was also a celebrated boxer. Lewis, who was born on October 29, 1856, in Chemung County, New York, eventually made her home in Cleveland, Ohio. An article, calling her an "amazon expert" boxer, in the *Syracuse Daily Standard* described her as follows:

> She is a tall, stately woman of masculine bearing, and walks with a firm, decided step. Her form is as straight as an arrow. She has a pleasing face, her lips are thin and firm, and her eyes clear and piercing. Her hair is of a bright, auburn hue, and is worn banged. The muscles of her arms and chest are hard as iron. A wiry bundle of muscle, lying from the collar bone to the armpit stand

out in great prominence. . . . She is . . . 5 feet 6 inches tall, and weighs 155 pounds.[75]

Lewis's talents as a boxer included fights with men. In January of 1885 she was said to have fought "a six round soft glove contest [with] Queensbury rules [against] Frank Stark of Sioux City at the Theater Comique,"[76] in Minneapolis, Minnesota. She also was said to have participated in "collar and elbow wrestling" matches in addition to her boxing.

Fighter "Lizzie Somers, the 110-pound female pugilist," was called out by the Troy, New York, fighter of some renown Nellie Malloy in an open challenge published in the *Sun*. In an article that ran a few days after the challenge, "Edwin Stevens, the plucky female featherweight trainer and backer, said that in case his protégé was matched he would begin her training by walking her from First Street to the Harlem bridge before breakfast."

Born in Brooklyn and nearing her twentieth birthday, Somers was described as "a pretty young women [with] a trim figure," with the writer adding that "any lady of her weight will have to 'mind her eye' in order to defeat her."[77]

Other female pugilists from the period come down to us from the *Police Gazette*'s publication of a series of brief vignettes about the state of female boxing in February 1885, just prior to the Stewart-Lewis fight. In their opinion, Libby Kelly was "the most scientific of her day."

Other boxers in the spotlight were "Carrie Livingston, Nettie Burk, Alice Livingston and Rose Marshall," although in their opinion "Libby Kelly was more a match for any of them."

The next grouping of women noted by the *Police Gazette* article included "Mabel Gray, Alice Jennings and Daisy Daley" along with "Hattie Stewart . . . Bertha McCoy . . . [and] Anne Lewis." The piece also had nothing but praise for Mlle. D'Omer, whom it was said now resided in Rochester, New York.[78] Hattie Leslie, who famously fought Alice Leary, and Hattie Edwards were also important figures in female pugilism in the period beginning in the mid-1880s.

Alice Ross of Canada, fighting in the early 1880s, gained notoriety, and Marry McNamara and Julia Perry, who fought a tough battle in 1888 where "vicious blows were interchanged," leaving both fighters "badly disfigured,"[79] also came to some prominence.

Jennie (Eugenia) Meade, originally from Cincinnati and trained by John Rowan, along with Marcia Meade, from New York "trained under John Donovan," fought a ten-round contest together at the "Olympic Theater, St. Paul, [Minnesota]" in March of 1887,[80] which gave them both notoriety in the sport.

Women's boxing in this era was not just confined to the United States. Women were known to have boxed and wrestled in France throughout the

19th century "in circuses, in music-halls, and at Fairs."[81] Female pugilists also began appearing on the British stage, and women were known to have displayed their science in Canada and Australia.

There were doubtless many other women who tried their hand at professional pugilism in this period. Some were dancers, gymnasts, singers, seriocomics, and other performers who found their way to boxing to expand their repertoire and marketability on the stage, while others, such as Hattie Stewart, just liked to fight. Whatever their reasons, they brought boxing to the fore and helped spur a movement for nonprofessional women to pick up the gloves if for no other reason than the sheer pleasure of the sport.[82]

CROSSING THE DIVIDE: SPARRING FOR THE LADIES AND OTHER SPORTS OF THE NEW WOMAN

Through the 1880s sports were beckoning women of all classes, as were the concepts of leisure and recreation. While some sports leant themselves more toward competition, such as pedestrianism, rowing, baseball, hockey, and bicycle racing, other sports were considered more leisurely and more in line with the feminine disposition. The latter included lawn tennis, croquet, dancing, gymnastic exercises (light), roller skating and ice skating, golf in the early 1890s, and with the development of the "safety bicycle," which sported newly designed wheels of equal size, bicycle riding.

The embrace of sports by women was not without strong opposition. The classic Victorian female was meant to conserve all of her strength for the rigors of childbirth and motherhood. Female competitive sports in particular were discouraged in favor of "healthful" displays of exercise. The Victorian conservative moralist Miss T. R. Coombs was one such person who argued against the sport of competitive bicycling by asking:

> Can we admire a girl, however beautiful she may be, whose face is as red as a lobster, and streaming with perspiration whose hair is hanging in a mop about her ears whose hairpins are strewn along the race-course, and whose general appearance is dusty, untidy and unwomanly?[83]

Boxing, while it remained on the periphery, at best, of acceptable sports for women, did begin to cut across class lines. Much as boxing and sparring had attracted "gentlemen" over the years, both in England and in the United States, the sport began to attract "ladies" as well. A case in point was the 1885 Sparring Club of Philadelphia's festival of games, an event hosted annually, featuring gloved contests between club members where ladies were present.

Under the heading "Philadelphia's Foibles. Young Ladies Studying the Noble Art of Self-Defence. Fair Hands in Boxing Gloves," the *New York*

Herald published a piece in January 1886 (and republished across the country) on the sparring craze among the privileged young women of that city since the festival. Couched in the idea that "The young ladies present ever in search of a new sensation, caught at the idea of learning to spar," the article described the difficulties of training them, where the "young ladies [have a] feminine passion for 'a strong guard' and a prompt 'cross-counter'" which the article's writer assumes is "likely to grow."

One boxing master is described as a "professional teacher of the heretofore exclusively 'manly art'" who had "met the best men of his day in this country and England, though never for money or with bare knuckles."

He had several students "but said, frankly, that he did not enjoy giving lessons, because he was in constant fear of accidently injuring his pupils."

His main concern was in ensuring that the young women's hands were properly gloved. To do so, he modified the design, adding "extra horse hair padding" as well as introducing an extra interior glove to help the women make a fist, while cutting of the top of the outer one. "Alteration [of] the gloves is rendered necessary," he said, "by the universal inclination among the female sex to strike with the hand open."

He continued and said, "It is the most difficult thing imaginable to teach a lady to close her fist. Even after you think she has been sufficiently warned of the danger she will impulsively lunge at you with her open hand—the fingers straight out and rigid." No explanation was provided for this phenomenon other than that the inclination was to slap rather than punch.

Asked if he felt that the sport was "a proper one for young ladies?" he replied,

> Why not? They are taught to swing clubs and dumb-bells at nearly every ladies' seminary in the country. I regard sparring purely as a sport. . . . It inculcates a poise on the feet that never can be secured otherwise and it develops muscles of the shoulders and back as no other exercise yet discovered does. [84]

An article published in April of 1886 about a woman in West Philadelphia who also taught sparring provided a different perspective on her young charges. She had taken up the gloves very reluctantly due to "failing health" and "weak lungs" at the behest of a brother with similar problems who'd found his way back to robust health through boxing exercises. After learning to spar, "she found the tonic of judicious exercise far superior to any preparation of bitters she had taken before" and "began to eat more," and "soon the roses of health drove the pallid hue of invalidism from her cheeks."

Having been badgered by her friends about her return to health, she imparted her "secret" and began to train one of her closest confidants. In the interim she devised a modified corset to pad the body from blows, and having done so she began teaching other young women. Her main focus was not only health but also helping her students through the "awkward" experience of donning their "air-cushioned boxing gloves," which ensured that the ladies would not be bruised. After some weeks, she was proud to say that they were able to spar four two-minute rounds, and as the author noted, she had become "a secret society female apostle of health."[85]

While the *Herald's* tone was dismissive and implied that the craze for sparring could easily be replaced by something more fashionable, the underlying notion that young women could and should participate in vigorous exercise was indicative of the new appreciation of health that was sweeping the country for middle-class men and women. This appreciation for the New Woman and her improved physical health was also an important message in the article about the "Lady" sparring teacher.

A third article, entitled "Boxing Ladies of Boston," originally appeared in a Boston paper and was republished in England in 1887 with a lead that began, "It is not society girls only, but shop-girls, typewriters, and even mothers of families who take part in the exercise of boxing."

The article continued that the boxing took place:

> At a well-known dry goods palace . . . the room given up to its female employees for luncheon purposes transformed almost every day at the noon hour into a boxing school, where the girls meet in friendly contest. . . . A tightly-blown football, fastened pendant from a hook in the ceiling by a piece of rope is generally the object of attack, and around this the fair young girls dance like so many Comanche Indians, striking out first with the left, catching the leather sphere squarely in the centre, then on the recoil sending it spinning again with a clever upper-cut or cross-counter, each time ducking so as to avoid a blow in the face as it comes back to its original position . . . they experience considerable trouble in mastering some of the feints, guards and leads [but] . . . on the whole, they are enthusiastic and persevering, and quick to acquaint themselves with pugilistic points, and, best of all, are very slow to engage in public exhibitions. They take to the sport for the physical good it does them, and for the development of mind and muscle.[86]

An interesting facet of all three articles was the decoupling of boxing as a competitive sport from sparring and boxing exercise. In the pieces about the Philadelphia boxing students, the teachers put a lot of effort into ensuring that their pupils would not be bruised or injured in any way. The male teacher, in fact, was at pains to maintain the well-being of his students. He was also very careful to dissociate himself from professional boxing, establishing very clearly that he had never boxed for money and only sparred as a "manly" pursuit. The female teacher had developed special clothing for her pupils to wear to keep them safe from harm and had taken the further precaution of using gloves that would not leave marks.

The article about the women who boxed in Boston clearly framed the endeavor as an exercise—though in praising the women's skills, the notion that they were "very slow to engage in public exhibitions" may well have been wishful thinking.

The boxing/sparring as exercise paradigm did, however, provide an outlet for vigorous physical activity which, though at the outer reaches of acceptable forms of sport, was nonetheless, a growing option for middle-class young ladies who were otherwise sheltered from pugilism's more "ugly" side.

The idea of boxing as exercise for the New Woman was also spreading. By the following year, an article reprinted from the *New York Mail and Express* in the *Semi-Weekly Interior Journal*, of Stanford, Kentucky, was published under the heading "Sparring by Ladies":

> An opinion in support of the efficacy of the exercise comes from one of the leading actresses of the day, who thus speaks of sparring by ladies: "If a lady engaged in theatrical or operatic work could select but one of the many accomplishments to which we as a class are devoted, I should recommend sparring. The stately carriage, without which none of us can hope to succeed, is made the more easy by knowledge of the principles of boxing, and it comes too, without any seeming effort. [87]

A ladies sparring club in Kentucky may have seemed far-fetched, but Hattie Stewart's experience of teaching women to box in Norfolk, Virginia, in the early part of the decade certainly gave a sense of its popularity. Stewart herself had been taught the sport in the late 1870s, and while her learning experiences occurred in her German-American ethnic enclave in Philadelphia, whether women were working class or members of the upper classes, the sport was spreading across the country.

THE GILDED AGE: FEMALE SPECTATORSHIP AT THE FIGHTS

Nellie Bly, born Elizabeth Jane Cochrane, was the most famous female reporter of her era beginning in the late 1880s. She made her reputation in 1887 when she "feigned insanity so successfully as to get herself committed to the lunatic asylum [in New York] for the purpose of writing a full and true account of the treatment of the inmates."[88] The success of the series of articles, published in the *New York World*, led to the publication of a book entitled *Ten Days in a Mad House* and solidified her stature as legendary journalist.

Two years later, in a first for newspapers, Nellie Bly traveled up to Belfast, New York, where the boxer John L. Sullivan was said to be training for his bout against his boxing nemesis Jake Kilrain. It is unclear if Bly had ever witnessed a prizefight (likely not, given that she was only twenty-three at the time) but her manner was engaging and her first-person account was filled with the boxers' interactions.

> "Mr. Sullivan, I would like to shake hands with you," I said, and he took my hand with a firm hearty grasp and with a hand that felt small and soft. Mr. Muldoon [his trainer] excused himself, and I was left to interview the Great John L.
> "I came here to learn all about you, Mr. Sullivan, so will you please begin by telling me at what time you get up in the morning," I said.
> "Well, I get up about 6 o'clock and get rubbed down," he began in a matter-of-fact way. "Then Muldoon and I walk and run a mile or a mile and a half away and then back. Just as soon as we get in I am given a showerbath and after being thoroughly rubbed down again, I put on an entire fresh outfit."

Her questions, less about the boxing world and more about Sullivan himself, put him at ease. In a later exchange she wrote:

> "Your hands look very soft and small for a fighter."
> "Do they?" and he held one out to me for inspection. "My friends tell me they look like hams," and he laughed. "I wear number nine gloves."
> "By the time I am ready to fight, there won't be any fat on my hands or face. They will be as hard as a bone. Do I harden them? Certainly. If I didn't I would have pieces knocked off of me. I have a mixture of rock salt and white wine and vinegar and several other ingredients which I wash my hands and face with."

Toward the end of their interview Sullivan said, "You are the first woman who ever interviewed me. . . . And I have given you more than I ever gave any reporter in my life. They generally manufacture things and credit them to me, although some are mighty good fellows."[89]

The article, published in the *Sunday World* edition on July 28, 1889, was not so much a sensation as another milestone in the complex relationship between women and pugilism. Bly's perspective was also interesting. Focusing on his physicality, his regimen, and ultimately, when it came to her focus on his hands, how they were not so different from her own.

The barrier having been broken, famed sportswriter Winifred Black, writing under the pseudonym Annie Laurie for the *San Francisco Examiner*, interviewed the likes of boxers Peter Jackson and James Corbett prior to their 1891 heavyweight bout. Her next exploit was to penetrate the work of boxing when she "infiltrated an all-male club in [June] 1892 to become the first woman to cover a prize fight for an American newspaper."[90]

The fight was a forty-one-round bare-knuckle rout that left the fighters "disfigured and swollen, their legs unsteady." The crowd, clearly out for more blood, was angry when the fight was called, but from where she sat, "Hidden in a perch overlooking the arena . . . it was a revelation."[91]

"I have seen men," she wrote, "not as women see them, but as men see them. . . . Men have a world into which women cannot enter. They have a being that women cannot understand. I learned all this at the prize-fight."[92]

The female spectatorship at the heyday of British boxing with its sparring venues for women was a thing of the past in 1890s America. The variety theater version of sparring, however, was as popular as ever with venerable stars such as Hattie Stewart filling theaters with their acts along with new stars and boxers such as John L. Sullivan who supplemented their boxing earnings by taking to the stage.

While women were performing pugilism in the prize ring, on stage, and even as a form of exercise with limited acceptance, women as spectators were still a taboo prospect in the 1880s and early 1890s. Yet, something had pushed Winifred Black to want to see a prizefight. The boxing scholar Kasia Boddy, through her extensive research, has shown how boxing became a topic of exploration in literary efforts in the period. Following up on the thought, she raised the idea that under "the influence of Darwinism . . . men (and later women) . . . became interested in boxing as a subject matter within which to explore the mechanisms of sexual selection."[93]

She went on to note, "The female assessment of a potential mate was central to many of Jack London's fight scenes, and more often than not his emphasis is on male excitement in realizing that this is the case."[94]

As early as 1891 the press began publishing reports of women in attendance at the fights. A brief notice in the *St. Paul Daily Globe* was particularly pointed in its condemnation:

> It is reported that quite a number of women attended the [Jack] Dempsey-[Robert] Fitzsimmons mill at New Orleans. What with women fighting prize fights in a twenty-four-foot ring, surrounded by a lot of drunken pugs, and other women attending mills between masculines in disguise, our boasted modern civilization appears to have been side tracked.[95]

While the emphasis on the breakdown in normative gender roles was discussed as indicative of a decline in civilized decorum, through the 1890s, women's spectatorship began to take on the sexualized connotations argued by Boddy. With the advent of cinema in this decade, the boxing film became an important mainstay of these early efforts, enticing audiences, including women, to become enamored with the images of half-naked men in the boxing ring.

These films began as short movies showing individual rounds of important boxing matches, with the fighters appearing shirtless and wearing short trunks or knee-length tights. Films of prizefights were also staged for the camera on specially created sets rather than in a live venue. Both types proved enticing and while boxing was still illegal in many states and locales, the popularity of these films further legitimized the sport while widening the audience even further to groups who might otherwise never have attended a match at a live venue.

The question of women's spectatorship at the fights was also seemingly resolved once and for all with the inclusion of female audience members at the much-anticipated Gentlemen Jim Corbett versus Robert Fitzsimmons prizefight in Carson City, Nevada, held on March 17, 1897. As has been established, women were in attendance at Fitzsimmons's 1891 bout, and Fitzsimmons's wife became a ringside fixture at other matches of his. The Corbett-Fitzsimmons prizefight, however, was a definitive landmark for female spectatorship for two reasons: It was marketed directly to women in an effort to push boxing toward a more mainstream form of entertainment and the fight was filmed in its entirely and later shown across the country as the first full-length feature film ever produced.

In the run-up to the long-anticipated match against Fitzsimmons, the coverage of the bout became frenzied with teams of reporters following both fighters and filled with evocative descriptions such as the "beautiful black eye" sported by one of Fitzsimmons's sparring partners. The coverage also featured writings by a female reporter. A first-person interview of Corbett entitled "Mr. Corbett Through A Woman's Eyes," published by William Randolph Hearst's *San Francisco Call* and written by Edna Edwina Edith Edgerton, was filled with romanticized images.

Stating her feelings about seeing Corbett for the first time, Edgerton wrote:

> Can I describe my emotions! Can I put in cold and chilling words the rapture with which I gazed on that form! Never! Ah me! Never! He has the head of a Greek god. His neck rises above his shoulders like a tower of ivory. He has the torso of Hercules, the arms and thighs of an Apollo Belvedere.

Edgerton, overwhelmed by the thought of "worshipping at the feet of Corbett," reported that she fainted, adding, "When I came to my senses again the great champion was bending over me." And having lifted her up and helping her to a "rude couch," he agreed to be interviewed, rattling off his itinerary for the day including that he'd eaten "ham and eggs for breakfast," and "play[ed] ball and skipped the rope for three hours."

At the close he told her she should "write me up every day until the fight comes off," with the closing note that this was said with "a roguish twinkle in the great athlete's eyes." And that while she would "interview Fitzsimmons to-morrow . . . tonight I dream of Corbett."[96]

As distinct from Nellie Bly's interview of Sullivan a decade before, the abjectly sexualized perspective promulgated by Edgerton presented her "women's eye view of Corbett," as a coquettish flirtation in which she relished the "eye candy" in front of her. Was it any wonder that women came to the fight and to the open practice sparring sessions at the arena in Carson City held a few days before the big event? The officials at Corbett's quarters "had their hands full in keeping the crowd which two-thirds were women, from encroaching too much on the space."[97]

Dozens of women were among the four thousand in attendance as Fitzsimmons and Corbett battled through thirteen hard-fought rounds. The fourteenth round, however, was the final reckoning for Corbett. According to one reporter, "The finish comes like a thunderbolt," when "Fitzsimmons springs forward with a great right-hand smash over Corbett's heart," to be followed by a "ripping left, flush in the pit of . . . [Corbett's] stomach."

Fitzsimmons's "amazon wife," who sat directly behind his corner during the bout, was described as having "sprung up to the top of her chair. Her cheeks . . . flushed and her eyes . . . blazing . . . [upon seeing] her reward for her Spartan attitude." She is further described as showing "not a tremor in her voice as she shrieks encouragement to the bloody man with the stilt-like legs standing over his fallen foe. It is the scream of a triumphant mother eagle, the paean of a Cleopatra for her victorious Antony."[98]

The theme of romantic aggrandizement promulgated in Edgerton's piece about Corbett was clearly carried through in the description of Fitzgerald's wife as "Cleopatra" to his "Antony." The sexuality of both the fighter and spectator are left in no doubt where male fighters stand in for hypermasculine images of maleness itself, and female spectators fulfill the role of sexualized and idealized feminine partners.

Interestingly, while Edgerton had swooned over Corbett, a tidbit published in the *Sacramento Daily Record* reporting the results of a poll seeking the female reaction to the Corbett-Fitzsimmons fight alluded to the real-world issues women faced.

> Salinas Index: Nine-tenths of the women are glad that Fitzsimmons whipped Corbett. They say that he wasn't true to his first wife, and that he abuses his second wife. Mrs. Corbett number one was a Santa Cruz girl, known as Ollie Lake before she married "Pompadour Jim."[99]

Two months after the fight, on May 22, 1897, the full-length feature film of the event debuted at New York City's Academy of Music on East Fourteenth Street near Union Square. The success of the film, the first to be distributed as a single cinematic event across the United States, played to packed houses in quality theaters and opera houses from New York to California. It was also said that women accounted for a significant number of tickets sold at showings in the United States. As noted by the *St. Paul Daily Globe*, during the film's run at the Metropolitan Theater in St. Paul, "The ladies too were out in force and appear to be making the most of this, their only opportunity to see just what a prize contest is like."[100]

The *Evening Times* also offered commentary when the film began its run at Washington, D.C.'s, New National Theater in September 1897:

> One of the remarkable features . . . is the great interest taken in the exhibitions by women. The reason is undoubtedly because the Veriscope allows them the opportunity of witnessing a clean scientific contest between two foremost boxers of the world, without being subjected to the necessity of seeing the men actually suffer from the effects of the blows, or having to undergo any of the little inconveniences encountered at an actual contest. [101]

Stuart's strategy to book the initial runs of the film in quality venues also furthered the opportunity to entice female audience members who otherwise only frequented the theaters for other entertainments. Special ladies' matinees were featured at some venues to spur attendance. The presentations in the first-run houses also included the presence of a master of ceremonies who delivered commentary during the showing—a not-unknown practice for traveling lectures that incorporated film—which may have further legitimized the showing as high-brow theater, certainly a first for prizefighting.

Scholars researching spectatorship of the film have noted that female attendance may have been somewhat overblown in some locales. Dan Stuart's promotion machine (and their practice of issuing press releases ahead of bookings) was said to have touted women theatergoers. Still, women did indeed view the film in large enough numbers to be significant, not only establishing a place for women at the fights, but also in no small way helping to usher in a greater legitimation for prizefighting.

As the boxing film became an important mainstay of theatrical showings of motion pictures, other films such as the Edison Company's 1901 short of the Gordon Sisters vaudeville sparring act also hit the cinema screen. The catalog noted it as follows:

> Champion lady boxers of the world. Here we depict two female pugilists that are really clever. They are engaged in a hot and heavy one-round sparring exhibition. . . . The exhibition is very lively from start to finish; the blows fall thick and fast, and some very clever pugilistic generalship is exhibited. [102]

The preponderance of the boxing films and the opportunities available to women to view such films—and even marvel at themselves—helped to set the stage for the legalization of professional prizefighting in many locales as the 1900s loomed.

This new paradigm, however, did not cross over into the realm of female professional boxing, which remained at best a sideshow performance on a variety theater stage.

Chapter Three

Boxing, Women, and the Mores of Change

The Jungle Woman is again with us.
—A sports page editorial, July 21, 1914 [1]

The New Woman at the turn of the century was on the cusp of dynamic change. Her clothing was less restricted, and she no longer expected to remain in the home. Daughters of the middle and upper classes attended college. Some of them even pursued careers, whilst working-class women could now aspire to something more than a factory job. Universal women's suffrage eventually became a reality in the United States with the ratification of the Nineteenth Amendment on August 26, 1920.

Boxing for women in the early years of the new century reflected the progressive nature of the era. Whether as spectators, including those female journalists who reported on the fights, or as practitioners—on stage, in the gym, or in the ring—women became publically associated with boxing more than ever. This participation, however, continued to be subject to the vicissitudes of public attitudes, the press, and fashionable trends. While boxing for men was increasingly legitimized both legally and in the eyes of the public, women remained on the periphery as marginal players at best.

The image of the female boxer, while still an anathema to womanhood in some quarters, was nevertheless a potent image by the 1920s, which saw the popularity of women's boxing matches spread as far afield as London, Paris, and Berlin, not to mention its continuing popularity in variety theater. Images of women in boxing attire were also featured in Hollywood films and magazine spreads. And, as distinct from the largely staged female sparring contests of the 1870s–1890s interspersed with occasional prizefights, the new century brought with it more recognition of "scientific" female boxing matches. The increased visibility of female prizefighting did not necessarily portend positive recognition of the sport or of the right of women to pursue it as headlines continued to decry boxing as shameful and the fighters as "Amazons." Still, the continued reportage and visibility meant that the sport was tacitly if not whole-heartedly accepted as an activity women were "given permission" to pursue.

Men's boxing was also subject to negative press and periodic calls for its banishment as brutal and inhumane even as many state legislatures were legalizing it. Despite the occasional calls from the pulpit to rid the world of the evils of the sport, boxing was becoming big business—attracting not only the 19th-century "sports" types but also the J. P. Morgans of the world. A bevy of politicians were also often seen alongside the newly crowned heroes of boxing.

The development of a well-regulated amateur boxing program under the auspices of the AAU—first constituted in 1888—also mitigated some of the negativity. Beginning in 1904, when men's boxing was featured as a demonstration sport at the St. Louis Olympic Games, amateur boxing enjoyed legitimizing of the highest order, especially after 1908 when it became a fully recognized sport by the IOC. Women's boxing was also demonstrated, but not as part of the Olympic Games. Rather, an exhibition match was put on under the auspices of the St. Louis Exhibition and World's Fair.

Amateur women's boxing, however, was not included as a sport under the AAU, despite the occasional "smoker" held at an AAU-affiliated boxing club. This meant that the opportunity for a robust program of boxing tournaments for women was denied to them as well as the development of sanctioned weights classes, unified rules, and amateur standings. It also meant that women were not given the chance to learn their craft in an amateur program governed by rules and regulations meant to ensure the safety of the participants, including the imposition of sanctions for clubs not adhering to the rules—something it would take nearly a century to enact in the United States.

The exclusion of women from a sanctioned amateur program also closed the path toward greater legitimacy for women's boxing as a sport. Amateur boxing contests in the United States did not begin to be sanctioned until the late 1970s and in many jurisdictions not until the mid to late 1990s.

THE FIN-DE-SIÈCLE WOMAN: GUSSIE FREEMAN, WOMAN PUGILIST

The fin de siècle woman is making rapid strides into the realm of man that it begins to look as though the weaker sex will become the stronger and man have to step aside in all vocations that have been exclusive his own.
—Brooklyn Correspondence, *Daily Argus News*, June 11, 1895[2]

The battling slasher Gussie Freeman is best known for her four-round battle against Hattie Leslie in November 1891 on the stage of Brooklyn's Unique Theater on Grand Street in East Williamsburg—a neighborhood fondly recalled as Dutchtown, so named for all the German immigrants that flooded the area beginning in the 1840s. Gussie was more than just a battling slasher though: She was a force of nature with a man-sized body on her large frame, a fierce will, and a fighting spirit that belied any frailties that might have beset her.

Gussie was born into poverty in the Ridgewood section of Queens of German parentage in or around March 1864. "I never had any education," she told a correspondent in 1895, seated at her newly opened saloon at 138 Cook Street on the corner of Bushwich Avenue in East Williamsburg. She added, "My mother was too poor to send me to school, and when I was twelve years old she send [*sic*] me to the rope walk to work." The ropewalk was the Waterbury Rope Works jute (hemp) factory at Waterbury and Ten Eyck Street where she worked well into her twenties before embarking on her colorful career as a boxer.

Even before she went to work at the ropewalk, some of her earliest memories were of setting out to find "wood and cinders for the family fuel." Once at the factory, she quickly rebelled against the fine needlework of women's work. "Whenever I could get out of the shop I would go to the yard and help load the trucks and before I was 14, I could do as much work as any man. I was larger and heavier than any woman in the shop.

"I wish I was more like a woman," she continued.

"I don't like to be so much like a man, but I can't help it. I must make a living and I am not fit for anything but the kind of work I do. I have a flat upstairs. It is the first home I ever had and the best thing I ever had."[3]

At the rope works, her hard labor hoisting bales of hemp gave her the strength of a man as she drew the reputation of defender of girls and women who were molested by the boys and men at the factory. As a scrapper, she also came to raise fighting cocks and fighting bulldogs, and was never afraid of a fight.

Gussie's life as a professional pugilist began when Hattie Leslie came to Brooklyn as "the leading feature" at an "Irving Specialty company" production at Williamsburg's Unique Theater. In the advertisements for the show, Hattie had issued her usual offer to give $25 to any male boxer at 135 pounds or any female boxer at any weight who could knock her out in four rounds.

Gussie, known as "Loney" or "Lonely," egged on by her pals at the ropewalk, took up the challenge and a four-round bout was scheduled. Fight night found the theater with a rambunctious sold-out crowd with the loge seats filled with the usual swells, the reserved stage seats with local Brooklyn politicians, and the rafter seats with the hooting and shouting of the boys and girls from the Waterbury Rope Works where it was said the tickets had been purchased for everyone to attend for free. A contingent of police from the Fifth Precinct in Brooklyn was also present in the wings under the command of its captain, Martin Short, just in case, it was said.

Some fifty years later in a remembrance published in the *Brooklyn Eagle*, one of her coworkers recalled that "All Dutchtown turned out to see her that night . . . the crowd went wild with excitement," as the women, looming large on the stage and with hard skills and definite science, battered each other from start to finish.[4]

The four-rounders then in vogue at the variety theaters across the country could be every bit as exciting as a regulation prizefight—and as one reporter put it:

> The Theater was crowded to suffocation.
>
> Mrs. Freeman . . . is big and powerful and weighs about 160 pounds. Her handiness with her fist has got her into innumerable rows and a majority of her opponents have been men, whom she has invariably thrashed. . . . [Patrick] Patsy Lantry seconded "Lonely," and Jim Brady of Buffalo, did the needful for Hattie [who] wore black fighting tights, a white silk tunic and a gold medal. Gussie was dressed in virgin white. Her hair . . . bound in a tight knot and tied with rope yarn . . .
>
> The lady scrappers walked to the centre of the stage, shook hands and came on guard. Gussie had a high, firm guard that contrasted favorably with the loose way that [Hattie] held her hands.

While Gussie was a natural bruiser with some skills, she was not a trained boxer, which began to tell as the fight wore on. Hattie threw a barrage of "scientific" punches, with Gussie answering and never letting up. As it was, both women launched stunning blows from end to end in the first round and eventually drew blood by the end of the second round when Gussie's waist-length blonde hair also let loose, swirling around her and partially covering her face (some accounts have noted it as happening in the third round).

At the suggestion of Hattie's corner, and seeing that the fight was a tough one, Hattie rushed out at the start of the third round swinging in a blaze of upper cuts, jabs, and straight punches, each answered by Gussie who was by now quite breathless but still very game. She was, however, clearly being beaten and to the deafening shouts of the rope works gang in the gallery, "Captain Short interfered and stopped the affair amid tremendous confusion," at which point "the referee, after being shouted and sworn at, gave the fight to Hattie."[5]

Even given Gussie's loss—which was immediately disputed and in press accounts over the years went from a loss in the third round to a draw in the fourth round and eventually to a win—the promoters of the show figured Gussie would be a real crowd pleaser and offered her the chance to join the tour as a sparring partner to Hattie. Sometime thereafter, likely in the winter/

early spring of 1892, Gussie left her life at the ropewalk to take up a stage career fighting in Hattie Leslie's company and was said to have even replaced her for a while after Leslie's death from typhoid fever on September 28, 1892, although the exact dates of Gussie's tour cannot be confirmed.

The tour took Gussie as far as Chicago before she returned—though according to Gussie, she'd been cheated out of her earnings. She also "was engaged to appear as a boxer with the London Sports company in the fall of 1893, and drew crowded houses for two weeks in Boston where she defeated twelve men, including Prof. Bagley and Tommy Butler, but her salary was not forthcoming at the end of the two weeks." Returning to the ropewalk, she worked as a brick handler, and in 1895 or so "bought the Cook street saloon."

Still, she was said to say, "If I only had some education, I would not be in this kind of business, but I must do something."[6]

By 1899 Gussie had not only worked as a prizefighter on stage but also run a saloon. If that wasn't enough, an article published in the *World* about an investigation into her job as a stevedore along Newtown Creek in the Greenpoint area reported the following:

> Miss Freeman is five feet ten inches tall, her fighting weight is 180 pounds and the foreman regards her as his best "man" on the docks. She is twenty-nine years old and has never been kissed by a man. . . . Being too strong to do needlework she trained and handled fighting dogs. Later she took up fighting chickens with success. She defeated men and women in the prize-ring. She challenged Corbett and Fitzsimmons, but they told her to get a reputation. . . . She figured as the star in several burlesque troops, but relinquished her career for her present occupation.[7]

Gussie was not only a pioneer of the ring but also a representative of working-class women who in a direct line to the fighters in 18th-century London lived by their fists and their wits as best they could. The rope works also spawned other women who took to the fistic science such as "'Limpy Sall' . . . the champion girl fighter; 'Lu' Raftery and also a once renowned female terror known as 'the Gouger.'"[8]

These women certainly did not set out to be boxers, but given the tough lives they lived, with little or no access to education, earning a dollar by loading bales of hemp, entering a boxing contest, or plying the boards with a boxing act was just one more way to ensure food on the table and a roof over their heads.

Gussie, outsized and living on her own terms in male-dominated occupations, captured the imagination of her community and the world at large that read of her exploits—so much so that a half-century later she still captivated those whose lives she touched. And while she may not have practiced the true sweet science, her perseverance and courage allowed others to always think of her as a real boxer.

APOCRYPHA: POLLY FAIRCLOUGH—LADY BOXER CHAMPION
OF THE WORLD

One of the more famous, if controversially so, of the female fairground
boxers at the turn of the century and beyond was Polly Fairclough. She came
to be known as Polly Burns or Mrs. Thomas (Tommy) Burns. Yet the peak of
her fame wasn't at the turn of the century when she actually performed in
boxing shows, but after she'd left the ring—first in the 1920s when she was
married to a former boxer and impresario named Tommy Burns on through
the 1940s after a series of articles hit the popular press in England and
Ireland where they settled.

According to the remembrances of her grandson, Patrick Dillon, Polly
Fairclough's actual birth name was likely Mary Agnes Taylor. As Mary
Agnes, she was born in 1881 in Whitehaven, Cumbria, Lancashire, a region
in the northwest of England near Liverpool. Patrick contended that her
father's name was James. As proof he had her birth certificate, which showed
his name as James Taylor, but there was also some indication that his name
might actually have been Thornton.

James was said to have been a horse dealer and trainer at local circuses in
Lancashire. When Polly was a small child, she allegedly watched her mother,
a trapeze artist, take a fatal fall. After the tragedy of her mother's death,
James is said to have married into "the famous fighting Fairclough family,"
although it is not substantiated.[9] Polly, along with her father and her new
"family," became full-time circus hands, where she picked up the gloves at
sixteen and began her career as a lady pugilist in the boxing booths at fairgrounds across northern Britain. Later accounts were further embellished
with stories of Polly having "wrestled lions and lifted ponies with her
teeth."[10]

These stories were included in a documentary about her life entitled *My
Great Grandmother Was a Boxer*, which appeared as part of the *True Lives*
series on Ireland's RTE network in the late 1990s. The film, directed by Niall
Byrne, a well-known film composer, followed Polly's great-granddaughter's
journey in search of the truth about Polly's life and times. The great-granddaughter claimed to be a descendent of Polly, although other descendants of
the family, including Polly's grandson, Patrick, knew nothing of her prior to
the publicity surrounding the film.

In terms of what can be substantiated about Polly's life, the English
census of the spring 1901 lists her as a twenty-year-old residing as a boarder
on London Road in the Southwark section of London, interestingly in the
same neighborhood where modern boxing began. The census also listed her
as married to a twenty-three-year-old pugilist named John Fairclough. Polly's occupation was listed as a "music hall artist."[11] Whether she became a
"Fairclough" through her father's remarriage—which thereby gave her the

chance to meet and marry John Fairclough—or whether the Fairclough connection in her youth was fanciful and, in fact, she married into the family herself, is unknown. What is very probable is her marriage to her pugilist husband in 1899.

Polly herself gave many interviews that embellished on her life and times, which as her great-granddaughter discovered years later left many tantalizing clues but little to substantiate her claims. In one, published in July of 1945, Polly was described as having been "a good-looking colleen, dark-haired and feminine, who was able to—and did—trade punches with the best fighters of her day." She was also touted as "one of the fastest, surest boxers ever to enter the ring."

The reporter went on to write about her appearance at traveling fairs where she would "appear on the platform while the barker challenged any man in the crowd to box three rounds with her for $50" and where "hundreds of disillusioned fellows" would emerge "with split lips and shiners after taking the beating of their lives." [12]

What can be substantiated are Polly Fairclough billings as a champion lady boxer in towns such as Seaham Harbour, where she appeared in 1903 at the New Theatre Royal along with other variety artists. A photograph from around 1900 also exists of her on the stage at the front of a boxing booth, a heavyset young woman with dark hair parted in the middle, pulled back in a bun. She also appeared at the Burton Statute Fair in a boxing booth and gained some notoriety there.

Other stories about Polly's exploits include her having fought 110 rounds in a single day at the boxing booths (possibly true given the long days and nights carnival boxers work); having exhibition fights with the famed American heavyweight champion Jack Johnson in Dublin; and sparring with Britain's answer to Johnson, Billy Wells. There are, in fact, two pictures of Polly and Billy from the 1920s in the RTE archives in Ireland taken out of doors on what appears to be a lawn. Given the existence of the photographs, if Polly actually ever did meet Jack Johnson it was likely under similar circumstances.

A photograph published in 1935 shows her in a playful boxing stance with Irish heavyweight Jack Doyle. She still looked quite spry as she extended her left in a jab toward Doyle's ribs. How the photograph came to be taken is unexplained, though it gives every indication that she had notoriety in her native Dublin at the time. [13]

One other famous story about Polly was that as a young girl of sixteen she fought a "hefty sailor" who "knocked out four of her front teeth and cut her lip." It is claimed she "walk[ed] down from the ring, sat down on a stool and had a doctor sew her lip with horsehair."

"Nobody ever knocked out Polly," she was to say. [14]

Toward the end of Polly's life, after the death of her husband, Tommy Burns, she fell on hard times financially, so much so she sold her story to the British tabloids. This brought her a minor celebrity in places as far-flung as Darwin, Australia, and the United States, and kept her name in the press until her death in near poverty in 1959 at the age of seventy-seven. A newspaper article that came out in the 1940s about her life was also the inspiration for a future boxer named Barbara Buttrick, who in reading about her was so enthralled she took up the gloves herself.

Alongside Polly plying the boards on both sides of the Atlantic as a champion lady boxer were such women as Annie Currie who appeared in a "scientific sparring exhibition" with C. J. Lewis, "a well-known instructor in the art" at the Wildwood Resort near Washington, D.C., in 1900.[15] "Lady Estella" Riche, the "Female Sampson" and "Champion Lady Boxer," "appeared in a vaudeville act," interestingly at a "moving picture theater" on Broadway, in New York City (and was also arrested for "project[ing] one of her muscular feet with such force against the anatomy of 'Shorty' Kuhn, a stage hand, as, in the parlance of the prize ring, to put Kuhn to sleep," having gotten into an altercation with him "after the close of the last performance").[16] The Gordon Sisters act that started in the late 1890s and was immortalized on film by Edison continued to play in East Coast theaters into the early 1900s. Their act consisted of scientific sparring as well as bag punching by Belle Gordon.

There were plenty of other aspirants as well, as this 1905 letter sent to the theatrical producers Thompson & Dundy, published in New York's *Morning Telegraph*, shows:

> Dear Sir—Can you use a fat lady Boxing act. One is knone as amelia Hill and Miss Mary Peters. Miss Peters weight is about 600 pounds height 5 foot 4. amelia Hill weight 475 pounds-height 4 foot 9. We do a little dancing. Miss Peters does a skirt dance and Amelia Hill does a little Oriental dance, making it a 15 min. act. We strip from dresses to bloomers for the Boxing act. Trusting this will meet with your favor
> Salary 50 joint.
> I remain
> Miss amelia Hill.[17]

TEXAS MAMIE: A WOMAN IN THE RING

> I've been up against some good ones and I've got some reputation, but Mamie trimmed me for fair.
> —Goldie O'Rourke, November 5, 1907

Mamie Winston Donavan (Dunaman),[18] known as "Texas Mamie," was born in Dallas, Texas, on April 25, 1883. She told reporters that as a young girl she had accompanied her parents to Montreal, Canada, before eventually settling in Philadelphia, Pennsylvania, with her invalid mother. An article in the *National Police Gazette*, introducing her, described her as "shapely, muscular and fine looking" and available "to meet any woman in America of her weight in a scientific boxing match for a good sized side bet."[19]

She started her boxing career as a bag puncher performing in contests and began prizefighting in private "smokers" around 1905. She became a stage performer in 1906 with a "scientific" pugilism act performed in such places as the Curio Hall in Philadelphia, where she called out any woman boxer to meet her on the stage with one hundred dollars given to the fighter who could last four rounds without being knocked out. Over the years her act grew to include wrestling, sparring, and bag punching. She was also alleged to have backed out of a fight with Polly Fairclough set to be staged in Paris sometime in 1900, but there is no evidence that this ever occurred, and there is every indication that Texas Mamie did not even box at that time. Given Mamie's later prominence, it is likely that a bout between Polly and Texas Mamie was wishful thinking on the part of one boxing impresario or another, or perhaps even Polly herself.

As a fighter, Texas Mamie gained much exposure in the press, beginning with her introduction to the boxing world by the *National Police Gazette*. She also had two widely reported fights in the summer and fall of 1906. She told the *Gazette* of how she boxed to support her mother and how she used the winnings from one of her fights to send her mother to Atlantic City for a week by the sea, something that seemed to resonate well with the boxing writers of the day.

The most famous of those fights took place on August 19, 1906, when Texas Mamie fought Ellen Devine in a prizefight held at a popular resort along the Delaware River. Devine, hailing from New York City, was in her first professional match. The diminutive women were both said to have weighed in at about 105 pounds and were in excellent fighting condition. Both Texas Mamie and Ellen Devine had been in training for some time prior to the match and so were ready for action, though little is known about their previous experience or what their training regimen consisted of. The fight itself followed Marquis of Queensbury rules, with the exception of their boxing costumes, which included the addition of a skirt worn over their tights.

The fight was lauded as the "fastest bout between ladies" ever seen with one witness describing the action as follows:

> Ellen done well in the first two rounds, but Texas took the lead in the third and Ellen was badly beat up by the Texas' rushing tactics. With a hard wallop in the sixth and last round and a right on the solar plexus, Texas doubled Ellen up and the New York girl was counted out by Referee Sam Devon of Camden.[20]

The knockout left Devine unconscious for some minutes. Luckily a physician was in the crowd and helped to bring her around. The press also reported that while Texas Mamie was on her way home she was attacked by a dog and bitten on the thigh. The wound did not become infected and it healed well after being cauterized by a doctor.

The Texas Mamie–Ellen Devine fight took place on a Sunday, and as if to preempt the possible outcry for boxing on the Sabbath (as had happened nearly twenty years earlier when Hattie Lewis fought on a Sunday), Texas Mamie was quoted as saying, "I wouldn't box on Sunday if it wasn't for mother. . . . I have to support her and the winnings come in handy."[21] She also proudly took home the $200 purse.

While most of the reporting about the fight was straightforward and lauded the "science" of the two boxers, the idea of two women engaging in fisticuffs—even scientific ones—did not sit well with all, and even for the less critical press, the "virago" meme was revived with such headlines as "Amazons Fight Six Hot Rounds."

Of the negative articles, the *Spokane Press* ran a headline that read "The Shame of 'Texas Mamie' and Another Female Pug." The text of the article was in the same vein with the author writing, "If there was anything needed to kill an outlawed, brutal sport, it was to have women enter the field," and ended with the idea that it "hurt" to watch.[22]

The *Minneapolis Journal*, while reprinting the basic facts of the fight from other press sources, added their own editorial content with a sub-headline that read "All Around Degeneracy Belt Seems to Belong to Philadelphia."[23]

Even given the backlash in some quarters, the fight proved popular enough that a local gymnasium manager named James O'Brien went about putting together a "smoker" between the two fighters set for the Labor Day weekend a few weeks away.

Following on the heels of her big win over Ellen Devine, the national press reported, Texas Mamie's next major fight was in early October when she gained a knockout win in the fourth round of her contest against Ida (or Ada) Atwell, a Bostonian who was the "directress of a physical culture school." The bout was fought "in front of 300 hundred or so sports," in Staten Island, New York, at the Corinthian Athletic Association clubhouse.[24] Texas Mamie was said to have "rushed from her corner at the sound of the bell and right across the ring at Miss Atwell . . . [landing a] left and a right" while "cleverly" blocking any counters. She defeated her opponent with a "hard cross counter to the jaw."[25]

Texas Mamie was applauded for her "side-stepping, blocking, feinting and general all-round gameness," so much so that "the Corinthians" voted to gift her with a "diamond belt" for being the "'real thing' in the female Fistians."[26]

Flush with the success of her fights, Texas Mamie came to New York City later in October of 1906 "to teach fellow members of the gentle sex the lady like art of self-defense" while still seeking "to defend her title of lady champion scientific boxer of the world." Setting up shop at "a new school for physical culture" said to have "blossomed in the Tenderloin," she was lauded as "the presiding genius there."[27]

The story was widely reported and garnered headlines such as "Texas Mamie To Open School, Boss Woman Boxer Will Teach Sisters the Art of Self Defense."[28] Snippets of ads in newspapers in 1906 and early 1907 give the impression that Texas Mamie divided her time between developing her variety theater act and her physical culture school, and catching what matches she could in private smokers in between her more formal prize-fights.

The next well-publicized bout was against British boxing champion Goldie O'Rourke in 1907. Press accounts noted that the fight was put on in North Bergen, New Jersey, at the Guttenburg Race Track with a ring erected in sight of the horse barns. Of interest was the fact that the chief of police himself was in attendance along with some "several hundred men and boys and a dozen women," a far cry from earlier female bouts that were routed by the police.

As the women entered the ring, Goldie was said to be 114 pounds and a few inches taller than Texas Mamie who weighed in at 103.5 pounds. As one reporter put it though, despite the weight and height differences, "'Dallas Bantam' as the sporting world knows Miss Donavan, proved too scientific for the English Champion,"[29] and knocked her out in the thirteenth round.

Another paper reported: "Miss O'Rourke has a black eye and her lips are cut and swollen . . . [and] Miss Donavan has several bruises on her face but is not otherwise injured."[30] The tone of the articles, which featured headlines such as "Texas Mamie Knocks Out Goldie O'Rourke in 13,"[31] were minus the disparaging remarks of newspaper accounts describing her fight with Ellen Devine—despite the fact they both had sustained injuries during their battle. Given Texas Mamie's evident technical prowess and popularity, the editorializing may well have been put on the back burner, as she proved her staying power as a figure in the boxing world.

Texas Mamie also worked hard to become a member of both the New York boxing and theatrical communities, gaining notice in the *New York Times* for participating in a charity boxing match at the 1908 edition of the theater group's annual field day held at the polo grounds. The event raised $5,000 for the New York Home for Destitute and Crippled Children. A highlight of the show was a wrestling match featuring Cora Livingstone, the champion female wrestler, and a fellow performer in variety theater. Livingstone was also known to participate in boxing shows from time to time, including a bout held in Buffalo, New York, against Bertha Smith, a Cincinnati-based fighter, in November 1911.

By 1909 Texas Mamie was appearing in Fred Irwin's Big Show with an unnamed partner, performing a physical culture exhibition that included fencing, boxing, and wrestling at places like the Gayety Theatre in Columbus, Ohio. She also appeared in the newly remodeled Ninth and Arch Museum in Philadelphia with a boxing act.

At some point, likely in late 1908 or early 1909, Texas Mamie suffered a tough defeat at the hands of Flora Ryan, a New York–based boxer. Flora Ryan's next bout, that spring, was against a Connecticut boxer named Kid Broad. Tippy Fay, Kid Broad's manager, put on the fight before a "select crowd of dead game sports" numbering about three hundred who had come out to see Flora, the woman who "gave Texas Mamie such a great battle."[32] Flora put on a fabulous exhibition of boxing at its best and defeated Kid Broad on points at the end of their ten-round bout.

From that point on, however, Texas Mamie seems to have receded into obscurity with little or no press, and beginning in 1910 there were seemingly no more notices of upcoming theatrical appearances or boxing events.

The fights of Texas Mamie recalled the bouts fought by Hattie Leslie, Hattie Stewart, and the other women who plied their trade as female boxers on stage and in makeshift rings across the country. Texas Mamie was also representative of a new breed of professional boxers whose exploits were more prominently featured in the world of sports and boxing enthusiasts.

AT THE FIGHTS

It has always been a supposition that boxing is a man's sport, but nowadays the women seem to be taking up all kinds of sports and they have included boxing in the list. So that settles it.
—T. S. Andrews, "Prize Fighting Becoming a Favorite Pastime for Women," July 28, 1914[33]

Yes, but that's part of the game. The excitement and nervous tension you are under when you are boxing makes you forget the pain of a blow almost as soon as you feel it.
—Helen Hildreth, 1917[34]

One of the more controversial aspects of boxing in the early 1900s was the increasing visibility of women at prizefights—whether as boxers, spectators, or even as boxing managers—on both sides of the Atlantic. One newspaper headline published in 1914 went so far as to state "Prize Fighting Becoming a Favorite Pastime for Women." The article went on to report on the attendance of more than one thousand women ringside at the heavyweight white championship of the world between America's Gunboat Smith and France's George Carpentier in London. So large was the expected crowd that the fight's promoter, Dick Burge, "engaged the services of a corps of female stewards."[35] A second match held in a different London venue, between Freddie Welch and Willie Ritchie, was also reported to have had a large number of women in attendance.

The surge in popularity was not, however, limited to London. Women attended boxing matches in Paris by the hundreds and were seen at boxing matches in New York and even in Milwaukee, Wisconsin, where boxing writer T. S. Andrews reported that women "thoroughly enjoy" watching boxing and further opined:

> Most women who attend these contests were very out-spoken and said that they could see no reason why the fair sex could not attend them just as well as watching a football match.[36]

Given that football then, as now, was known for its violence on the field, the notion was a potent one, though the brutality of boxing, pitting two fighters against one another in the ring, was certainly more readily identified as "violent." The presence of women at the prizefights, as noted earlier, while a subject for public debate, played into the hands of boxing promoters who in looking to further legitimize the sport from the earlier stigmas sought out the presence of women to prove that boxing had crossed a threshold of respectability. The pervasiveness of gloved fights versus the predominant bareknuckle fighting of a generation before was another selling point in proving that prizefighting was no longer the brutal sport it had once been. The fact that women were more familiar with boxing, both as spectators and perhaps not as contestants so much as denizens of boxing gymnasium programs geared toward exercise and light sparring, also took the stigma from spectatorship.

An amateur boxing charity event to benefit the city's poor held at the Sixty-Ninth Street Armory in New York City, including a contest held between police and fire department boxers, drew in excess of two hundred women—said to be the largest number of women to have ever attended a boxing card in the city—was a case in point. The presence of so many well-heeled men and women, alongside the city's political and social elite plus a veritable "who's who" of boxing champions including Bob Fitzsimmons—considered a "dean" of the boxing community—gave credence to the idea that prizefighting was not only becoming mainstream but also embracing a full spectrum of spectators.

In 1917 the *Tacoma Times* even ran a series of three articles penned by Elizabeth Tucker, touted as "the only woman boxing manager in the world." Elizabeth gained notoriety acting as boxing manager and trainer for her twin brother, Lonnie Tucker, and a younger brother, Frankie Tucker. In one of the articles she wrote, "If the entrance of women into politics and all the other lines so long held by men is going to do good, I don't see why a woman managing professional boxers won't help." She went on to argue, "Lots of harm has come to the boxing game because of unscrupulous tricks by some boxers and promoters. I would certainly stop anything of that sort if I [k]new of it and no doubt I would find out."

The brilliance of her argument was in aligning her very femininity, and therefore one was to presume her forthright scrupulous nature, with being an instrument to further "cleanse" boxing of its illegitimacy by ensuring its respectability, saying as much when she wrote, "My intention is to do everything I can to regain for boxing the prestige which it once held." She furthered her goal by her support for a national boxing commission—something that is a "gleam" in the "eye" of boxing reformers to this day. The fact that the newspaper ran a series of articles by her also further legitimized both her presence in the boxing world and the notion that women were actually good for boxing. [37]

A full-blooded Cherokee originally hailing from Oklahoma, Elizabeth and her brother Frankie were shown running along side of each other down a street in St. Louis in September of 1916 ahead of his bout against Harry Atwood (which Tucker subsequently won in a twelve rounder). The article about her, entitled "Trains Her Brother to Be a Fighter," noted:

> When Frank Tucker, a pugilist of St. Louis goes on the road he knows he must do some real work. He can't sit down and rest without doing his three miles like some fighters do. "Sis" Elizabeth Tucker, his trainer and manager, goes along to see he does his work. She appears in the ring also as his chief second. The boy believes she is going to make a great fighter of him. Anyway, she is large[ly] responsible for his present winning form. [38]

Elizabeth began by managing and training her twin brother, Lonnie Tucker's, boxing career. A featherweight, he began fighting in 1912. She also told a newspaper that she was going to accompany her brothers on a trip to Australia in late 1916, telling the reporter, "Why shouldn't a girl manage a fighter? I have to look after my brothers anyway and what's the difference if I manage or let someone else do it. I think my interest in them makes me the proper person to do it." The article also stated that she'd been a "delegate from Oklahoma to the Progressive convention where she led a demonstration for Roosevelt" and otherwise rode "the range on her own ranch, which she manages capably." [39]

Her notoriety didn't end there. She was also an early motorcycling enthusiast, horsewoman, swimmer, and expert publicist who kept herself and her brothers in the news as late as 1921 when she proclaimed, "The fight game offers opportunities for individuality, financial remuneration, plenty of diversion and business ability,"[40] all of which is well within the reach of women.

Women's prizefighting also began to subtly change with the growth in popularity of the sport in France alongside the French boxing variant—not dissimilar from modern kickboxing—known as savate. Roughly following the popularity of boxing in England and the United States throughout the 19th century, women began to participate in both savate and regular boxing. Female boxers came to notoriety in France, and stories of their fights made the newspapers in Europe and in the United States.

The French female boxer who seemingly garnered the most attention was Mlle. Marthe Carpentier. Her first notices in the American press were in March 1914, having defeated Mrs. Lucie Warner, "wife of an English fighter, in four fast rounds," of a six-round bout. The prizefight was put on at "Chantilly before a large audience of fashionably-dressed men and a surprisingly large number of women." The report continued that "the English woman had the better of the fighting in the first three rounds," but in the last round, "Mlle. Carpentier rallied" and after "landing a heavy blow on Mrs. Warner's jaw," put her on the canvas. The fight was over when "after the count of seven her seconds threw up the sponge."[41]

English reports of the fight from the *Central News* wire were not so enamored of the bout. With a headline screaming "Disgraceful Scene in France," the crowd was described as "about 400 jockeys and stable lads." The write-up of the fight itself was also decidedly negative, describing an unsatisfactory event where "After the first two rounds the combatants fought rather wildly, and the referee was obliged to interfere very frequently to compel them to observe the rules."[42]

The disconnect between the two reports of the fight is telling of the continuing social and cultural concerns being raised by the sight of women in the ring. This is especially so when considering the descriptions of the crowds as being made up of well-heeled men and women versus horseracing louts—the latter reminiscent of the crowd description of the Hattie Leslie v. Alice Leary fight thirty years before near Buffalo, New York.

Within a few days, having been proclaimed the "world's champion woman boxer," Mlle. Carpentier, in an article by United Press and widely distributed throughout the United States, was described as "a good looking French brunette, 18 years of age," who had been trained for six months by a Monsieur Albany, "an expert boxer and jiu-jitsu instructor." Although the first press accounts had described her as being twenty-five, it is difficult to ascertain her actual age at the time she entered boxing. The United Press piece went on to note "her first serious match will be with Miss Grace Cleveland of Geneva who has signed up for a ten round contest."[43]

Carpentier's championship match with Cleveland was scheduled for April. Despite the popularity of Mlle. Carpentier's previous bout and the rise of female spectatorship at boxing matches in Paris, however, the promoters encountered problems putting on the fight, for what they believed would have been a very well-attended night of boxing. As stated in an article date-lined Paris, France, April 18, "the proposed match in which [Mlle. Carpenti-er] and several other female boxers had promised to appear, has been forbid-den by H. Henion, prefect of police," due to the "many protests against the match on the ground that it would foster brutality among women."[44]

By the end of April 1914, however, Mlle. Carpentier was headlining on stage at the Royal Hippodrome in Liverpool as part of a show entitled The Lady Boxers, along with Miss Lucie Warner, Miss Adele Neilson of Nor-way, Mlle. Alice Fleury of Belgium, and a "Miss Vera Caine [of England], who introduces a ball-punching exhibition." In the tradition of many variety theater boxing shows, Carpentier also issued "a challenge to any lady of her own weight . . . in the world."[45] The show was noted in September of 1914 as having been put "together by Gus Onlaw, a well-known French sports-man."[46] Carpentier also occasionally boxed local male fighters in three-round sparring matches and was known to have sparred with Charlie "Rip-per" Matthews and Jack "The Fighting Barber" Matthews in October of 1914.[47]

The year 1915 also saw Carpentier make appearances in theaters in Eng-land in the lady-boxing show and against other male opponents. One such show included a three-round sparring contest with a local Newcastle boxer named Nichol Brady and, in the second show of the day, in a bout with fighter Jim Berry, "the leading bantam-weight" from Dinnington.[48] The Lady Boxers show did continue to appear, though the newspapers advertise-ments no longer featured the other fighters in the troop so it is difficult to ascertain if all of the same women were still part of the act. One notice, however, from June 1915, showed the troop intact and also made special mention of Alice Fleury as having "won numerous contests at the Moulin Rouge in Paris." She was also said to have issued a challenge to all comers in her weight class. The notice for the show made an inference as well of the impact that the Great War, as it was known then, was having on women.

> Through the general replacement of men by members of the "gentler" sex, the
> exhibition of boxing . . . by sports-women . . . last night was not quite as great
> a novelty as it might have been in normal times, but it is sufficiently novel for
> the occasion, and the spectacle, if not exactly edifying, was rather attractive.[49]

Not two weeks before, the *Aberdeen Evening Express* had run a commentary on an advertisement that had made that precise point:

> "Boxers (experienced females) wanted."—"Daily Chronicle." Bombardier
> Wells is stated to have rejoined the army, and his brother-pugilists should now

have no hesitation in following his lead since there are experienced ladies ready to fill their places in the ring.[50]

If the war was beginning to have an impact on the place of women in Great Britain and likely in France, the United States, as a noncombatant state and firmly isolationist in this period, could not count on the war as having an effect on the perception of women and the roles they could enact as yet. For female boxers in Britain, however, the connections were certainly being made between "male roles" and the allowance for women to begin to "stand in" for their male counterparts in what had been thought of as highly masculine endeavors such as boxing.

By 1916 advertisements for Carpentier's female boxing troop seemed to dry up, although Vera Caine, who had a punch-bag act, continued on in her own right. Other women plying the boards as lady boxing champions in England at that time included Madge Young who brought down the house nightly with her blindfolded boxing exhibition. Miss Billie Wells also began to make a name for herself and by 1918 had an act that included "singing, dancing, comedy and boxing."[51]

Back in the United States, boxers such as Myrtle Havers, a seventeen-year-old from Flint, Michigan, born in December 1894, were making a name for themselves. Havers was best known for knocking out Mabel Williams. At twenty-two, Williams, originally from Grand Rapids, was renowned as the best female boxer in Michigan until she was put "into dreamland with a stiff upper cut after having severely punished Miss Havers in the early part of the seventh round," leaving her with enough bruising on her right eye to close it. The women had been scheduled to fight a ten-round girls' championship bout.[52] It is said "friends of the winner picked her up on on their shoulders and decorated her with the club colors pink and white."[53] They also "sent to Chicago for a bronze medal emblematic of the girls' boxing championship of the state."[54] News of the fight was published as far afield as England and Australia.

By 1910, Havers had already begun work as a leatherworker in an auto factory. There is no word on how she got into boxing or whether she continued on in her career. She otherwise continued to hold jobs in the auto industry, including working as a machinist, before becoming a beautician in the late 1920s. She continued to live in and around Flint for the rest of her life, before passing away in 1971.

Another boxer who gained notoriety in the period was Helen Hildreth. She boxed on the vaudeville stage from about 1916 to 1921. Her main sparring partner was John (Johnny or Jack) Atkinson. Both weighed about 105 pounds and the pair put together a three-round boxing act that excited audiences with Hildreth's evident "science."

Hildreth, a widow (though not much is known about her marriage), was said to have come to boxing after a bout of poor health, although in an interview she gave in 1918, she claimed to have been in a railroad wreck. According to another press account, after getting herself to the gym, she developed a gradual interest in the sport through bag-punching and light sparring with her brother. She also claimed to have studied boxing with Billy Grupp at his boxing club in West Harlem.

Aside from boxing with Atkinson, Hildreth's exploits in the sport in 1916 and 1917 included private exhibition sparring sessions with the likes of "Benny Leonard, lightweight champion; Pete Herman, bantamweight champion; Kewpie Ertle, former bantamweight champion; and Johnny Dundee."[55] Her act was often billed under the title Helen Hildreth & Co. and noted her as the "'Champion Lady Bantamweight Boxer'—the only woman to ever publicly box before a licensed Boxing Club."[56] The fight alluded to in the advertisement was the boxing match that wasn't—her fight at the Grupp Athletic Club on West 116th Street in New York, for which she became most well-known.

As one newspaper headline put it:

WOMAN BOXES ONE ROUND AND THEN—
Naughty Police Order Helen Hildreth from Ring at Grupp's A. C.[57]

Hildreth's fight was claimed to be the "first time a woman . . . attempted to box in a licensed club since the Frawley law was enacted." She was to box only one clean round against Atkinson before Police Inspector Ryan along with four members of his squad stopped the fight by approaching her in her corner at the end of the first round. Other newspaper accounts, however, claim the fight was stopped well into the second round. Either way, she was said to have given Atkinson a beating.

The Frawley Act, under which auspices the police chose to end the bout, was in effect from 1911 to 1917. It legalized boxing in New York State by, among other things, limiting sanctioned bouts to ten rounds. The most controversial aspect of the new law was it only allowed fight decisions based on one or another fighter being knocked out. The act also established an athletic commission and regulated boxing clubs. In the absence of official boxing results, the general practice was for a select group of boxing reporters to determine winners and losers by decision, although officially fights were noted as draws.[58]

According to reports by the International News Service and Billy Grupp, the owner of the gym (and also Hildreth's trainer), the commission regulating boxing had previously sanctioned the bout. Regardless, Hildreth's foray into the ring, while not strictly illegal per se, attracted enough attention to bring the police to the Grupp Athletic Club—whether as a test case or not remains unknown.

The fight had been well attended, and as one newspaper put it, "They sparred like veterans" after the first two preliminary bouts on the night's fight card. Helen's appearance in the ring was described as causing "a gasp of astonishment," after she "threw off her bathrobe and disclosed a graceful figure in white tights and a close-fitting jersey." Her fighting ability, however, won over everyone in the crowd and the consensus was that she won the round handily on points.

Other aspects of the fight that were of a controversial nature included the use of pneumatic or air-filled gloves, rather than standard boxing gloves, and Hildreth's appearance in tights. The use of the pneumatic gloves was likely in place to forestall any possible interference by the authorities—and as for her boxing costume, it was fairly standard for the era. As a disappointed Hildreth put it:

> I don't see why they should stop me. Perhaps it was the tights. You see, Mr. Atkinson and I do boxing and dancing on the stage and as Mr. Grupp has given me lessons we thought we would return the compliment and box at his club. The Boxing Commission gave permission and we thought it would be all right.[59]

With the publicity from the fight Hildreth, billing herself as "The Boxing Girl," went back onto the stage with Atkinson in a show entitled "Fighting It Out," playing on the vaudeville circuit with an act that drew increasing notice. She also sought out well-known boxing champions to spar with her in an effort to increase her standing as a boxer in the public's eye—as well as to garner frequent press coverage.

In 1917 at the beginning of America's involvement in the Great War, Hilda Hildreth was asked about women in the boxing ring. Her response was in relation to America's war efforts:

> There is no reason why women as well as men shouldn't interest themselves in physical culture. They owe it to themselves and now they owe it to their families. Now with the nation at war and with Uncle Sam mobilizing every resource, domestic as well as military, she owes it to her country.[60]

As with the British in 1915, Americans in 1917 were working through a thicket of questions around issues of nationalism, patriotism, and the place of normative gender roles in time of war. Hildreth's call to physical culture as part of one's patriotic duty was no less inspired by nationalist fervor than the Spartans' belief that strong women made for strong warriors.

Even before the United States entered the war, an article published in the *Brooklyn Daily Eagle* made mention of the changing world:

> In these days when women of Russia are taking up arms and are fighting in the
> trenches, one has no right to laugh at the woman boxer. Certainly, it would not
> be well to laugh in the presence of Helen Hildreth . . . [who says] boxing is the
> one sport in the world that requires both courage and nerve.
>
> Courage is the control of one's mentality over the moral or physical sys-
> tem. A man or woman without courage has a yellow streak and is a coward. [61]

As with many other female boxers of her era, Hildreth continued to take her
act to the stage. By 1918, however, she was also doing her "bit," bringing her
boxing show to soldiers and boxing in charity events, and in 1919 she appeared at the Chateau Theirry Club in Manhattan's Beekman Hill to entertain
"wounded heroes" with her boxing prowess. [62]

Not much is known about Hildreth after 1921 or so, although at the time
of the census in 1920 she was living on Manhattan's West Side with her
widowed father, widowed sister, and Jack Atkinson. She had listed her occupation as "actress."[63]

Chapter Four

Encountering the Modern: Flappers, Mae West, and the War Years

The girls will be taking a whirl out of the mits soon—you watch. They are great at a fight; they fizz up so easy. All you have to do is land a punch, wink, look sassy, and you've got them in their hallelujah.
—Jess Willard, April 4, 1915[1]

In the post–World War I era of the late 1910s, 1920s, and 1930s women steadily became fixtures at ringside. Movie stars like Mae West, who was taught to fight as a young girl by her pugilist father, "Battling" Jack West, were closely associated with boxing, and West's image was used in a 1936 *Popeye* cartoon entitled "Never Kick a Woman." Hollywood films depicted women in boxing gloves, such as in the 1927 silent film *Rough House Rosie* starring the irrepressible Clara Bow. Coincidently, that same year the German film *The Fighting Lady*, about a woman who learns to become her own defender by taking up the gloves, was released.

The popularity of boxing extended even to charity events—many in support of veterans—that featured well-known doyens of society, such as judges, cozying up to such boxing giants as Jack Dempsey. Certain highly publicized fights were also social events for the well-heeled who came out in tails and evening gowns as if it were a night out at the opera. Images of women were also featured at ringside, sitting alongside their dates, in rapt attention.

The fitness crazes in Europe and America incorporated boxing techniques and images of athletic female boxers became normal in Weimer Germany. Female boxing also rose again in popularity at carnival sideshows in Great Britain as well as in vaudeville and burlesque acts across America. Popular images of fit women were a mainstay of American World War II propaganda, including the incorporation of boxing motifs on the covers of such popular comic books as *Dixie Dugan* and *Wonder Woman*. These images, however, continued to play on the Amazon theme, and, in the case of *Wonder Woman*, drew a direct parallel to the Roman goddess Diana and the Amazons.

OBSERVING WOMEN: VIOLENCE, BOXING, AND THE BODY

The writer Djuna Barnes, who was to become part of the literary circle of the "lost generation" in 1920s Paris, got her start as reporter in the mold of Nellie Bly. Writing in the 1910s, she penned first-person articles and exposés on issues of the day for Joseph Pulitzer's *New York World*.

Her first boxing article was entitled "My Sisters and I at a New York Prizefight." In writing about her "sisters," she stated, "They do not appear self-conscious, nor is there anything in their behavior to indicate that anything is unusual." To her mind:

> They look indifferently upon the raised square with its shivering taut ropes, its limp towels and scarred brown pails, the stools in the corner, the sponge in its pool of water that widens ever and drips to the floor below. And they finger their chatelaines [belts] and speak of the boxers' build.[2]

What is striking about Barnes's writing is her elegant prose as she presses her viewpoint about the essential blasé nature of women bearing witness to the rituals of the ring: "Some lean forward with hands, palms outwards, thrust between their knees and . . . women who dared the ringside . . . balanced between wonder and apprehension."[3]

Her lasting impression is of a woman "who had cried out just before the finish—'Go to it, and show us that you're men!'"[4]

The following year Barnes interviewed Jess Willard—who had famously defeated Jack Johnson for the heavyweight title in Cuba the previous April. Willard's comment to Barnes that women "fizz up so easy" watching boxing was a clear indication of the prevalent idea that men in boxing rings were attractive to women. Barnes's next boxing article, written in 1921, explored this issue further. She interviewed heavyweight champion Jack Dempsey ahead of his highly touted bout against the French fighter Georges Carpentier (no relation to Marthe Carpentier)—but it quickly came to the subject of women. Dempsey had been on record with his views that women were good for the sport of boxing.

> Women are beginning—as they should—to take up boxing seriously as they take up swimming, riding and other athletics. It is all the working out of the theory that a sound body and a sound mind travel together.[5]

In her interview with Dempsey, Barnes did not so much talk about women in the ring as hint at the fetishism of the male boxing body as a sexual object—a continuation on the trajectory that had begun with the gushing reviews of Gentleman Jim Corbett and his famous pompadour in the 1890s.

"Of course the women will all be on Georges Carpentier's side," said Jack Dempsey. The champion heavyweight paused as if to let that sink in, then continued: "It's not longer enough to have speed and a good right arm to be the favorite. You have to be good-looking, too, now that ladies go to the fights. Well I am willing to do my bit."[6]

This was a far cry from the novelty and outcry at the idea that "dainty" women would be subjected to the violence of the ring, which permeated the writings about female spectatorship not ten years before—although when it came to articles penned by women, Barnes's writings seem more like a continuation on the trajectory that had begun with the Corbett interview, minus her admissions of "fandom." What was clear from her work was the idea that women ogled male boxers as sexual objects—frankly and without concern.

Another author on the cusp of fame who wrote about women at the fights was Ernest Hemingway. In an article penned for the *Toronto Star Weekly* in May 1920, he observed that women, present for the first time at a boxing event in Toronto, were not only game to watch, but quickly garnered the intricacies of the sport and the ultimate boxing cachet: the knockout.

The fight had been marketed to women as a chance to see the French heavyweight boxing "idol" Georges Carpentier—the doyens of Toronto society among them. From Hemingway's perspective, Carpentier's good looks were not, however, the only draw. Hemingway strongly felt that the boxing itself, with all of the attendant blood and gore the fistic art could muster, was perhaps an even greater lure than the half-naked male boxing bodies in the ring. In Hemingway's estimation, what he was witnessing was a redux of the Roman Forum, which he insisted had at one time or another seen a greater proportion of women in attendance.

WOMEN'S BOXING: SELF-DEFENSE AND SELF-IMPROVEMENT

At the time of World War I, women had been lacing up the gloves in the salons of the middle classes and the vaudeville stage regularly since the 1880s, yet women's fighting was still taboo and difficult to come by. The self-reflexive strands of modernity had, however, begun to imbue women's participation with a sense of themselves and their own possibilities—especially when equating boxing with self-defense.

Boxer Vera Roehm seemed to embody some of that spirit—having started in vaudeville, she graced the pages of the *National Police Gazette* in 1917, and used her position to promulgate boxing as an important tool in the arsenal for a woman's ability to stand her ground. Billing herself as a "physical culture expert, boxer and all-around athlete," Roehm firmly believed "women would do well to learn boxing. It would teach them to take care of themselves at all times," and from her perspective would help "the vast majority" of women who "are helpless at present if insulted or attacked, as often happens."[7]

Born in Baltimore, Maryland, of Austrian parentage, she claimed to have been trained as a nurse, though this is hard to substantiate given that she began appearing in the highly popular vaudeville act Will Roehm's Athletic Girls as early as 1911. Will Roehm, likely her father, had earlier promoted Cora Livingstone as the champion lady wrestler of the world in 1908.

Vera Roehm, though a member of the Athletic Girls troop, began drawing notices of her own in such places as Fort Wayne, Indiana, in 1914. There she gained notoriety as a physical culturist and all-around athlete in the five-woman show that consisted of boxing, wrestling, fencing, exercises, and bag-punching routines.

Her main claim to boxing lore, however, was her participation in what was likely the first female boxing film teaching self-defense. Distributed in 1917, by Paramount-Bray, the short, entitled *The Womanly Art of Self-Defense*, was marketed as an educational two-reeler. A review described "the usefulness to women of knowledge of boxing." Vera Roehm was described as "one of our finest feminine exponents of boxing." She was lauded for demonstrating a myriad of boxing techniques and for explaining boxing lexicon. "Here we learn what is meant by the kidney blow, the solar plexis [*sic*] blow, and various other important movements," she was said to have described. The review also complimented her for the "forceful illustration" of how "a woman may maintain her right to sit on a park bench unmolested."[8]

The year 1917 also saw Roehm syndicate a series of articles marketed as health tips. Her simple exhortations to women were on such subjects as gaining enjoyment from exercise, the importance of stretching, and how to get rid of a scrawny neck, all featuring her in posed photographs wearing a sleeveless form-fitted top and tights.

She was, however, an interesting contradiction—on the one hand, an advocate for women's physical development in the boxing ring, on the wrestling mat, and even in her own home doing exercises; and on the other, as late as 1919, on record as claiming that women didn't belong in the professional boxing ring. It was also reported that while she had watched sparring events between men, and even lightly sparred with male boxers on occasion, she had never actually been to the fights.

By 1922, Roehm was marketing herself as a physical culturist and stage beauty, promulgating the secrets of the stage to share her tips with women through her exercise regimen that took a mere ten to fifteen minutes a day. She also marketed body building and physical culture courses.

Another woman whose fame as a "champion" boxer coincided to some extent with Vera Roehm was "Countess" (as in a boxer's ten count) Jeanne La Mar (alternatively, she was known as Jeanne Lamar and Jeanne La Marr). La Mar was purportedly born in France, though a 1930 census entry shows that she was actually born in New York of French parentage in 1900. Given that she had a son named Marcel who was born in 1912, her likely birth year was closer to 1890. La Mar was married to Paul Lamar until sometime before December 1927.

She seems to have begun appearing as a French boxing "champion" around 1921 when she bag punched to music at Stillman's Gym in New York City. Known as a ballet dancer, she was remembered fondly by gym owner Lou Stillman decades later. Most accounts show her fully engaging in the New York boxing scene in the early 1920s, though how she learned the art before coming to Stillman's is unknown. Aside from boxing, she also enjoyed some renown as a soprano on the vaudeville stage and appeared in occasional dramatic roles.

Claiming to be the French female boxing champion, the five-foot, two-inch boxing dynamo was skilled not only at the sweet science but also at effectively garnering publicity for herself. La Mar, in a bid for boxing notoriety outside of the realm of the vaudeville stage, took the tact of working with well-known boxing promoters. Her aim was to get a fight at the world-renowned Madison Square Garden. To do so she sought out no less a personage than Tex Rickard's boxing organization at the Garden (Jack Dempsey's promoter and an architect of bringing in female spectators to the prize-fights—known as the "Jenny Wren" section) and his longtime matchmaker Leo P. Flynn (who went on to manage Dempsey).

After some negotiations, La Mar successfully signed with Flynn. With over sixty fighters in Flynn's stable at the time, La Mar, as the first female boxer under contract, solidified her place of preeminence in the boxing world. Once under contract, she set to work attempting to get a match against Miss Mae Devereaux or alternatively an exhibition bout against a male boxer to be named. As for Devereaux, in the mid-1920s Dempsey, a strong proponent of women who boxed, was most impressed with the actress and dancer, whose real name was May O'Hara. Having been trained by her brother Eddie O'Hara—who also trained Dempsey—she had the skills of a true champion, skills Dempsey believed could knock out a lot of male bantamweights. Having taken up boxing for fitness, she also boxed to keep herself from the mashers walking along Broadway.[9]

La Mar's real goal at this time, however, was to obtain a boxing license from the New York State Athletic Commission (boxing had become legal again in the state in 1920). Her efforts to obtain a license proved unsuccessful, but La Mar remained undaunted.

She further legitimized her prominence by claiming to have sparred with such French male boxing champions as George Carpentier (who had just lost to Jack Dempsey) and Eugene Criqui. Given that she had visited France in 1919, where her husband had been a second lieutenant in the American Expeditionary Forces, it is possible that she had opportunities to show her prowess in the ring at that time. Regardless of whether she actually sparred in Paris, however, La Mar's intention was to solidify her place as a trailblazer in the ranks of female professional fighters.

As it turned out, she was unsuccessful in her bid for a fight at the Garden, but she continued to garner press coverage for her feats in the ring, including sending the boxer Johnny Watson to the canvas in the third round of an exhibition bout in Reading, Pennsylvania, in 1922. La Mar appeared on the stage presenting a series of boxing exhibitions, where she followed in the long tradition of female pugilists from the 1880s and challenged women in the audience to box with her.

Eager to maintain her insistence that she was an actual boxing professional versus a stage performer, she put in appearances at professional and amateur boxing shows wherever she could. These exhibitions included fights with other fistic women (on the vaudeville stage or in boxing venues) including bouts with Princess Henry, so named because she was married to pugilist Prince Henry.

Although it is unclear when she and Flynn parted ways, she eventually signed with boxing promoters Joe Woodman and George Lawrence in 1923, who helped La Mar perform in three-round exhibitions against the likes of the fighter Bugs Moran, the gangster. At around the time she signed with Woodman and Lawrence, it was reported that she secured a professional boxing license, the first ever issued to a woman in the state of New Jersey. Her aim was to fight a sanctioned bout against Kiddy McCue, a boxer out of St. Paul, Minnesota, or Princess Henry of Allentown, Pennsylvania, with whom she had already been performing in shows. It is unclear if any of these bouts actually occurred, as a press notice in September of that year stated that none of her challenges had been accepted. It has also been claimed she was granted a license to box in the state of Texas at some point—but it remains unsubstantiated.

By 1924 she was featured on WHN radio in New York, both singing in French and English (in her guise as a soprano) and giving talks on such topic as "Self-defense for Women." Press accounts of her boxing, however, were starting to dry up, and as the decade wore on, her radio work seemed centered on her singing. Advertisements in *Variety* emphasized both her boxing and dramatic stage appearances. She also appealed to Actor's Equity in this period to ensure that no other artists could use her stage name.

In late 1927 she moved to Los Angeles with her second husband, Thomas Failace (or Faye). The marriage came to an abrupt end a few weeks after their arrival when police were called to their Hollywood home, apparently responding to the culmination of weeks of brawling since their wedding in early December. There is no mention of what happened to her first husband, Paul Lamar. Some accounts note that he died—though the record is spotty—and one reporter researching her life claimed that at her husband Paul's death she was the beneficiary of a large insurance claim, which she was said to have lived on as her main source of income through the mid-1930s. Added to the mystery, however, are census records that indicate Paul had remarried and remained quite "alive."

At about this time, in 1931, La Mar was also flatly turned down in her bid to be granted a boxing license by the state of California. Her history in this period became somewhat murky as she struggled to maintain her place in the limelight. By the early 1930s she was pulling such stunts as calling out the famed Olympian Babe Didrikson to meet her in the ring. Shortly thereafter, in 1935, La Mar decamped from Los Angeles to live in her cabin on a piece of land above Big John Flats Mountain near Wrightwood, California, about an hour and a half northeast of the city. Once there she became embroiled in a mystery worthy of any 1930s Hollywood potboiler.

Still identified as the French female boxing champion, La Mar began to drink heavily, and as her cash flow apparently dried up she sought out pickup bouts in local venues. Though no longer married, she lived with a younger man identified later as Gustave M. Van Herran, known locally as Gus. La Mar claimed he was her nephew whom she raised since childhood. Undoubtedly this was the same "Marcel" identified as her son on her first husband Paul's passport application from 1920. The best guess is she called Gus (Marcel) her "nephew" to maintain the fiction of her purported age which, as time went on, got younger and younger.

In 1937 or so Gus disappeared rather mysteriously only to have his skeletal remains discovered alongside a rusted-out hunting rifle. His remains were found on La Mar's property about a year after his disappearance. An investigation at first concluded that Gus, who had been shot in the head, was murdered; however, the cause of his death was eventually changed to suicide. The Associated Press news report at the time, published in the *New York Times*, stated her nephew had been released from Stockton State Hospital where it was reported he had apparently threatened to commit suicide a month or so before his disappearance. La Mar disputed the findings, but nothing ever came of it. At about this time, she herself left the mountain for parts unknown and was said to have died in the early 1940s nearly destitute. A reporter looking into her story in the 2000s brought to life the claim that she had confessed to murdering Gus, though the actors in the sad tale were long since gone.

For all of the drama of her story, punctuated by many acts of self-promotion that kept her in the public eye for decades, La Mar, through her attempts at legitimizing her standing as a professional boxer—some successful, some not—remains an important figure in women's boxing at a time of great transition.

As with Roehm, she sought to promulgate women's boxing as a means to self-actualization. Through her talks on self-defense, although she differed from Roehm, who did not see a place for women in the professional side of boxing, La Mar very much supported women in the professional prize ring and sought prominence in the sport she came to love for herself wherever she could.

The struggle for acceptance of such figures as Roehm and La Mar bracketed the legitimization that women had successfully garnered for themselves at the ballot box. Other women in other sports also pushed for success. One figure, Ida Schnall, had come to prominence with her failed bid to become a member of the 1912 U.S. Olympic Team. A champion swimmer and diver, her efforts to compete in Sweden, where women's swimming events were added to Games for the first time that year, were thwarted by the U.S. Olympic Committee secretary, James E. Sullivan. The following year, as captain of the New York Female Giants baseball team, Schnall was to write a letter to the editor of the *New York Times* complaining about the denial of women in such prestigious sporting outlets as the Olympics.

Despite her being denied a place in the Olympics, Schnall gained notoriety as a female sports figure and advocate for women's physical cultural. Schnall's life intersected La Mar's in 1923 when La Mar accepted Schnall's very public challenge to fight. Various news reports had them fighting for the featherweight, junior lightweight, or lightweight championship, and Schnall was photographed, with a baseball bat in hand, as she readied for the bout.

The match was set for May 12, and an application to the New York State Athletic Commission was lodged; however, a permit for the bout was not forthcoming—and the women, though determined to fight, were minus a venue. At the time, La Mar pointed out that nowhere in the rulings were women forbidden to fight, but regardless of her interpretation, their boxing bid was denied.

Other women who boxed with some notoriety in the era with an eye on women's fitness and health included Americans Laura Bennett and Gertrude Allison, French boxer Mlle. Gonraud, and the English fighter Miss Annie Newton, who along with other members of the Women's Boxing Club in London, founded by her father, Professor Andrew Newton, were said to have been featured in a Gaumont newsreel piece in the 1920s.

In this same era, female boxing characters put in appearances in films—with the boxing as self-defense meme clearly embedded in the characterizations. Most famous of them in the United States was Clara Bow's *Rough*

House Rose, first shown in 1927. The film was produced by Adolph Zucker and Jessie L. Lasky, and directed by Frank R. Strayer for Paramount Pictures, and as noted in the trailer (the only surviving portion of the film), it is the story of a girl who "got her men treating 'em rough." The images show her socking a boyfriend, cheering on another boxer boyfriend at ringside, and bits and pieces of a boxing dance number at the nightclub where she was a headliner.

The German film *The Fighting Lady*, also produced in 1927, incorporated the boxing-as-self-defense theme as an antidote to troubled political times and the physical threats that lurk in the dark. The heroine takes up boxing after being mugged in the park. Her newly found confidence and prowess, however, have a detrimental effect on her relationship with her fiancé, who feels threatened by her ability to take care of herself. Angered by his lack of understanding she storms out and, walking in the same park where she was mugged before, she fends off a would-be attacker with three swift shots that knock him down to the ground. Her fiancé comes upon her, having followed her for fear that she was cheating on him. Together they drag the would-be criminal to the police—followed by images of newspaper headlines lauding her for defending herself. The close of the film opines that by the year 2000 women will be the protectors over men.[10]

Other strands along the theme of self-improvement were articulated by such women as actress Vicki Baum who took up boxing in the early 1930s and viewed it as a means of measuring her own strength. Baum, joined by such luminaries as the iconic Marlene Dietrich and Germany's elite boxing royalty including Max Schmeling, worked out at a boxing club opened by Sabri Mahir in Weimar-era Berlin. Said to have originally been a soccer player from Turkey who left at the time of the Second Balkan War, Mahir was also purported to be a German named Sally Mayer, originally from Cologne. Whether Mahir or Mayer, he took the name "Terrible Turk" and gained fame boxing four opponents at a time at Germany's first boxing venue, the Circus Busch.

Mahir's gym on Tauentzien Street in West Berlin, at the southern end of the Charlottenberg district, catered to men and women. The pervading philosophy was that boxing training—whether for professionals, recreational boxers, men, or women—was all the same. Men and women contented themselves with the same difficult regimens, workouts, sparring schedules, and principles of asceticism. Something of a salon—where Mahir held court spouting his ideas about perfecting the body—the gym attracted a wide assortment of people from bankers to artists to boxers.

The idea of measuring strength and such things as stamina, the bulge of growing muscles, and the confidence that came from executing boxing's myriad exercises, not to mention the intricacies of the sweet science itself in the ring, were a new means of expression for women taking their place in the post–World War I world. And whereas boxing prior to the war was still somewhat hidden inside salons, gyms, the closed doors of hosted boxing smokers, or on the vaudeville stage, the images of gloved women were increasingly slipping into the mainstream.

So too were images of women in "unclothed" states, as images of fighters like Texas Mamie—clad in full-length tights, a form-fitting shirt, and short skirt from the 1900s—gave way to even skimpier outfits, which revealed sleeveless low-cut tops, a scarf around the waist, and something akin to modern bicycle shorts.

Female boxing bouts unheard of prior to World War I also became popular in Germany—particularly in Berlin's growing cabaret scene—beginning in the early 1920s. The bouts were said to be hard fought, as distinct from the women's boxing "acts" prevalent on the American vaudeville stage. Jack Dempsey, visiting Berlin, witnessed one such evening of boxing and was impressed by the ferocity and great skills of the young fighters, but fearful of the potential dangers.

Under the sway of Weimar culture, however, boxing's popularity extended far beyond male and female spectatorship and participation in the ring and the "salon" boxing gyms. As a recreational sport, it even extended to such places as German luxury cruise ships where lessons and sparring were offered to the men and women of the upper decks.

The popularity of fistic women in Germany, though unsanctioned, was indicative of yet another rise in the physical culture for women that had begun in the 1880s. More than ever, women in England, on the Continent, and in the United States were taking up sports ranging from tennis to swimming, golf to baseball, and swimming to boxing, as well as other martial sports including competitive wrestling, judo, and jiujitsu (the latter two having been introduced in the early 1900s by Japanese masters of the respective arts). In the meantime, the French boxing variant, savate, continued to enjoy a renaissance that included many female practitioners both in the gym and in bouts. Championships in the sport were also held, and by the early 1930s, several newsreels and short documentary films featured savate, including films that taught the basic rudiments of the game. Some of these films also featured women such as the highly recognized fighter referred to as La Belle France who appeared in newsreels distributed by British Pathé. In the brief film, she is shown demonstrating a number of savate techniques with a male savate practitioner. In another newsreel short, a group of about twenty young French women are shown performing a series of exercises.

In the United States boxing as self-actualization also continued to gain traction for recreational boxers who met to box regularly in classes and gyms. One such group, cited by writer Kate Sekules in her memoir *The Boxer's Heart: A Woman Fighting*, was the Busters Club of Flint, Michigan, which she reports was started by a group of stenographers who took up the gloves. How many women were in the club and how they started is un-known—although according to Sekules, at some point they were banned from practicing at the local YMCA.

WOMEN AND THE WORK OF BOXING

The 1930s was a time of deep anxiety and fear in the United States. The Great Depression and its aftermath—racial strife, the rise of fascism, and the coming of World War II—put tremendous pressure on men and women as they negotiated the changing landscape of their world. Cheap entertainment in the form of movies, and boxing and wrestling shows, saw a rise in atten-dance and the emergence of women as a meaningful fan base, just as vaude-ville started to die out. Radio also leaped to the fore for entertainment of another kind, entertaining Americans seated in living rooms across America.

In the work of the ring, women had been laboring in one capacity or another for decades as entertainers, fighters, managers, and even trainers. In the 1930s that labor extended to such things as licensed fight promotion and refereeing. Most notable among them was Belle Martell, who became the first licensed referee in the state of California on April 30, 1940, after more than nine years of involvement in the sport alongside her husband, Art. Prior to her career in boxing, Martell had been a dancer and contortionist in vaude-ville. It is also where she met her husband, a former boxer in his native Australia.

With the rise of talkies, the landscape for vaudeville changed dramatical-ly. Belle and Art left the business and after moving to Van Nuys, California, Art set up a boxing gym in his garage and began training amateur fighters. Belle figured she'd retire and be a housewife for a change. Fairly soon thereafter, however, Belle grew tired of sitting around doing nothing and took to the sport herself. Before long she was good enough to train the boys as they came into the gym—and also helped with the business side of things. Quickly garnering success with popular fight shows, Belle and Art also man-aged amateur fighters. Shortly thereafter they came to the attention of none other than the "Great White Hope" himself, Jim Jeffries, who in his retire-ment had set up a boxing gym in Burbank, converted from an old dairy barn on his property. They began managing fight nights for Jeffries, which proved all the rage, and brought them to the attention of the Hollywood set who worked in the studios nearby.

By the mid-1930s Belle and Art were fixtures in the Los Angeles amateur boxing scene. Leaving Jeffries's big red barn, they managed amateur boxing nights at the Grand Olympic Auditorium in downtown Los Angeles. Com-monly referred to as the "Olympic," they attracted large crowds: young and old, men, women, and kids. They also charged nothing more than fifty cents or a dollar to be entertained by a great boxing card and the chance to hobnob with the likes of Mae West, Barbara Stanwyck, and other Hollywood stars—many of them women.

Aside from co-promoting the bouts alongside her husband, Belle also began doing the honors as the ring announcer and gained a license to appear in that capacity at boxing matches, along with a license to act as a timekeeper which she did on a regular basis. On nights when she acted as the ring impresario, she cut a striking figure dressed in a black velvet evening gown and used every decibel of her twenty-two years of stage training to garner the attention of the crowd.

Speaking to a reporter about it, she said, "I had a tough job convincing the fans that they wanted to listen to a woman announcer. It just took a lot of nerve and a gift of gab. They thought they'd scare me, but I tossed back remarks as fast as they were made."[11]

As an experienced trainer, timekeeper, and ring figure—and by 1940, running a well-respected gym called the Los Angeles Athletic Club with her husband and partner—she had a fair amount of notoriety, and what she thought of as "clout in the business."

Belle's next move was to gain her referee's license. Taking it very seriously, she enlisted former lightweight champion Willie Ritchie to help teach her the fine points of the referee's ring duties and to help her prepare for the state licensing exam. Newspapers reporting on her at the time wrote that she aced the test with the score of 97½—the highest ever recorded, though she'd actually failed portions of it on her first written attempt. Undertaking an oral exam in front of the five-member panel of the California Athletic Commission the day after her written test, she passed with flying colors.[12]

Belle Martell's triumph, however, was short-lived and controversial. While she had been cheered at ringside for her previous endeavors inside the velvet ropes, the response to her role as the "third man" was another matter.

"First Woman Referee Puts Pulchritude in Pugilism," read one headline emphasizing the story along the lines of "feminine" interests. The photo, showing her with two young fighters, took more notice of what she was wearing than of her refereeing duties: "What the well-dressed referee is wearing becomes a fashion note as Mrs. Belle Martell makes her bow in Southern California as the first woman fight referee."[13]

Another reported she handled her work "as well as any man."[14]

But others in the press in California were less kind, vilifying her ring appearances—not so much for her performance, but because of the belief that "women have no place in a prizefight ring."

Even the state was unsure of its own decision to grant her a license and limited her first appearance as a ring official to one bout only. Of that one fight it was reported "the inspector's report to the commission" was thought to be "favorable."[15]

Nine days after her license was issued, Martell officiated on a busy fight card at the weekly amateur fight night in Pasadena. She is said to have officiated at eight fights that night and even counted out a young fighter named Jimmy Archuleta who'd been floored with a knockout punch.[16] One paper went so far as to praise her for her "workmanlike manner" in that fight.[17]

She managed to officiate a few more matches before the California Athletic Commission issued new rules barring women from acting as referees in amateur and professional boxing matches after May 24, 1940. It read in part, "No license will be granted to members of the female sex to referee, second or manage in the ring when other performers are of the opposite sex."[18]

Reacting to the cancellation of her license, and referring to herself as the first licensed female referee in the country, Martell was furious.

> "The Commission found no fault with my work," declared Mrs. Martell, "but based its action solely on the fact that I am a woman.
> "If it continues to discriminate against me by refusing me assignments, I may take the case to the courts. Several women's organizations are rallying to my aid and plan a protest to Governor Olson."

A few days later, Belle felt beaten down by all the controversy. She had dedicated the better part of ten years to running amateur boxing shows with an unmatched dedication to the fight game and to the youngsters she had taken under her wing. Disgusted and sickened by all that had transpired, one month and one day after being granted the referee's license she had worked so hard to obtain, she announced she was "giving boxing back to the men."

She'd decided to retire from day-to-day activities ringside at the end of June. Explaining her reasoning she said, "The stupid and ridiculous charges stirred up during the past month have brought about my decision to step out and give the men, who have been blasting so loudly, a chance to see what they can do for boxing."[19]

Even with her pronouncement and the suspension of amateur fighting at the Olympic, she and her husband went on to found Martell's Arena, known fondly as Belle's Arena, and continued to promote amateur fighters. Belle approached her work there with the same determination and spirit she'd always had—minus the hope of ever being an official inside the squared circle.

Other women also took to the business side of the ring in this era. In the spring of 1934, the wife of boxing promoter Archie Leary took over his duties at the Leary Arena in Fairfield, Maine, and put on mixed boxing and wrestling programs to enthusiastic crowds. She even added in a musical component to entertain the crowds between bouts.

During the war years, Helen Zivic, the wife of ex-welterweight champion and future International Boxing Hall of Fame fighter Fritzie Zivic, became the first woman to become a licensed promoter in the state of Pennsylvania. With her husband, a corporal in the army, off in San Antonio, Texas, Zivic not only took over her husband's promotional duties but ran a stable of five fighters. Her view, however, was that she was only taking it on temporarily until he came home.

Juanita Yeargain, known as the "First Lady of Boxing" in Topeka, Kansas, had been a girdle-fitter before taking over the role of promoter for the Topeka Auditorium's boxing and wrestling shows in September 1943. Her husband, Max Yeargain, a former fighter turned matchmaker and fight promoter, had taken the call to join the navy. Similar to Helen Zivic's story, Juanita took over the reins, but in her case she never looked back. She promoted highly successful weekly sold-out shows that were proving more popular than her husband's. Her NWA national championship wrestling cards included some of the best in the business. Her boxing fighters were also well-respected—one of whom was Chilean heavyweight fighter Arturo Godoy who'd fought and been knocked out by champion Joe Louis in 1940.

Another woman of the ring was Dorothy Bodeen. Following in the footsteps of Belle Martell, she became an officially recognized boxing promoter in California in 1945. Based in Oxnard, California, she began promoting a series of amateur boxing nights at the El Rio Stadium with the blessing of the California Athletic Commission.

Most famous of all the female boxing promoters from that era, however, was Aileen "The Redhead" Eaton, who began her career in boxing as a troubleshooter for the owner of the Olympic when business profits started to go bad in 1942. Bringing in a boxing commission inspector, Cal Eaton, the two worked side by side overhauling the promotion at the theater. They married some six years later with Aileen eventually taking over the business entirely upon Eaton's death in 1966. Aileen helped build a veritable empire of fighting that is legendary to this day, with her best work hitting its stride in the 1960s and 1970s.

Her involvement in the sport included a three-year stint as a commissioner with the California State Athletic Commission. She is also the only woman (as of this writing) to be inducted into the International Boxing Hall of Fame. She was inducted posthumously in 2002, following her death in 1987. She also promoted the first women's bout at the Olympic Theater in May 1976—shortly after the state of California legally sanctioned women's boxing.

During the war years, women continued to box. From fighting teams of coeds in California to female soldiers and sailors boxing in makeshift squared match sites on base or aboard ships, images of women in the ring also extended to photos of "lady" seconds at boxing matches. One such match was held by the Royal Australian Air Force, as shown in the January

30, 1943, edition of the *Milwaukee Journal*.[20] The women, attired in uniform shirts and shorts, appear to be soldiers themselves and, if not, women involved in some sort of women's work corps.

Newspapers also continued to tout boxing as exercise for women to improve their health and their figures—especially their "busts" by developing the pectoral muscles.[21]

In popular culture, boxing-themed movies were hitting the theaters with regularity. The Betty Grable vehicle *Footlight Serenade* featured her in a boxing number, "I Heard the Birdies Sing." Her signature number tells the story of how falling in love is like hearing the "birdies" from a knockout and includes an innovative sequence where she boxes her own shadow.

The area inside the velvet ropes where boxing took place remained a male domain when it came to fighting or even refereeing. While the new modern woman certainly boxed in many guises in the period from the end of World War I on through World War II, there was also an apparent overriding discomfort that denied women the opportunity to fight as professionals in any meaningful or sustained way despite their growing success in the wrestling ring. The house side of the fight game, however, was another matter as women did make important inroads as spectators, managers, and promoters in the sport in the years between the wars.

Chapter Five

Boxing in the Age of the "Mighty Atom"

She is a girl who really likes to fight and we can't keep her out of the gymnasium.
—Mickey Wood, owner, Mayfair Gymnasium, April 7, 1949[1]

Barbara Buttrick, popularly known as "The Mighty Atom of the Ring," was a British boxer who took up the gloves in the late 1940s. She became representative of the new post–World War II female boxer who held her own in the gym and went her own way in finding opportunities to ply her trade—whether performing in a carnival sideshow, in the back lot of a feed store, or in an actual arena. Buttrick came to the United States in the early 1950s and, along with other pioneers such as Phyllis Kugler and Jo Ann Hagen, forged a career as a professional fighter, retiring with a claimed record of thirty wins, one loss, and one draw.

The 1950s and 1960s became an era when boxers pushed at the strictures against female boxing in Great Britain, the United States, and Canada. Along with Kugler, Buttrick was able to gain a license to box professionally in one of the states—Texas in 1957—something that hadn't happened in the United States since the early 1920s when Mlle. La Mar was licensed to box in New Jersey. (A sanctioned fight in West Virginia was fought in June of 1950 between Jo Ann Hagen and a Chicagoan named Nancy Parker, though it is unclear if they were issued formal licenses to fight.)

These boxers of the 1950s joined the many women who were staying in the workforce regardless of the entreaties to stay at home to raise a family. And while many women were forced to trade in their blue-collar war-related factory jobs for more traditional pink-collar work as secretaries or shop girls, boxing women—and their close cousins, "lady" wrestlers—were staking a claim for legitimation and acceptance.

Wrestling, in particular, grew in popularity with regular circuits and fighting opportunities for women. Despite the seeming acceptance of "lady wrestling," however, boxing remained out of reach as a sustainable professional venture for at least one of the "old" reasons: The male domain of boxing was unsuitable for women. Professional female wrestling matches on the other hand were viewed as entertainment and not as brutal sport. In an attempt to rectify the barely visible impact of "girl" gloved fighters on the boxing scene, promoters and trainers like Belle Martell put their considerable talents toward developing a new generation of women to fight on legitimate amateur and professional fight cards, unfortunately without a lot of success.

Even though regular employment as fighters was hard to come by, these women continued to train and work in and around boxing. Ofttimes they were isolated figures in the boxing gyms of the day where they kept their skills sharp and earned the respect of their male counterparts, however begrudgingly. In the United States in particular, it also meant riding the wave of gender expectations that pushed at domesticity. However improbably, cracks in the veneer were shining through as more and more women entered the labor force—including boxing women who continued to make gains in the sport as promoters, trainers, managers, boxing gym managers, and officials.

BARBARA BUTTRICK: THE "MIGHTY ATOM" OF THE RING

At four-feet, eleven-inches tall and weighing just nintety-eight pounds, Barbara Buttrick, known variously as "Battling Barbara" and "the Mighty Atom of the Ring," could very easily have hidden behind a free-hanging heavy bag and never have been noticed. What she lacked in physical stature, however, she more than made up for in hard work, grit, heart, and determination—all the attributes necessary to ply a trade as a boxer inside the velvet ropes of the boxing ring. She was also not unlike her moniker, a force to be reckoned with in a tiny package: hard charging, combustible, and mean when she needed to be.

As a "mighty atom" she was also something more: a postwar woman unafraid of taking the hard road and equally unapologetic about the path she chose to get there. Nor did anything in her makeup align her with the flighty images of powder-puff girls in boxing costumes that permeated popular images from the 1930s. She was a Rosie the Riveter in boxing gloves: ready to take charge with fists of steel whether fighting women or men despite her diminutive size.

Barbara Buttrick was born in March of 1930. She was the only child of a shopkeeper and his wife who raised her in the village of Cottingham in

Yorkshire, England, northwest of the city of Hull. The family home was on 18 Linden Avenue—a street barely three blocks long. Her home, like the others on her street, was a two-story semidetached brick house with a large back lot and fronted by a small garden. Across the street was a row of trees that bordered the narrow grassy wedge between it and the main railway line.

Always "sporty" (in the parlance of the time), Barbara Buttrick's interest in boxing began by chance when she was fifteen years old. Coming into a friend's house after playing soccer, her friend's mother handed the girls pieces of the newspaper, admonishing them to wipe the dirt from their shoes before tracking it into the house. What caught Buttrick's attention, however, was not whether she'd managed to remove all of the offending mud but an article featuring a story about the women's champion boxer Polly (Fairclough) Burns, purportedly entitled, "Polly the Champ."

What intrigued Buttrick were Polly's stories of having boxed men in the fairground boxing booth shows that made their way up and down the countryside following the age-old circuit of fairs that had dotted Britain for centuries. Thoroughly enthralled by what she had read, Buttrick dropped the idea that had been percolating in her head to start an all-girls soccer team in favor of taking up boxing.

Speaking about it years later, Buttrick said that she got a book entitled *The Noble Art of Self-Defense*, written by the champion flyweight Jimmy Wilde—to whom she was later compared—and began teaching herself to fight with a punching bag she set up in the backyard. She also wrote to Polly Burns who responded to her and noted that since there weren't very many girls fighting, it would be hard to get onto boxing cards. Buttrick wrote to other fighters, and even the *Boxing News*, but the replies were even more discouraging.

That didn't stop Buttrick, however, and as she improved her boxing know-how, she began sparring with the neighborhood boys and any girls when she could. It was in those early fights that she developed a good chin and learned how to give up weight and height—becoming more and more skilled as a counterpuncher in the process, a trademark of her later success in the ring. She also received encouraging support from Len Smith, a young former bantamweight amateur boxer (and her future husband), who was of the opinion that if she wanted to box, she should.

What was also clear was Buttrick's commitment not only to learning the sport but to having a career as a fighter, so much so that she's been quoted as saying, "My mum used to look at our family tree to find where it [the boxing] came from."[2]

When Buttrick turned eighteen, she managed to win her parents' permission to go south to London to train at Mickey Wood's Mayfair Gymnasium (and Tough Guys agency), arranged by Len Smith. Soon after her arrival, she got a job as a secretary where she typed by day. After work, she went to the

Mayfair Gymnasium on Great Portland Street near the Baker Street tube and worked out for three hours before making her way to her room at the YMCA in Bloomsbury. She mostly trained with Len Smith at the beginning. At 118 pounds, Smith was a fitting size and weight for her to spar with as she began learning the finer points of how to box. She also received instructions from the well-known veteran trainer Wally May on the nuances of the fight game.

It was Buttrick's perseverance and skill that brought her to the attention of the Mayfair Gymnasium's owner, Mickey Wood, who signed her on as a "tough girl." Wood, the former British lightweight wrestling champion and a commando instructor during World War II, ran a stunt school and talent agency based in his gym, and taught various fighting techniques and such feats as how to jump from a moving car and other action-oriented stunts for the movies.

No doubt Wood's theatrical background in combination with Buttrick's evident skill and unrelenting desire to pursue professional boxing led them to introduce Buttrick to the sporting world in October of 1948—a mere three months after her arrival in London. It was Buttrick's intention to box as a professional, and Wood was only too happy to assist her by bringing in the press to garner as much publicity as possible.

So successful was her introduction to the denizens of London's Fleet Street, she received press attention all over Great Britain and as far away as Australia and the United States. In one article that ran on October 12, 1948, a photograph of Buttrick showed her in a boxing stance with a caption that read she was "prepared to accept any challenge from an opponent in her own weight [class]" and that "when fully trained," it was her desire "to start a boxing club for women only"[3] as "England's first woman professional boxer."[4]

The response was equally well reported, most notably with a series of articles about three women in Australia who were training to meet Buttrick's challenge. One story that ran in the Hull paper in her native Yorkshire noted that Buttrick had received "three offers from Sydney." The women were introduced as "Fay Lynch (18), 114lb., 5ft. 3in; Pat Bailey (17), 112lb., 5ft. 2in.; and Cath Thomas (18), 117lb. 5ft. 4in."

The article also quoted Buttrick's mother who upon hearing of the challenge said, "I have told her she is not to box in public. Boxing is only a hobby for her."[5] Clearly mother and daughter had different ideas.

Meanwhile an Australian paper reported that the women were feasting on "oysters and underdone beefsteaks—and drank 6 pints of milk." The three fledgling pugilists were also reported to "train 3 periods a week at home." Fay Lynch further described their training regimen, stating, "We run, skip, use both the punch-ball and punch-bag, shadow box and spar." The article gave every indication that Lynch, under the tutelage of a "well-known Sydney trainer," was as serious about boxing as Buttrick. "We try to eat and live like professional boxers," she was reported as having said. "We don't bother about feminine fashions, but stick mostly to a sporting style of dress. But we use lipstick and powder."[6]

A British account opined, "The Sydney girls use lipstick and powder as a concession to convention,"[7] with both papers also reporting Fay's comment that they all wished they'd "been born boys."

Arrangements to bring the three young women to England could not, however, be finalized. Of the three, Cath Thomas became the most dedicated to boxing and had the temerity to box a man in an exhibition fight in December of that year in Fairfield, on the outskirts of Sydney. Her exploits, while applauded in some circles, invoked the ire of the authorities and she was "banned from giving public performances in New South Wales . . . by state officials."[8] Her promoter, Stan Easton, who had been planning a bout for her in the Sydney suburb of Hornsby, was also told to desist.

Speaking of it to the press, Thomas said, "I'll never give up fighting now that I've broken into the game. They can't stop me boxing in my home-made ring."[9]

Thomas kept to her word and continued to defy the ban, fighting at smokers in and around the Sydney area. By February 1949 it was claimed that she had fought a total of "14 fights against men, for five knockouts, two technical knockouts and five wins on points. She has been knocked out twice," all of which gave her a 12-2 record.

She also reiterated her defiance of the ban and said, "I will take on anyone between 8.6 and 9.0 [stone]. They can forget I'm a woman and hit as hard as they like. I like them to hit me first. It seems to rouse me."[10]

February 1949 marked another flurry of press coverage for Buttrick, including a newsreel piece that played in the theaters throughout Britain.[11] She was also booked to perform a boxing bout on stage at the Kilburn Empire Theater on March 7, 1949, against the London-based middleweight Bert Saunders.

Reacting to the news, the Variety Artistes' Federation (VAF), a theatrical trade organization, in an unprecedented act moved to have the other entertainers slated to appear on the same bill boycott the show. The VAF's general secretary, Lewis Lee, in calling for the action stated he felt the show would be "degrading to the best interests of society, public entertainment, the boxing profession and womanhood."[12]

Mickey Wood, who had been instrumental in promoting the fight and had by then become a fierce defender of Buttrick's right to fight, said, "There are women lion tamers, snake charmers, trapeze artistes. Why should not this girl box?" Finishing up his comments, he added, "She lives for boxing. In seven months she has trained two hours a day without any injury."[13]

VAF next issued a letter to the theater's manager, Nat Tennens. According to one press account, the letter expressed VAF's "repugnance and opposition" to the show and threatened "appropriate action [would be] taken to prevent the presentation."

Tennens, standing his ground, said, "The VAF are in a difficult position, for they are trying to be dictators, censors and trade unionists at the same time. The Lord Chamberlain had no objections to Barbara appearing, nor have the LCC [London County Council] or the police."[14]

He was also quoted as saying, "I see no more harm in displaying the skill of a girl boxer than in staging strip tease acts, nudes, and adagio dancing in which girls are flung about in an undignified manner."[15] Equating a young woman's boxing demonstration on stage to snake charmers and trapeze artists was one thing, but equating it with a "girlie" show appeared to push the boundaries of the exhibition he was touting into another realm entirely and would hardly have helped his cause.

Within a few days, Tennens received notification from the LCC that his theater-operating license would likely be revoked if he allowed the performance to continue—a not unexpected outcome given the negative publicity and the notion that Buttrick's show was "indecent" at best.[16] The British Boxing Board of Control (BBBC) also warned Bert Saunders of possible punitive actions if he were to appear on stage with Buttrick. Tennens, complaining that he'd had booking orders from all over the country, had no choice but to cancel the boxing match against Saunders; however, when it came to Buttrick, he told the world that she would still perform "an exhibition of training, shadow boxing and punchball work."[17]

Subscribing to the theory that when life gives you lemons make lemonade, Tennens took the tact of advertising the ban as a way of putting more theatergoers in the seats. The headline of the advertisement for her one-week engagement read "Battling Barbara Buttrick/The Girl Boxer Banned By The Variety Artists Federation,"[18] and in true boxing tradition, her act was the "main event," appearing last on the bill.

Tennens himself took to the stage to introduce her to the audience. Standing under a spotlight, he gave an oration on the important role that women played during World War II, followed by a further speech on how it was wrong to keep women out of the boxing ring. When he was finished, he motioned Buttrick to join him to fanfare and a drumroll.

Buttrick walked out from the wing wearing all white, and after clasping her hands in the air toward the audience, removed a silk boxer's robe. Underneath she wore a white cardigan sweater and white silk boxing shorts with a side stripe. Even her hair sported a white ribbon. After acknowledging the applause, Buttrick got right to work skipping rope to music and working out on a spring ball before a heavy bag dramatically descended from the ceiling, at which point Tennens shouted out, "The terrific punch of this little girl is estimated at over 700 pounds."[19] Completing several minutes on the heavy bag and some minutes on the speed bag, her act finished in a wash of green light as she shadowboxed around the stage.

The notices the next day also left no doubt that the public missed out when her sparring match was canceled. Commenting on her shadowboxing, one reviewer wrote, "She showed remarkable speed and good footwork." She was also quoted as telling the audience, "Unfortunately I have been prevented from meeting an opponent, but I hope my exhibition has entertained you."[20] The audience's rousing applause certainly gave every indication that she had.

The week at the Kilburn Theater aside, Buttrick was dead set on competing. A "secret contest" between Buttrick and an unnamed female boxer from Leamington Spa, Warwickshire, was announced to the press and set for late April 1949 at an undisclosed location in London. To keep the mystery going, the press also reported that a small audience of invitation-only fight fans would be in attendance.

In preparation for the fight, Buttrick—who had just turned down an offer "to tour with a London production" because they would not let her spar—traveled back up to Cottingham with Len Smith to train. Met at the train station by the local press, Smith, when asked how Buttrick was doing, told the *Hull Daily News* reporter that after "nine months" at the "Mayfair Gymnasium . . . [she] was shaping well."[21] Smith also mentioned that she would be working on her plans to help other women who wanted to box, and would be looking for a possible space to open a women's boxing club as well as weighing other opportunities including an offer from a promoter in New York.

Buttrick's opponent for the clandestine bout turned out to be Kathleen Turpin, sister of three boxing brothers. Oldest brother Dick became the first "colored" boxer in the modern era to win a title fight in England, having been awarded the Lonsdale Belt as the British Middleweight Champion in 1948. Not to be outdone, Randy Turpin, two years Kathleen's junior, was to later defeat boxing great Sugar Ray Robinson for the middleweight title of the world in a hard-fought fifteen-round shocker in London in 1951. A third brother, Jackie Turpin, also won a championship (BBBC title) and made a name for himself while fighting as a featherweight.

With thirty pounds on Buttrick, Turpin was certainly going to be a challenge. This was especially so as she was pictured in the press hard at work on a double-ended bag in the boxing gym where she trained—and presumably, having been around boxing all her life, she had at least some modicum of skill.

During this period, Buttrick also challenged Cath Thomas, who was continuing to make a name for herself in Australia. The hope was that the two women would fight for an Empire women's championship title, with Buttrick ceding twenty or so pounds in order to fight. The challenges of getting the two women together proved to be too great to even consider. Both were banned from boxing in their home countries and there was the vast geographical distance between them. As it was, Thomas "demand[ed] expenses, and a guarantee, before accepting the bout."[22] The two women, fierce competitors both, were never able to meet in the ring. Thomas seemed to slowly dissolve into the recesses of history with very little more that can be found about her boxing exploits past 1948.

For unknown reasons, the fight between Buttrick and Turpin was never listed on the "official" record of fights that Buttrick maintained over the years.[23] It is possible that the Buttrick/Turpin fight did not take place at all. The venue owners may have pulled the bout, fearing repercussions from promoting a clandestine match. Furthermore, there is little, if any, information on Turpin herself after this period, nor reports on whether she ever fought at all after the Buttrick challenge.

As the spring wore on, Buttrick also pressed for permission to fight professionally by requesting the BBBC reverse its long-standing ban on female boxing. Issues raised include the canard that women needed special rules, not to mention "protective devises to prevent permanent injury to girls who slug each other."

The ringing endorsements of Buttrick's trainers to the press were couched in language that left no doubt that women's fighting was not the equal to men's.

Wally May opined, "Any fight between women with which I have anything to do would have to be a lady-like exhibition."

Even Len Smith said the fights should be "short" with "big gloves and a new code of foul blows," to help "overcome some of the old objections to girls in the ring." He did, however, go on to say, "a bloody nose now and then wouldn't hurt them."

Mickey Wood's tact was to speak about Barbara Buttrick herself, saying:

> She is a girl who really likes to fight, and we just can't keep her out of the gymnasium. . . . She would crawl in through the window if we shut the door. We have decided to give her the best of our professional skill. She is in prime physical shape, and what a slugger! I don't want my chin to get in the way when she swings.

Buttrick herself, in making her case to the public, said, "Girls are in most sports and should do well in boxing. I've just got to convince the boxing boards it is safe, and anyway, I'm not afraid of getting hurt."[24]

The BBBC did not agree and maintained the ban.

By this point it was obvious that there were no particular opportunities for Buttrick to fight an actual boxing match—other than sparring in the gym or risking the possible repercussions of fighting in clandestine matches. The only recourse was to follow in the footsteps of her heroine Polly Burns by taking to the boxing booths still plying English fairgrounds from one end of the country to the other.

Buttrick's first appearance was with Tommy Wood's boxing booth show on Derby Day, June 4, 1949, at the fair held annually at Epson Downs. She fought male opponents, taking on all comers who were within a thirty-pound swing range of her ninety-eight-pound frame. As was the normal course in the boxing booths, Buttrick took on all female comers in her catch-weight range from 90 pounds to 130, and in the absence of women, boxed men, her usual opponents. Boxing as many as thirty or more rounds in a day, Buttrick became an efficient boxing machine, and to her recollection, was never bested by a challenger.

Next up, Buttrick toured the West Country, with Sam McKeowen's Boxing and Wrestling Show. The boxing show became a perfect venue for her "professional" fights, as they would take place on the fairgrounds well away from the prying eyes of the VFA, BBBC, or the LCC in a duly licensed venue.

According to Buttrick's official record, as the summer wore on she tallied three fights, two in July and one in September. Of the three fights, Buttrick won the first by TKO in the second round against Margaret Johnson in Penzance, England—a well-known stop on the boxing booth circuit even if the location was remote at the edge of the peninsula jutting out into the Celtic Sea. Buttrick won her second fight against Joan Fletcher by KO in the second round in Brixham, England, and won her third match on points after four rounds of boxing against Sheila Craig in Paignton, England—just down the road from Brixham.

Interviewed by a West Country boxing magazine, the article on Buttrick noted that the "objects of her tour with the booth were to gain experience and encourage other girls to take up the sport!" The piece also reiterated Buttrick's desire to "start a gymnasium" of her own and went on to proudly mention a West Country woman, the wife of boxer Alf Wright from Plymouth "who could hold her own" in the ring.[25]

For the next boxing booth season in 1950, she switched to Professor Boscoe's Boxing and Wrestling Show, which plied her home county of Yorkshire. Buttrick received top billing as "Britain's Leading Girl Boxer," and drew considerable crowds of men, women, and children. Boscoe, acting as her promoter, sought out professional fights for her, although with little success.

One such fight in July 1950 was to have been fought against Elsa Hoffman, a young German woman living in the town of Dewsbury. Set to be held at the Dewsbury Feast on the fairground, "Elsa failed to turn up" for their "four two-minute round" fight. Speaking with the press about the planned fight, the mayor of the town, J. E. Brown, said he felt the fight was "deplorable" and was "glad that nothing came of it."[26]

Even though the sold-out match was canceled, Buttrick received challenges from the crowd. In all, she fought four "official" fights—winning three by KO and one by TKO between July and September. This was in addition to the daily rounds she fought in the booth.

Despite the shock and dismay that women might have a boxing contest at the fairgrounds, there was a long tradition of boxing women in boxing booth shows stretching back to the late 1800s. In the 1910s, '20s, and '30s in England, such shows as The Moore Family of Athletes featured not only the sons but also the daughters of the shows proprietor, Professor Moore. The same was true of the Hickmans, a boxing family that claimed to go as far back as the 1820s champion Tom Hickman. The Hickmans traveled in the 1920s with the Pat Collins Boxing Show.

Winnie Davies boxed in Jack Lemm's athletic and strongman shows in the late 1920s and early 1930s (he was her father). Davies was even occasionally featured on the show bills as the Flyweight Champion Lady Boxer. Other boxing booth notables included Alf Stewart, whose wife and daughters—while not boxing—shared duties as timekeepers, ticket takers, and all of the other jobs that kept the show running.

Boxing booth work was by no means easy for boxers. Fighters had to work all day and well into the evening before packing up the show and hitting the road for the next destination, where the long workday started all over again. Hardest were rainy days when the crowds stayed away and very little money came into the till. Packing up in the rain was also difficult as was the near-constant travel from town to town.

As with male boxers, the fairground shows gave women fighters the opportunity to learn their trade and come in contact with other fighters and entertainers seeking to earn a living by their fists. While it could be difficult for women in particular—because they were subjected to negative attention by the authorities—the female fighters were at least able to practice their trade and, as in Buttrick's case, out of sight of the boxing officials who would rather she not jump in the ring at all.

In 1952, with Smith by her side, Buttrick took off for a season of touring the French countryside with a boxing booth show there. The retinue traveled the length and breadth of France in such places as Joinville, Neufchateau, Vitre, and Dale, and—as with her British boxing booth tours—aside from daily bouts, she racked up six more wins to her running tally of "official" fights. It is difficult to know if the women she fought were actual boxers, savate fighters, or just women who were eager to challenge her. What is clear is that in France, as in England, women were only too eager to pick up the gloves. Speaking about her time in the boxing booths, she told a reporter:

It was an exciting life . . . we moved from town to town and I didn't feel tied down. We'd put up the tent and then I'd fight at night. If the girls that come up could last three rounds with me, they'd win a prize. Many of them would fancy their chances with me because I was very small. But I never had much trouble.[27]

Following her travels through France, Buttrick and Smith decided to give the United States a go, where they'd heard that women were starting to box professionally. It was to be a momentous decision, one that saw Buttrick and Smith marry earlier in the year, in June 1952, and leave England for good with a view to making a life for Buttrick as a professional boxer, hopeful of the potential for greater opportunities.

BOXING BEAUTIES: WOMEN'S BOXING IN THE 1950S

I went at her with a combination attack—left jabs to the head and hard rights to the body. Girls can be beaten with body punches. After three rounds of all the punches I could throw, Miss Hagen was finished.
—Mrs. Lancaster (Pat Emerick), March, 1972[28]

In an era of bathing-beauty contests, "Susie homemaker," and visions of the Cold War beginning to stir in the public's consciousness, women's boxing in the United States had begun to pick up in the late 1940s. There were pockets of opportunity for actual fights in something other than the nightclub venues plied by Mickey Walker's all-girl boxing troupe in the mid-1930s. This was due in no small part to the rise of women's wrestling and the newcomer to women's sports Roller Derby, which in the late 1940s and early 1950s aired as many as three times a week on television.

Such wrestling stars as Mary "The Fabulous Moolah" Ellison, June Byers, Millie Stafford, Mildred Burke, Ella Waldek, Mae Young, and former boxer Bonnie Bartlett were wrestling stalwarts in the late 1940s and on through 1950s. The popularity of these fighters led to the growth of women's wrestling in all parts the United States, Canada, and Mexico. The acceptance of women in the wrestling ring also helped open the door to bring female boxers as a feature on fight cards.

In June 1950 Jo Ann Hagen, billed as the women's world featherweight champion, came from South Bend, Indiana, to fight a six-round match against a Chicago fighter named Nancy Parker at the Radio Center in Huntington, West Virginia. Hagen won the bout by decision after both women boxed to the adoring hoots, whistles, and shouts of the three thousand fans who'd poured into the arena to see them fight—one-third of whom were women. For the contest, Hagen and Parker boxed wearing sixteen-ounce gloves—presumably for their protection and likely to satisfy the authorities.

A newspaper reporting on the fight claimed that the fight was lackluster at best because the fighters both wore twelve-ounce gloves. The article also stated that it was only an exhibition fight, which meant there was no decision issued.[29] The discrepancy in the glove size was not addressed.

This first female boxing bout in the state of West Virginia was reported to be a fully sanctioned event, although the state's "athletic commissioner J. Patrick Beacom protested the bout as being against 'common decency.'"

Luckily for Hagen and Parker, the fight—promoted by Dick Deutsch, a local boxing and wrestling promoter—was not opposed by B. W. West, the commission official responsible for the Huntington jurisdiction, who opined that he "knew of no law prohibiting women from boxing." Deutsch himself was a well-known promoter who the year before had put together a wrestling card featuring seven women in a variety of pairings and went on to promote Joe Louis's wrestling appearance in Huntington in 1956. Speaking of the boisterous female fans at the Hagen-Parker fight, whose number even surprised Deutsch, he went on to say, "Maybe they learned some pointers on how to deal with hubby when he gets rough," perhaps speaking truth to an all-too-common occurrence that harkened back to the meme of women's boxing as self-defense.[30]

Unfortunately, West Virginia's foray into the world of women's boxing was short-lived. Within a week or so of the contest, the West Virginia Athletic Commission voted to ban female boxers from the ring. Patrick Beacom, who had objected to the Hagen-Parker fight from the onset, led the call for the banning, claiming that participation in boxing "may cause such physical harm to the women boxer as to do great injury to the already sick boxing game." He gained the support of the National Boxing Association (NBA) in his call for the ban.[31] While recommending the ban, the NBA had no power to enact any decisions—those were left to the individual state athletic and boxing authorities. In another blow to the sport, the French Boxing Federation announced a ban on female boxing the following November, even though the women affected by the ruling contested it strongly.

Jo Ann Hagen (shortened from Ver Hagen and originally a sandlot baseball player) was known as "the Bashing Blonde from South Bend." She boxed for trainer and manager Johnny Nate, who popularized women's boxing in and around South Bend. The women worked out in a space below Nate's tavern on North Hill Street, where there was a heavy bag, an area for sparring, and other boxing equipment. Nate himself had been a bantamweight, achieving some notoriety as a Golden Gloves fighter in the early 1930s. His older brother, Georgie Nate, also came to prominence as a boxer in the Midwest.

At some point, Johnny Nate turned to training and managing female fighters, including Jo Ann Hagen and Phyllis Kugler. Phyllis fought under the name "Phil" Kugler in the 1950s until someone figured out that the apparent amateur boxer fighting in the arena was a girl. Kugler, a self-professed "tomboy," had grown up in the sport with a father who had been an amateur boxer and brothers who all took up boxing. In an interview with the *South Bend Tribune* decades later, Kugler recalled "her mother had different feelings":

> My mom had a problem with it, especially when I broke my nose for the fourth or fifth time in a fight down in Texas. . . . But my mother wasn't the only one. It took some people around here a long time to accept what I was doing.

On the topic of boxing, clearly her main interest, she also told the reporter, "What really worked for me was a double left hook followed by a right cross."[32]

Hagen—said to be the 126-pound champion—featured in an earlier bout against Arvilla M. Emerick, billed as Pat Emerick, another South Bend fighter, who'd taken up boxing in 1948 at the age of nineteen. Emerick's workout at that time consisted of practicing her punches on the heavy bag, sparring, and running five miles a day along a path that bordered the railway line not far from the University of Notre Dame. She likely also spent at least some time training with Johnny Nate. When she wasn't boxing, she worked first as a ticket taker in a movie theater and then as a store manager.

In 1949 Hagen and Emerick fought a six-round co-feature main event at the Moose Auditorium in Council Bluffs, Iowa, promoted by former boxer and current wrestling star Champ Thomas. It was to be the town's first public women's boxing match. Stories about the fight in the local paper began appearing a week before on an almost daily basis.

One surviving photograph of the fight popularized on the Internet shows the taller five-foot, seven-inch Hagen delivering a hard left to Emerick's face as the five-foot, four-inch fighter threw a right to Hagen's midsection. The caption from an unknown newspaper erroneously reported that the fight took place in Cincinnati, Ohio. In another photograph, published in the local Council Bluffs paper, Emerick is shown shooting a straight right to Hagen's chin.

Hagen was reported to be the more active and aggressive fighter during the first three rounds of the bout, but in the fourth round, Emerick came on strong, taking "all the steam out of the South Bend blonde who passed out at the end of the round." Hagen was revived by her corner, but declined to enter the ring for the fifth round, giving Emerick the TKO win.[33]

Recalling the fight in 1972, Emerick remembered it as only lasting three rounds before Hagen took to her stool:

> I went at her with a combination attack—left jabs to the head and hard rights to the body. Girls can be beaten with body punches. After three rounds of all the

punches I could throw, Miss Hagen was finished; couldn't answer the bell for
the fourth round. They gave me the championship on a TKO.

Emerick stated that she gave up fighting in September 1950 after a serious
car accident in Indiana. She went on to marry Robert Lancaster in 1955 and
raised ten children with him. She also recalled that in the nearly two years
that she fought professionally, she had traveled in and around Indiana, Nebraska, and Iowa, earning as much as $250 for a title fight, "before deduc-
tions," but otherwise earning very little.[34] She was purportedly given a trophy with a golden glove on top for the fight against Hagen.[35] In all, Pat
Emerick claimed a record of eighteen fights with only one loss—her first.

Hagan, although she lost the fight against Emerick, was featured in a
gimmicky "rasso-boxing" match against wrestler Bev Lehmar in the same
theater the following week. The five-round boxing/wrestling match allowed
mat work and straight punching, with both young women reported to have
"pitched and tossed to a stormy . . . draw," with Hagen having "survived an
early series of body slams."[36] The women fought in front of a roaring crowd
of 875 fans—the largest to that date in the series of matches held at the
Moose.

Not to be outdone, promoter Champ Thomas continued offering women's
wrestling, but boxing proved to be so popular that by the middle of December of 1949 local girls were clamoring to take up the sport. This led Thomas
to bet on fights with local "talent." Although the girls were relatively untrained, he nonetheless added the matches as a feature of his Tuesday night
fight cards. For the first outing Jean Hansen, a Council Bluffs native, fought
against Ida Spaulding, who hailed from Oklahoma.[37]

Another outgrowth of the Hagen-Emerick boxing match was what the
local press called the "invasion by women and girls of the rougher and
tougher fields of competitive athletics" from Council Bluffs and the surrounding towns in southwest Iowa. The paper cited boxing, wrestling,
mixed-gender wrestling, and even the case of a ten-year-old girl who showed
up for a football clinic "figur[ing] she could play football as well as the
boys."[38]

Out in California, Belle Martell was back in the fray working to promote
female boxers alongside her husband, Art. Martell believed "boxing as a
competitive sport is dead." In her view the advent of television was killing
boxing because more and more fights were being marketed for the television
audience—with few spectators showing up at the arenas, and no opportunity
for budding boxers to develop their talent. In her opinion, the best course to
save boxing—and taking a cue from the successes she saw in the promotion
of wrestling—was to wow the crowd with really skilled female boxers. To
undertake her endeavor, she advertised to the public for potential fighters.

Overwhelmed by the response, she told a reporter she received in all "150—everything from movie extras, Earl Carroll showgirls to plain Amazons."

Putting the women through a training regimen, she and her husband signed Jacqueline O'Neill along with ten of the other women who showed the most skill and aptitude to be future champions. O'Neill, a 125-pound fighter, was viewed as their first potential title winner—and with Belle pushing to get California to abolish its rule banning female fighting, she promoted O'Neill's debut fight for viewing on television in the fall of 1951.[39]

Given the Martells' record of success with amateur boxing beginning in the 1930s, they were hopeful that their promotional acumen would help kickstart these sorts of entertainments, but ultimately not much came of it. Absent in the discussion was who the sanctioning body or bodies would be that might confer women's boxing titles. There was also no discussion on what sort of regional and national network was to be put in place to promote the female fights—something akin, perhaps, to wrestling's NWA—with the added understanding that men's boxing at the time didn't fare much better. As it was, titles for women continued to be conferred on a local level through the auspices of sponsoring organizations and promoters themselves who awarded the titles as an add-on to their fight-card marketing. The NBA also continued to prove itself wholly unsympathetic to the cause of women's boxing.

The advent of television had hurt the gate receipts for the kinds of shows the Martells were famous for. After closing up shop at the Olympic and running Belle's Arena, they were looking to the women's fight angle as a way to stay in the game. While not much came of it, they did end up taking over the Hollywood Legion Stadium's Thursday night amateur program in 1954, a highly popular venue for wrestling as well. One facet of their renewed amateur night program, however, was the seeming absence of female fights on their cards.

Into this mix of burgeoning boxing promotion and opportunities for professional fights between skilled female fighters came Barbara Buttrick. After coming to America, she made appearances with a boxing-and-wrestling act on the American carnival circuit, picking up true boxing matches where she could.

According to her record, her first fight in the United States was against Pat Emerick. They were purported to have fought in Omaha, Nebraska, with Buttrick winning their six-round bout on points in December 1952. While Emerick claimed to have been retired at this time—given that it was two years after her accident—it is possible that she fought against Buttrick, if not in a sanctioned bout then in an exhibition bout.

Buttrick's next fight was in St. Louis a month later. Her opponent turned out to be Nancy Parker, a veteran of the Hagen fight in West Virginia. In the match, despite Parker's size and weight advantage, Buttrick bested her with a third-round KO win. Buttrick went on to fight four more boxing matches in 1953, traveling a circuit of boxing shows throughout the Midwest and the old border states. In between fights, Buttrick settled in Waterloo, Iowa, working as a boxing trainer at the Elks Club, teaching young boys of color the rudiments of boxing.

In this period she also began fighting in wrestling matches for promoter Karl Pojello, a Lithuanian by birth who had wrestled in the United States in the 1930s. Pojello, based out of Chicago, famously promoted such wrestlers as Maurice Tillet, the "French Angel." The relationship between Buttrick and Pojello came to an abrupt end, however, when Pojello died in September 1954.

A genius at wrestling promotion, Pojello had Buttrick fighting on all manner of cards. One such fight card, in November 1953, found her battling Dorothy Ford with a thirty-minute time limit. Another part of the card featured "'Battling Betty Bear,'" a "175-pound black bear" and her trainer, "Walter Gatlin," a black wrestler "from Memphis."[40]

Another card in February 1954 saw Buttrick participate in the main event: a mixed-gender, mixed-race tag-team bout. The match, along with the undercard fight, was featured at the Playdium Theater, a combination nightclub, bowling alley, and bar located in downtown Sheboygan, Wisconsin. The top billing on the card was for an African-American wrestler, Irene Cobb, and her father, John Cobb, based out of wrestling's mecca: Dallas, Texas. The father-daughter pairing was set to fight Buttrick, partnered with Big Jack Bernard (as in 240 pounds big), from Nashville, Tennessee. An advertisement, featuring a full-length photograph of Irene Cobb dressed in an elaborate bathing costume in a strong-woman pose, promised a "Mixed Tag Match!" with "Girls!" and "Men!" as the main event.[41] One newspaper also referred to the show as "The colorful mixed tag team match" on the weekly card at the Playdium.[42]

While Buttrick and Bernard lost to the Cobbs, the fight itself was a sensation. The local Sheboygan paper published a photograph of the ring extravaganza featuring Irene Cobb, who easily outweighed Buttrick by forty pounds or more, dangling Buttrick behind her on her back. The caption read in part, "Little (100 pounds) Barbara Buttrick refuses to release her leg-lock despite the fact that Irene Cobb manages to standup and put her in an upside-down position."[43]

Other Buttrick wrestling matches were contests on less flamboyant fight cards with one or two women's wrestling events among the four or five fights on the card. Speaking about her experiences to an Associated Press reporter a couple of years later, she noted she was not very enamored of wrestling and had left the sport in favor of boxing, adding, "Boxers don't last as long as wrestlers, and I figure I can take up wrestling when I am through with boxing." She was often paired with women who outweighed her by forty to fifty pounds, which could not have been easy for her. The truth was, as a highly-skilled practitioner of the sweet science, the rough and ready world of wrestling was well out of her wheelhouse.[44]

Buttrick was able to jump back to boxing in July 1954, when she fought Audrey Burrows, listed as the "United States Bantam Champ." Burrows was another South Bend fighter who weighed in at about 116 pounds. The eight-round world championship fight was billed as the main event on a five-fight card featuring local and regional talent. Buttrick was given top billing as the "British Champion." Rather than hold the bouts inside a theater or arena, the promoters put together an outdoor affair in Dickinson, North Dakota, at the American Legion baseball field.

A press report in the *Bismarck Tribune* touting the contest was less than flattering in the lead-up to the fight:

> In one corner, wearing Devil's Delight lipstick and chartreuse trunks, will be Barbara Buttrick, "champion of the British Isles." Opposing her, with a Tony "natural wave" and an off-the-shoulder ensemble will be Audrey Burrows from South Bend, Ind. The respective weights of the fistic femmes are their own darn business.[45]

Most press reports were in actuality positive when it came to female boxers in the period, and the notices announcing the outcome of the match were no exception. Buttrick had defeated Burrows by KO with the *Billings Gazette* reporting:

> Briton Wins—Barbara Buttrick, champion woman boxer of the British Isles, won over Audrey Burrows in a boxing match at the American Legion baseball field Friday night. The bout went three rounds.[46]

The local *Dickinson Press* was also positive and led with:

> Battling Barbara Buttrick of the British Isle scored a third-round knockout over Audrey Burrows. . . . In the main go, Burrows carried the fight to the British girl for a round and a half before hitting the canvas in the second round for a seven-count. Referee Pat Conlon tolled out the full 10 in the third when the girl from Indiana stopped a volley of Buttrick blasts and wound up on the deck.[47]

If there was any controversy at all it was in sorting through whether the fight went three or four rounds, as noted on Buttrick's official record.

Buttrick's next boxing match was held on September 9, 1954, and was the toughest in her career as a professional boxer. Signed by boxing promoter Jack Berry, the now five-foot Buttrick was set to battle Jo Ann Hagen, who had a full seven inches in height and at least thirty pounds in weight over her.

The fight itself was the "semi windup" to the main event to be held at the Victory Pavilion in Calgary, Alberta, Canada. A poster for the fight featured photographs of both fighters with the title "In This Corner" as the lead-in. Buttrick was featured as the "British Empire Girl Champion" and Hagen as "America's Finest Girl Boxer." Further text noted they were "two of the classiest girl boxers in the world."[48]

Both fighters were certainly well matched, as they were both seasoned pros with several years of boxing experience. The height and weight differences, however, placed Buttrick in an exceedingly disadvantaged position going into the eight-round bout. The promoter didn't consider it an issue and more than happily arranged for the fight to be broadcast on radio—a first for women's boxing anywhere in the world.

A photograph of the boxing match first published in the *Calgary Herald* shows Hagen, a statuesque blond with light-colored trunks, white boxing shoes (modified ice skating boots), and a white shirt, towering over Buttrick. Hagen's gloved right hand is extended and pushing Buttrick's head back as she connects with a right to Hagen's chest underneath her left arm. The image of Buttrick, who sported dark trunks with a Union Jack on the right leg and a white shirt, seems to be that of a child attempting to fight an adult.

As could have been predicted, Hagen, who came in thirty pounds or so heavier than Buttrick, proved to be too overpowering. Still, although Buttrick lost to Hagen on points, she showed remarkable skill and tenacity that kept her upright except for two brief trips to the canvas in the fourth and the seventh rounds.

In an article published in the *Calgary Herald* the next day, the reporter was quite obviously impressed with both fighters, touting their match as "an action-packed" bout. He also stated Buttrick and Hagen "showed an amazing knowledge of the art of self-defense as both came up with some clever bits of Boxing."

The piece pointed out that Hagen "possessed too much of an advantage" over Buttrick, who was nonetheless "game against the powerful hitting Hagen." It also reported that while Barbara was suffering from a bad head cold, she overcame it as best she could and "won the plaudits of the crowd as she weaved her way in on her American opponent continuously and in fact was the aggressor throughout the bout."

The reporter stated that "without exception the bout provided plenty of action and the crowd in its entirety ate it up."

In postfight interviews, Hagan said she thought Buttrick was "the best and toughest fighter she'd ever met" and was quoted as saying, "I have a split lip and cut nose to prove it." Buttrick, reported to be in a "jovial mood, and unmarked," was equally ebullient about Hagen saying, "She was big, she was strong, she was tough and she won. JoAnn is the best boxer I have ever been up against, but I would like to meet her again when I am in better shape." It was to be the only loss Buttrick claimed to have suffered in her career.[49]

Buttrick didn't fight any more boxing bouts that year, in part due to the difficulty in finding women to combat, and in part having suffered an injury to her back. She pulled up stakes with her husband and relocated to Dallas, Texas, in 1955, thinking the climate for fighting might be better there. Len Smith got a job as a physical culture instructor at a club in Dallas, while Buttrick went into training with local veteran trainer Mickey Riley. A former lightweight, Riley, known as "The Singing Boxer" (renowned in his boxing days for singing to the crowd before each fight), hailed from San Antonio, Texas. He fought from the late 1910s through 1935, with most of his bouts contested in Texas, though he occasionally went as far afield as Oklahoma.

Speaking about Buttrick to reporters, Riley declared she was "the finest boxer he ever had seen" and, taking a cue from Buttrick's earlier promotional endeavors, "issued a challenge to any woman in the world to take [her on]." He also rated her as "better than most men her weight."[50]

Following this challenge, Buttrick claimed success in two more fights: one in July 1955 against Juanita Lopez in Tyler, Texas, whom she bested in a six-rounder on points, and the other in Reynosa, Mexico, against Rosita Gonzalez, who hit the canvas giving Buttrick the KO win in the third round. Boxing for women, however, was still illegal in Texas, so any fights there, or in Mexico for that matter, remained unsanctioned. Attempts by Riley to seek out fights in other locales with matchmakers and promoters were also difficult to bring to fruition—including one that would have brought Buttrick to Australia had Riley been able to solidify plans made with San Francisco-based promoter Bill Newman.

WOMEN, BOXING, AND POPULAR CULTURE

In the decade of the 1950s, the juxtaposition of women and boxing also became a theme in other aspects of popular culture.

Active female boxers were also seen on television. Boxer Jo Ann Hagen put in an appearance on the popular game show *What's My Line* on July 22, 1956, signing in as a "professional boxer," to the wows of the audience and the panel. She also appeared alongside fellow South Bend fighter and sparring partner, Phyllis Kugler, on the November 18, 1956, airing of the highly rated television variety program *The Steve Allen Show*. During the segment, Hagen and Kugler came onto the stage in dresses and Hagen chitchatted with Steve Allen before they both left to change into their boxing trunks. Both Hagen and Allen then donned boxing gloves, and after batting around with Steve Allen, Phyllis Kugler came out and she and Hagen spent a minute giving a light sparring exhibition.

Another feature of this period was the growing popularity of boxing on television and the marketing of the sport as family entertainment. *The Ring* magazine, boxing's premier publication of record, even put a woman on the cover of its 1955 TV Fights edition. In the cover illustration, a family of three, a mother, a father, and their son, are shown actively engaged in watching a fight on a large console television set. This was no family of working-class stiffs. Their dress and manner were clearly meant to show a middle-class suburban family. The choice of showing a domestic scene that was a variant on a Norman Rockwell view of the family was clearly in line with the objectives of bringing sports content into households during the "family hour" at the end of the work and school day. And no wonder: Boxing was hugely profitable to the sponsors, chiefly Pabst Blue Ribbon beer and Gillette, and could be seen on most nights of the week.

A woman was even featured as a sports writer named "Mickey" Riley on the *Dear Phoebe* television program, which ran from 1954 to 1955. On the show, Riley opined about sports from baseball to boxing and joked about her attendance at boxing matches.[51]

The sight of gloved young women neatly attired in trunks and white shirts in boxing's squared circle, however, seemed an anathema on television and in the corridors of athletic commissions—this despite the attention showered on women who touched upon boxing on game shows or comedy programs. Seemingly, as long as women remained outside the ring they could be tolerated. The view also carried over into the day-to-day lives of the women who plied the boxing circuit. As noted by Kugler, reminiscing about her experiences, from time to time, padlocked doors greeted fighters when they showed up in the hours before the scheduled bout because local authorities had canceled the match. This even happened at one of Johnny Nate's scheduled shows at The Arena in South Bend because the authorities didn't like the fact that "Phil Kugler" was actually "Phyllis."

"We had a huge fight out of the ring just to get into the ring," she said. "It was very hard."[52]

The fans were another story. There was a ready acceptance of these women by the paying public who came out to support them—and by the trainers and promoters who worked with the women and insisted on pushing for opportunities in the sport they loved, even if for some promoters it was just an opportunity to make a buck or two.

Some in the boxing world were genuinely supportive. During her trip to New York with Kugler to appear on *The Steve Allen Show*, Hagen met Jack Dempsey at his restaurant in New York. She told a reporter that after she had asked him for his autograph, he'd asked her for hers. Given how Dempsey had lauded women in the ring as early as the 1920s, it is no surprise that he would have shown some excitement at meeting Hagen.[53]

In Kugler's case, acceptance—or at least opportunities—meant following her trainer Johnny Nate's keen advice to wear dresses outside of the squared circle. She also tried to drum up fights by keeping herself in the public eye. Kugler was an attractive blond with cascading hair that fell past her shoulders. She put on exhibitions of her speed-bag prowess at such places as "car shows, openings and other [promotional] events," putting her own spin on it by doing it blindfolded. Despite all of her efforts at self-marketing and fitting in long hours in the gym to perfect her craft, it was not until her appearances on television that her family and others in her community in South Bend began to accept what she was doing. Even then, it did not stop her mother from being upset when she came home with a broken nose.

All the publicity work by Hagen and Kugler pushing for acceptance on a national stage seemed to pay off when their originally scheduled November meeting—postponed so the pair could go to New York—was rebooked for December 13, 1956. The match was billed as a "world's women's championship," and was the main event at a planned variety show to be held at St. Joseph High School in South Bend, a two-minute walk from Johnny Nate's place on North Hill Street. Press coverage was local, though with reporters as far afield as Kugler's home state of Michigan set to attend, Kugler hoped that one or more articles might make it onto the wires.

From the opening bell of round one Hagen was clearly the attacker against Kugler (who had for some unknown reason insisted on wearing a helmet in the ring) and continued as such through the first three rounds. The fourth round, however, saw Kugler come back—and people ringside were of the impression that Hagen was stunned as she walked back to her corner at the end of the four-round fight.

Fans were certain that even with Kugler's flurry in the fourth, the outcome would find Hagen the victor, whom they judged as winning the bout three rounds to one. Despite this general consensus, Phyllis Kugler ended up being given the nod by split decision along with the title of women's boxing champion. As the scoring was announced the crowd let loose a torrent of boos and shouts.

For most in the crowd, including some reporters, Hagen seemed the "clear winner . . . [having sent] Kugler to the canvas once . . . drawing blood from her nose." Fans did concede that Hagen was a bit dazed at the end, but it did not stop the general feeling that Hagen had been robbed. [54]

At the time, there was talk that the fight was fixed and a couple of newspaper articles were said to have implied it. In an interview in 2005 with Hagen's two brothers, Vic and Harvey Verhaegen, both stated their belief that Johnny Nate arranged for Kugler to win to make some extra cash off the fight, but offered no proof other than to speculate on the stories that had circulated soon after the fight.

In the immediate aftermath of the contest, Hagen had been interviewed and was quoted as saying she was "very anxious to meet Phyllis again—but I'm strictly against her using head gear." Sometime later, though, she told her brother, "That's it, I am done with it." True to her word, and apparently embittered by the experience, she left boxing, eventually joining the U.S. Marines. After she mustered out she married and had a family, rarely speaking of her boxing career. In all, she was said to have fought seventy-seven fights, including some wrestling matches.

Reminiscing about their sister, who died at the age of seventy-three on February 5, 2004, the brothers proudly traded stories, including an alternative version of how she'd been recruited to box. The story most people had heard was that she'd been "discovered" while playing in a sandlot baseball game. In their version of the story, "She punched a fellow worker" who was "getting fresh" at the local Bendix plant. One of Johnny Nate's brothers worked at the plant and happened to see her and figured with a fist that could be thrown that hard, she should get into boxing. While Hagen worked with Nate, she helped him build the boxing gym and tavern on North Hill Street and also "tried to teach other women boxers" how to fight—including Phyllis Kugler.[55]

A few weeks after the Verhaegen interview, Kugler responded to the reports of the fix. Kugler stated:

> I fought my heart out and I never heard anybody ever say it [was fixed] until I read that [speculation]. . . . I think she knew I did [win]. We were not best friends but there was never any animosity. The night it was over, there was never any question about it.
>
> Asked about the headgear, she said, "Actually, it's hot and heavy, and it's hard to see. . . . I never wore one after that. . . . I thought if she got by [without it], I didn't have to [wear it]."[56]

Years earlier Kugler admitted that the fight had put a strain on their friendship—and that in fact it was Hagen who had brought her into the gym to meet Johnny Nate after she'd "begged Jo-Ann to let her work out with her at the gym." They both worked together at a bowling alley in South Bend at the time, before she left to work in a plastics factory as a pressman.[57]

Their fits and starts of getting onto fight cards very much mirrored the experiences of Barbara Buttrick, who had been struggling to make it as a professional boxer since she first came to London in 1948. By the end of 1955, her career had pretty much come to a standstill with no reported fights for nearly two years until she was offered the opportunity to box Phyllis Kugler in August 1957, followed by a second match in October.

For their first fight, Kugler and Buttrick were slated to meet in a four-rounder at the municipal baseball field in Pompano Beach, Florida. The fight was apparently a first for the state. The card was sponsored by the local

Fraternal Order of Police, and was promoted as a title match to be awarded by Glenn Sheppard, who was not only a boxing promoter but also a member of the Florida Boxing Commission. Both women agreed to wear twelve-ounce gloves for the bout, something Buttrick found "too paddy," and they also both agreed to help out with promotion. Kugler sparred with "Rocky Randell, the Georgia lightweight, on the showroom floor of Sheppard's Buick Dealership," while Buttrick touted her fight "at the Magic City Gym in Miami Beach" where she trained ahead of the match. [58]

As usual, Buttrick came in shorter and lighter. Having not fought in a while may have been telling as well since the four-round bout was called a draw. Along with the boxing show, Kugler was given an award as the "Fraternal Order of Police, Woman Boxer and Boxing's Beauty Queen of the Year." [59]

The second meeting between Buttrick and Kugler was momentous on several fronts. To begin with, the fight's promoter, Jimmie Scaramozi, a former lightweight, was able to do something no one in memory had achieved—a fully sanctioned women's boxing match complete with duly issued boxing licenses from the Texas Commission of Labor for both Buttrick and Kugler. Additionally, it was one of very few—if any—boxing matches between female fighters held in Texas, and while women's wrestling had become a popular feature in San Antonio, no one had ever thought to promote a female boxing bout. Scaramozi also planned on taking the two fighters on an exhibition tour shortly after to capitalize on the fight and to help promote future fight cards.

The six-rounder, billed as the "Women's World Championship Fight," was to be held at the San Antonio Municipal Auditorium as the co-feature to the main event between middleweights Eloy Ellez and Sanitago Guttierez, two up-and-coming Texas fighters. On the handbill for the card, Kugler was listed as "Indiana's Blonde Bombshell," while Buttrick was headlined as "England's Mighty Atom Of The Ring." [60]

Both women came to San Antonio two days prior to the fight to appear in a public workout at the Downtown Athletic Club, giving the press their first look at them. It was Buttrick who impressed the crowd of onlookers. A reporter for the *San Antonio Express* began his piece, "A large number of San Antonio Fans got away from their television and radio sets . . . to watch a little English Girl workout," further noting "the group agreed [she] knows a thing or two about the manly art of self-defense."

In the workout, Buttrick sparred "two Fast Rounds with Earnest Ramon, a San Antonio Bantamweight" who "learned early" that she "knew how to use her fists." Her shots were reported as "straight and true" with particular emphasis placed on her left jab–right cross combination. [61]

On fight night, Buttrick proved to be unstoppable, assaulting Kugler with a continuous barrage of hard shots that saw Kugler with a dark shiner under her left eye midway through the match. Buttrick easily won every round and came away with the decision and the first sanctioned women's boxing title.

As the *San Antonio Light* put it:

> The fiery little Britisher won every round and blooded the nose of the blond from South Bend, Ind. Buttrick displayed a sharp left jab and a grim determination as she forced the fight with her outclassed opponent, billed as the world's women's bantamweight champion.[62]

The Associated Press also put out a story and a photo on the wires that was reprinted across the country extolling Buttrick's "deadly right." The photo carried the headline "Female Fury in Texas Boxing Ring."[63]

The *San Antonio Express* also lauded Buttrick's abilities, writing: "From the opening Round, Little Barbara, quick as a cat, peppered her foe with lightening lefts to the head and face and followed through with right hand shots to the body."[64]

While the fight was a success, the box office numbers were not. The stadium, which held thousands, only brought in 731 paying customers, though Scaramozi contended that he intended to bring in more female fighters to contest in San Antonio.

The next blow came two days after the fight when the state athletic commission canceled the planned Buttrick-Kugler "fistic tour." The reason given was that the weight difference between the two fighters—reported to be 23½ pounds—was greater than the regulation six pounds. As one paper put it, "The laugh is that [Barbara] defeated Phyllis, who wasn't in Barbara's class as a boxer, is the weightier one." The writer also opined that Kugler would have to lose an arm to make up the weight difference.

Mickey Riley, Buttrick's trainer, was incensed, stating, "This is discrimination. Women boxers are required to weigh in. Women wrestlers are allowed to give an estimated weight."[65] Regardless of the arguments, what had seemed like a promising new beginning for women's boxing turned out to be something of a bust. Still, *The Ring* magazine recognized the fight for what it was when it listed it in its Fights of the Month section, along with a photograph from the bout.

Buttrick did not have any fights following her decisive win. Apparently the boom/bust cycle of women's boxing was still in effect, although, as reported in the *Albuquerque Tribune*, Buttrick signed on for a bout against boxer Mary Himes, another South Bend fighter who weighed in at about 128 pounds. The match was promoted by Louis "Red" Valencia and scheduled to be put on at the Civic Auditorium in Albuquerque, New Mexico, as the lead-in to the main event, between two welterweights, but it seems that it never came to pass.

In the interim, Buttrick moved to Miami Beach with her husband and began working out at the world-famous Fifth Street Gym. Becoming a regular at the gym, she worked out as often as she could—the only woman in the gym—and was instantly respected by the fighters and trainers there for her toughness. She was even sought out by fighters close to her weight looking to tune up for fights, and she otherwise kept her ears open for opportunities.

Of Buttrick's time in the gym, Angelo Dundee, famed for training Muhammad Ali at the Fifth Street Gym, was quoted as saying she was "a perfect English Lady until she climbed through the ropes. Then she transformed from a duchess into a lioness in the blink of an eye." She also worked alongside such boxers as the young Muhammad Ali (known as Cassius Clay at the time), Emile Griffith, and Willie Pep.[66]

Her next—and, as it turned out, last—professional fight was held on October 1, 1959, at the North Miami Armory. The fight was a four-rounder with Chico Vejar—having just gone ten rounds himself on the card's main event—acting as the referee. A first for women's boxing in the Miami area, the fight was against Gloria Adams who, while weighing in at 116 pounds, was at least 145 pounds when she walked into the ring. The contest was very hard fought with Gloria able to land her "jolting left" on Buttrick's jaw, but she proved no match for Buttrick, who out-boxed her throughout the bout to take a unanimous decision.

Buttrick continued to train following the fight, but stopped in 1960 after learning she was four months pregnant. Her heart remained with boxing throughout her life and especially so when she became active again in the sport on the other side of the ropes beginning in the 1970s.

When measuring the skills and abilities of women boxers in the 1950s, the boxing matches between Buttrick, Hagen, and Kugler stand out. Each fought one another in tough matches with evident skill, ring savvy, and toughness. That some of the fights were contested or unnoticed seemed par for the course. But to the enduring credit of these outstanding practitioners of the sweet science, their love of the sport kept them in the game.

For Buttrick, that love meant leaving her home in England to find opportunities to box in America—opportunities that were still hard to come by and necessitated her to don wrestler's togs in order to fight at all. For other women it meant enduring the ridicule of family and the hardscrabble life of working by day and boxing by night just to get a chance to fight.

Chapter Six

Burning Bras, Taking on the "Sheriff," and Winning the Right to Fight

[I'm] not in this for publicity, I'm not going to be merely a figurehead. I'm going to be the promoter.
—Pat Boardman, age eighteen, Tampa, Florida [1]

With the first stirrings of the women's movement in the late 1960s on through the 1970s, girls and women began finding their way into the boxing gym (and the ring) in greater and greater numbers. The era of the perfect wife and the perfect mother was being rapidly replaced by a consciousness-raising that extended to women's control over their own bodies—including their right to play sports wherever and whenever they wanted. The period also saw the parents of young girls finding it acceptable for their daughters to box alongside their male peers.

Beginning in the 1970s there was a huge push by American women to legalize their participation in professional boxing. Boxers such as Jackie "The Female Ali" Tonawanda and Marian "Lady Tyger" Trimiar, who led the way for legalization of women's boxing in New York State, were willing to go to court to press their legal claims.

Women also sued to be able to officiate at boxing contests as judges, referees, managers, and even trainers in the 1970s. Carol Polis and Eva Shain's efforts won them the right to judge professional fights in Madison Square Garden. These legal contests resulted in a growing coterie of female fighters, officials, referees, judges, and managers who were engaged in all aspects of the professional fight game. This coincided with the historic enactment of Title IX, which regulated fairness and gender equality in education, including athletic programs, by Congress on June 23, 1972. It went into effect three years later on June 21, 1975.

FROM PEARLS TO LOVE BEADS: WOMEN EMBRACING
THE RING

With a dateline of January 1, 1960, the *Los Angeles Times* ran an Associated Press story with the headline "Teen-age Miss Set to Stage Florida Fights." The story featured an eighteen-year-old named Pat Boardman with an eye to begin promoting fights at the Tampa Armory. Boardman grew up with boxing as the daughter of a boxing manager and promoter named Sam Boardman and the sister of a respectable lightweight boxer, Larry Boardman. When the promoter resigned his post at the Tampa Armory, Pat Boardman was there to jump in.

Boardman brimmed with confidence. As she stepped into a new decade, she seemed to portend the enormity of the changes the decade of the 1960s would bring. Telling a reporter, "I'm not going to be merely a figurehead, I'm going to be the promoter," she felt she would "lean heavily on" her father for her first foray, but "after six months or a year," she'd be very much on her own.

She'd decided to enter the promoting game some months after she and her family had moved to the Tampa area from Connecticut where Sam Boardman had been successful in the fight game. Immediately after local Tampa promoter Jimmy Tolisano announced that he was leaving his job with the arena, Pat Boardman leapt up to take his place.

"There was no stopping her," her father said, though he was still "inclined to think she's too green," even though she'd grown up in the sport. [2]

True to her word, but perhaps a little later than anticipated, she staged her first fight card in May 1961, bringing in a crowd of six hundred—a good night for the Armory—to see five fights, including a ten-round main event between two middleweights that ended in a draw.

Women had successfully promoted fights since the 1920s, and with the advent of World War II more and more women entered the game. Through the 1950s, figures such as Aileen Eaton emerged as true powerhouses in the world of the business of boxing.

Originally from Vancouver, Canada, Eaton moved to Los Angeles as a teenager, and had even attended two years of law school. She eventually married an osteopath named Martin LaBell and they had three children. In 1941 Eaton's husband died suddenly after an accident he sustained swimming, leaving her as the sole supporter of her family. Never one to succumb to her troubles, she went to work as a private secretary for Frank A. Garbutt—then the president of the Los Angeles Athletic Club.

Among the assets of the club was boxing's mecca in Los Angeles, the Olympic Theater, which was seemingly in dire financial straits. Aware of her background in law, Garbutt tasked Eaton to find out why the Olympic was bleeding money. She quickly ascertained there were probable shenanigans with the books. She urged Garbutt to hire Cal Eaton, a well-respected boxing commission inspector. By then Aileen Eaton was hooked on boxing. Partnering with Cal to get the Olympic back in the black, their personal lives intertwined and the two married several years later.

Taking over professional boxing and wrestling promotion at Los Angeles's Olympic Theater, Eaton molded a reputation as a tough and able promoter whose business acumen built the Olympic into a premier venue for top-notch fighters. Strong willed, with a reputation for being straight as an arrow and uncompromising, Eaton promoted a nationally broadcast fight in 1958 between Carmen Basillo and Art Aragon that was widely reported as the "biggest petticoat promotion in ring history"—and never mind the "petticoat," it was the largest payday for a fight to date in history, period.[3] The contest, in fact, set a new record for gross receipts in the state of California: $236,521.10.

By the 1960s Eaton was a boxing icon, who, when her husband Cal died in 1966, took over the business outright and ran it until 1980. She went on to fill a position with the California Athletic Commission as a commissioner in 1982 and served for a total of three years. In all, she was said to have promoted over "10,000 professional fights" in her career and "staged more than 100 world championship matches." Of her years as a promoter, the *Los Angeles Times* columnist Jim Murray wrote: "Red-haired, blue-eyed, pound for pound she was as tough as any welterweight who ever came down the aisle."[4]

Eaton was given many honors over her lifetime and posthumously. Acknowledging the role of women in the sport of boxing, the Boxing Writers Association chose Aileen Eaton and Washington, D.C., promoter Helen Ahearn as honorees at the 1967 Barney Ross Memorial Dinner—the association's first-ever coed event.

Female managers were also making headlines, including Bonnie Coccaro. Coccaro began managing fighters after working alongside her husband, ex-featherweight boxer Tony Coccaro, at the Millville Athletic Club—a gym he had started to train amateur fighters. Much like the Martells in California, the New Jersey–based pair promoted amateur fights in nearby towns including Vineland and Atlantic City. When it came time for heavyweight Morris "Mo-Man" Williams to turn pro, it was Bonnie who stepped up to manage his career.

As she told famed New York City–based columnist Sidney Fields, there were disadvantages to being a woman in the fight game. For one, she generally wasn't allowed to be with her fighter in the men's locker room before a bout. She also couldn't stand in his corner between rounds. So "when I want to tell my fighter something I don't want anyone to hear, I pass it on to my trainer," she said.

During the day, she managed the Millville bus terminal, including the luncheonette—a seven-day-a-week job. At night she spent her hours in the gym, "eyeing the amateurs and her own fighters," keeping them on the straight and narrow. "I can be a rough bully when I have to," she said, but then her soft side would come out: cooking for her fighters on the day of their match, or giving them free meals at the bus terminal.[5]

The 1960s also brought women into the ring as announcers. Following in the footsteps of Belle Martell, whose stints as a ring announcer were seemingly forgotten, one young woman named Rhonda Kay decided to give it a go. A fight fan, Kay, twenty-two, worked at a local radio station. One day she approached a boxing promoter who'd come to the station to talk about an upcoming card and told him "if he wanted to get a big crowd at his fights, why not have a woman do the announcing."[6] He apparently mulled it over and gave her the job as the first female ring announcer at the Akron Armory's fight shows in Akron, Ohio.

Appearing in a long multicolored, wide-legged, sleeveless one-piece outfit, Kay, who had tuned up at a local club show, admitted to being a little frightened at first. "Scared to death to tell you the truth," she said, "but when I saw the fans were enjoying it, I began to enjoy myself too." She also hoped it was the beginning of a "long association with the sport."[7]

Model Lorna Anderson, her hair in an "updo" and sporting a block-patterned sleeveless minidress, was the ring announcer at a ten-round boxing match in Toronto, Canada, between heavyweights Bob "Pretty Boy" Felstein and Archie McBride held on June 27, 1967. Marion Bassett, a female boxing promoter, had promoted the fight.

In the ring, women were continuing to appear in fights, although those seemed to be less numerous and, when fought, were reported as if each was the first time women had ever appeared in the ring. A fight held in June 1959 that was called "Canada's first women's boxing match" was hardly the first ever held. And whereas the bout between Buttrick and Hagen had been positively viewed, the bout between grandmother June Lounder, thirty-seven, and Myrna McConvey, twenty, who earned her living as a stenographer, won the moniker of "mama stay home."

Viewed in the press as nothing more than a joke, the match, held in front of 672 fight fans, had been Lounder's idea to help pep up the regularly held Monday night fights programs. It had the desired effect, but unfortunately neither woman was particularly skilled, so the outcome of the fight was decidedly negative. Even though Lounder was given the win, the bout didn't advance the idea of women fighting seriously in the ring—and neither woman took up the gloves in a match again.[8]

The roster of fighters for women's boxing matches had seemingly slimmed down and fights were harder to come by. Boxing bouts between women did continue to be scheduled; however, many of the fights in the

Midwest were now associated with wrestling. The cards were proving popular with the fans, although the boxing matches were clearly less disciplined displays of the sweet science.

Two well-respected wrestlers who began making noise as boxers were Betty Niccoli and Jean Antone. They had often been paired as one-on-one or tag-team opponents in the wrestling ring, but began facing each other in boxing bouts as well. They appeared on the same marquee as wrestling—trading in break falls and body slams for boxing gloves. Their typical boxing bouts were five- or six-rounders. They fought together essentially as a boxing act from the mid-1960s on through the mid-1970s, adding Rhonda Jean, another wrestler who took up the gloves, to their wrestling cards.

Jean Antone also boxed in a series of fights against wrestler Kay Noble—where more often than not the fights were advertised "gloves to be thrown in." A match that drew a lot of attention between the two women was held on October 5, 1965, in Abilene, Texas, at the Fair Park Auditorium. Noble "floored" her opponent at 1:45 into the third round.[9] The two women held a "rematch" three days later where Noble again knocked Antone out with a "round house right to the chin at 1:03 in the fourth round."[10] The two women continued to oppose each other on the circuit, but generally fought wrestling matches, although they would sometimes mix in boxing. In one match, held in June 1966, the women boxed for two rounds before switching to wrestling, in which Antone won the bout.[11] Theatrical to the last, many of the boxing matches held between female wrestlers seemed to end in KOs.

What was also obvious in these events was that the main purpose for the fighting was to give the crowd what they wanted. Whereas female boxers such as Barbara Buttrick and Jo Ann Hagen had taken to the wrestling mat in order to have any sort of career in the ring, the wrestlers who fought boxing matches did so at the behest of the promoters to entice fans to their shows. Not to be lost, though, was the enduring popularity of women's boxing even if the contenders were not wholly trained in the sweet science. The authorities also paid much more critical attention to "pure" women's boxing matches with the wrestler's boxing bouts pretty much left alone.

Boxing matches by trained female professional pugilists were harder to come by than their wrestling-boxing cousins. Even when they were offered, some shows were never actually realized. In one, a purported title fight was scheduled for July 9, 1966, at the Garden Auditorium in Vancouver, Canada, as a co-feature of the main event. Promoted by Windsor Olson, the fight was a matchup between a twenty-three-year-old ex-marine named Toni Bratton from Washington, D.C., and Billie Howell, a twenty-two-year-old "farm girl" from Omaha, Nebraska.

Olson had previous gained notoriety when he "barred women" from attending a fight card at the Garden Auditorium the previous April "on the grounds that boxing was the last stronghold of the male sex." His stance, however, did not sit well with the boxing community, who banded together to act as ushers. On fight night, they showed female fight fans to their seats—thus overturning the ban—in what was reported to be a peaceful defiance of Olson's stated position. [12]

Undeterred by his stance against women as fans, Olson next shopped the world heavyweight championship match in Butte, Montana, between his two female fighters along with another twenty-two-year-old fighter named Terry Fisher, from Olson's hometown of Seattle, Washington. His idea was to pit two of the three fighters against each other and then see if other bouts could be promoted. The request for the bout was brought before Troy Evans, chairman of the Montana State Athletic Commission; however, prospects did not look good even though there was no particular rule against it.

Speaking with a reporter, Olson stated, "They use the standard gloves and there is no wrestling or hair-pulling in connection with their fights." Despite his efforts, the fight was never held.

Boxing also saw a bevy of young girls take up the gloves. In 1969 Laura Bloomberg, a "sports minded" twelve-year-old, was the only girl to regularly box at the Manomet Boys Club in Manomet, Massachusetts. Although she originally came to the boys club to play basketball, she became enamored of boxing when she watched other kids at the club picking up the gloves. Shortly after she joined the club, trainer Charles "Babe" Woods, a former New England middleweight champion himself, who over the years trained or worked the corner for such fighting luminaries as Rocky Marciano, Sonny Liston, and Renaldo Oliveira, set up a boxing clinic at the boys club on Fridays.

Bloomberg came along with the other kids to give it a go. Learning she was a girl, Woods, a little uncertain of how she'd do, figured he'd give her a shot, especially since they boxed with twelve-ounce gloves. Bloomberg proved impressive from the beginning with excellent raw physical talent, a terrific work ethic, and a genuine flare for the science of fisticuffs. Woods even went so far as to compare her to middleweight Paul Pender. She was also made an honorary club member and came out a winner in all of her fights. Her boxing prowess, however, ran afoul of the Massachusetts State Boxing Commission because of her gender when they learned she would be fighting at a boys club fight night open to the public. The show was to have been a benefit for the club and included a roster of professional boxing stars set to fight three-round exhibition bouts.

As reported in the press, the commission chairman, Eddie Urbec, stated that Bloomberg's participation in a boxing match was "in direct violation of the state laws" and would be "turned over to the State Police." He added, "This is serious indeed. One punch and she can be hurt for life." [13]

Bloomberg's father, a retired Marine Corps master sergeant, fully supported his daughter, saying:

Laura is very sports minded. . . . When she first came home and told me that she wanted to do a little boxing I went to see Babe Woods. . . . He explained the program to me and I watched some of the bouts. I can't see there is any real danger. As soon as the fighters get tired, the round ends. . . . Laura gets hit harder playing sandlot football . . . [though] this will be her last year of contact sports anyway.

Woods, although a keen supporter of her throughout, still advised her parents that they "get her some golf clubs and have her take lessons . . . because when she gets older she can't very well play football or box."[14] Clearly, though, Bloomberg's coach and parents supported her fighting. They were in agreement that while she could participate as a child, once she hit adolescence her sports options should be limited to "girls' sports."

At a meeting held with all parties shortly before the club show benefit, it was determined that Laura Bloomberg's fighting days were over. The meeting attendees included Urbec, two detectives from the district attorney's office, the show's promoters, trainer "Babe" Wood, and Laura Bloomberg's father. Eventually, they came up with one face-saving compromise: Bloomberg's evident talent for boxing would be honored in the ring by none other than Paul Pender himself, along with boxers Lou Brouillard and Dick Hall—champions all.

Celebrating her boxing abilities under the headline "Battling Little Laura Ends Boxing Career," the lead paragraph of the *Boston Globe* article detailing her saga read: "Twelve-year-old Laura Bloomberg of Manomet will retire tonight as the only undefeated girl pugilist in America."[15]

In a similar case in 1972, a twelve-year-old girl named Jackie Fuller from South Oxney, England, was a boxing phenomenon at her amateur club, winning all of her bouts. She was poised to move up in class when a medical examination revealed she was a girl and she was forced to quit. Her coach, Bill Green, was quoted as saying, "That girl is the best boy I have ever trained. It wasn't until her medical that we discovered the truth." He continued, "She was real championship class. But now it is over. It's illegal for girls to belong to a boxing club."

In response to queries by the press, Jackie is reported as having said, "I just prefer boys' games. Netball was too soft so I joined the boxing club."[16]

Not all girls were prohibited from boxing. Three months after the Bloomberg episode, at the Hoffman Estates Boys Club northwest of Chicago, girls were welcomed to join in club activities on a series of "Ladies Nights." Participating in everything from darts to boxing matches, the girls were allowed to compete against each other with boxing gloves and given instruction on the finer points of how to throw a jab.[17]

A boxing trainer named Doyle Weaver, feeling committed to the idea that young girls should be given the chance to box, made his Dallas Junior Gloves

Club coed in 1966. With the popularity growing, he started a Missy Junior Gloves Club two years later with a mantra of egalitarianism and a same-size-fits-all training philosophy. The program he set up trained girls from the ages of six to sixteen, and despite extreme pressure to stop his efforts, he persevered. The payoff was that three hundred girls signed up in 1972—"more than had ever participated in his boys' boxing efforts."[18]

In places as far flung as Port of Spain, Trinidad, women were also clamoring to fight in the ring—and in 1965 Beatrice Clarke, a former bicycling champion, made a splash challenging any and all ring opponents to compete against her. With a plan to legalize females in the ring in 1966, a local promoter, H. A. Clark, promised to put on women's boxing events.[19]

Even "Dear Abby" got into the act with a column on female boxing. A reader signed "Milwaukee" asked if there was a "danger factor" if women picked up the gloves as opposed to wrestling. The columnist responded, "Medical authorities agreed that repeated blows to the area of the breasts CAN be dangerous to women" if they didn't wear "protective covering" so "skip the boxing" without it. "As for wrestling," she opined, "you can bend each other into pretzels if you like."[20]

At the time Bloomberg was prevented from fighting, the National Organization for Women (NOW)—founded in 1966—though barely three years old, was strongly and very publicly advocating for women's equality. The Bloomberg case also occurred fifteen months or so after President Lyndon Johnson issued Executive Order 11375, which put a stop to discrimination based on gender for federal employees and all organizations contracted with the federal government.

Johnson's order led directly to ending the practice of listing employment advertisements under the headings of "male" or "female" and, as amended, was used as the basis for lawsuits against institutions and other large corporations that discriminated against women either through labor practices or pay equity. It was also a pivotal forerunner for future legislation, including Title IX of the Civil Rights Act of 1964, which granted equal rights to women in education. While aimed at ending discriminatory practices in education based on gender, Title IX is most closely associated with providing female students equal access to competitive athletic programs on par with those offered to male students.

When it came to professional competitive sports, however, the impediments to legality versus illegality were clearly in the domain of athletic governing bodies at the state, county, or city level. In the realm of amateur sports, lawsuits eventually won women the right to compete, citing civil rights statutes in effect. As long as women's boxing was restricted by the statutes of states or other lesser jurisdictions and their governing-body rules and regulations, women would be denied access to the licensing necessary to perform as boxers, judges, referees, trainers, or any of the other licensing categories required on a jurisdiction-by-jurisdiction basis.

Positive changes were also in the offing. When it came to female reporters, the New York State Athletic Commission began allowing properly credentialed members of the fourth estate into dressing rooms at boxing and wrestling matches—as long as the fighters were reasonably dressed. The June 1972 ruling also allowed women to sit in the press row—alongside the bastion of cigar-chomping sports writers of the old school. The ironclad "men's only" club had, however, already been "breached" in Seattle, Washington. When a female reporter joined the elite ringside row at a bout in 1970, some of the old-timers were alarmed.[21]

Another facet of boxing's "men's club"—judging at ringside—also fell when Carol Polis, a former stockbroker and mother of four, fought her way into the judge's chair in early 1974. Polis, the wife of a part-time boxing referee, had become enamored with the game. Before working as a professional judge, she'd scored fights on the backs of the fight program, her acumen spot-on in comparison with other boxing aficionados.

Describing herself as a "very, very bored housewife," Polis took the step of undergoing "three months of ringside apprenticeship and a series of tests administered by the Pennsylvania Athletic Commission." Having successfully passed her examinations, Governor Milton Shapp of Pennsylvania swore her in as a boxing judge on February 1, 1973. He was quoted as saying her certification represented "a solid blow against male supremacy."[22]

A little over three weeks after gaining her appointment she officiated at a ten-round bout between Ernie Shavers and Jimmy Young that ended with a TKO in the third round, with Shavers coming up the winner. Describing the fight, she recalled being "in shock because there were 17,000 people there."[23] She told a reporter at the time that she was "'a little nervous' before the bout and later said 'I'm glad it was a knockout.'"[24]

Polis's one pet peeve in the early days of her judging was that she wasn't allowed to sit ringside in between her judging duties. Though not an actual "rule," she found that when she wasn't actually officiating she was forced to scramble for a place in the stands and was often "expelled by a ticket holder."[25]

By October 2, 1974, Polis managed to breach the citadel of male boxing in New York State when she was issued a license there, thus paving the way for two other women to take on judging duties: Eva Shain and Carol Castellano (wife of fellow boxing judge Tony Castellano), who were both licensed on October 1, 1975. Shain had the distinction of being the first woman to judge a heavyweight title fight at Madison Square Garden, on September 29, 1977. She gave Mohammed Ali the nod over Ernie Shavers in their fifteen-round war, scoring the bout 9-6 along with fellow judge Tony Castellano. The referee had scored the bout 9-5-1 also for Ali.

As discriminatory barriers to women began to fall under the banner of the "women's liberation movement," boxing commissions and other boxing-related organizations began to feel the heat. The visibility of women climbing into the ring or officiating at ringside helped ferment a miniboom in the number of women picking up the gloves and fighting for their right to box. These women, steeled by the struggle of their "sisters," began using civil rights and other legislative precedents to fuel their cause, which in turn gave rise to greater numbers of females willing to fight for their right to box.

"I'LL SEE YOU IN COURT!": THE FIGHT TO GAIN LICENSES

Jacqueline Garrett, claiming to be twenty-six—although she was likely forty at the time—and fighting under the name Jackie "The Female Ali" Tonawanda, wanted to box professionally. It was October 7, 1974, and she did what every other amateur fighter wanting to turn pro did in New York State: She applied for a boxing license at the New York State Athletic Commission (NYSAC) office. In her case, though, another female boxer, twenty-one-year-old Marian "Lady Tyger" Trimiar, hailing from the South Bronx, also wanted to turn pro—and a slew of reporters and photographers who documented their every move accompanied them.

Tonawanda trained with such boxing old hands as Connie Bryant and Freddie Brown at Bobby Gleason's legendary boxing club, Gleason's Gym, when it was still in the Bronx before a move to Manhattan in 1974. Tonawanda originally took an interest in the sport when she dated a boxer. She'd follow him to the gym and after a while began banging the heavy bag during his workouts, eventually learning the intricacies of the sweet science. At five feet, nine inches tall and around 175 pounds, Jackie could hit every bit as hard as a man, and as late as the 1990s she was still no slouch in the ring. As remembered by former Junior Welterweight Commonwealth Champion turned boxing trainer Lennox Blackmoore, who knew her in the early 1980s, "When she hit you, man, you felt it."[26]

As for Lady Tyger Trimiar, an attractive 130-lb. fighter, she heeded the sign that invited women in to box at Gleason's Gym, training with Mack Williams, who had her full-out sparring with men. She first came to the attention of the press in May 1974 when she made her amateur boxing debut at the Audubon Ballroom in Manhattan's Washington Heights (most famously known as the hall where Malcolm X was assassinated). A piece in the *New York Times* noted that as she made her way down her block the night of the fight, "Children called her name and followed her down the sidewalk, shadow boxing with mailboxes, parking meters and one another. Passing motorists slowed down and shouted 'Good luck, Tyger.'"

She'd been training at the Wagner Center with Mickey Rosario, working out seven days a week including daily runs and sparring with whoever would take her on—with one sparring session even costing her a front tooth. For her debut bout, a friend named Diane Corum had agreed to box with her. Even though Diane, known as "Killer Diane," outweighed her by at least fifty pounds, Lady Tyger was game.

When it came time to fight, though, an official with the local AAU came up to the ring apron and yelled, "The girls cannot fight on this program. All other bouts must be completed." The two women obliged, and though by the time they got into the ring the crowd had definitely shrunk, they were wildly applauded for "every punch for three rounds." When it was all over, Lady Tyger was asked about the fight, to which she replied, "I'm going to do it again [and] go to court if I have to."[27]

A month before her bid for a license in early September, Trimiar sparred in a boxing show at the famed San Gennaro Festival on Mulberry Street, in New York City's Little Italy. Touted as "Women's Lib" entering the ring, the boxing festival was put on by Madison Square Garden promoter John F. X. Condon, in part to promote Vito Antonfermo, a middleweight set to fight a few days later at the Garden. Condon was intrigued by the idea of a female fighter and—hoping to arouse the crowd's interest—matched Lady Tyger against a fourteen-year-old male lightweight comer on the amateur scene named Miles Ruane.

In the ring Lady Tyger proved more than capable, impressing the audience and the reporters in attendance with her taut fighting style and liberal use of the jab in her one-round exhibition against Antonfermo. Her two-round "bout" against Ruane, for which they had agreed to forego body shots, was called a "draw." Lady Tyger felt she was on a mission. "Right now," she said, "I'm the only woman boxer and I'm trying to convince the American Olympics officials that there ought to be a girls' boxing team."[28]

With dreams of a possible fight between Trimiar and Tonawanda at Madison Square Garden, the press went to Gleason's Gym to talk to both women about their background in boxing ahead of their planned trip to the NYSAC office. The reporters quickly established that both women had been solidly trained, but it was in the more probing questions that the women started to open up.

Tonawanda, in response to a query about why she kept boxing even though she wasn't fighting, said, "It's loneliness or wanting to be a part of something." She also talked about how she'd met great fighters over the years working out at the gym, including the likes of Joe Louis and Rocky Marciano in between her gigs as a singer, with some even showing her a trick or two. The boxing came in handy, she said. "Once in San Francisco, a guy came up and grabbed my shoulder. I hit him once in the jaw, once in the stomach, and down he went. He kept saying 'I can't believe it, I can't believe it.'"

Tonawanda also spoke of how the gym had been hers and hers alone until Trimiar came. "'I showed her what do,' [she] said, 'but I was too heavy to box her. I guess I'll have to take off a lot of weight. Training is good for that. I run a couple of miles at six every morning [and] work out a few hours in the gym everyday.'"

As for Lady Tyger, she reemphasized how entangled her bid for a license was with "women's lib." In fact it was so important to her, she'd "had chest protectors designed for herself and Jackie to use in their match."

Closing out the interview, Tonawanda said, "This is a big thing for me, though. People used to ask me what I was training for, and I'd say I was training for a fight. Now it's true."[29]

Having made it down to the NYSAC offices at 270 Broadway, the two women filled out their applications and paid their five-dollar fees. After being fingerprinted, they sat down at a desk in front of Commissioner Ralph Giordano and with raised right hands were sworn in. Afterward, they stood in line with other fighters to wait for their medical examinations. On hand to support them was the Garden's John Condon.

Speaking of the experience, Tonawanda said, "I think other girls will apply if we get our licenses." Trimiar added, "One of my reasons for applying is to open the door for others." A clerk at the office named Emma Elizando chimed in, "I think it's great . . . [t]his is where it will start." One of the fighters in line also added, "I'll fight one of them." As with the other fighters, the full NYSAC was set to review the applications at a meeting in early November pending any issues with the women's fingerprints slated to be sent off to Albany to be checked.[30]

November came and went, however, without a ruling from the NYSAC. Any potential for a fight between the two women was also seemingly lost—though both continued to work out at the gym as diligently as before. Finally in December, with no word having been issued, Tonawanda, through her attorney, served notice that she would seek legal redress. In response, the NYSAC adamantly insisted that her application, along with Trimiar's, was still being considered.

The NYSAC made the point that since women's boxing was illegal, rules prohibiting female fights would have to be overturned before the licenses could be issued. A spokesman for the commission added that it takes "four to six weeks to clear [fingerprints] through the FBI and the State Criminal Investigation Division." He also stated, "The chairman sent a general letter out, polling people within boxing . . . people like promoters, managers, referees, judges and doctors for their reactions. The most important reactions and opinions will be that of the doctors." The latter, of course, related to the ongoing idea that female physiognomy lacked the stamina and physical attributes to withstand "vigorous" sports.

In response to the long delay, Tonawanda filed a sex discrimination complaint with the state's Human Rights Commission, claiming that the NYSAC's "refusal to act on her application . . . had violated her constitutional rights." Her attorney, Stanley N. Soloman, claimed the delay was "unduly denying [his client] the right to earn a living."[31]

With headlines that read "Girl Boxer Loses Round," the press reported on a letter issued by the NYSAC denying Tonawanda and Trimiar a license to box in New York State. The letter read:

> Your application for a license to box in New York State was considered by the Commission at a meeting on January 16, 1975.
>
> The matter of licensing women boxers is regulated by Rule 2015.15 of Part 205, the Commission Its Powers and Procedures, of the rules promulgated by the Commission which reads as follows:
>
> 205.15 Disqualification of women. No woman may be licensed as a boxer or second or licensed to compete in any wrestling with men.
>
> Please be advised that the Commission after considering your application and reviewing its rules and regulations unanimously denied your application for a license to box in this State.[32]

From the perspective of Tonawanda's legal counsel, the argument in part came down to an interpretation of the rule. Soloman argued that since it allowed wrestling between women, it must also allow women to box. The only prohibition was against women who wrestled male opponents, and since Tonawanda was only asking for a license to box women, it was moot. Chairman of the NYSAC Edwin B. Dooley didn't see it that way, vehemently stating, "The rule was passed by the state legislature in 1928 and it is our duty to enforce it. The board feels that the rule means 'no woman may box'—period."

Aside from the ruling, Tonawanda had sought and been granted a "show-cause order demanding that the board tell the court why a license should not be granted," to be answered in New York State Supreme Court in early February, pending any last minute motions.[33]

In an affidavit issued to the court on February 4, Commissioner Dooley argued:

> The image that boxing presents to the public is all important to its acceptability as a professional sport. It is "the manly art of self-defense". The licensing of women as professional boxers would at once destroy the image that attracts serious boxing fans and brings professional boxing into disrepute among them, to the financial detriment of those whose livelihoods depend upon this activity.
>
> Neither is the Commission satisfied that women boxers would not be unduly endangering their reproductive organs and breasts; despite the use of

whatever protective devices may be available. The avoidance of serious physical injury is a major responsibility of the Commission.

Finally, the Commission is not satisfied that there are a sufficient number of qualified women available as professional competition for petitioner. [34]

While waiting for the next move in court, and hoping to impress the NYSAC with her prowess as a boxer, Tonawanda agreed to participate in a kickboxing exhibition against a 155-lb. male kickboxer from Philadelphia named Larry Rodania. The bout was to be a "keynote" of the Oriental World of Self Defense show promoted by martial arts impresario Grandmaster Aaron Banks. Scheduled for the main arena at Madison Square Garden on June 7, 1975, the show had previously been held at the Felt Forum. Banks had moved it to the arena the previous year and managed to fill the stands with twenty thousand fans—an unheard-of number for a martial arts show. He was hoping to top that record with his mixed-gender kickboxing bout. Not only would Jackie Tonawanda be the first woman to fight in the ring at Madison Square Garden, but also she'd be doing it fighting against a man.

Kickboxing was a brand-new sport that had gained popularity since it was first established in Japan in the early 1960s. It incorporated elements from traditional martial arts such as karate with a sprinkling of Muay Thai and other more traditional fighting styles thrown in, plus Western-style boxing. Not unlike French savate, kickboxing is actually contested in a boxing ring rather than on a mat, as with traditional martial arts competitions.

The sport was unbounded by boxing and wrestling commissions, so women were able to compete unfettered by the legal wrangling that so many female boxers faced. International karate competition in particular had opened itself to allow women's divisions, and kickboxing had already seen mixed-gender fighting in the United States.

In preparation for the fight, Tonawanda trained vigorously with David Vasquez, a well-respected bantamweight champion, and even managed to drop down to 160 pounds, hoping to be lighter on her feet as she entered the ring. "The less I weigh the faster I can move around in the ring, and I have to be fast to counter his feet kicks," she was quoted as saying. [35] Speaking with another reporter, she told her, "I've got my whole purse riding on a second round knockout," and went on to predict that her win would be in the second round by none other than a KO. [36]

True to her word, Tonawanda used her superior boxing skills to knock out her opponent with a hard right in the second round of the five-round bout. Speaking about the match a few days later, she expressed disappointment that the outcome of the match was barely reported. "I did what I predicted and took him out in the second on a solid punch. So why is it that everyone is asking me three days later, who won the bout?"

Ultimately it didn't matter. "Hear[ing] the crowd chanting 'Jackie, Jackie'" spurred her on, and she loved that it took her "nearly two hours to get out of the place because everyone wanted autographs. And you'd better believe I signed them all."[37]

Approximately ten days after her fight, the Supreme Court came out with its ruling on Jackie Tonawanda's case. This time the NYSAC had put in a countermotion arguing that the case be thrown out based upon her alleged failure to state a cause of action—meaning since the NYSAC had answered why the license wasn't granted, the case should be thrown out.

Justice Harry B. Frank, writing for the court, felt otherwise. He ruled in part that the denial of professional boxing licenses to women was based on "highly questionable" arguments. He further wrote, "Patronizing male chauvinism of this type not only has no place in our legal system, but should not be countenanced at any level in our society." Finally arguing, "This court will not hold that women should be precluded from professionally exploiting whatever skills they may have in the sport of boxing merely because they are women," he directed that Tonawanda should amend her petition to sue the NYSAC for denying her a license to box.

While the law had not been struck down per se, the speciousness of the arguments offered by the NYSAC were such that in the justice's opinion, Tonawanda should sue to do precisely that: have the law overturned. Having chosen not to, the rule remained in place.

Another case was opened on the other side of the country in Virginia City, Nevada. Caroline Svendsen, a thirty-four-year-old construction worker, part-time cocktail waitress, mother of a nineteen-year-old daughter, and grandmother of a five-year-old grandson, had taken up boxing in her spare time. She eventually met up with boxing manager Ted Walker, who thought she had the talent to become a fighter. Walker also believed it a good time to promote women in the boxing ring.

On July 3, 1975, a couple of weeks after Jackie Tonawanda's win in New York State Supreme Court, Caroline Svendsen walked into the Nevada State Athletic Commission (NAC) office in Garnerville, Nevada, and filled out the application forms for a license to box. Svendsen was hoping to become the first woman in Nevada to become legally sanctioned. Her plan was to have her debut bout on a professional fight card scheduled for September 19 in Virginia City, a fight card that her manager was helping to put together.

Seemingly wanting to give it a fair hearing, the commission agreed to review Svendsen's application at their regular monthly meeting the following Thursday. The executive secretary of the NAC, Jim Deskin, had told reporters that they would be seeking a "medical evaluation from three Las Vegas doctors as to whether a woman boxer could be injured by punches to the breasts" ahead of their decision. Deskin also expressed skepticism about the whole thing, asking rhetorically, "Who's she going to fight?" given that she was the only woman applying for a license to box.[38]

The following week, the NAC met and actually granted her a license—making Svendsen the first woman in the state of Nevada to hold a professional boxing license. According to Bill Dickson, who became an important promoter of women's boxing beginning in 1976 and through the 1980s in Nevada, this was not their first go-around with the NAC. While the newspapers had dutifully reported on Svendsen's application and the NAC's rapid approval, Svendsen had actually already been turned down once before, and it was only due to the impending threat of a lawsuit that the NAC relented and gave her the license.[39]

Quoted in the press after Svendsen had been granted her license, Walker said, "My fighter probably will start her career in September by taking on another woman in Virginia City."[40] The first order of business was to come up with a likely opponent and ensure that she would be licensed in time for the September 19 card under the promotional hand of Charlie Palmer, a regular on the Nevada fight scene.

By mid-August, the NAC was beginning to get cold feet, with reports that they were delaying approval of the match set to be on the undercard of the ten-round heavyweight main event between Terry Hinke and Harold Carter. The delay in part was due to the absence of a confirmed opponent for Svendsen.

Three weeks later, at the beginning of September, Jim Deskin decided to voice his concerns about the fight with the announcement that he was recommending that the NAC only allow the fight to go forward if it was labeled an exhibition.

"Nobody has seen two women fight," he said. "Two women haven't fought in the United States yet." While he evidently had no knowledge of the high caliber of women's boxing that had taken place in the 1950s—or of the fact that Barbara Buttrick and Phyllis Kugler had fought a licensed bout in San Antonio, Texas, in 1957—he also seemed unaware of the pockets of terrifically skilled female boxers who were fighting to get licensed in other locales.

Svendsen was disappointed to learn of the change, and although she told the press, "It doesn't make any difference to me," she clearly wanted the fight to be sanctioned. She went on to say:

> I'd like it to be a fight. We've got to start somewhere. I definitely want it to be a real fight. I wouldn't want to spend my whole career fighting exhibitions because no state wanted to be first. I think they're trying to keep me out. I have my license and I'm qualified. As long as it's going to be a girl fighting another girl, why should anyone object to it?[41]

As this was going on, Ted Walker had found a likely opponent in Connie Costello, a twenty-eght-year-old woman from Drain, Oregon (though some accounts showed her as coming from Salem). He wasn't ready to announce it just yet. When Walker did, the following day, the matter of the bout being an exhibition was settled. Costello, who was also a novice in the ring, was accepted as an opponent, and the four-round match was approved on the fight card as an exhibition bout.

The next order of business was to continue training for the fight plus the usual array of prefight promotion, including the public workouts scheduled over three days during the week before the match.

Svendsen had been in training for the bout at the Clear Creek Job Corps Center since July, but the ritual of the open workout was something new for her. In fact, she'd never had an actual fight other than sparring sessions during her training. Reporting on the public opening, to which the press was invited, Steve Sneddon of the *Reno Evening Gazette* headlined his piece "Caroline Svendsen Scared?"

Set at the Silver Queen Saloon in Virginia City, Svendsen in a moment of candor told the press, "I can't say I'm not scared." She went on to say, "I've talked to guys about their feelings in their first fight, but there aren't any women to talk to about it." She also told the press she had no idea what she was afraid of but "[w]hen I thought of working out in front of people I almost threw up." [42]

She followed up her remarks saying that while "the publicity bothered her at first . . . 'just punching the bag last night I realized I could block the public out.'"[43]

Her jitters aside, she went through a sparring session with fighter Benny Casing in front of two hundred or so fans, acquitting herself well. In fact, she did so well, Connie Costello pulled out of the bout with Ted Walker, telling reporters, "She felt Caroline was too good for her." Whatever the real reason, Walker was able to replace her the day before the fight with Jean Lange, a thirty-four-year-old fighter originally from Los Angeles but then living in Phoenix, Arizona.

Lange had previously had one unsanctioned boxing match in 1973—on an Indian Reservation near Sacaton, Arizona—against the well-known wrestler Princess Tona Tomah, who'd been on the scene since the late 1950s but took to boxing in the 1970s. Lange, a meat cutter by trade, was also said to have "wrestled in exhibition matches," although no mention was ever made as to where or when the bouts occurred. With Lange on board, Walker was able to garner the support of the NAC, which dutifully licensed Lange to box in Nevada, turning around her application in one day pending a medical examination.

One other final accommodation was made for the "safety" of the women during the match. On fight night, they would both be wearing breast protectors. While nothing more than plastic bra inserts, Svendsen described them as looking "like two Jello molds." [44] The women also were slated to wear heavy foam "pelvic protectors" said to be "similar to the equipment worn by women bull fighters in Spain."[45]

When fight night came, Svendsen, weighing in at 138 lbs., entered the ring like a champ with gold boxing gloves, and within fifty seconds of the first round landed Lange on the canvas after having been hit with two stunning left uppercuts. Lange, who'd weighed in at 134 lbs., lay there for a full twenty seconds after the ten-count before moving. Svendsen had proved that she was indeed a fighter, in front of the twelve hundred fans seated in the outdoor bleachers in the parking lot of the Delta Saloon.

Elated by her win—and having decided to go for a knockout, thinking a decision for a four-round exhibition bout would soon be forgotten—Svendsen told reporters, "[I] couldn't believe it when I knocked her out." Though she admitted, "The scary part was that she didn't get up after the count of 10."

She also told reporters, "I was really nervous about this fight but now the first fight jitters are out of me." She was ready for the bouts her manager had put in motion for her in Oregon. Asked about Lange, Svendsen said, "Either they get hurt or I get hurt. She was out to get me down fast . . . only I was stronger."

Lange said she was impressed with Svendsen's fighting ability, though she couched it by saying, "She showed me a few good punches . . . but that's about it. Next time I'll be in shape to take her." Lange also claimed that she'd only had one day to prepare for the fight and hadn't been in the gym for six months.[46]

The next big hurdle for Svendsen was gaining permission from the boxing authorities in Oregon to fight. Nick Sckavone, chairman of the Portland Municipal Boxing and Wrestling Commission (Portland Boxing Commission), was quoted as saying:

> My first reaction, and it's a personal one, is that I don't care for it. It's rude and it's crude, two women fighting in a ring. . . . I'm certainly not going to fight Women's Lib. I'll go along with the majority and trend of time, I'll have to.[47]

Despite his feelings, he called for a special commission meeting to vote on the issue. At the meeting, authorization was given by a margin of 3-2 to hold a boxing match between Svendsen and boxer Jennie Josephs from Menteca City, California. Sckavone himself had cast the winning vote, breaking a 2-2 tie.

The bout was set for October 23 at the Multnomah County Exposition Center and, as agreed, would be "a regulation match, not an exhibition."[48] This all boded well for a successful first women's fight in Oregon, and in the days leading up to it everything seemed to be going well. There was no further interference from the Portland Boxing Commission and both fighters were in training. The day before the fight, however, Jennie Josephs had to withdraw having come down with a bad case of the flu and laryngitis.

Walker, wanting to make sure the fight would still go on, wasted no time. He immediately got in contact with Jean Lange. As if she'd only been sitting by the phone waiting for the call, she flew from Phoenix to Portland on two and a half hours' notice. Lange was game for the challenge, telling the press she'd been training "ever since [Caroline Svendsen] beat me the first time," and had also kept her weight to 134 lbs.[49]

The fight itself, though historic in the context of the 1970s, was less than stellar technically. Neither fighter had a plethora of boxing skills and, as reported by the Associated Press, they were subject to occasional boos from the crowd accompanied by disparaging remarks interspersed with cheers for the harder flurries. The AP article itself wasn't particularly flattering either, noting that the first round "For the most part . . . was an alley fight complete with flailing arms and wild punches." The reporter also noted, "When solid blows connected, their bodies did not absorb the force and both were knocked off balance."[50]

Lange's prefight boast was telling, as the fight went four full rounds. Svendsen was given the decision—her first actual "official" fight—but she had to work hard for it. Lange was said to have given a stronger showing than her first time in the ring. She attributed it to "a lot more conditioning. I had one day in the gym for the [first fight], because I had been called in as a substitute. This time I trained every day, hoping I could get a rematch." Svendsen, clearly tired at the end of the fight, was quoted as saying, "She just wouldn't go down, no matter how hard I hit her."[51]

While Caroline Svendsen's fight for the right to box legally in Nevada had been very public, with national press coverage throughout, the matter of women's boxing in the state of Arizona took a different tack entirely. The Arizona Athletic Commission, by a 3-0 vote, agreed to legalize women's boxing in the state in early October, and even held their first legally sanctioned women's bout on October 10. It was held with barely any press coverage and only became a national story when the Associated Press put it on the wire in the middle of November.

The change in the Arizona rules stipulated that women who applied "for the $5 license must be between 18 and 38 years old, physically fit and must have had 'a little experience boxing other women.'" The rules also specified that women wear "steel-and-sponge protectors . . . for the breasts and a sponge protector for the pelvis."

The commission chairman, Nicholas Kondora, said, "I don't like the idea of women boxing but we had to go along with [it]. They told us women are doing it all over the country." Another of the commissioners, Mike Quilhuis, "an ex-boxer," was "enthusiastic about admitting the female leather push-ers." Weight brackets would be the same for both men and women, though no mixed-gender fights would be allowed. [52]

Arizona had already had its share of controversy when it came to wom-en's participation in the ring. Seven months before, in March of 1975, Mar-ion Bermudez, a twenty-three-year-old nationally ranked karate champion—with a third-degree brown belt at the time—chose to enter the Phoenix Gold-en Gloves in the 125-lb. novice class. Originally from the Bronx and of mixed Puerto Rican and Trinidadian heritage, she had transferred to Arizona State University from a small college in Nebraska where she had been the recipient of an athletic scholarship.

Bermudez had taken up karate—a highly popular form of self-defense for women at a time of rising crime rates when many felt unsafe walking alone on the streets—in 1972. For some it was also a gateway to competitive karate, one of the few contact sports where serious competition was open to them. In accordance with the rules of the many associations that were spring-ing up, mixed-gender competition was also allowed in certain of the martial arts forms (including kickboxing).

As the date for the Golden Gloves championship loomed, Bermudez and her karate coach, Fred Stille, thought about having her apply, mostly to provide her with cross training to enhance her competitive karate skills. Both felt this was a key way of learning the "inside" game, as opposed to karate, which was traditionally fought with considerable distance between the oppo-nents.

With just seven hours of boxing training in the ring over a period of a week, Bermudez showed up for the weigh-in held on March 7. Her presence caused something of a stir between the coaches, fighters, and tournament officials in attendance. Rather than tossing her out, the officials decided to let her fight despite their trepidation—although mainly because they did not want it to become a contentious issue. As Ben Hinds, a tournament official also acting as a referee, put it, "This is definitely not a woman's sport, but if we try to stop her I think she could turn around and sue everyone for violating her civil rights."

The state tournament director, Harry Ginn, agreed: "I've been in boxing 30 years and I've never heard of anything like this before. I don't think women should be boxing, but she stands a chance if she fights a turkey. Otherwise, she doesn't have the experience to fight inside." The sponsoring organization of the Golden Gloves, the AAU, took a dim view and warned that there might be consequences.

Bermudez forged ahead. Upon winning her first bout by split decision, Hinds said, "The young lady surprised me. I didn't think she'd have the power that she did." She eventually lost her second fight. Hinds, acting at referee, stopped it in the first round after she'd taken two standing eight counts. As it happened, the fighter she had lost to ended up as the divisional champion. Bermudez was upset about the fight being stopped, saying that she wasn't hurt and had been pulled from the fight too soon. Later even Hinds agreed, but in the moment he was more concerned about her getting hurt and the possible ramifications.[53]

Win or lose, when Bermudez entered the ring, she had the crowd behind her. One woman, "the wife of a boxing coach [even yelled out], 'We do it at home with rolling pins and frying pans; no reason we can't do it in the ring with left hooks.'"[54]

Unfortunately for the officials who had allowed Bermudez to fight, displeasure with the decision was the least of it from the perspective of the AAU. Believing that it was firmly against AAU policies to allow women to compete, both Al Fenn, president of the Arizona Golden Gloves Association, and Harry Ginn were indefinitely suspended for allowing Bermudez to compete.

Asked by the press for her reaction, Bermudez said, "I don't think the AAU was right . . . I feel really badly about it. They really stuck their necks out for me and I'd like to help them any way I could." She did say that she intended to continue boxing as part of her training "as long as my coach feels it's beneficial."

Summing up what the tournament had given her, Stille said, "Both matches were a good experience for her. The second one kept her from having a swelled head—intellectually speaking." He added, "We only trained about a week before the Golden Gloves. If we had had three months, I and other boxing coaches who worked with her think she could have had a good chance of winning her division."[55]

Bermudez went on to compete in a karate championship in New York, defeating a male opponent—winning $500 and the moniker of a professional karate competitor. She also finished her bachelor's degree in electrical technology at Arizona State University, the first woman to do so. Her life revolved around the study of martial arts, and as she contemplated the future she spoke of why she was embracing boxing in addition to karate.

> At first, when I was looking at boxing, it really didn't look like anything too complicated. My eye was untrained. Talking to some of the good amateur boxers and some of the pro boxers, there's really a lot more to it than meets the eye. . . . People that really get into boxing seem to get the same thing out of their art that people in karate get out of theirs. It's a matter of getting to know yourself and self-confidence. It's kind of like testing yourself.[56]

By the time October rolled around, Bermudez was ready to take on yet more challenges. With women's boxing now legal in Arizona, she signed up to compete in the state's first legally sanctioned women's bout, a three-rounder against another karate student named Karen Mast, at the Tucson Community

Center Exhibition Hall. Bermudez was decidedly the more experienced of the two and, although a sanctioned boxing match, it was actually a kickboxing fight billed as a "karate-boxing" exhibition. Not surprisingly, Bermudez defeated Mast by TKO at the end of the second round in front of the crowd of fifteen hundred cheering fans.

Mast, a green belt in karate, working at a karate school as an instructor, had taken the fight with one day's notice and was not too pleased with the outcome. She'd agreed to participate "willingly" but in truth hadn't known what to expect. As she told a reporter a couple of months later, "I didn't train as a boxer, and I don't know much about it, but everyone said, 'don't worry about it.' That's the attitude they said I should have. It wasn't a good attitude."[57]

A second female bout in Arizona—this time an actual boxing match or rematch of sorts—was set for December 10, 1975, between Jean Lange and Princess Tona Tomah at the Phoenix Civic Plaza, and perhaps a repeat of their previous outing. Not much is known about the fight, although Tomah's son, Piper Carle, recalled that his mother had won the first official women's boxing match in Phoenix. He claimed it was a six-rounder and that his mother defeated her opponent by unanimous decision. He also recalled that she "had boxed 13 men before she was allowed to box women legally."[58] Tomah was an important figure in the wrestling and boxing scene in Phoenix, where she even eventually trained amateur boxers under the auspices of the AAU.

The state of Indiana, once the home of an active women's boxing scene in the 1950s, became embroiled in controversy in early November of 1975 when a women's amateur boxing match was canceled. The bout was between Jo Crumes, a local boxer and member of the Anderson PAL, and Barb Napier, Ohio's women's bantamweight amateur champion. They were to be a feature of the second annual Veteran's Day boxing card held to benefit the Anderson PAL. Napier had won her title at an amateur boxing show held at the Dayton Gym Club in Dayton, Ohio, six weeks before—with no hitches reported—and, in fact, was accompanied to the fight night by Ed Shock, chairman of the AAU in Dayton, Ohio.

The hometown fighter, Jo Crumes, was a twenty-one-year-old nursing student at Ball State University who'd recently played for the league-winning Madison County Women's softball team. She'd also played basketball and even football on a pick-up team. Crumes, in a talk with reporters, called herself "daddy's little tomboy," and told how she'd been "shadow boxing, jumping rope and working out on the bags," in preparation for the fight. She'd also sparred with male fighters, including some "highly rated local boxers."[59] Her father, Wendell Crumes, was the Anderson PAL club's boxing coach and a former Golden Glove fighter who had been taking his daughter with him to the fights since she was a little girl. He'd also overseen her training—giving her the same regimen as his male fighters and proudly expressed confidence in her abilities.

The fight itself had initially been brought to the attention of the two governing bodies—the State Athletic Commission and the Indiana AAU—four weeks before. At that time, both parties had said they'd look into it and after a while told the PAL officials there was "nothing wrong" with putting a women's bout on the fight card. A few days before the fight, it was announced that the fight had been postponed, but by the afternoon of the day before the fight the "differences had been ironed out," and as a result, it was back on. Ten minutes before the scheduled start time of the PAL fight card, however, the bout was summarily canceled, although the rest of the fight card was allowed to continue without a hitch. It was said that the crowd had swollen by an extra hundred people to around three hundred paying customers in anticipation of the Crumes-Napier fight. [60]

At issue when the controversy erupted were such technicalities as what the women were required to wear in the ring. The rules stated, "A fighter must wear a protective cup," as well as mandating that "a fighter must either be in the ring topless or wear a T-shirt with nothing under it." AAU official George DeFadis along with State Athletic Commission official Kelse McClure were uncomfortable with the lack of clarity and told the PAL they'd pull out the rulebook if the fight went ahead. Speaking to the issue, PAL club president Sgt. Roy Springfield was frustrated and, noting the shirt rule, said "that rules out any protective clothing, even a bra"—something both women anticipated wearing.

To punctuate the seriousness of the AAU and State Athletic Commission requests to pull the bout, Anderson police chief Paddy Jamerson had been contacted, requesting that he stop the fight in the event that two women were allowed to proceed. Springfield agreed to drop the fight from the evening's bout sheet, telling a local reporter:

> I'll say this, in Indiana we go by the book and that's good. I understand there are rules being written for women's boxing right now but it takes something like this to get people to act. It's discouraging to have [to] call the fight off, but that doesn't mean we won't try again. [61]

Equally frustrated with the proceedings was Ohio AAU chief Ed Shock who said he was considering a lawsuit on behalf of Barb Napier, although action was never taken.

As originally planned, Crumes and Napier had been scheduled to fight two bouts: one in Indiana and one in Dayton, Ohio. With the first fight canceled, it was just a matter of getting the two women the hundred-plus miles from Anderson to Dayton where they were to be featured in an amateur show at the Dayton Club Gym, the same club where Napier had won her title.

The bout, labeled in Ohio as "the fight that couldn't be staged in Indiana," was Crumes's debut match—but the crowd wouldn't have known it based on her performance. From the opening bell, Crumes proved herself to be a boxer's boxer. She showed terrific focus and fortitude and was able to drop Napier to the deck with a "short left hand punch" at 1:15 of the first round, giving Crumes the KO win. Crumes's triumphant performance wasn't enough for her father, who said "He was tired of the controversy [and] would ask his daughter not to fight again."[62]

Napier went on to break ground again on December 9, 1975, when she fought Ann Roberts of Tyler, Texas, in a four-round bout at the Eagles Club in Milwaukee, Wisconsin—a fight said to be the first sanctioned women's boxing bout in the state. In this case, promoter Harry Simos presented his fight card to Vern Woodward, the secretary of the Wisconsin State Athletic Examining Board.

Noting that the decision would be put to a vote by the three-member board, Woodward said:

> There's no rule against it, but there's no rule at all. I don't know whether we have the right to approve or disapprove the bout. I'm going to check with the Attorney General and then poll the members of the board. I know women have fought other places, but we've never had to deal with it.[63]

While there had certainly been women's wrestling matches in Wisconsin, it is hard to say if any of the barnstorming women's boxing matches in the 1950s had actually been fought there—at least legally. Within a few days, though, the board agreed to allow the bout to go on as scheduled by a vote of 3-0.

Simos generated a lot of publicity ahead of his fight, with one newspaper noting the Napier-Roberts fight was garnering more attention than the main event. The crowd on fight night reflected the excitement of seeing female boxing in action with a nearly record-breaking audience of 1,126 fans and total receipts of $3,726. The boxing prowess of the two fighters, however, did not live up to the expectations of the crowd—even though they only fought one-minute rounds.

Both young women, as one reporter put it, "looking young with their hair in pigtails, did not fight with enough gusto to please the fans." Audience members liberally booed the fighters for inactivity, only livening up in the third round during some good exchanges. Even then, the mood of the crowd was mean with lots of jeering and catcalls thrown at the two fighters. At the end of it, Roberts, who outweighed Napier by twenty pounds, won by split decision.[64]

After the fight, Roberts said, she had been "nervous" and admitted she "just didn't fight a good match, I don't know what was wrong, I think the size of the crowd had something to do with the way we fought." Napier had a cut below her right eye from the brief encounter and said she didn't know what had happened, but despite that said she'd "whip her the next time."

While neither fighter had shown particular skills when they boxed, both women were game to be in the ring and proud to have won the right to pound on each other legally. They were also inspiring others—even with their less-than-perfect boxing prowess. Arlene Townsend, who'd come to see the bout with her boxer husband, said, "I would have like to see them fight longer. It was too short. In fact, I wouldn't mind fighting myself. The idea of being injured doesn't bother me in the least."[65]

Much as Jo Ann Hagen's fight against Pat Emerick in Council Bluffs, Iowa, circa 1949 had caused a sensation among local women, who inundated the promoter with requests to learn to box, the publicity surrounding such fighters as Caroline Svendsen got out the word that women could make it into the ring. Some fights appearing on regular boxing cards were even televised, which further spurred women to consider taking up the gloves. The breaking down of long-held barriers to active participation in boxing, whether under the banner of "women's lib" or not, produced an enormous change in the perception of what women could and could not achieve.

And despite crowds that may have been less than enthusiastic, one-minute boxing rounds, and uncomfortable chest protectors, women embraced the idea of boxing as a well-won right, with every cut and bruise a badge of honor for those who crossed through the velvet ropes into the ring.

Chapter Seven

A Ring of Their Own

I didn't even know I had a black eye until I looked in the mirror. Then I thought, oh well, I'll just take out my makeup. . . . I proved I had tough skin.
—Pat Pineda, age twenty-two, San Pedro, California.[1]

As the 1970s advanced into the 1980s, women continued to advocate for the right to box professionally in the United States, as well as to open the door to amateur competition. States such as California and New York finally acquiesced and let women in the ring—although not without controversy. Female fighters were less successful when it came to amateur contests, and while individual state organizations allowed some women to enter amateur tournaments, the AAU continued to cite dubious medical reasons for keeping female fighters out of its contests. In one instance, nineteen-year-old Jill Lafler sued to compete at the Golden Gloves amateur tournament on the basis of sex discrimination only to have her case denied by the U. S. District Court for the Western District of Michigan when they sided with the prevailing view and allowed the continued exclusion of women from amateur competition.

On another front, female fighters were castigated as "women's libbers," an uneasy moniker that was fraught with political meaning at a time of huge transition in the place of women in American society.

BE CAREFUL WHAT YOU WISH FOR

For the women who successfully campaigned to enter the boxing ring, a chance to box often meant they were entering the ring as professionals with little or no ring knowledge. Many others were lured by a combination of their own enthusiasm and the excitement of seeing women slugging it out on television or reading about it in the newspaper. This desire to box met up, in some cases, with unscrupulous promoters cashing in on the novelty by adding women's bouts to fight cards. Unfortunately, promoters' desire to put a few more bodies in the seats meant that, at times, little or no concern was given to the actual fighting abilities of the women or for their safety. Fights also ranged from one-minute rounds to three-minute rounds, changing state by state and, in some cases, fight by fight, in a system that was haphazard at best—even though men's fights had standard three-minute rounds with the exception of youth amateur contests.

Sue "Tiger Lily" Fox, a twenty-five-year-old mother of three, is a case in point: A woman who entered boxing with enthusiasm, but felt "sucker-punched" after her first bout, and though she went on to a successful career in boxing, it took its toll.[2] Fox was a black belt in karate whose first experience in the ring was not so dissimilar to Karen Mast's professional debut bout in Arizona. Fox had been a competitor in light-contact competitions throughout the Northwest and was just beginning to participate in full-contact matches. Overall she had been undefeated in a total of about thirty amateur karate bouts.

Making her home at the time in Vancouver, Washington, Fox was watching the news one evening when video highlights of Caroline Svendsen's bout against Jean Lange were aired. In a recent interview, Fox said, "I saw it on TV and it was absolutely amazing, though I have to tell you, thinking about it now, the boxing was terrible! At the time I thought it was great."[3]

Here were two female boxers who were paid to box for four rounds—when, as she put it, "I was actually paying to fight in karate tournaments!"

The next day she set out to find a boxing gym, which eventually brought her to the attention of a man claiming to be a women's boxing fight manager named "Abe T." He seemed to her to be very nice and accommodating, but as Fox explained, "Little did I know, my newly-found manager did not appear to have my interests at heart."[4]

Sue was hoping to get a fight with Caroline Svendsen or Jean Lange, figuring that she would have a chance given that their skill levels were about on par with her own—basically nil. Unable or unwilling to put together a bout with either Svendsen or Lange, Abe told Sue of a fighter named Theresa "Princess Red Star" Kibby, twenty-two, from California, who was looking for her first fight. Kibby also saw the fight between Svendsen and Lange, and had actually been in the stands. Abe talked up Kibby to Fox, mentioning that she had maybe a couple of years of boxing experience, but was basically a novice. Fox was happy with the prospect and excited by the idea of getting into the ring.

Setting the contest for February 12, 1976, the fight was promoted as "karate" versus "boxing"—something that harkened back to the rasso-boxing contest Jo Ann Hagen fought in at Council Bluffs. One important distinction was Fox would not be allowed to use any of her karate techniques in the ring other than punching. Perhaps because the fight was set up to pit a "black belt" against a "novice boxer," no thought was given to Fox's training, other than to have her continue with her normal karate regimen. This meant she had neither boxing training nor any time in an actual boxing ring in the weeks leading up to the fight.

Fox persevered, although she grew uneasy in the days before the fight when she learned that her opponent was from a prominent boxing family. As it turned out, Kibby's father was a well-respected Native American boxing trainer named Dave Kibby Sr., who had founded the Del Norte Boys Club and managed the River's End boxing and baseball teams. He also sat on the board of the Indian Action Council of Northwestern California, along with Theresa Kibby's sister, Darlene Buckskin. Her two brothers, Dave Kibby Jr. and Roger Buckskin, also boxed professionally—and both would be fighting opponents on the same fight card as Kibby and Fox. If that wasn't enough, Theresa Kibby had been boxing since she was a kid alongside her two brothers, and although she'd never had an actual official fight, she'd been sparring for years. As with other fighters of the period, she excelled in other sports and had played on the Smith River girls' basketball team along with her sports-minded sisters who were also skilled in the science of the ring.

There were other surprises as well. The bout between Fox and Kibby was originally slated for four two-minute rounds—an oft-used practice for women's bouts as they became legalized, though not standard by any means—but as the fight drew near, it was switched to four rounds of three minutes duration each. All of this proved to be a self-described "disaster" for Fox, who was outboxed at every turn and unable to defend herself from Kibby's counterpunching abilities. By the third round the referee had seen enough and waved off the fight, giving Kibby the TKO win.

After the match, Fox was quoted as saying, "I'm glad they stopped it because I was getting woozy. But this was fun. When do I fight again?"[5] Years later, Fox put it this way:

> The referee stopped the fight in the third round, after I was too stubborn to fall down. What was unfortunate for me . . . was that I had been duped, and by taking away my powerful [karate] leg kicks, I was just a "*bad boxer.*"[6]

Kibby was said to have "stalked her red-haired opponent relentlessly in the entertaining match that was the pro debut for both," telling reporters, "This was all worth it, I can't wait for my next fight."[7]

In truth, Theresa Kibby had boxing pretty "wired up" by the time of her first bout, with a strong network of support and a proper training routine that included daily runs and plenty of opportunities to spar experienced male boxers. The strength of her family ties also meant that they had enough pull to see to it that her early fights would be family affairs. All of this meant her experiences were fairly unique. In California, boxing gym manager and trainer Dee Knuckles had been making a name by seeing to the training of young women at the San Pedro Locker Club—part of the Harbor View Housing Project community center in San Pedro, California. Knuckles (her real name by way of a marriage) attempted to provide the kind of support young male boxers received, though with mixed results.

Starting in 1974, at the behest of some local girls, Knuckles ran a boxing class for teenage girls and young women. Initially a once-a-week class, it became increasingly popular and grew to two evenings a week after Knuckles enlisted a friend from the Los Angeles Police Department to train the girls. Eventually, her star pupil, a former "street fighter" named Pat Pineda, also helped lead the classes. The boxing students jumped rope, learned boxing fundamentals, and sparred, but most importantly, it gave "the girls [something] to do so they wouldn't be standing on street corners"—a not uncommon theme for boxing programs aimed an adolescent boys.

For Pineda, who dropped out of the tenth grade to get married and became the mother of two young children, it brought focus, a return to the books "to get her diploma," and her eventual entry into college. It also helped her get a job at the local YWCA working with kids. Along with other girls at the gym, she had the chance to show off her talents in a series of exhibition bouts in and around San Pedro.[8] She was also an exhibition sparring partner to up-and-coming male boxers on cards put together by Don Fraser, the promoter at boxing's Forum venue.

In early January 1976, Pineda—with Dee Knuckles at her side—made her way to the California State Athletic Commission (SAC) to apply for a boxing license. The year before, the SAC had indicated they were beginning to study the feasibility of legalizing women's boxing under some conditions. Pineda was reportedly the first woman to apply after California had begun changing its rules to allow women to box. The requirements for the license included a medical examination and a "screen[ing] for professional skill and ability as a boxer," something most other states did not require. Given that Pineda was the first to apply, the commission had not yet worked out how to test her—nor had they determined what, if any, protective equipment would be required or to decide on any other regulations specific to women.[9]

By early March, all indications were that the SAC would be willing to use an actual fight between Pineda and an opponent as a test. While it is unclear if the SAC contacted Dave Kibby Sr. directly about the test, arrangements were made for Pineda to fight his daughter, Theresa Kibby, in a bout billed as the boxer Kibby versus the puncher Pineda. As usual, one of Kibby's brothers was also on the fight card.

Two weeks later, Pineda traveled to Stateline on Lake with Dee Knuckles to prove to the SAC officials gathered there that she could indeed fight well enough to receive her license to box professionally in the state of California. She was set to fight Kibby at the Sahara Tahoe Hotel & Casino just across the border from South Lake Tahoe, California, in Stateline, Nevada. It was also Pineda's debut bout as a professional boxer.

The four-rounder was fought in front of twelve hundred fight fans on March 18 with Theresa Kibby in fine form for what was her third professional contest. Kibby took the fight by decision, but it was not a walkover. Pineda acquitted herself well, delivering what was described as a "jarring punch to [Kibby's] chin in the second round." Sportswriter Steve Sneddon went on to write, "It was the kind of punch that often turns fights around. . . . Pineda [then] moved in and roughed her up."

What he saw in Kibby, though, was even fiercer. He thought her without equal in the burgeoning world of women's boxing and noted, "Her opponent paid dearly for the momentary success," when Kibby's "killer instinct" kicked in—something he'd not seen in either of her brothers.[10]

By the fourth round, Pineda's left eye was swollen and her nose was examined to make certain it hadn't been broken. Throughout the retaliatory barrage of the third and fourth rounds, Pineda had managed to withstand the onslaught of jabs and combinations and never went down—something that left everyone feeling they'd truly watched two professionals in action. Mindful of why the fight was being contested, Dave Kibby Sr. told the waiting reporters, "Those people were really enthusiastic and I would have to say the [California] State Athletic Commission people were impressed." The state inspector was described as "amazed. He didn't believe it. He said they boxed better than some men pros."[11]

The upshot was the SAC felt comfortable enough to begin granting licenses to women for both professional and amateur contests. As Inspector Roy Tennison put it, "The girls were pretty well schooled in the art of boxing and in defending themselves. Both of them. It wasn't a helter skelter affair." The SAC noted the next step would be to write up specific rules and regulations, but in the interim issued guidelines that would allow women to begin to contest fights legally in California. The requirements included the stipulation that all fights be four-round bouts of two-minutes duration for each round, that all women wear breast protectors, that the gloves be ten ounces, and that there be no mixed-gender fights. The women were also required to certify that they weren't pregnant or menstruating.[12]

With the hurdle of gaining a license to box in California finally over, the next step was to come up with a bout. Promoter Don Fraser, who had watched Pat Pineda spar with some of his fighters in the past, provided the answer. He added a four-round women's bout to his fight card slated for April 28, 1976—just five weeks after Pineda's debut contest. The fight was set for the Forum in Inglewood, California, and would be on the undercard of the highly anticipated Danny Lopez v. Octavio Gomez fight.

A "worthy" opponent was found in Kim Maybee, an eighteen-year-old recent graduate of Marshall High School in Los Angeles who lived in Hollywood. She stood six feet, one and a half inches tall, had played basketball in high school, and was looking to join a professional woman's football team as a receiver. She carried a mean wallop, but had no professional fights, nor much time—if any—in the boxing gym.

Ahead of the fight, Maybee described herself as a "street fighter," telling reporters, "I learned to fight in the street. When somebody jumped me I'd jump [them] back." Maybee also said she eventually began developing her boxing skills with help from her brothers, although she had never trained with a true boxing trainer.[13]

Eleven days before the historic encounter between Pineda and Maybee, the first approved amateur women's bout in the state of California was held on April 17 in the town of Eureka. The contest pitted one of Dave Kibby Sr.'s boxing students, sixteen-year-old Cheri Sutherland, against a fighter from nearby Oregon, Karen Steward. Sutherland won the bout by a split decision, although both girls performed well in front of 1,458 cheering spectators—a sell-out crowd for the venue.[14]

That amateur fight out of the way, Fraser arranged for a crescendo of press coverage—and the inevitable opinions. While most reactions to the fight were muted, some in the press expressed dismay, stating promoter Don Fraser should be "ashamed of himself" for "playing off ladies' wrestling and roller derby."[15]

Columnist Jim Murray of the *Los Angeles Times* was also appalled at the prospect, writing, "Apparently the Bill of Rights includes the right to a detached retina, or a subdural hemorrhage, or a nose bleed, aphasia or any of the traumas of the prize ring. Women don't want men to be having all the fun."[16]

Other articles were careful to state it was not a "women's lib" thing, while still more reveled in the perceived incongruity of a woman boxer. A half-page spread on Pat Pineda by Rich Roberts of the *Independent Press-Telegram* began with a *What's My Line?* game-show-inspired question. He offered up such possible guesses as: "a belly dancer in a Greek restaurant," "a channel swimmer," or "a professional pizza twirler." He also opined that any boxing decision in her upcoming bout "may be that the whole affair was almost as ridiculous as some of the other bouts the commission has sanctioned." While not exactly a resounding endorsement of fighting between female boxers, at least it made mention that some of the fights between male boxers had been less than up to standard.[17]

A *Los Angeles Times* piece written by Cheryl Bentsen provided an in-depth look at the circumstances surrounding the fight and included some quotes from the SAC. George Johnson, an SAC inspector, described Pineda and Maybee as having "limited" skills. He went on to explain:

Maybee and Pineda are hesitant—well maybe that's not the right word. They're not mean enough. I watched two girls box in Eureka recently. They were amateurs, but they didn't have the ability to adjust constantly during the fight, to see the openings. They are conscious of their looks and consequently think about defense and not offense.

The latter issue of appearances became a theme in many of the articles, from the standpoint of not wanting to see women get hurt to purported squeamishness by the boxers themselves at the prospects of getting punched in the face. In Bentsen's piece, however, the fighters themselves dispelled some of the myths.

Pineda said of getting hit, "When I'm in the ring I hear people going, 'Oooooh! Aaaaah!' Like they feel every punch [but] it's not so bad." Pineda and Maybee both pointed out their rough beginnings in neighborhoods where people fought regardless of gender. Pineda related a story of how in one fight "one of the girls kicked me in the back while I was on top of another girl, hitting her in the face and cutting her eye. . . . I fought this girl about three times, and finally I got her by the hair, threw her and said, 'You can't even fight.'"

Maybee also told of her days fighting in her neighborhood, whether it was kids on the street or her brothers, saying, "Hey, I've fought so many times since I was a little kid, it's ridiculous!"

A member of the SAC had expressed such concern over the matter of "girls" fighting that he went so far as to contact the world-famous retired tennis player Althea Gibson about it. She had recently joined the New Jersey Athletic Commission, which was responsible for boxing and wrestling there. From her perspective, girls fighting and boys fighting were not different, contending that in the kind of neighborhoods she'd come from it wasn't a big deal.

If it was "okay" for girls from the "ghetto" to wale on each other alongside their brothers, then the question of maintaining a feminine appearance could not be so readily dismissed. Even Kim Maybee self-reflexively asked how she would contend with Pat Pineda's perceived good looks in the ring.

"'One thing I worry about is Pat's face,' she said. 'She is pretty. Wow! If I hit her—I've seen the aftereffects of hitting someone in the jaw. Sheeeewwww! I figure, one round. That's all I need.'"[18]

Both fighters seemingly dispelled the questions surrounding female appearance in the boxing ring, although the questions by no means went away. The promoter, however, attempted to turn the conversation to the usual publicity surrounding well-publicized fights. Both women participated in open workouts and press events held at the old Main Street Gym in Los Angeles. This was a good strategy as the gym was the stomping ground for all of the great fighters in L.A. and a popular locale for "boxing pressers" (publicity events for sports reporters prior to fights).

Along with Pineda and Maybee, Fraser was also promoting Danny Lopez and Octavio Gomez, who participated in the press events. Fraser's focus, however, was clearly on getting the word out about the historic nature of the Pineda-Maybee bout as the first fully sanctioned professional female fight in California. Fraser even had both women spar with Danny Lopez, who, when asked to pick a winner for the bout between Pineda and Maybee, chose Maybee because she was the harder puncher.

The pressure of the upcoming fight was not to be underestimated, especially for Pineda. The day before the fight she had an argument with Dee Knuckles. Knuckles had big plans for Pineda after the contest: visions of a boxing tour with stops in Hawaii, Germany, Paris, South Africa, and maybe even Madison Square Garden. She was also worried that Pineda "might blow it." Pineda's response was to say, "Dee and I don't see eye-to-eye about all this stuff. I don't know what it all means. It's my career right now, but may not be for long. I only worry about today. I could be dead tomorrow."[19]

Pineda's comments proved to be somewhat prophetic. At the weigh-in, the five-foot, five-and-a-half-inch Pineda came in underweight while Maybee came in at 165 pounds—five pounds over the weight limit. Pineda went out to gain weight—eating a double meal of Chinese and Mexican food to come in at 154, while Maybee went off to shed five pounds by sitting in a "sweat box" and going for a long run. When she came back she weighed exactly 160 pounds. By fight time, however, Maybee not only had an eight-inch height advantage, but she also had gone back to her original weight—with no word on what Pineda actually weighed at fight time or how all that food may have affected her. While the issues Pineda and Maybee faced with making weight was nothing new in boxing, Maybee was clearly an entire weight class larger just before their ring debut at the Forum.

Still, the fight went on. Both women came into the ring wearing long, flowing red satin robes, reminiscent, one reporter said, "of the hoopla of televised wrestling matches" from the 1950s. Underneath, though, they showed none of the flamboyance of the earlier era, with both wearing plain boxing shorts and T-shirts, their breast protectors tucked into their bras.[20]

From the opening bell, it was clear that the fight was a "ms-match" as one paper put it. The lanky, muscular Maybee pummeled Pineda at will with Pineda showing none of the crispness or fortitude of her first fight against Kibby. In the second round, Maybee continued her onslaught through the early going. Maybee even showboated a bit, wowing the crowd of 7,540 spectators with her rendition of the "Ali shuffle." Once she began to "land consecutive lefts and rights to the head" in the second round, referee Marty Denkel called an eight-count and, not liking what he saw, stopped the bout at fifty-seven seconds into the second round of the scheduled four-round match, giving Maybee the TKO win.[21]

The spectator's reaction to the bout was mixed. Some were clearly aghast. One man, identified as a dentist from Santa Monica, said, "Is this sick, or is this sick? It's insanely sadistic to watch two women fight." A boxing trainer who viewed the fight said, "Anybody who puts a woman in the ring ought to be in jail. Women aren't built for fighting; it's inhuman." A female spectator who watched the bout was clearly excited and seeing the possibilities for her own career in the ring said, "I think the money's going to be good."[22]

After it was over and Pineda was in her dressing room, she told reporters she had "pulled some punches." The disappointment clearly showing, she added, "I wish I could have got a whole K.O.—not a technical one." She then went on to announce her retirement, saying, "That was my last fight." In actuality, she had one more fight—a four-round rematch against Kim Maybee at the Olympic the following October which she lost by decision, making Pineda's record 0-3.

The exuberant Maybee didn't respond to Pineda's pronouncement, but when asked about the stoppage told the reporters, "It was fine. It was fine. She couldn't take no more." The press, clearly fascinated with speaking to a female boxer, also asked if she "did the things other gal teen-agers do." Maybee responded, "Yes. I know how to knit but it's a waste of time. But I can cook." After a beat, the smiling Maybee said, "Now I want to see my friends."[23]

For their efforts the two women were reported to have received anywhere from $250 to $350. One tidbit for the fight night was that if Kim Maybee had not made weight, Diane Syverson, a twenty-six-year-old former professional Roller Derby player, who was the third woman to have been licensed by the state of California, would have replaced her on the card. She is said to have fought Maybee in Fresno in June 1976. Syverson gave Maybee a twenty-pound advantage in the bout, but won with a decisive fourth-round TKO. The contest, however, is not officially listed on any of the boxing record websites—a not uncommon occurrence for many of the female bouts at that time.

THE AVALANCHE: WOMEN'S BOXING "INVADES" THE RING

> If the (women) boxers aren't taken off the card, people like you, for putting on the card, and the women boxers will have to be killed. . . . This letter is by no means a joke.
> —Typewritten death threat mailed to Aileen Eaton and Don Chagrin, May 1976[24]

The "firsts" continued with bouts in other states including Montana—where there was to have been a never-realized fight ten years before—and the legalization of women's boxing in Canada for professional and amateur matches, which led to some cross-border opportunities for Americans looking to compete. No mention, however, was given to the earlier professional bouts that had been held in Canada over the years.

What was becoming increasingly clear was the growing popularity of the sport in spite of the controversy and negative reactions from some fight fans and the press. There was also no shortage of women who wanted to try their "fists" in the ring, with women's bouts in California beginning to appear more and more often on fight cards.

A big "win" for women's boxing was the announcement that the Olympic Theater—once the province of Belle Martell and now under the watchful eye of Aileen Eaton—would add its first female bout to a professional fight card. The contest was actually a rematch between Theresa "Princess Red Star" Kibby and Diane Syverson. Kibby and Syverson had met in a boxing contest held on May 5, 1975, at the Civic Auditorium in San Jose, California. After four intense rounds, the fight was called a draw, but as one newspaper put it, the matchup was the "San Jose thriller that overshadowed the main event."

The rematch at the Olympic was announced in mid-May and scheduled for May 27, 1975, ahead of the Memorial Day weekend. Given the press notices that Kibby and Syverson had received, the choice was a good one. It also looked as though there wouldn't be any controversy associated with the bout. That was all to change, however, when the press was informed that a death threat had been mailed to Aileen Eaton and the Olympic Theater's matchmaker, Don Chargin. Fighters Theresa Kirby and Diane Syverson were also explicitly threatened.

The typed missive complete with several misspelled words and signed "THE BOXING FANS" had been postmarked in San Bernardino a week before the fight—and was received just four days before the bout was set to go on.[25]

The *Independent Press-Telegram* printed excerpts from the letter in its article on the threat: "If the (women) boxers aren't taken off the card, people like you, for putting on the card, and the women boxers will have to be killed. . . . This letter is by no means a joke."[26]

None of the threatened parties were deterred by the letter, which was turned over to the FBI for investigation. Kibby's father, notified of the letter's content, said, "I'm not worried about that. We have a contract to fulfill and we intend to honor it."[27]

Although a bit unnerving, the good news was that the bout was going to be televised live on KCOP (Channel 13) along with the main event—a ten-rounder between heavyweights Howard Smith, ranked four, and Dan Johnson.

Fight night came with a flourish. *Los Angeles Times* columnist John Hall began his report of the fight this way: "So it's come to this . . . Olympic ring announcer Jimmy Lennon: 'In this corner, in a black one-piece boxing ensemble.'" Hall continued,

> That was Diane "Blondee" Syverson being introduced en route to her split decision win over Princess Red Star in the "first-ever" at the old downtown fight club. . . . The women were livelier than heavyweight headliner Howard Smith, the crowd roared, TV ratings were the best and promoter Aileen Eaton says she will continue to feature females as often as she can make suitable matches.[28]

The ratings for the fight had taken a big jump during the time when the two women fought, outdistancing the men's bout and "all but rivaling the network telecast of the pro basketball playoffs the same night—at a more inviting time."[29]

Kibby's camp was less than happy with the split-decision outcome for obvious reasons. Asked for his reaction, Dave Kibby Sr. said, "It was the damndest thing I've seen in all my born days. . . . Theresa went straight in, around and in back and punched from the opening bell to the end." He continued, "In the third round she rained punches on Syverson and had her so confused she didn't know what was going on." Kibby also said that Don Chargin had told him, "It was Theresa's fight," but having been impressed by the professionalism shown by both fighters intended to "bring them back."

Regarding the death threat, Kibby noted there'd been extra security and that they had even been "met at the plane by former heavyweight boxer Mario Silva," who "escorted" them "to and from the arena." Security personnel were also on hand in the ring with two assigned to each corner. What made the night worthwhile—even with the loss—was Kibby's report that Aileen Eaton had told him, "I'm happy and proud the way things turned out. They were good weren't they."[30]

Aside from the two Kibby-Syverson fights, the month of May was a busy one for women's boxing.

The Hyatt Tahoe at Incline Village, Nevada, added its first women's bout to a fight card on May 5, 1975: a four-rounder featuring Caroline Svendsen and newcomer Ersi Arvizu, with referee Mills Lane in attendance. It proved to be Svendsen's only loss—a TKO in the second round of the fight.

In Portland, Maine, on May 20, 1975, not one but two female fights were held on a three-fight card. The first was between Cathy "Cat" Davis, a New Yorker who picked up the gauntlet from Jackie Tonawanda and "Lady Tyger" Trimiar to sue for the right to box in New York. She fought against Bobbi Shane with Davis taking it with a KO in the fourth round. The second female bout on the card was a three-rounder between Gwen Hibbler and Margie Dunson. Hibbler won the bout by unanimous decision, and went on to fight Lady Tyger the following year. As for Dunson, she fought Cat Davis no less than four times—losing each of the bouts.

The month of June also had a number of fights. Marion Bermudez, the karate champion who had defeated Karen Mast in the fall of 1975, fought a boxing match against Ersi Arvizu, defeating her by TKO in the third round at the Hyatt Tahoe on June 9. A bout between Diane Syverson and Kim May-bee was fought on June 12 on a card that included Dave Kibby—a card Theresa Kibby was originally scheduled to appear on.

Also in June, New York fighter Cathy "Cat" Davis fought a bout against Nickie Hanson, who was making her debut in what was scheduled to have been an eight-round bout at the Seattle Center Arena. Davis won the contest held on June 29 by KO at fifty-six seconds into the second round. The next night, on June 30, Theresa Kibby went back into the ring to fight a four-rounder against LaVonne Ludian, a Las Vegas blackjack dealer, at the Silver Slipper in Las Vegas, Nevada, the first of a regular series of women's bouts there. Kibby took the fight by unanimous decision. The Olympic, however, took a hiatus from putting women's boxing on their fight cards until September 30 when Marian "Lady Tyger" Trimiar fought a Japanese female boxer named Masako "Taka-Chan" Takatsuki, defeating her by unanimous decision after four rounds of boxing.

As matches were being scheduled and fought, fighters like Sue Fox were also seeking out gyms and trainers to gain the necessary experience to succeed in boxing. In Fox's case, it meant uprooting her life and moving to California. She began training at a gym in Westminster, California, but once there, had to go through the ritual of a beat-down in the ring with an experienced male bantamweight sparring "partner" to begin to gain any sort of acceptance at all. Acting as if it were the most natural thing in the world, she'd even agreed to spar with him the next day—in effect a second day of punishment—but he never showed up. Fox eventually learned the fighter had been told to knock her out. Fox's will of iron, and the kind of heart that had already buoyed her as a competitive karate fighter, meant that she had refused to go down. "I loved boxing that much," she said. As for the bantamweight, according to Fox "he was too humiliated to return to the gym."[31]

Fox's experience was in no way unique, and truthfully the proverbial beat-down was a known quantity on the men's boxing side—a technique to measure how tough fighters really were and whether they understood just how much of a commitment boxing really required. For women entering the ring with little to no experience, and not having had the opportunities to fight as youngsters, the entire process was a huge shock to the system. Women were also ignored in gyms, finding it hard to get attention or any sort of assistance during their early forays. If these fighters continued to show up, seek out sparring partners, and in all other ways persevere, they were more often than not received with some begrudging respect and, over time, could team up with the same trainers who worked with their male counterparts. It was by no means a perfect situation, but at least women were beginning to learn the intricacies of boxing rather than just walking into the ring as "fresh meat" for a beating.

The political side of women's participation in the sport was also never too far from the fore in this period. At the beginning of 1976, fighters "Lady Tyger" Trimiar and Gwen Gemini had appeared alongside former heavyweight champion Rocky Marciano on the *Mike Douglas Show*, a popular television talk show. The two women had come on the show to promote their four-rounder at the Arena in Philadelphia—the first sanctioned female bout in memory in Pennsylvania—but with Lady Tyger's newly shorn bald head they were something of a "freak show." The two women had previously fought a sanctioned exhibition boxing contest in Connecticut in December 1975, the first female bout in memory in that state. That bout went unscored, but Lady Tyger was considered to be the clear winner by everyone watching the fight. She was also deemed skilled. Gwen Gemini had little or no experience before entering the squared circle; however, she proved to be a quick study and by the following year was very well respected by her peers and considered one of the sport's best fighters.

The fact that the Philadelphia match at the Arena was planned as an exhibition did not deter the promoters from the usual hoopla surrounding fights. They also didn't shy from having Lady Tyger and Gwen Gemini appear on an eight-fight boxing card. Lady Tyger even put in an appearance at Joe Frazier's Gym in Philadelphia the day before the fight, which the press attended.

As a prerequisite for the fight, the Pennsylvania Athletic Commission required women to don an aluminum bra—a precaution against injuries to the breasts, although the impact on a fist, even a gloved one thrown at full force onto a chest protector, did not seem to be a consideration. Lady Tyger had refused to wear her aluminum bra during the bout.

"Don't tell anyone," she told reporter Gary Smith from the *Philadelphia Daily News* after the fight. "I'll get in trouble if they find that I didn't wear the aluminum bra we're supposed to wear. Please don't write that."

Smith did. Letting his readers in on the "secret," he wrote, "Sorry, Lady. Can't sit on a scoop like that." Smith went on to quote Gemini who said, "I WORE my aluminum bra," having clunked on it making a "loud knocking sound."

The Pennsylvania State Athletic Commission had, however, already determined not to allow a decision—opting to hold off until the commission decided further on which boxing rules were to apply to women's bouts. As with their previous bout the month before, the fight was called a "no contest." In the eyes of the crowd and other boxing aficionados, however, Lady Tyger won handily, showing off her superior boxing skills and some flourishes including an "Ali shuffle."

Smith's article was less interested in any skills Lady Tyger might have shown and continued in a bemused and nearly feckless tone as he turned his attentions to Gwen Gemini:

> Another reporter approached, searching for the social significance of two women boxing, digging to see if the soul of a women's libber lurked beneath Gwen Gemini's aluminum bra.
> "What IS women's lib, anyway?" asked Gemini. . . . "I love to stay in the kitchen to cook. . . . I'd cook myself to death."[32]

Bob Wright, a sportswriter with a boxing beat for the *Philadelphia Evening Bulletin*, wrote a piece that began by intoning a "but why?" query about Lady Tyger's shorn head. "Because it's me. Clean, unique. And it's very convenient."

To the "Why fight?" question she offered, "I don't fight, I box. I'm an athlete and this is my sport." As for being "unladylike," she said, "Men! I'm a lady. You can be a lady and be an athlete too."

He did, however, give her the opportunity to espouse her perspective on women's rights, including the fact that she'd voted no on the Equal Rights Amendment because "I found out at the last minute and didn't really know what it was all about." She continued:

> Mostly I'm for equal rights for people. I think anybody should be able to do anything they're able to do. As a girl, I haven't been able to get all the exposure and experience guys get boxing amateurs. But I think when it comes to where we can get the same background; you'll find a lady can do the job just as well as a man.[33]

While not all female boxers shaved their heads or were clear in their perspectives on the issues of the day, the inanity of the questions was vexing at best. Underlying them was the discomfort with the continued push against the legal barriers to full unfettered participation in all aspects of society.

In boxing in particular, those arguments also became nuanced in the "jargon" of boxing lore. Were women practicing "science" or were they merely brawling—or worse, "cat fighting?" This sort of question was sometimes at the heart of whether to legalize female boxing. The California Athletic Commission had raised just such issues in their rather public deliberation on whether to sanction women's boxing. The queries, however, very clearly revealed the biases of the commission members. As an example, one commissioner adjudged that female fighters were less aggressive because of concerns about their appearance. Such opinions played out in the press, as did the general castigation of all female boxers as a bunch of "women's libbers"—a euphemism for man-hating troublemakers or worse.

Not to be lost, though, was the fact that many of the women were not particularly skilled. And that was putting it kindly. From the point of view of the boxing fan who'd come to an arena to watch a fight card with every expectation that the skills the boxers displayed would be at least adequate, seeing fighters flail around the ring with no science was painful to watch. Throwing gender into the mix made it that much more unpalatable to a subset of fight fans who reacted whenever a fighter was perceived as missing a certain level of competence. One retired boxer who had been at the Pineda v. Maybee fight put it this way: "Those girls were dragging it; you can't change the rules for them; they sell fights here, and it's a fraud if they don't produce what they promise. Make 'em fight proper; let 'em get in there and kill each other."[34]

WOMEN'S BOXING LAS VEGAS STYLE

They're real pros. . . . When the girls fight it's SRO. They are worth the $250 apiece, plus expenses, for the four-rounders. I know one thing: When they fight it's on the dead level and they're in shape.
—Mrs. Bill Miller, promoter, Silver Slipper Casino, Las Vegas, 1977[35]

By the fall of 1976, there were a considerable number of women who were fighting with some regularity in regional pockets of the United States. Venues in the state of Nevada in particular were finding an upside to featuring women's bouts: more bodies to fill the seats at the fights, to buy drinks, and to play in the casinos.

Boxer LaVonne Ludian, who'd lost her debut bout against Theresa Kibby in June at the Silver Slipper Casino in Las Vegas, began to appear regularly on fight cards at various venues in Nevada.

Ludian faced a series of female fighters making their debuts on the Wednesday night fight shows at the Silver Slipper beginning on September 15. She also appeared at the Hyatt Tahoe and the Sahara Tahoe in their regular shows. Ludian's many appearances in the ring quickly pushed her record to 6-1 when she faced Kibby again on December 8, 1976, at the Silver Slipper. She lost for the second time to Kibby by unanimous decision—but it didn't keep her from a spot on the January 5, 1977, card against Andrea Chandler, whom she trounced for the second time with a first-round KO. (Their previous fight had been at the Hyatt Tahoe in October.)

The interest in women's boxing in Nevada had started with Caroline Svendsen's first fight. In fact, the Silver Slipper, under the promotional hand of Bill Miller, had put on the casino's first women's bout on October 22, 1975, one month after Svendsen's first bout in the state. The contest was a four-rounder between Britisher Tansy "Baby Bear" James and Aggie Henry, with James getting the nod on points. It was a debut for both of them. Henry went on to fight against Ludian in November of 1976 at the Sahara Tahoe, losing to her by KO in the first round.

Bill Dickson, the promoter for the Hyatt Tahoe, began putting women on the fight cards at the urging of Caroline Svendsen's manager, Ted Walker, and as noted, the first fight was in May 1976. It's quite possible that there was an earlier bout, but if so, it did not appear in the official records. Dickson also put LaVonne Ludian on the card at the annual Gardnerville, Nevada, 4th of July celebration (held on July 10)—a four-rounder pitting her against Sharon Blain in her debut bout that Ludian took by KO. Taking on duties at the Silver Slipper in 1977, Dickson became the matchmaker responsible for the Wednesday night fight shows, including the female fighters under promoter Mrs. Bill Miller, who had taken over for her husband after his death by heart attack in 1976.

Many of the women in the shows were one-fight wonders, although some persevered through two, three, or more fights, becoming regulars with growing followings. Fighters such as bantamweight Karen Bennett, appearing in six shows between January and June 1977, was a particular favorite at the Silver Slipper. While Bennett lost her first two bouts—her debut, against Masako "Taka-Chan" Takatsuki, and her second against karate champion Marion Bermudez—she was hooked on boxing and won her next four fights with KO wins.

Takatsuki had been around boxing since getting her license as a trainer in Japan where she taught boxing at Tokyo's Saitama Chuo Boxing Gym in the early 1970s. A featherweight, she was the only woman licensed to train boxers by the Japan Boxing Commission after having successfully gained her boxing manager's license. She also made regular appearances in exhibition fights with men at Tokyo's famed Korakuen Hall.[36]

Written about in *Boxing Illustrated Magazine* in 1973, Takatsuki had received a challenge from Millie Golden—a California-based woman living in Anaheim with a light background in the sport—but nothing ever came of it.[37] Takatsuki eventually came to the United States in 1976 to gain her license to box women.[38] As noted, she lost her first bout in the United States to Lady Tyger Trimiar at the Olympic Theater on September 30, 1976, on points after four rounds of boxing, having taken a mandatory eight-count in the first round.

Sue Fox—who'd lost her rematch against Theresa Kibby in Missoula, Montana, at the first sanctioned female bout in that state, on October 23, 1976, by TKO in the third round—also began fighting at the Silver Slipper, the Sahara Tahoe, and the Hyatt Tahoe. By then, Fox had hooked up with Dee Knuckles who began managing her along with others who fought in Nevada in 1977 and 1978.

By March 1977, Don Riley, writing for the Knight Ridder news service, published a piece with the title "Women Boxers a Smash in Vegas." Riley posed several questions in his piece, among them, "Would you believe that recently a middleweight feminine swatter from California won the 'fighter of the month' honors?"

Likely he was referring to two separate welterweight bouts that had been called fights of the month: the February 2 fight between Sue Fox and Charlene Anthony at the Silver Slipper, which ended in a unanimous decision for Fox, and Fox's March 1 bout against LaVonne Ludian at the Hyatt Tahoe, which was called a draw. He also singled out Fox as the "red-headed pig-tailed southpaw swinger who throws 100 punches a round."

He published the startling fact that female boxers could "command $100 more per fight than their male preliminary counterparts." He backed up his claim by writing that a recent fight at the Silver Slipper "upstairs ballroom" was jammed with "1,100 fans" who'd shelled out "nearly $10,000 to watch the festivities which were clearly highlighted by the girls' bout."

Mrs. Bill Miller, who took credit for putting on the shows, told Riley:

> They're real pros. . . . When the girls fight it's SRO. They are worth the $250 apiece, plus expenses, for the four-rounders. I know one thing: When they fight it's on the dead level and they're in shape.[39]

The positive press was bringing attention to what had once been called a sideshow attraction in the mix of entertainment at the casinos. The economics of that sideshow were another matter, and women's boxing began to attract big-time promoters. According to Bill Dickson, Bob Arum of Top Rank, upon hearing the hoopla about women's boxing, came to the Silver Slipper to watch a bout. It happened to be the third matchup between LaVonne Ludian, who was becoming a major draw on the fight cards, and Princess Red Star Kibby.

Their two previous outings had ended in the win column for Kibby on points. For this go-round, Kibby had added a new weapon to her arsenal—she would switch to a southpaw stance at opportune moments during the fight. The bout itself was a regular Wednesday "Strip Fight of the Week" contest, although it was being promoted as a welterweight championship bout. Given Ludian's popularity and the moniker of a "title fight," the night's draw was $6,400, a record haul. The promoters even held up the start time to allow the maximum crowd to come into the ballroom. To garner even more publicity, promoter Tim Miller had put in a request to the Nevada State Athletic Commission to up the number of rounds to either five or six, with the argument that both fighters were experienced. Permission wasn't granted, so the women were held to the original four-rounder.

The fight, held on March 9, 1977, was "action-packed" from the start, and although Ludian was three inches taller with a longer reach, by the end of the fight she was said to have had two black eyes. The verdict after four rounds of boxing was a draw—to the consternation of the crowd of around eight hundred fight fans, who gave the win to Kibby. As one newspaper account put it, the verdict was "lustily booed" by the "standing room only" spectators.[40] Reporters and even Ludian's own team, if Kibby was to be believed, scored the fight in the win column for Princess Red Star. This included the UPI account, which gave Ludian "a slight edge in the opening round" due to her "lethal jab," but Kibby the other three for outworking Ludian by "land[ing] numerous left and right hooks and overhand rights."[41]

Princess Red Star was understandably upset, telling columnist Don Terbush, "They wanted to give me the [title] trophy but I said no. If it was really a draw I couldn't take the trophy."[42]

Whatever the actual scoring for the fight, Bill Dickson claimed that Bob Arum was "very impressed" with what he saw. Arum was so impressed that he spoke to Dickson about arranging for Ludian and Kibby to appear on the undercard of his upcoming Ernie Shavers versus Howard Smith fight at the Aladdin Hotel—to be televised nationally on *CBS Sports Spectacular*.[43] The card was to be broadcast on Saturday, April 16, 1977, at 4:30 p.m. (EST) and was also to include the pro debut of Olympic gold medalist Michael Spinks fighting Pat Barry. (It was eventually even on TV listings as the Women's Middleweight Championships.)

The Ludian-Kibby fight—a fourth rematch—would also come with an enormous payday. Both women would be paid $2,500—a record for professional women boxers as far as anyone knew—plus national exposure for the sport that was taking Las Vegas by storm. Also added to the fight was an additional women's undercard bout between Darlene Buckskin and Sue TL Fox. They, too, would be given a huge payday, but because of the difference in their weights, their bout was to be called an exhibition.

Within a few days, Top Rank disclosed it wanted to sign each of the four women to an exclusive one-year contract. According to the contract, each of them would not only fight on April 16 but also be offered the possibility of three additional fights with successive paydays of $4,000, $5,000, and $6,000. For fighters who at the time were earning a couple of hundred dollars a fight, that was extraordinary money and opportunity.[44]

Fighter LaVonne Ludian, in speaking about the offer some time later, told a reporter:

> Boxers have a short amount of time to make money. Especially as a female, I have a shorter amount of time. Why take 30 fights all over the country when I can get the same amount of money in three fights? You always have to think about a broken nose or a cut.[45]

On fight night at the Aladdin, the crowd was decidedly behind their hometown favorite, LaVonne Ludian, to win the Nevada State Women's Welterweight Championship. The fight, though, belonged to Princess Red Star from the moment of the opening bell. She "bobbed and weaved," slipped punches and swarmed Ludian with punches, later telling reporters that "sparring and . . . harder workouts really helped" her prepare for the fight.

Kibby won over the crowd from the second round and by the fourth had "stunned [Ludian] up against the ropes with a right hand to the face," and she was given the unanimous decision at the end of the fourth and final round—along with the championship.[46] Brief notices about the fight in the press the next day noted that she had "pounded out a unanimous decision."[47]

What went unreported was that "Ludian had the flu and was very ill . . . [but] fought anyway." According to Sue Fox, the response from the television-viewing public was "negative" leading Top Rank to "later withdraw their offer"—a huge setback for all four women.[48] Arum had been quoted as saying, "Women's boxing is ridiculous. Women should be home making babies."[49]

Years later, in 1987, Arum claimed Ludian started crying from a blow—embarrassing him and the CBS executives watching the bout:

> Women's boxing is ridiculous. I promoted one bout for CBS-TV in 1977. It was between an Indian woman [Princess Red Star Kibby] and a woman casino dealer [LaVonne Ludian] in the Aladdin Hotel in Las Vegas. When [Princess Red Star] hit the dealer in the nose the dealer stopped fighting and started crying all over the place. The people booed and the network complained and I swore that Saturday afternoon that I'd never promote another women's bout.[50]

Arum reiterated his perspective in 1994, having remained true to his word; however, he did begin to promote women's boxing shortly thereafter when other promoters' fights began to hit it big-time on pay-per-view.

The fight scene in Nevada recovered quickly from the unfortunate turn of events surrounding the Top Rank promotion of the Ludian-Kibby fight. Bouts were still as popular as ever. Sue TL Fox, along with fighter Gwen Gemini, who had been meeting with success boxing in the Nevada and California boxing shows, both appeared on Tom Snyder's late-night program, *Tomorrow*, in July of that year. For the episode, a boxing ring was set up in the studio and the two put on an exhibition fight before joining their manager, Dee Knuckles, on camera to talk about the sport.

About midway through 1978, however, the fight scene in Nevada began to slow down. Bill Dickson recalled that there were problems getting fighters, and those who did fight were often badly mismatched. Fights between women were still occurring in other locales—including California, Oregon, Illinois, Ohio, Utah, and Texas—which kept the sport alive, although the Cincinnati Boxing and Wrestling Commission "refus[ed] to all women to box because of 'the difference in their anatomy to men,' in January 1977 even though female fights were legal elsewhere in the state."[51]

Sue Fox, speaking of the end of her professional career in this period, said she "couldn't get any fights except tough, tough, fights." Elaborating, she said, "When I first went into boxing I was scientific. At the end of my career I was a little slugger. I [even] had my jaw knocked out three times." Tired of the struggle waged out of the ring to get recognition and a fair shake, she also began to worry about her future. After three years in the mix she hung up her gloves, in part because she didn't want to risk further injury and because it was time to pursue a "real" job. For her, that meant joining law enforcement where she enjoyed a successful career for many years. [52]

Las Vegas's position as the center of women's boxing continued for some period to come. Printed ratings for the top women's boxers began appearing in *Boxing Illustrated* magazine. According to Sue Fox the ratings listed under the heading of the Women's Boxing Federations were based on the relative popularity of the fighters and were selected by a group in Las Vegas that included Vern Stevenson, who later formed the Women's World Boxing Association (WBBA) followed by the International Women's Boxing Association (IWBA) a few years later. They also didn't just include the names of fighters in the Nevada scene—although many, particularly in the welterweight division of those early rankings, often fought there.

By November 1977 a sampling of the ranked boxers included such fighters as Margie Dunson from Maine, listed as the welterweight champion (though this was questionable because of her many losses to Cat Davis). Others in the division included Diane Syverson, Theresa Kibby, and LaVonne Ludian.

In all, there were about thirty-five fighters listed in the November 1977 ratings. The ranks swelled up to around forty by August of 1978, and by April of 1979 the listing had grown to some fifty names, reflecting the changing landscape of professional women's boxing. This included a growing number of states that were legalizing female participation in sport, which in turn created more opportunities for fights and the potential for more women to enter the ranks. [53]

THE AMATEURS: ROUND ONE

The controversies surrounding women's boxing continued fairly unabated despite a growing professional boxing scene. Problems still swirled around jurisdictions that refused to allow women to fight and the sensationalism surrounding those who managed to win court cases. Opportunities to fight in the amateurs were also proving difficult, even though a healthy amateur boxing program would be the best avenue to allow young women the opportunity to learn their craft under the supervision of trainers, coaches, and the strict set of rules that governed amateur contests.

One case involving an eleven-year-old girl named Amber "Jim" Hunt from Salt Lake City, Utah, drew a lot of notoriety nationwide. Hunt's amateur boxing career called into question not only "girls' boxing" but also the point at which sensationalizing such endeavors becomes exploitative, especially when it comes to children.

Amber Jim Hunt was mad for boxing. In December 1976 she began making her way through the local junior Golden Gloves, bloodying the nose of her first opponent and knocking out her second opponent one week later "at 55 seconds into the second round." She also made it into a national press that couldn't resist her fondness for the kind of poetry Muhammad Ali loved to espouse prior to his bouts. She recited one before her second fight:

> You asked me who?
> Freddie's his name.
> He'll go out in round two.

Hunt had come with her brothers to a boxing training program for kids, and as her trainer, Mike Bullock, said, "They quit. She stayed." Hunt, who once told a reporter she was a reincarnation of Babe Didrikson, also excelled at other sports including track and swimming, but as she said, "I like to beat up boys, to show them what a girl can do." Her father, Jack Hunt, a practicing Buddhist, also spoke to reporters, telling them she'd initially gotten into sports at the age of seven because she was overweight. He was also identified as being unemployed and on welfare.[54]

The following January Amber Hunt hit the national press—but not for her boxing prowess, which included an 8-0 record. Beginning in early December she had struck up a correspondence with convicted murderer Gary Gilmore shortly before his execution, telling the press she wrote him "because I thought he might be lonely."

He had given Hunt and her family over $1,200 worth of gifts, including a "complete 8-millimeter movie outfit," so that Jack Hunt could take movies of Amber's fights to help "refine her style." Asked about the gifts, Hunt said, "Until Gary started helping out, we were too poor to give Amber the things she needed for her career."[55]

In mid-February, Hunt hit the national press again when she participated on a local Golden Gloves-PAL card. She entered the tournament with a 9-0 record, but lost a three-round decision to her eleven-year-old opponent. The decided crowd favorite among the three thousand fans viewing the fight at the State Fairgrounds Coliseum in Utah, she wore a shirt emblazoned with the words "Knock 'em out for me," the last words Gary Gilmore had written to her. Clearly disappointed, Hunt said, "Everybody loses. You can't win all the time, but it [defeat] doesn't feel good." As for the shirt, Hunt told the press it was her father's idea.[56]

By April Hunt had amassed a 13-4 record with ten knockouts. She still professed her love of the sport and stated her goal was to fight in the Olympics. As she readied to appear in an exhibition bout on April 26, 1977, at the Intermountain AAU Senior Boxing Championships, however, the AAU banned her from further participation in the sport. The ban included any regular competition or exhibition matches held under the auspices of the AAU, although she did actually win a unanimous decision over her opponent in a bout fought at the event despite the ban.

At issue was a letter sent by National AAU Junior Olympic Committee chairman Jerry Dusenberry to Harry Miller, the chairman of the Intermountain AAU Boxing Committee. In it, Dusenberry stated his belief that Hunt was being used as a "drawing card." He went on to write, "There is no need to 'circus-ize' or prostitute our sport to generate interest" what with the "excellent caliber of boxing in your area as well as competent coaches."

It was true that Hunt had been attracting attention as a fighter. Her determination, grit, and fortitude were of interest to people and she had developed a true base of cheering fans—win or lose. From the perspective of the AAU, however, "Permitting a girl to participate in the Junior Olympic or AAU program is unequivocally contrary to the AAU rule and unacceptable." Going even further Dusenberry rehashed the notion that repeated blows might cause "breast cancer as a result of trauma to the mammary glands" and that "severe force to the abdominal or pelvic area is extremely dangerous to a pregnancy."

Although Dusenberry acknowledged that it was unlikely that Hunt was pregnant, he nonetheless added, "But you and I know better. Open sexuality is increasing among younger people today. There are increasingly reports of pre-adolescent abortions at most medical centers."

Hunt's family came into possession of the AAU letter sometime in the late spring or early summer. Reading it, they were aghast at the tone of it and the implications that an eleven-year-old girl might be sexually active. They hired Ronald Stanger—the lawyer who represented Gary Gilmore—to look into filing suit against the AAU. A suit was eventually filed in November in the U.S. District Court of Utah seeking "$100,000 for punitive damages, injunctive release and attorney's fees," but it went nowhere.[57] The underlying issues, though, were never truly dealt with. On the one hand was the question of whether an eleven-year-old girl had been unfairly exploited by her family and the local boxing officials. On the other was the question of the spurious science that was underlying the AAU's refusal to allow girls and women to compete in its amateur programs.

The state of California had dealt with the pregnancy issues—as had other jurisdictions—by having fighters attest to their not being pregnant or even menstruating on the day of a fight. Some states were even more invasive, requiring medical evidence or examinations, but the net effect was to sanction women's professional fighting. When it came to breast "health," states were requiring breast protectors—which were uncomfortable and had cost at least one fighter a bout when she began adjusting one of the "cups" midfight and got "clocked"—but, again, women were still allowed to fight.

Whatever the outcome with Amber Hunt, the fact that she boxed at all was impressive to some. Writing twenty years later, a woman who had been the same age as Amber remembers feeling that she and her friends were "the children of a new era [who] aspired to greatness." "That message was reinforced by the newspaper I read. There were stories about amazing kids like Amber Hunt, 11, who was boxing with boys," a feat that resonated with her throughout her life.[58]

Two other jurisdictions in the late 1970s or early '80s also contended with AAU regulations with mixed outcomes. As early as 1975 women began boxing on the campus of the University of Minnesota at Duluth in a program started by Bill Paul, a student and former Air Force regional heavyweight champion. Within a couple of years Paul had about fifteen or so regulars who came to his classes. In speaking with the press about it in June 1977, he told a reporter, "I believe we had the first female boxing bouts in the country on June 1, 1975, at the Duluth campus."[59] While not exactly true, they were likely the first bouts at the college.

Later in the summer, Paul, along with three of his fighters, Colleen McCann, Mari Stack, and Sue Carlson, started the International Women's Professional Boxing Association (IWPBA), hoping to convince Minnesota to legalize women's professional boxing and promote fight cards. Not too much had come of the IWPBA, but the core group of amateur boxers in the original class were continuing to practice at the University of Minnesota. In the spring, Paul attempted to get a group of boxers onto an AAU boxing card but was prevented from doing so. He was told, "They can have their own bouts to determine state champions in May"; however, the group was described as "bitter" about it and planned to protest by pairing two of the fighters, Joan Marcolt and Debbie "Ginger" Kaufman, to battle "for the state female bantamweight championship."[60]

As the month wore on, the IWPBA, representing the women, negotiated with the AAU director, Harry Davis. At issue was the gaining of permission to stage an all-female amateur tournament sponsored by the University of Minnesota's women's boxing club under the auspices of the AAU. The date picked was May 12, 1975.

Given the AAU's track record in other jurisdictions, there was not a lot of hope that it would agree to allow the bouts to go on. In late April, however, the AAU acceded to the request and helped to charter the IWBA, under whose auspices the tournament was allowed to go forward. This was a first for women's amateur boxing, although it did not necessarily translate into other similar organizations nationwide.

Another case involved Jill Lafler, a nineteen-year-old student at a local community college in Lansing, Michigan, who was interested in pursuing opportunities to box in the amateurs. As a member of the Lansing Community College Boxing Club, she already had one successful sanctioned amateur match—defeating her male opponent by unanimous decision at the end of their three-round bout. She loved winning and wanted more of it, and as she said later, "There is professional boxing for women, but you can't just say, 'Hey, I'm a pro.'"[61]

With one win under her belt, the 106-pound fighter sought to compete in the Golden Gloves—then an all-male boxing competition—against men. There was nothing on the books in the state of Michigan that prohibited male-female boxing contests. The rub was the state's claim to have adopted an amateur boxing rule barring female participation, promulgated by the U.S.A. Amateur Boxing Federation, that had gone into effect in Michigan three years prior—and there was cause for some dispute as to whether the ruling had in fact ever been adopted.

The national press gained wind of her case with a story picked up by the Associated Press with the headline "Battles Sex Bias In Ring," and by United Press International, under the headlines "Woman Boxer Fears No Court, No Man" and "Woman Boxer Not Afraid of Men."

When asked why she wanted to enter the Golden Gloves, Lafler replied simply, "Because there is no other competition around."[62]

Once Lafler's application was filed, however, the deputy director of the state's Department of Licensing and Regulation, Virgina Zeeb, had no problem denying Lafler the right to compete, stating, "I do not want to preside over the first girl in the state of Michigan, or in the world, dropping dead in the ring."[63]

Pushing aside the hyperbole of Zeeb's comments, Jill Lafler, with the encouragement of her coach, sought out attorney Paul Rosenbaum, a Golden Gloves winner, a former Michigan State house member, and a promoter affiliated with burgeoning Toughwoman and Toughman contests in the state. Rosembaum jumped at the opportunity to take the case on, and in speaking of a planned lawsuit against the ban, was quoted as saying, "Here's a person who wants to fight, knows how to fight, and the only reason she can't is because she's a woman."[64]

At first, it seemed that Jill Lafler might prove successful in her bid to compete, when a temporary restraining order was issued by Michigan's Ingham County Circuit Court suspending the final outcome of the Golden Gloves championship in her weight category—flyweight—pending the outcome of her case. In its ruling, the court alleged that Lafler was being discriminated against on the basis of sex discrimination in violation of the equal rights clauses of the United States and Michigan Constitutions, the federal

Civil Rights Act of 1964, and the Michigan Civil Rights Act, known locally as the Elliot-Larsen Act.

The Michigan Athletic Control Board and the other defendants reacted immediately to the state court's ruling by moving the case to a federal jurisdiction. When the court papers were filed they requested that the judge dissolve the restraining order, which would allow the Golden Gloves competition in the flyweight division to continue.

By moving the case to a federal court the defendants effectively deflected the circuit court's support of Jill Lafler's discrimination suit until the decision—to either keep the restraining order in place or lift the ban—was resolved. What this meant for Jill Lafler was a waiting game—plus keeping herself at her 106-pound weight and an intensive training regimen.

Within days the case was placed on the docket of the U.S. District Court for the Western District of Michigan and assigned to Judge Wendell Miles, who issued his ruling on February 9, 1982—one day prior to the Golden Gloves flyweight championship round.

Judge Miles issued an eight-page opinion dissolving the restraining order effectively barring Jill Lafler from the 1982 Golden Gloves competition, while leaving the door open for further litigation.

The ruling by Justice Miles cited a 1977 court case requiring that a plaintiff have the substantial likelihood of success on the merits and proof of suffering irreparable harm. In Justice Miles's opinion, the plaintiff, Jill Lafler, would not succeed on her merits—meaning she had very little chance to win—nor would she suffer irreparable harm, even though she would be denied immediate access to the amateur experience she needed to adequately prepare her for a professional boxing career.

As for her discrimination case, Judge Miles wrote that because her application to compete was to the Golden Gloves, a private organization—which followed state and federal rules barring mixed-gender amateur competition, previous court rulings, and even Title IX regulations calling for separate male and female teams or programs for contact sport—this meant that the basis for her case was questionable.

Judge Miles stated: "Separate competition for men and women is even more likely to be constitutionally permissible in the context of a contact sport such as boxing."[65] He continued, "It is unrealistic to believe that women could enter the sport of boxing and operate under the same rules with no detrimental effect on the safety of the participants."

The court ruling was widely reported in the press and came as a tremendous blow to Jill Lafler and her cause. "I don't know what happened up there or why it took the turn it did," Jill Lafler said, adding, "It went the opposite of the way I thought."[66] The door had been left open for her to continue litigation in federal court, but after careful consideration, she opted to work with Dennis Sprandel of the Michigan chapter of the U.S. Amateur Boxing

Federation, having extracted a promise that Sprandel would work hard to form a separate sanctioning body for women. This followed on the heels of the state-based Michigan Athletic Board of Control's unanimous decision to institute a special set of rules for women's boxing.

Jill Lafler's dreams of amateur competition had come to an end with the concurrent announcement that she'd just learned of her pregnancy, and while she had not filed a motion to dismiss her lawsuit, her days of fighting for equal opportunity for women in the boxing ring had come to an end.

Image from a Chalcidian black-figured hydria depicting Atalanta wrestling Peleus at the funerary games of King Pelias. The background shows the prize of the duel, the skin, and the head of the Calydonian boar. Dated between c. 540 and c. 530 BCE. Staaliche Antikensammiungen (Bavarian State Collections of Antiques), Munich, Germany.

From the Tower manuscript, combat manual from between the late 13th and early 14th centuries depicting defensive and offensive sword techniques between a woman named Walpurgis and a priest. National Museum of Arms and Armour, U.K., online collection. Copyright Royal Armouries.

Hattie Stewart, 1884. Known as the female "John L. Sullivan," Hattie Stewart began boxing in the early 1880s. She toured the country in boxing shows and boxed both men and women. She was prominently featured in the *Police Gazette* along with a handful of other female pugilists from the era. *National Police Gazette*, Boxrec.com.

Glass plate negative of two women boxing at Freshwater, Australia, photographer possibly Arthur Phillips, 1895. Phillips Glass Plate Negative Collection, Powerhouse Museum, Sydney, Australia. Gift of the Estate of Raymond W. Phillips, 2008.

Boxing was first introduced as a sport during the third Olympic Games held at the St. Louis World's Fair in 1904. While not invited to participate, two female boxers put on an exhibition match during the games. Women did not officially compete as boxers until the London Games held in August 2012. IOC Olympic Museum Collection.

Fraulein Kussin (left) and Mrs. Rose Edwards boxing match on March 7, 1912. George Grantham Bain Collection/Library of Congress.

Eighteen-year-old English boxer Barbara Buttrick (right) in training with a male sparring partner at Mickey Wood's Mayfair Gym, London, February 4, 1949. She is training for an exhibition bout at the Kilburn Empire, despite protests from leading figures in the boxing world, who are opposed to women's boxing. Buttrick went on to world championship titles in the flyweight and bantamweight classes and later founded the WIBF. Photo by Keystone/Hulton Archive/Getty Images.

Jo Ann Hagen (left) handed Barbara Buttrick her only professional loss. The two competed at Victoria Pavilion, Calgary, Alberta, Canada. This image was originally published in *The Albertan* on September 11, 1954. Glenbow Museum Archives/ Glenbow Museum, Calgary, Alberta, Canada. Photographer Jack De Lorme.

Jackie Tonawanda working out at Gleason's Gym, near the old Madison Square Garden, in 1974. Rogers Photo Archive/Keystone Media.

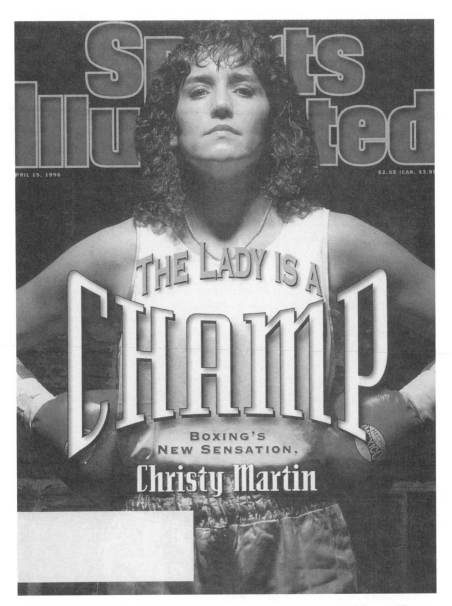

Christy Martin was the first female boxer to appear on the cover of *Sports Illustrated*. The April 15, 1996, edition of the magazine appeared on the stands shortly after her triumph in the ring. *Sports Illustrated*/Getty Images. Photographer Brian Smith.

Christy Martin sporting a bloody nose after her triumphant win against Deirdre Gogerty on March 16, 1996. The six-round fight was promoted by Don King and appeared on the undercard of a pay-per-view extravaganza featuring a Mike Tyson heavyweight championship bout. Hulton Archive/Getty Images. Photographer Al Bello/Allsport.

Former IFBA featherweight champion Bonnie Canino and her trainer, Burt Rodriguez, during Canino's title defense against Canadian contender Nora Daigle. Canino won the ten-round "Satin Storm" fight by unanimous decision. The bout was held on June 26, 1998, in Las Vegas, Nevada. Photographer Mary Ann Owen; used by permission of the photographer.

Boxer and author Kate Sekules training at Gleason's Gym, Brooklyn, NY, in 1997. Magnum Photos. Photographer Bruce Davidson.

Former kickboxing champion Lucia Rijker (left) from the Netherlands became an unstoppable force in women's boxing, ending her career with a perfect 17-0 boxing record. She defeated Diane Dutra with a third-round TKO in a bout at the Hard Rock Hotel and Casino in Las Vegas, Nevada, on August 8, 1999. Rijker also appeared in the 2004 film *Million Dollar Baby* as Billie "The Blue Bear." Photographer Mary Ann Owen.

Boxer Layla McCarter lands a huge left hook against Victoria Cisneros. It was McCarter's first outing after breaking her hand ten months earlier against Canadian boxer Jelena Mrdjenovich. McCarter won her bout against Cisneros by unanimous decision at the Sky Ute Casino in Ignacio, Colorado, on April 1, 2006. Photographer Mary Ann Owen.

Boxer Melissa Hernandez lands a straight right against Lisa Brown. The two fought at the Shaw Conference Centre in Edmonton, Alberta, Canada, for the WIBA Super Bantamweight Championship title. Hernandez won the hard-fought ten-rounder by unanimous decision on November 4, 2006. Photographer Mary Ann Owen.

Ann Saccurato (right) defeated Canadian hometown favorite Jelena Mrdjenovich in the main-event fight at the Shaw Conference Center in Edmonton, Alberta, Canada, for the vacant WBC Lightweight Championship title. Saccurato had a 10-1-2 record coming into the fight, against Mrdjenovich's 18-1. Photographer Mary Ann Owen.

Chevelle Hallbeck (right) is renowned for her punching power and physique. Hallbeck's career began in 1997 and has spanned two generations of fighters. She defeated her opponent, Terri Blair, by unanimous decision in an eight-round bout on July 2, 2007, at the Pechanga Resort and Casino in Temecula, California. Photographer Mary Ann Owen.

Women's boxing star Mia St. John holding her WBC Female Light Middleweight Championship belt. She defeated Christy Martin by unanimous decision on August 14, 2012, and Martin announced her retirement from boxing shortly after the fight. The two first met on December 12, 2002, when Martin won by unanimous decision. Photographer Mary Ann Owen.

Olympic gold medal winner Claressa Shields (right) competing in the National PAL Tournament in 2011. Shields was sixteen and won the middleweight title. She is shown delivering a straight right to former champion Andrecia Wasson. Photographer Sue Jaye Johnson.

Chapter Eight

These Ladies Love the Ring

You know that in five years of research at the University of Arizona, they've found that women's pain tolerance is higher than men's and that their leg strength, pound for pound, is stronger than men. It all revolves around child-birth. I tell you, women's boxing is going to catch on.
—Lady Tyger Trimiar, 1980[1]

I always respected women and have been a supporter of women's lib. But in the boxing ring, no. I can't stand to see women cutting each other up and spilling blood in the ring.
—Floyd Patterson, commissioner, New York State Athletic Commission, 1978[2]

As the decade of the 1970s came to a close, it was hard to believe that women's boxing had come so far in such a short span of time. Multiple jurisdictions had legalized the sport and women were successfully pushing the limits—even extending bouts from four round to upwards of ten rounds. Women were continuing to sue for the right to box in those locales where boxing was still restricted to only men, and there was a sense that their lawsuits would eventually prevail, given the recent track record.

Watching Barbra Streisand on the big screen in her comedic turn as a boxing manager in her 1979 film *The Main Event* may well have seemed incongruent, but—if nothing else—it was a commentary on the changes that had been wrought over the decade: Women had gained the right to be inside velvet ropes and were planning to stay.

Even public television had broached the subject when they aired a docu-mentary by filmmaker Jane Warrenbrand entitled *Cat, A Woman Who Fought Back*, tracing Cathy "Cat" Davis's journey to become a licensed boxer in the state of New York. The film went so far as to show Cat in the ring—giving audiences who might otherwise never have observed a gloved female bout the opportunity to watch a women's fight in action.

New women's boxing organizations sprang up: conferring championship titles, promoting opportunities, and advocating for the sport. Those female fighters who had managed to stay in the game through the late 1970s were now poised to benefit by winning championships and finding themselves with a greater number of venues to ply their trade.

By the early 1980s, however, the women's side of boxing began to perceptibly fall off the radar. It was no longer a new sensation, and while fights still played out in local markets and even ended up on television, there seemed very little indication that the sport would continue to grow in popularity. Women's boxing was also succumbing to the kinds of controversies that had long plagued the men's side of the game, even touching women's boxing's first national star, Cathy "Cat" Davis.

Such things as fixing fights, mismatches, overstating fight records, and other unsavory aspects of the business infiltrated women's boxing, sullying whatever positives there were in the sport, and making it more difficult to gain recognition and acceptance. The major promoters of the day also steered clear of women's fights, questioning the quality of the fighting and the amount of money that could be made. The downturn in the economy and a falloff in support for men's boxing may also have played into the calculus of the decline.

The period at the end of the 1970s and the beginning of the 1980s also saw the rise of Toughman and Toughwoman fighting contests, pitting novice boxers against each other (some of whom were less than novices, having had no training whatsoever). As a test of strength, fortitude, and as some would say, stupidity, the contests were wildly popular. For many women they offered an opportunity to actually box (after a fashion), and had tremendous appeal for women fighters who were having difficulty finding boxing matches—not only for the fun of it, but as a chance to earn cash prizes.

As the decade progressed, and the fitness craze that had begun in the 1970s began to truly take hold, boxing also became popular as a form of exercise with more and more gyms offering opportunities for women to hit the bag. This included some of the more serious boxing gyms that found the general decline of interest in boxing meant there were fewer men coming into the gyms. By opening their doors to a new female clientele these gyms were not only bringing in a greater cash flow, but also catering to an entirely untapped market of enthusiasm for the sport—an enthusiasm that was to have an effect on gym-based competition as it entered the "white collar" era.

THE GOOD AND THE BAD: BOXING'S FIRST "GOLDEN" GIRL

Cathy "Cat" Davis began making a name for herself in boxing in 1976. Originally from Winnfield, Louisiana, she had fenced at Louisiana State University and won several championships (some sources claim she went to the University of New Orleans).[3] The five-foot, ten-inch blonde with Farrah Fawcett hair initially got interested in boxing to cross-train for fencing and as a form of exercise. She moved to New York to further her fencing opportunities and for a hoped-for fencing scholarship, and eventually met up with trainer Sal Algieri who coached youngsters at a local PAL club in Hopewell Junction, New York, about thirty minutes south of Poughkeepsie.

Algieri, a former boxer with a checkered past (having admitted to taking a fall in at least one fight in Sydney, Australia), had been a spectator at the 1975 fight in Connecticut between Lady Tyger and Gwen Gemini. A few weeks after the fight, Algieri put out a call—published in the *Evening News* in nearby Beacon, New York—"recruiting women between the ages of 17 and 22" who were "interested in becoming professional women boxers." He told the paper he believed "women's professional boxing will become a big thing in the United States in the near future."[4] While he subsequently denigrated the skills of both Lady Tyger and Gwen Gemini, telling a reporter "both of them didn't know what they were doing," he had been clearly hooked on the potential of bringing female boxers into the sport as professionals at the time he placed the notice in the paper.[5]

Responding to an inquiry from Cat Davis, Algieri was immediately smitten and began training her at his gym in Hopewell Junction. Given that Davis was already a competitive athlete who'd been an admitted tomboy growing up, she caught on very quickly, impressing Algieri with her work ethic and her strong left jab.

Soon Algieri began arranging exhibition fights for her. He also helped set up the Women's Boxing Federation (WBF)—in part (as has been substantiated) to promote Davis's fights and provide a mechanism to confer championship titles, a very smart bit of promotion. Al "Scoop" Gallello, a former boxer, well-known boxing "operator," and Sal Algieri's former manager when he fought in the pros, was tapped to head the WBF while Algieri was listed as a consultant.[6]

As previously noted, Davis fought Bobbi Shane in Portland, Maine, in May 1976—winning by KO. Although it was not Davis's debut fight, it is the first fight listed on her current record of fights. Unofficially, she had also fought a woman named Jean Silver, defeating her by KO in the second round, although not much else is known.

Her next official contest was negotiated as an eight-round "championship" match in Seattle, Washington, against Nickie Hanson (or Hansen), allegedly an Arizona-based fighter. A press release issued before the fight by the promoter Global Productions Limited had claimed that Davis and Hanson were "two of the finest women fighters in the world," and further claimed that Nickie Hanson had a 7-0 record coming into the bout. (Very little other information has been uncovered about Hanson except that she also lost a fight to Davis the following April in Pennsylvania.)

The press release also provided further information on the WBF, noting it as "a recently-formed organization created to bring some form to the rapidly-growing area of women's boxing." It also claimed the WBF's four directors were "former featherweight champ Willie Pep, Al Braverman, Paddy Flood and Dee Knuckles" with the note that Knuckles also served "as co-chairman for the WBF's West Coast affairs."[7]

The crowd at the venue numbered eight thousand on fight night, with a lot of expectant fans eager to see an eight-round women's title bout. Hanson didn't last long, though, going down by KO in the second round of the fight to give Davis the WBF lightweight title. Once Davis's win was made official by the ring announcer, she was "presented with a five-foot-high championship trophy" conferred upon her by the WBF.[8]

Prior to and after Davis's fight with Hanson, Algieri put together other matches for her, for which she was getting paid anywhere from $200 to $500 per fight, plus expenses in some instances. By this point the two had also become romantically involved—their intended nuptials were announced in a Liz Smith gossip column, a testament to how quickly Davis's star rose.

Boxing Promoter Lou Duva, looking to see what women's boxing was all about, took an interest in Davis shortly after the Hanson fight in June. He had seen Davis knock out Las Vegas-based fighter Joanna Lutz after only nineteen seconds of the second round of a bout held at the Silver Slipper.[9] Duva had been struck by the exuberant fight fans that were overflowing the second-floor venue and was eager to translate some of that success to women's fights on the East Coast. He had it in mind to put together an exhibition bout between Cat Davis and Arizonian Jean Lange (the same Jean Lange who fought Carol Svendsen).[10] The plan was to hold the event outdoors at the Hinchliffe Stadium in Patterson, New Jersey, and then contact Athletic Commissioner Althea Gibson to see about getting the bout sanctioned on that basis.

Gibson, who'd been taught to box by her father and had already weighed in on women's boxing in California, agreed to give it a go. Before a crowd of twenty-four hundred excited fans, Davis and Lange squared off in a four-round exhibition that was a co-feature of the main event.

Lange proved no match for Davis and was felled by a stiff left jab that had followed "two rights to Lange's chin." The combination of punches sent Lange to the canvas twenty seconds into the second round. A reporter speaking with Gill Fuller, an associate of Althea Gibson, quoted him in a less-than-flattering article about the bout: "[Gibson] said she would have to take a long look at any other women to be sure they were really fighters before she sanctioned any other bouts."

Duva, on the other hand, was ecstatic, while his son Don Duva gushed, "We had one of our largest crowds ever because of the women."[11] Years later, Lou Duva said that Althea Gibson and the then New York State boxing commissioner James Farley Jr. met in a room at the stadium after the fight to talk about whether to confer licenses on female fighters. Duva said, "I honestly thought it was better for women to go into the amateur shows or the Olympics rather than go right into professional [boxing]. They needed to have more experience. Then you could go ahead and issue them a license."[12]

Davis, who was beginning to gain notoriety, continued to fight—most notably with Margie Dunson in a series of four contests that spanned the twelve months from November 1976 to November 1977. In that period Davis also amassed an impressive record of wins, but it was difficult to know which fights were actually sanctioned professional bouts and which were only exhibitions, given that Algieri, through the WBF, maintained the records.

The first bout between Davis and Dunson was held in Dunson's hometown of Portland, Maine, at the Exposition Building. Cat Davis was able to defeat her handily, taking the fight by KO in the third round. Dunson had previously fought Lady Tyger and Gwen Hibbler, losing both bouts. It is unknown what other fights she might have had before meeting Davis, or what boxing experience, if any, she'd had before launching her professional career.

Their next meeting was in Allentown, Pennsylvania, in February 1977. That bout ended when "Davis floored Dunson after 48 seconds were gone in the second round of a bout scheduled for six, two-minute rounds."

Dunson had just "stunned Davis with a hard right to the blonde's left eye, [when] Davis countered with a left-right combination, sending Dunson to the deck for the full count." Dunson was apparently flattened by the blow and was said to have needed help not only getting back to her corner, but to the dressing room.

The bout had been promoted by John Florio and was another case where a Davis fight was the featured bout on the card alongside the main event. Florio claimed having the Davis v. Dunson fight brought in double the usual number of fight fans, and he promised to put on more women's bouts in the future.[13]

Davis and Dunson also fought a month later at the Wagner Ballroom in Philadelphia. This time around the contest was promoted by Barry McCall, with Dunson losing by KO at 1:54 into the third round—her third straight loss to Davis. A hand-typed note about the battle by an unknown writer described Davis as having thrown a "series of overhand rights until Dunson went down," although Davis ended up "with a swollen knuckle on her right hand from banging Dunsons [*sic*] face."[14]

Their fourth and final fight was set for November 11, 1977, in Fayetteville, North Carolina—a co-feature under the main event: a heavyweight bout between Sandman Parker and Terry Denny. Both women were listed on the advertisements as "Women World Champs": Cat Davis as a lightweight champion and Margie Dunson as a welterweight champion. As confirmed by the November Women's World Federations rankings in *Boxing Illustrated*, both were title holders, although where and when Dunson had "won" her title was a mystery, given her purported win-loss record.

The fight card, promoted by Ringside Promotions Limited, was only the second fight night in the state of North Carolina since boxing was legalized (the state had banned the sport in 1890). As could be readily predicted, Davis was victorious again—this time taking "exactly 2 minutes 34 seconds of the first round" to send Dunson to the canvas. Speaking with a reporter, Davis explained her win saying, "I know that if you put two boxers out there and one has four or five years' experience and the other is just starting you're going to have a boring match."[15] Given that the pair had started out in boxing at around the same time and had already fought three previous times, it was not hard to surmise that Davis's explanation was disingenuous at best. Both women were, however, being paid and questions about the manner in which Davis won her bouts were raised again and again as her career continued.

In parallel with her boxing outside New York State, as early as March 1976 Cat Davis had applied for a license to box in New York State, but was turned down. She applied again in June 1977, and with no license in the offing, Algieri helped her obtain counsel to see what her options might be. In the end Davis and her team decided to pick up the gauntlet—first thrown down by Jackie Tonawanda and Lady Tyger Trimiar in 1975—and sue the New York State Athletic Commission (NYSAC) in 1977. She was able to prevail and won her suit six months later in December.

Davis's case had been predicated on two separate points. The first contention was that the regulation of boxing was not within the scope of the NYSAC. The second and more potent contention was that she was being denied equal protection under the Fourteenth Amendment to the Constitution and Section 11 of Article I of the New York State Constitution, the same argument advanced by Jackie Tonawanda (Garrett)—reportedly using the same court papers as the basis for the suit.[16] The NYSAC had countered "that women should not be licensed as boxers for the reason that there is insufficient administrative experience . . . to support the promulgation of boxing standards." The state further argued "women's boxing would cause sensationalism and subject women boxers to exploitation."

Justice Nathaniel T. Helman, in his opinion on the case, cited the precedent set in the Tonawanda (Garrett) case two years before by Justice Frank, which "found the regulation invalid under the equal protection clauses of the State and Federal Constitutions."

Because "no judgment was settled upon the reported decision" (Tonawanda had not pursued the case beyond the initial state court's ruling), the dreaded New York State rule number 205.15, denying women the right to box in New York State, still stood.

Writing that the arguments made by the NYSAC in the Davis case were "unimpressive," Justice Helman continued by stating that upholding the denial of the license would mean "much need[ed] change would never take place," and that such things as the possible "exploitation" of women boxers could be handled under existing "labor and contract laws."

Concluding that the "cross-motion" by the state was denied, Justice Helman found in favor of Cathy Davis by invalidating rule 205.15. In so doing, he directed the NYSAC to "promulgate rules for the licensing of women as boxers, with due consideration for the protective needs of women."[17]

Overturning the rule, which had been the bane of female wrestlers and boxers, did not mean that the NYSAC would act immediately—in fact the NYSAC filed an appeal to the appellate court in February 1978. By May, perhaps in response to the threat of further lawsuits, the NYSAC "took a major step toward the licensing of women boxers . . . when it requested permission to drop its appeal." In their request, they noted that the commission "would have 90 days to draw up rules for women," after which time, applications from women "will be accepted and processed by the commission."[18]

Bowing to the inevitable—and joining forty-two other states that had already legalized women's boxing—on September 19, 1978, the NYSAC issued its first boxing licenses to the three women who had worked the hardest to see the ban overturned. The first license was issued to Cathy "Cat" Davis, much to the annoyance of Jackie "The Female Ali" Tonawanda (Garrett) and Marian "Lady Tyger" Trimiar. Lady Tyger felt that she and Tonawanda had labored longer with the previous court actions that eventually paved the way for Davis to succeed. The commission, however, issued the first license to Davis because it was her court case that had directly led to the legalization of women's boxing in New York State.

In true "boxing" style, Lady Tyger said, "I challenge the 'Cat' to fight right here and now." Davis reportedly responded, "You'll have to learn to box first."

Associated Press columnist Will Grimsley wrote, "The two made menacing gestures toward each other, and aides joined commission officials in keeping them apart."

"The Cat's been ducking me for a long time—meow! meow!" Tyger said, adding, "I'm going to get her soon."

Grimsley also reported that while pithy dialogue between Cat Davis and Lady Tyger might have seemed manufactured solely for the many representatives of the press that had come to watch the proceedings, there was still a genuine animosity between the pair, stemming from earlier attempts to put together matches—and ongoing questions about Davis's record. [19]

While waiting for the NYSAC to finally lift the ban against female boxing in New York State, Davis had continued to pursue her boxing career. She also sought a more national platform.

Davis's statuesque figure, good looks, long blonde hair, and apparent "girl next door" wholesomeness were beginning to make her a media darling and a poster girl for women's boxing. It certainly helped that she had been to college, spoke with a soft southern drawl, and was considered "articulate." She also projected an image that was the antithesis of a "bra-burning" feminist activist—something Lady Tyger, a black woman who sported a shaved head and was an outspoken critic of the status quo, would have been automatically associated with, even if she had never uttered a word.

The issue of class, color, and gender affectation was also never far from the surface in relation to women's boxing. Algieri was quick to point out, "I'd expected to find the ugliest chick in the world. Bald. Terrible, who knows what? When she came up I said, 'Hey you don't wanna fight, man, you wanna be a model or something.'" He told a variation of that story whenever he described his first meeting with Davis—sometimes adding that he thought she'd be short and squat. Whatever the stereotypes for what a woman interested in boxing might look like, being a tall, slim, pretty blonde who didn't look muscle-bound and who wasn't obviously working class, "ethnic," or black or Hispanic, was something that Davis and her team exploited—perhaps, it could be argued, to the detriment of other female fighters.

Just after the New Year in 1978, Cat Davis accepted an invitation to join twelve other female athletes (all Caucasian) at the "Sports Superstars" tournament in Freeport, Bahamas, to be held on January 23 and 24, with parts of the competition shown on ABC television. The concept of the show was to take a group of "star" athletes from various sports and pit them against one another in a series of competitive events. In previous years, tennis star Billie Jean King had even participated. To be included with the potential for a lot of additional publicity was quite a coup for Davis. The eventual 1978 winner was speed skater Anne Henning (her third win in a row), but regardless, it gave Davis tremendous national exposure and established her in the minds of the media as a face of women's boxing—if not the face.

Returning home, she shot a segment for *CBS Sports Spectacular* television program at the Hilton in Las Vegas in February. The piece showed her sparring with Algieri and included an interview with her. She also appeared on *The Today Show* in this period.

In an article by columnist Jeff Meyers that ran about the same time, it was claimed that Davis had "signed a contract that guarantees her $70,000 for her next three fights." [20] That was an extraordinary amount of money. Considering that Bob Arum offered $15,000 for a three-fight deal the year before to LaVonne Ludian, Theresa Kibby, and Sue TL Fox, it was an enormous escalation in the apparent value of female fighters. What was absent was information on who was offering the guarantee and when the fights would occur.

By then Davis was claiming a 16-0 record with fifteen by KO and one by decision. Aside from her boxing, she was also earning money as a model, performing exhibition bouts with Algieri (one famously at the New York Coliseum's auto show a year later), and even speaking engagements. One thing Davis wasn't really doing was boxing—not until two planned fights: a nontitle bout in Atlanta, Georgia, in June against boxer Ernestine Jones meant as a tune-up for a later title defense against Jo Jo Thomas in, of all places, Monaco. Surprisingly, the latter fight had also been announced as a twelve-rounder to be contested at the venue in Fayetteville, North Carolina.

Ahead of her bout against Jones, *People* magazine ran a story about Davis in their May 15, 1978, edition—another first for Davis and for the sport of women's boxing.

Telling *People*, "I never want to be considered a jock," Davis went on to say, "There's the image that to be a boxer you've got to be dumb, have a nose that's spread across your face and cauliflower ears. If you're a woman, you have to weigh at least 180 pounds and swear like a sailor."

The author of the piece, in playing off Davis's statement, wrote, "Cat (née Cathy) weighs 132 pounds, has a comely set of ears and a pug (not pug's) nose and speaks like a lady in accents Louisianan." It also described her training regimen ("rises at 9 a.m., eats an orange and drinks tea with honey, then jogs three to five miles. . . . By noon she is at a dingy Lodi gym where Algieri . . . helps supervise her two-and-a-half-hour workout"). By then Davis and Algieri were living together in a new apartment in Lodi, New Jersey, and while the article didn't gush too much about their love affair, it did mention they were engaged to be married.

Clearly following the script set by Davis and Algieri of presenting her as a clean-cut young woman who preferred training to actual fighting, the puff piece continued the depiction of Davis as worlds apart from the perception and reality of boxing.

The interesting tidbit about her upcoming battle was that the article stated Davis would be fighting "10th-ranked Connie Smith in a nontitle fight in Atlanta" as a stepping-stone to her title fight with Jo Jo Thomas. Her championship fight was reported to sport a payday "of upwards of $35,000." That was an astronomical purse for a women's bout, and showed that Davis was truly hitting the "big leagues" as a fighter—and by inference, bringing other fighters with her.[21]

Unfortunately for Davis, the match against Ernestine Jones (called Connie Smith for the fight), a black Chicago-based fighter, proved to be a disaster. Right from the start Jones clobbered Davis, sending her to the canvas in the first round of their battle with a stinging left. Jones was able to hit her at will, and Davis hit the deck one more time in the second round and again in the third before Algieri threw in the towel. Davis, so it seemed, had her first loss by TKO, complete with pictures splattered all over the papers showing Smith tagging Davis with a hard right.

Immediately after the fight, Sal Algieri contested the outcome, proclaiming that Jones "had used illegal tactics," and hollered for a no contest, which he received two weeks later. An article in the *Sydney Morning Herald* dredged up Sal Algieri's past indiscretion—that he admitted he'd taken a dive against Australian fighter Rocky Gattellari in the 1960s. Denizens of the fight game in Sydney certainly hadn't forgotten or forgiven him, and figured Algieri was "true to form" when he "started ranting and raving" to have the fight declared a "no contest."[22]

An article in the *Chicago Tribune* (Jones's hometown) also thought it suspect to call for a no contest. First off, Ernestine "Queen Steen" Jones claimed when she got to Atlanta, Davis's people said they wanted her to box using the name Connie Smith—with no explanation given. Jones's trainer, Randy Tidwell, claimed to be equally mystified. "I think maybe they did it so that later they could say 'Connie Smith doesn't exist,'" he said. As Connie Smith, however, Jones had "signed a one-year contract with an Atlanta firm."

Given that the *People* article had already identified Davis's opponent as Connie Smith (a boxer from Hawaii), it is possible that the planned fight fell through and, not wanting to cancel the bout due to all of the attendant publicity, Jones was sought out as a replacement and told to box under the assumed name, but that is speculation. Whether Jones's management was also in collusion is an unknown—though they rigorously denied knowledge of it later on. As Jo Jo Thomas was also mentioned in the *People* piece, some contact had already been made between the two groups; so the question comes down to whether Ernestine Jones was part of the original package or not, and whether Davis's people had intended to substitute Jones for Smith all along.

As for the fight, the article claimed that Davis "went out cold" after being tagged by Jones in the first round. Tidwell put it his way:

> They had invested a lot of money in her. She had signed a TV contract and had a big spread in Ring Magazine. So the referee is counting, 'One . . . get up, get up . . . two . . . get up, get up . . .
>
> Before the fight, they said you couldn't be saved by the bell. But I counted 28 seconds she was down before the bell rang and they got her to her corner.
>
> Jones flattened Davis again in the second round. "This time, they dragged her to the corner . . ." said Tidwell.[23]

The rationale for the no-contest claim was predicated on a few points that were articulated at different times. In July reporter Randall V. Beriage wrote that Davis claimed "her opponent drugged her drinking water and then stepped on her ankle." He also quoted Davis as saying, "It was foul tactics on the part of my opponent's camp."

Beriage also wrote, "She had good reason to want to remove the blemish from her otherwise undefeated record," as Davis told him, "I've been signed by NBC Sports for $110,000," seemingly all the rationale necessary to want to contest a bad beat down. Beriage had met up with her at a dinner for Ring 30 (the chapter for a boxing veterans aid organization covering the Bronx and nearby suburbs), founded and presided over by WBF head Scoop Gallello.[24]

In September, at the presser where she received her New York State boxing license, Davis told reporters, "My opponent kept pushing me down in the ring and falling on top of me, hurting my leg. But I have never been seriously injured."[25]

Aside from her claim of a deal with NBC, the proverbial "elephant in the room" was the article about Cat Davis in the August edition of *The Ring*, which had already hit the stands. Sal Algieri himself had a byline for the article, entitled "'Cat' Davis, Woman Boxer, Could Be Start of a New Breed."

It was a big deal.

The Ring—boxing's self-proclaimed bible—had put a photo spread of Cat Davis on the front page. Never in the history of the magazine had a woman appeared on the cover (and as of this writing it remains the only time).

The article was a three pager with accompanying photos showing Cat Davis in varying boxing poses. Another puff piece, it was told as a first-person narrative—expanding on the article in *People* and relying on materials provided in Davis's press releases. It also made note of her increasing popularity as a gate draw, describing her as "the missing link between Ali and other fighters."

The controversy over her fight in Atlanta, however, was not included, as the article had gone to press before it erupted. Algieri did drop four names of possible future opponents, noting Davis would be fighting "two of the top four in the Women's Boxing Federation list [including] Connie Smith of Hawaii."[26]

For the professional fighting world, the inclusion of Cat Davis on the cover of *The Ring* was an endorsement not only of her as the face of women's boxing but of boxing itself. Stated differently, it was a way of saying that the sport was accepting the "fact" of the female side of game—although in truth it hadn't. A more nuanced perspective would have been to say that women's boxing had at the very least been acknowledged, even if there were forces in boxing (a strong majority) that would have preferred the women's game to go away entirely.

A couple of weeks after New York State issued boxing licenses to Cat Davis, Jackie Tonawanda, and Lady Tyger, a bombshell hit the press in the form of an attack on Davis and Algieri. New York City's *Village Voice* published a page-one story by writer Jack Newfield entitled "The Great White Hype."

The article was all about Cathy Davis and Sal Algieri, alleging that they had fixed fights and padded Davis's record with phony names. Accompanying the front-page portion of the article was the UPI photograph of Davis getting her head snapped back by a straight right thrown by "Ernestine Jones (alias Connie Smith)." Newfield was unsparing in his condemnation of Davis and Algieri, and purposefully provocative in choosing to make the allusion to "The Great White Hope" moniker of the Jack Johnson boxing era. Writing that "Cat is a lady boxer who is white, blonde, and pretty," he added:

> Cat is also not what she appears to be. And her manager-boyfriend, Sal Algieri, stands accused of trying to fix her fights, of controlling a fake "commission" that regulates women's boxing, and of using phony names for her opponents.

Among Newfield's allegations, he claimed that Ernestine Jones "says she was told by Algieri to lose." Newfield also published a copy of the check made out to Jones's manager, Jack Cowen. It showed the payday as $535 with a handwritten note on the upper left-hand corner that read "PURSE FOR CONNIE SMITH AS PER AGREEMENT."

The check was dated June 7, 1978, written on the Pyramid Promotions Inc. account, and it featured two "Payment Stopped" stamps on it. Davis's lawyer, Robin Suttenberg, also signed the check, and although she claimed she was not part of the Pyramid Promotions organization, Newfield uncovered that she was listed on the incorporation papers as the "lawyer."

As it stood, Ernestine Jones was never paid for her efforts and had been involved in what was at the very least an unethical scam—a fact Newfield attributed to some degree to her being an unknown black Chicago-based boxer.

Cowen also told Newfield that two weeks after the fight he had received a telegram from "Al Gallello, 'chairman of the Women's Boxing Federation,'" which stated that "the fight was officially being changed to 'no contest' because of dirty tactics." The telegram also claimed that Jones's trainer, Randy Tidwell, and Connie Smith were being suspended for six months. The WBF was able to take that step due to an absence of any actual boxing commission with jurisdiction over fight (there was not a boxing commission at that time in Atlanta). Since the WBF claimed to be the "sanctioning" body for the fight, they conferred upon themselves the right to overturn the TKO decision.

In response, Cowen filed a "notarized affidavit" with NYSAC in August 1978. In it, he attested to the commission that he had been told to have Ernestine Jones fight under the name Connie Smith. Cowen also wrote, in part:

> Two days prior to the fight, Mr. Algieri made several attempts to myself and Randy Tidwell for Ms. Jones to lose the bout, stating she "had to lose" in order that Mr. Algieri's television arrangements would not be affected by a loss. Mr. Algieri also stated that if Ms. Jones lost, it would mean a television appearance by one of our other female boxers.

Newfield credited the "find" to a sportswriter, Malcolm "Flash" Gordon, who wrote and distributed an independent newsletter, *Flash Gordon's Tonight's Boxing Program & Weekly Newsletter*. Gordon's mimeographed boxing programs already had a track record of exposing illegal shenanigans in boxing, including a Don King scandal in 1977 that involved phony records and payoffs to justify having subpar fighters on an ABC Sports boxing tournament.

Flash had written in his June 29, 1978, edition that there were other instances of Cat Davis's opponents boxing "under phony names," and that Davis had KO'd "the same opponent four times under different names" in what he coined "Sal Algieri's 'dive caravan.'"[27]

Not much more came of the accusations leveled by Newfield in the press—at least not overtly as no one really picked up the gauntlet in the press—except to rehash portions of the accusations and to look more skeptically on the legitimacy of some fighters and of women's boxing. What did happen was Cat Davis was pretty much ignored by others in the fight game who were too busy trying to make a go of it to worry about the machinations of Sal Algieri and his "friends"—aside from "skirmishes" between the growing number of rival women's boxing organizations and the WBF. Davis's career never recovered.

The entire affair left a scar on women's boxing as a whole, and meant that fighters outside the Algieri organization had to work much harder to prove their legitimacy. The WBF—the organization started by Algieri—was almost universally dismissed, although it continued to operate and pump out materials on Davis, as well as to sanction other belts through at least 1981.

A documentary featuring Davis that had been filmed in 1978 aired in May 1979 as part of a documentary series on public television. The one-hour work by Jane Warrenbrand, entitled "Cat, A Woman Who Fought Back," followed Davis's "fight" to get licensed in New York State, including footage from her July 14, 1978, bout against Mona Hayes, a substitute for California fighter

Toni Lear Rodriguez who had canceled at the last minute. (A clear mismatch, Davis defeated Hayes by KO.) The documentary also featured brief comments on women's boxing from heavyweights Muhammad Ali and Joe Frazier—none of it particularly flattering.

Davis, who had been so much on the ascendant prior to the debacle in Atlanta, fought very few fights after the Newfield article and none of the "promised" fortune came her way. In her next big battle, the following year on July 2, 1979, she faced off against the purported German women's boxing champion, Uschi Doering, in what was billed as a twelve-round WBF championship bout at the Exposition Building in Portland, site of Davis's earlier triumphs.

The much younger and taller Davis handily defeated Doering, although Doering had managed to tag Davis with what was described as a "head-snapping" straight right early on—seemingly the only photo from the fight that was circulated over the wires on the UPI feed. Other than the moment of that photograph, Davis was seen to dominate throughout the fight, refereed by ex-fighter Willie Pep, who had been part of Davis's coterie early on in her career. He "halted the fight less than a minute into the sixth round as Davis was peppering Doering while she remained hunched in her shell." It was considered to be a good stoppage.

This time around, however, there were less than two hundred fans in the crowd, and the press questioned Davis's right to call herself a lightweight champion, since she had dropped to "number five on the Boxing Illustrated list"—with Lady Tyger, her nemesis, listed as champion. [28]

Perhaps the most scathing article published about the fight was reserved for *Sports Illustrated*. The short piece raised the question of how the fight could have been called a championship bout because "that billing will be disputed by":

> (1) Ernestine Jones, who is credited with having knocked out Davis last year in Atlanta, which Cat vigorously denies, and (2) Marian (Lady Tyger) Trimiar, also known as the Black Kojak because of her bald pat, who insists that she, not Cat, is the world lightweight champ. [29]

The commentary by Newfield regarding race and class did not go away either, but neither were his points dealt with in any meaningful way. As a promotion "machine," Algieri and the WBF had certainly mined an untapped vein of opportunity: that of a white, educated, pretty, middle-class young woman who happened to earn her living as a champion female boxer. While it called into question the editorial priorities of the publications that "drank the Kool-Aid," and the public's fascination with the seeming incongruity, most seemed to have little stomach to ask the harder questions about the swirling issues related to race, class, and gender. It seemed that, while they reported on "women's libbers" entering the heretofore vaulted domain of the manly art, few were willing to dig down into the deeper societal issues that were continuing to plague the United States.

That WBF and Algieri also cheated their way into getting Cathy Davis to the "top of the heap" was also unfortunate—and proved, perhaps, that when it came to boxing, no one was incorruptible, even a pretty "white girl" from the "right" side of the tracks.

A lifetime later, and long since out of the game, Davis (who in 2005 lived and worked as a chef in South Africa's Kruger National Park) reflected on the controversies for a piece in *Sports Illustrated.* In answer to a question as to whether "racism had played a role in the editors' decision to feature the white Davis rather than the black and arguably more accomplished Trimair," she responded,

> A lot of what we did got distorted [by the press]. Boxing is all about oppressed people fighting their way up in society, and women's boxing was a mirror for the rising women's movement.[30]

Certainly that was true, but issues of race and class were also never far from the surface and were important considerations, which continued to be unresolved as the sport unfolded in the 1980s and 1990s.

WIN SOME . . . LOSE SOME

As the drama associated with Cathy Davis unfolded, women's boxing continued on. Fights were fought, new fighters entered the game, and fighters who had been there at the beginning of the 1970s boom began to bow out of boxing. Promoters in Nevada and California, still working the vein of gold they'd discovered, even began putting on all-female fight cards with some success.

According to Bill Dickson, by 1979 he'd staged eighteen or nineteen women's fight cards at the Hyatt Lake Tahoe. He explained, "At first they were very inexperienced, but as they started to learn more, fans realized [they were seeing] some [well-fought] contests. Some good girls started coming along, and you could feel it. It was no longer a novelty."[31] He did say that he was hedging his bets on promoting an all-female card, claiming that women often bowed out at the last moment. By putting on a "bonus bout" between male fighters, he had "insurance" in case any of the women's contests fell through.

In California, where there were at least twenty-five licensed fighters, promoter Sammy Sanders felt none of Dickson's trepidations. Familiar with the women's fight scene and impressed with the women who boxed at the Hoover St. Gym in the Southland area of Los Angeles, Sanders put together what was likely to have been the first professional all-female fight card in California.

The bouts were called the "World Premiere All Girls" boxing show and were presented at the Hawthorne Memorial Center on February 11, 1979. The bouts were also promoted as elimination fights for the planned World Championships to be held in July. The main event was a six-round battle between Lady Tyger Trimiar and Carlotta Lee, a former kickboxer with a 17-1 record in the sport who had taken up boxing after seeing Lady Tyger fight at the Olympic two years before. Lee, who traveled as far as Japan to compete in kickboxing events, had also recently graduated from the University of Houston with a bachelor's degree in nursing, proving that Cat Davis was far from the only college woman in the sport—which, in fact, had many.

Other fighters on the card included: Cora Webber (another kickboxer, and twin sister of boxer Dora Webber, both of whom were considered among boxing's best), Lydia "Squeaky" Bayardo (who was quickly becoming known as a very strong fighter), Dulcie Lucas (a college student at Cal State in L.A.), Valarie Ganther, Shirley "Zebra Girl" Tucker (who went on to successfully campaign to get the California State Athletic Commission to extend the limits on the number of rounds allowed for women's fights to ten), Toni Lear Rodriguez (who had canceled a fight against Cat Davis in July 1978 and was considered a powerhouse fighter), up-and-comer Garcielo Casillas, and Candy Smith.

The evening also sported at least a thousand excited fans who were treated to what writer Alastair Segerdal described as an evening of boxing "that would rival any male championship card." At ringside were the "glitterati" of women's boxing at the time, including women's boxing promoters Johnny Dubliss, who was big in California, and Eric Westlake, who put together shows in Las Vegas.[32]

Boxing in California was also experiencing growing pains. As Don Fraser, who'd promoted the first show at the Olympic, put it, "Everybody followed my pioneering and then it lost interest. The novelty wore off."

Aileen Eaton had also become cool, stating, "I won't say I wouldn't use women again, but most likely I would not." In her experience, women didn't necessarily understand what it meant to actually make weight or other requirements that male boxers took for granted. Even knowing that women were new to the profession and needed time to learn the ropes didn't make it any less vexing to her.[33] She did, however, put on fights through the early 1980s.

The second all-female card in California was held in July at the Los Angeles Sports Arena. Billed as the "First California State Triple Crown," the show featured three championship bouts with arguably some of the best women boxers on the West Coast scene. This time, Carlotta Lee was matched against Cora Webber in a title match along with two other championship pairings: Lilli Rodriguez v. Toni Lear Rodriguez, and Dulcie Lucas fighting the Canadian fighter Britt Van Buskirk, who was rapidly becoming known as a very good boxer. The other three fights on the bill were Lady Tyger v. Ernestine Jones, Graciela Casillas v. Karen Bennett, and Squeaky Bayardo v. Toni Bryant.

"Good" boxing wasn't only confined to Nevada and California. In fact there were increasing pockets of strong female fighters all over the United States with prominent fighters in Indiana, Minnesota, Kansas, New York, Arizona, and other states. British native Tansy "Baby Bear" James, who'd come south from Canada to California as a teenager, was among the first boxers in Nevada in 1975, but had since fought all over the country. In 1978 she opened a women's boxing academy in Kansas City, Kansas, and passed the state test for her referee's license in the same year.

Baby Bear's boxing career included being banned from doing battle in Cincinnati along with Joanna Lutz in 1977. She also fought in a ten-round featherweight championship battle against Toni Lear Rodriguez that was sanctioned by the recently formed Women's World Boxing Association (WWBA), headed by Vern Stevenson.

Baby Bear was outpointed in the contest, attributing the loss years later to a bout of hepatitis. "I was so drained by the hepatitis," she said, "I had no stamina. Toni Lear was just too strong for me." She retired from boxing after losing a rematch a year later at the Olympic in L.A., in early 1979.[34]

Baby Bear refereed many men's bouts, but one of the most memorable of the fights she officiated in was the Women's Boxing Federation[35] bantamweight title fight between Bonnie Prestwood and Debbie "Ginger" Kaufman, a fight that was held at her own "Baby Bear Boxing Arena" and promoted by Vern Stevenson. Prestwood, a housewife and a product of the Muncie Police Athletic League, fought a ten-round war against Minnesotan Ginger Kaufman—among the original coterie of boxers at the University of Minnesota who'd taken on the AAU and won the right to fight an amateur tournament there.

The bout between Prestwood and Kaufman was an all-action affair almost from the start. Prestwood, "who had never been floored," went down twice in the second round from two "sledging rights," the second of which "dropped her flat on her back." Hanging on until the bell, Preston came out swinging in the third round with a "series of right uppercuts and left hook combinations to the head" that left Kaufman stunned.

The fourth round saw Kaufman land "a straight right to the button" as Prestwood was coming off the ropes. The shot "spilled her face forward" and left her "glassy eyed" as she forced herself up from the canvas at the count of nine. Baby Bear let the fight continue, and after Prestwood and Kaufman tangled again, Kaufman let loose with her "fearsome straight right hand that had been the difference all night," putting Prestwood on the deck again.

By then the crowd was wild. Prestwood was able to push back in the fifth and sixth rounds, landing her "short inside right uppercut and combination[s]" with tremendous effect. In the seventh round, however, "the co-ed from Minnesota figured out the right uppercut and contained it with clinching at close quarters." Going into the eighth round, the two fighters battled toe to toe, with an observer giving the advantage to Prestwood until she was hit with a "crackerjack right hander" that put her "through the ropes."

No sooner had Baby Bear pushed the two women apart than the fierce battle began anew with Kaufman throwing another straight right hammer that put Prestwood on the deck for the last time, giving Kaufman the KO win and the title.

Vern Stevenson, admittedly a fierce advocate for the sport, but nonetheless a fair judge of skills in the ring, proclaimed the bout "the greatest ladies battle ever fought," with a reporter on the scene adding, "It very well could have been."[36]

Under the auspices of the WWBA, Stevenson was promoting fights wherever he could. In 1980 he turned his sights to Miami after receiving a call from Dave Lewin, the president of the House of Champions boxing club, who had a proposition for him. He and his associate, Luiz Izquierdo, wanted to add a women's bout as a main event to the boxing show they were putting on at the Jai-Alai Fronton center in Miami.

Lewin had gotten it in mind after meeting the former women's boxing champion Barbara Buttrick. Although she had retired from the ring twenty years before and had been raising her two daughters while working as a bookkeeper, she was still an active member of Ring 31, the Miami chapter of the National Veteran Boxers Association. In speaking to Lewin, Buttrick had taken it upon herself to educate him about the state of women's boxing. Lewin learned about the WWBA and the growth in women's boxing in other states from Buttrick. Doing a turnaround, Lewin decided that a women's boxing match would be just the thing to add as a novelty.

With terms set, Stevenson signed on two WWBA-ranked super lightweights. The first was a thirty-year-old boxer named Blanca "the San Antonio Rose" Rodriguez. Decidedly older than many of the boxers coming on the scene, she was nonetheless skilled. She also was the mother of a nine-year-old son and worked as housekeeping supervisor in a nursing home in San Antonio, Texas. Her opponent was a student at a junior college in Tacoma, Washington, named Tina O'Riley, who was twenty-two years of age. The plan was to have the pair fight in an eight-round main event bout—the only female contest on the six-fight card.

With Vern Stevenson in town, Buttrick acted as an ambassador of sorts to ease Stevenson's and his two fighters' way into the Miami boxing scene. Buttrick, of course, had been keeping abreast of the resurgence in women's boxing since the early 1970s. She had even given some consideration to returning to the sport, but after working out at the Fifth Street Gym for a few days, it became apparent to her that her fighting days were over. She also thought about training women—something she had considered as a young woman—and placed advertisements in a local paper. The response, however, was not what she had hoped, and consisted of a lot of "obscene telephone callers" as it had run next to the ads for massage parlors. Undeterred, she thought of other ways to reenter the sport and eventually affiliated herself with the WWBA.

On the night of the fight, Buttrick had the chance to work "the corner for Rodriguez," and even brought along her twelve-year-old daughter, Beverly, to help her—handing out flyers for women's boxing lessons, among other things.

Stevenson for his part met with the press. Stevenson felt the acute need to establish the legitimacy of his organization and of women's boxing in general as the Davis/Algieri affair was still fairly fresh in fans' memories. Tackling the problem straight on he said:

> With us, credibility is the thing. It's been a long, uphill battle, but we're starting to get acceptance. This isn't just a show, a gimmick. It's for real. These women are good boxers. You can't keep women out of the ring, it's against the law to discriminate. We've got women plumbers and telephone linemen and mechanics, why not boxers?[37]

As the fight card unfolded, the arena was sparsely attended through the preliminaries and even the main event. Regardless, when the two women came into the ring, they put on a tough hard-fought show for the crowd. Rodriquez had the height and reach advantage. With a stiff left jab, she was able to score a lot of points in the early going. O'Riley, having figured out her opponent's jab, took over in the middle rounds, scoring often. The momentum swung back the other way in the last couple of rounds—which was all that was needed to give Rodriguez the edge on points in a close fight that saw neither of them hit the canvas.

After the match was over, O'Riley, sitting next to Buttrick in the dressing room, tried to describe her feelings about the contest:[38]

> I was really scared before the fight, but I know I went in there and did an athlete's job. I know I went eight rounds of boxing, something that most men couldn't have done. It's hard to put it into words. I'm still high from the whole experience.

As women continued to box across the country, other boxing opportunities began to offer themselves in the form of the Toughwoman boxing contests. First begun in 1979, the Toughman/Toughwoman concept was simple: Put together a tournament with as many contestants as could be garnered into each weight class represented and let them have at it with few provisos except that the entrants must have had no more than five amateur fights. Each bout was limited to three rounds, each of one or two minutes duration, and contestants wore heavily padded gloves. Winners were to be awarded cash prizes of varying amounts. Events were also shown on local television, not only piquing interest but creating a carnival atmosphere at the events, which could be thought of as a hybrid of professional wrestling fine-tuned for the masses.

Organized by Arthur Dore (with assistance from former Olympic trainer Dean Oswald) for his company Ardore Ltd., the tournaments took on a life of their own. Local contestant winners were then given the opportunity to apply to enter into the higher-level "toughest men" events, where they could garner huge payouts if they made it to the finals. The first such men's competition, held in Pontiac, Michigan, was advertised to pay out $50,000 to the heavyweight winner, $20,000 to the other finalist, and $5,000 to each of the semifinalists.[39]

The first Toughwoman contest was held in December 1980 in Sioux City, Iowa. It proved so popular that a second contest was held in May 1981 with twenty-five contestants vying to be the "toughest woman in Des Moines"—each trying to win the $1,600 top prize. This contest adhered to the same rules as for men and consisted of three rounds of two-minute duration. Promoter Kathy Eisenhauer was quoted as saying, "The women are just as talented as the men [and] a lot of them are even better fighters. They take it seriously."

One of the requirements for the contest was that each female entering "must train at least thirty days prior to the bouts and have no previous boxing experience." Winners of the women's contests in each weight class also had the opportunity to compete in the newly formed "national Toughwoman contest."[40]

While the contests were controversial due to the specter of having untrained fighters waling on each other, the fights and tournaments did not run afoul of the local courts. Still, injuries and even deaths occurred, which made the contests something more than just a lark. For the women entering them, Toughwoman contests were often the first opportunity they had to enter a boxing ring—an opportunity that led some women to later take up boxing and other martial sports professionally.

THE EXPERIMENT: GLEASON'S GYM

We were in the 1980s and the recession was going on and I said, "Ira, we're cutting off half of the population of the country. Women want to come in here to box, they want to work out and when we go to the bank in the morning, they don't say, is this female money or male money, they'll just take it."

—Bruce Silverglade, owner, Gleason's Gym, July 10, 2013[41]

With the coming of the women's movement in the 1960s came a resurgence of interest in martial sports. There were opportunities to take self-defense classes, and for those women who wanted more thorough training, classes in karate, judo, and eventually kickboxing that allowed them to progress far enough in their sport to obtain black belts and beyond. When it came to boxing, however, there were few classes designed for women. That meant that any boxing training was old school: in a boxing gym one-on-one with a trainer, and encompassing lots of roadwork, calisthenics, and shadowboxing before rounds on the heavy bag, the speed bag, slip rope, and sparring in the ring. What was missing were opportunities for women to learn how to box systematically and safely without being subjected to the kind of "beat down" that Sue Fox had experienced. Worse perhaps was being completely ignored in the gym for months at a time, unable to find a trainer who would work with them, and having learned very little by way of actual boxing skills or pointers on what to do in the professional boxing ring. The situation was very reminiscent of what women experienced in the 1950s, when the pioneers of that era worked out in gyms as the sole woman in a sea of men.

Dee Knuckles—in her San Pedro gym actively seeking out trainers for girls' boxing classes—was a rare exception. When it came to boxing programs, most were geared to school-age boys. Girls were only rarely accepted: perhaps a girl or two, and these often dropped when it came to any competition because of pressure from outside organizations. Some "professional" gyms were friendlier to female boxers than others, but there were really very few established programs that taught boxing geared specifically to women who might have had no prior experience with the sport.

One boxing club of renown that began to consider bringing women in for lessons was Gleason's Gym in New York. A traditional boxing gym, Gleason's was the home to countless champions—first in its quarters in the Bronx, and then on West Thirtieth Street at Eighth Avenue, a few blocks from Madison Square Garden. It had never been particularly averse to accepting the occasional female boxer as one of its own, and had even been quite inviting to women in the early 1970s, although a year or two might go by when no women were training.

In that period, Jackie Tonawanda became a fixture at the gym. A big woman, boxing as a heavyweight, Jackie could always hold her own against the men she sparred with. She also had decent ring skills and possessed a work ethic that rivaled any of the serious male fighters who worked out there—although her claims of having fought and won many fights as a professional were certainly suspect.

According to Bruce Silverglade, the owner of Gleason's Gym, Yvonne Barkley, the sister of former champion Iran "The Blade" Barkley, was another highly talented fighter. "She taught Iran how to box, and she was tougher than Iran," he said. "She looked like a guy in the ring, and she was just really tough so she held her own in there," just like Jackie.

Yvonne Barkley also boxed professionally for a time, facing top female fighters from the period such as Lady Tyger (another Gleason's alumni), Gwen Gemini, Squeaky Bayardo, and Sue Carlson.

Given that there were so few women boxing at Gleason's, individual women were usually on their own and if they sparred it was against men, who made it a point to pull no punches just because they were boxing a female. It wasn't that a woman had to be "tougher," but she did have to prove that she had real boxing skills, heart, and the willingness to train the same way the guys did.

"I was a little bit in awe of their abilities," Silverglade went on to say. "The fact that they would come in the gym [and were such] good athletes, in great condition, doing a heck of a tough sport."

While Gleason's could accommodate the occasional female fighter, what they didn't have were the facilities or the space to handle a possible large influx of women who wanted to learn to box. The gym's owners were also in a quandary about how to handle women boxers. Silverglade's partner, Ira Becker, was a "traditionalist" and would say, "No, no, we don't want women in the sport."

Bruce Silverglade, on the other hand, was much younger and figured that if women wanted to learn to fight, the gym ought to figure out a way to bring them in. A realist, he was also concerned about the "bottom line," and the gym was feeling the pinch of the early 1980s recession that was affecting his gym membership. Silverglade was also speaking to women who would wander into Gleason's asking if they could learn to box, and seeing that the trickle was becoming a trend, wondered if there was a way for the gym to begin offering lessons, perhaps lessening their financial troubles.

The problem was the facilities at the gym were not really adequate for bringing in women. The space consisted of two rings, hanging boxing equipment, and only one dressing area. The shower and bathroom facilities were down in the basement.

Talking it over together, Silverglade and Becker decided to try an experiment. They would close the gym early three nights a week, let women come in, and see what happened.

The first group had six very eager women in it. "I had two trainers and we trained in a group, and it proved to be very, very successful right away and the numbers grew. Eventually he had groups of 12 women training at one time," said Silverglade.

"We had models, business women, you name it. But women would come, not to make money, not to get out of poverty like the boys do but because it was a challenge for them. Most of them were highly educated and already had good positions and so this was a challenge. It was very easy to teach them, too, because they'd come in and say 'listen, I don't know how to box. Teach me.'"

What Silverglade found was women were more ready to learn than their male counterparts because they had no preconceptions about how to box—or the notion that they already knew how to box coupled with a lot of bad habits that needed to be "unlearned." Since his female students were starting from scratch they had no such ideas and with so much motivation they learned readily, becoming quite skilled very quickly.

Silverglade was also adamant that there would be nothing to distinguish between the way men and women were trained. The regimen was the same: "We were going to teach the sport of boxing and it progresses to sparring." The women quickly took to that as well, sparring amongst themselves—and sometimes even sporting a shiner or two after three or four rounds in the ring.

In 1985 Gleason's needed to find new space, and eventually found a locale in what is now the "trendy" neighborhood of Dumbo, Brooklyn, but at the time was an area that was dodgy at best. While it was under construction, Silverglade insisted that they also build a facility with areas just for women: a separate locker room, bathroom, and shower area. Even given the locale in a sparsely inhabited industrial area, the women's program took off through word of mouth.

The popularity of the women's program at Gleason's rubbed off on other local boxing gyms, and larger health club chains even began putting up heavy bags and speed bags, and offering rudimentary boxing training.

But in Silverglade's estimation, the popularity of the sport really took off once amateur boxing became legal for women in the early 1990s. Opportunities to compete in the Golden Gloves in particular—spurred on by a lawsuit by Dee Hamaguchi, a graduate of Gleason's female training program—were particularly inviting to younger women because of the Golden Gloves' storied history. This gave Gleason's a decided edge over other gyms in the first several years, since they had been the first to develop women's boxing talents and had a long history of training amateur fighters aiming to be Golden Gloves champions.

As Silverglade pointed out, while in some things women and men are intrinsically different—such as the physical attributes of the body that may make a male heavyweight that much bigger and stronger than a female of the same weight class—it doesn't take away from having equal skill sets in the ring or the savvy to outfox an opponent through ten grueling rounds. With the experiment, Silverglade had wanted to give women the opportunity to box. What he found was that the opportunity profoundly changed how women were viewed as athletes and competitors, a view that continues to reverberate to this day.

THE PROBLEM OF RECOGNITION

When you say "girls boxing" you think that they just slap each other around.
But . . . it ain't like that at all.
—Bob Silver, boxing trainer, August 15, 1987[42]

A brief article that appeared in the *Sacramento Bee* in the spring of 1985 seemed to sum up the state of women's boxing ten years after it was legalized in Nevada: "Women Fight Discrimination in Battle for Bouts."

Johnny Dubliss, a former boxer who became involved in promoting women's boxing in the mid-1970s and went on to start the Women's Boxing Board (WBB), was frustrated with the state of women's boxing.

"You run into discrimination all over the country, things like you can't use women fighters a certain time of month. . . . The result of this is it's hard for women to get matches. There are no more than 100 active women fighters in the U.S."

To further his point, he emphatically stated that "fans like it" when women fighters are on a card. "They provide something special in lieu of a big main event," and should be getting on more cards, not less. He added, "We had a recent card in Baltimore that made money that way. . . . It's a novelty. It could turn into something profitable."

For her part, Lady Tyger Trimiar said, "When you're a pioneer, it's hard to get going. I've gone as much as two years between fights. I'm a lightweight, but I fought in Baltimore as a middleweight because I wasn't in the best condition."

The money for fights was also very low, ranging from $300 to $1,200, with fighters, even of Lady Tyger's renown and prowess, being pressured into turning up at fights without their own trainers to save the promoters money. At the Baltimore fight, Lady Tyger was in that exact position. It proved to be a big mistake. With "no cornerman there for me," she said, "I had to borrow another fighter's, an old man with shaky hands. He lost my $60 mouthpiece. I didn't come home with much money; just enough to buy a jogging suit. It's discouraging."[43]

The early stars of the ring in Nevada had also left the sport, and the will for promoters to put on fights in those locales had also petered out. Venues such as the Hyatt Tahoe at Incline Village were barely putting on fights for male fighters—never mind female bouts—and even Las Vegas had many fewer boxing shows, with no women's bouts on the cards.

Women fought where they could, places where small pockets of boxing activity were creating a "buzz" among the women who picked up the gloves. One such place was the Benton Bombers boxing club in Waterville, Maine. Promoter Jerry Thompson actively put on women's bouts in Waterville, and the state of Maine permitted an active amateur program to flourish.

Newcomers Cheryl Brown and Laura Holt excited the crowds in Maine with at least six bouts against each other in 1983 and 1984, including a fight for the North American Women's Super Featherweight title, which Holt won. Both Brown and Holt had also won state boxing championships during the period. Brown even set a record during her second ring appearance as an amateur by scoring a TKO win ten seconds into the fight over fighter Pat Poland, the fastest in the history of boxing in the state of Maine for men or women.[44]

Holt started boxing when she was about twenty, having called up a local gym to ask if she could come in and train. She came from a family of fifteen children and had long since been "boxing" in one fashion or another with her five brothers.[45] Brown, on the other hand, had been an all-around athlete, running cross-country and playing softball and basketball. What intrigued Brown was an ad placed by Jerry Thomson seeking a heavyweight fighter. Although she was a lightweight she "went down anyway," one of "15 women answering the advertisement."[46]

Other fighters that were doing their best to continue boxing were Lady Tyger, Toni Lear Rodriguez, Diane Clark, Britt Van Buskirk, and twin fighters Cora and Dora Webber. Cora Webber and Laura Holt, ranked number one and two respectively, met in a fifteen-round Super Featherweight WWWB Championship fight in March 1986. Their main event was held at the Radisson Hotel in Denver, Colorado, and, by all reports, was a war. In the end, Holt took the unanimous decision by ten rounds to Webber's four—with one round being called a draw.[47] Maintaining her home in Maine, Holt's win even made the local papers, proving that in some locales, female boxers were still newsmakers.

Fighter Del Pettis from San Diego also started having some success in the early 1980s fighting other women who had entered boxing between 1979 and 1983 such as Nancy Thompson, Louise "Frisco Kid" Loo, Joann Metallo, and Brenda Myers. Pettis won her early fights, but began running into trouble when she stepped up in class to fight the likes of Toni Lear Rodriguez and Laura Holt.

In 1987 Pettis was slated to fight Laura Holt in Johnny Dubliss's WBB Super Featherweight Championship main event bout held on August 15. In the presser the day before the bout, Pettis was in a fighting mood, remarking, "I'm good-looking and I can fight. People who think pro women boxers are ugly and do more slapping and wrestling than boxing will be in for a surprise. I plan to knock out Holt and win the first of four titles before I retire and get married."

Holt's response was short. "She'll be in for a long evening," she said, adding, "The only other thing I'm saying is that I will win the title. I prefer to do my talking in the ring."[48]

The fight proved to be a tough one for both with Pettis bearing the brunt of the punishment. Women still were required to wear breast protectors, which meant that fighters typically did not go to the body much. In the case of the Pettis-Holt fight the pair went toe to toe, with Holt connecting the majority of her punches to Pettis's eyes. By the fifth round, one eye had nearly closed into a "bloody mess." Clearly concerned that any more battering might lead to serious ocular damage, referee Stanley Berg waived off Holt and stopped the fight. A reporter who viewed the bout wrote, "It should have been stopped a round or two earlier."

Pettis, however, refused to go down. Holt stated afterwards, "I don't think I ever hit anyone that solid before. I've never seen a woman who could take a punch like that." She went on to say, "It's hard when you hit someone with everything you've got and then she just smiles and comes right back at you."[49]

The fight was the first women's bout held at the Lakeshore Athletic Club in Chicago. With around two hundred excited fans in attendance, most were satisfied, some finding it to be the fight of the night—and at least as good as the other fights on the undercard: four- and six-round bouts between male boxers, with three ending by TKO.

Both women had earned a $1,200 payday for the fight, with Pettis taking a long retirement before coming back to boxing in the mid-1990s. Holt also hung up the gloves shortly thereafter, but had already won the esteem of her trainer and the owner of a boxing gym in Maine, Bob Silva.

With the paucity of women's professional fights, even when women could get bouts, they faced enormous pressures. The women's side of boxing was routinely ridiculed in the press, noting everything from whether a fighter was physically attractive to what her hairstyle was (or wasn't) to minute dissections of her skill sets. Women were also forced to wear uncomfortable and thoroughly unnecessary breast protectors. Depending upon what state they fought in, women had to abide by whatever limitations were set: from the number of rounds they could fight (still four in some jurisdictions), to the duration of rounds (generally two minutes), to the type of medical information they had to divulge (including the need to get a pregnancy test before being allowed to fight). The major promoters—who thought nothing of issuing strong statements condemning the sport in the press—were also ignoring them.

In April 1987 Lady Tyger organized a hunger strike with Pettis and Joan Metallo to raise attention on the plight of female boxers and their ill treatment at the hands of the big promoters. Under the auspices of her group, Friends of Lady Tyger (FOLT), the stated goals of the hunger strike were fairly straightforward. They spoke to the need for equity in the sport between men and women and the frustrations that women felt trying to earn a living as professional boxers. A flyer developed to publicize the women's boxing hunger strike listed seven goals along with a plaintive request that said, "Please support our struggle. We don't want to die." The goals listed were:

1. Major Network coverage for women boxers.
2. Compensation from Networks/Promoters for loss of a livelihood.
3. Equal corporate sponsorship of Womans [*sic*] participation in boxing.
4. The promotion of boxing for girls and women as a means of self-esteem and self-defense
5. Economic parity for Women on all professional boxing cards.
6. The promotion of boxing as an amateur and professional sport for Women.
7. The licensing of all qualified female applicants in their respective states.[50]

To draw attention to their action the women picketed the WBC Middleweight Championship bout between "Marvelous" Marvin Hagler and Sugar Ray Leonard at Caesar's Palace in Las Vegas. Their object was to bring attention to their plight and to Bob Arum in particular, whom they viewed as "openly prejudiced" against female fighters. They also hoped to draw the attention of Don King to convince him to put women's fights on boxing cards—something King would eventually do, but not at that time.

Given that Sugar Ray Leonard's win rocked the boxing world, the actions of the three hunger-striking women were lost in the noise generated by the Leonard-Hagler outcome. It did not deter the three from continuing, nor stop the support—if limited—that they were receiving. An article that appeared in the *Chicago Tribune* in mid-April noted that two promoters, Marshall Christopher (a former police officer in Chicago), and his partner, Kristin Newman—who had put on successful amateur women's boxing, drawing as many as two thousand fight fans—were raising money in support of the fast.

Lady Tyger, still buoyant and full of fight, admitted that while "starting to think about oatmeal," she was still incensed by the ill treatment and lack of opportunity for women in the sport. As she told a reporter, "Mud wrestling and jello wrestling can get on television, but [boxing] can't." [51]

By April 28, Lady Tyger was the only one of the three who was still fasting. She'd lost close to "30 pounds since starting her water-only fast," but had lost none of her fervor as she prepared to picket in front of Don King's office in New York City with some of her supporters. Telling reporters boxing is "my heart, it's my love," she went on to say, "Unless women get more recognition, we will be fighting just as a novelty for the rest of our lives. There will be no future."[52]

A few days afterward, realizing that the inaction of Bob Arum and Don King were not worth the further risk to her health, she ended her fast. Talking about it a few months later, she told a reporter that she would continue her activism on behalf of women's boxing, adding, "Women should not be treated as weirdos to box. People say women have to be lesbian or crazy to box. That's not true and it's very unfair. They don't say that about men." [53]

What she touched on was a growing truism of the perception of women who participated in the sport—the vision of the female boxer as unattractive, muscle-bound, and likely or not, a full-on "dyke" with a motorcycle. These were the stereotypes that had been hiding in the shadows of female athleticism since the late 1890s. It had haunted Babe Didrikson during the early years of her athletic career and it had plagued "lady" wrestlers, footballers, Roller Derby "babes," and female boxers for decades. The negative connotations also impacted the hopes that had been stirred with the passage of Title IX. While equality on the playing fields was beginning to unfold in school gymnasiums and on college campuses, women still had to fight their way into acceptance in sports.

Lady Tyger had voiced very real questions about the place of women in the world of boxing. Unfortunately the organizations that undergirded the sport were also fractured. Promotions for "name" fighters were in the hands of a few, with no true national umbrella to help regulate how the sport was conducted. When it came to women, the situation was much worse. Without money or support, there was very little an individual fighter could do, except to try to ply their trade with dignity and the opportunity to earn enough money to at least cover their expenses.

While the obstacles were huge, women continued to enter the sport, hopeful that each would be the one to break through. In so doing—despite all the problems—the number of women athletes boxing across the country grew, and with that growth came a stronger resolve to break down the remaining barriers to women's full participation in the sport they so dearly loved.

Chapter Nine

Christy Martin and the Pinking of the Velvet Ropes

I didn't know anything about boxing. I'd never hit a heavy bag or done anything like that in my life. But I was an athlete. Athletes are cocky. I liked the challenge.
—Christy Martin [1]

Christy Martin became the public symbol of women's boxing almost from the beginning of her professional career in the early 1990s. Known for her aggressive, no-nonsense style, she brought a little something extra that all boxers of renown of either gender seemed to share—a savvy acumen for promotion that propelled them above the crowd.

With her trademark pink boxer shorts and pink boxing gloves, Martin pushed her way inside "big" promotion to get her fights televised on the biggest fight cards of the day—something no female boxer had been successful in doing before. She also pushed her earnings higher than anyone in women's boxing had before.

Martin's desire was so great that she thought nothing of getting bloody and bruised in her efforts to win, training that much harder in the gym every chance she could, and spending hours and hours of focused effort to develop a hard, aggressive boxing style and the ring savvy to give her knockout wins.

Like other women who were taking up the gloves in the late 1980s and early 1990s, Martin pushed against the prevailing winds of discouragement to fight whomever, wherever, and whenever she could. She was also part of a movement of women who participated in everything from Toughwoman competitions and "boxercise" classes to the first female forays into amateur boxing competitions.

Christy, along with countless other women, was becoming a fixture in boxing clubs all across the United States. In the show-not-tell world of boxing, "walking the walk" began to trump gender as women proved that they could box with science—putting in the hours of training, roadwork, and whatever else was asked of them.

These factors—an increasing number of highly skilled fighters, the growth of new promotional opportunities, sponsoring organizations, and the advent of the amateurs—led to the second boom in women's boxing in the mid-1990s. All of the increasing popularity aside, the true "birth" of women's boxing in the mind of the public was the night Christy Martin fought an Irish fighter named Deirdre Gogarty on March 16, 1996.

Their fight was on the undercard of Mike Tyson's otherwise lackluster heavyweight title challenge against the British champion Frank Bruno on a Don King Promotions pay-per-view extravaganza beamed around the world from the MGM Grand Casino in Las Vegas, Nevada.

What happened after their bout was nothing short of an exponential leap into the stratosphere for women's professional boxing.

The immediate aftermath saw a veritable stampede by promoters to bring female fighters onto more and more pay-per-view cards in more lucrative venues. This resulted in a growth of women's boxing in both large and small markets across the United States. Martin's fight also brought forth boxing superstars such as Lucia Rijker, a former kickboxing champion from the Netherlands, and Mia St. John, who seemed undefeatable in the boxing ring and was a former *Playboy* model.

WOMEN'S BOXING: IF NOT ONE WAY THEN ANOTHER

Women's boxing in the period of the late 1980s and early 1990s was still primarily consigned to minor markets and tiny hole-in-the wall venues—one cut above topless boxing, yet another variant on so-called foxy boxing and mud wrestling. Controversy often surrounded those fights and the question of the legitimacy of female contests was still a continuing issue plaguing the sport.

A case in point was the reaction to the first sanctioned professional female boxing contest in the state of Ohio. The match occurred on August 27, 1986, between a twenty-seven-year-old U.S. Army sergeant, "Lady" Debra (Debbie) Kennedy, and her thirty-three-year-old opponent, Sharon Harrington, a welder working for General Motors. The four-round bout played out in front of a packed house of more than fifteen hundred fight fans who alternatively cheered, laughed, and applauded the hard work of the two novice boxers who were both making their professional debut. The capacity crowd erupted into boos, however, when the bout was ruled a draw by the three judges.

While notable as a first, the reaction of former heavyweight champion Larry Holmes, in attendance at the fight, was in keeping with the prevailing view that women did not belong in the ring—period. "Boxing is just not for ladies," he said later, opining, "Though I think it was an interesting fight."[2]

No less a boxing aficionado than Joyce Carol Oates, whose book *On Boxing* had become part of the sport's canon almost from the date of its publication in 1987, famously derided women's boxing as something monstrous.

Many women rejected such sentiments and learned to box, believing it was their right to do so. If they couldn't get enough experience in the gym, they tried their luck in the ring and hoped for the best, training as hard as they could and sparring with whomever was willing to lace up the gloves against them. What women in the ring in this period did not have was the chance to fight competitively in an amateur boxing contest before entering the fray as professionals. Their only options were Toughwoman contests, burgeoning "white collar" club fights in boxing gyms, or male-driven fantasy "catfight" foxy boxing shows.

Women were garnering some training in the gym, but whereas a young male contender might have had five, six, or even seven years of training and competitive experience before turning pro, a woman might have had limited exposure, amounting to just a few months or a year or two (at most) learning the basics of boxing from a professional trainer before their first pro fight.

The dilemma created a self-fulfilling prophecy of sorts: Without the chance to truly learn their craft outside the corona of klieg lights of a professional fight, many performances in the ring were subpar at best and, at worst, dangerous for the participants. The first female death in a Toughwoman contestant—Stacy Young, age thirty, in 2003—is a terrible reminder of what can happen when an ill-prepared fighter is let loose in the ring in an unsanctioned bout.

Young, a mother of two and in her first fight, was hit repeatedly in the head and was clearly shown on videotape barely able to walk back to her corner at the end of the third round, while being sucker punched a few more times by her opponent. Young suffered a seizure, collapsed, and was subsequently declared brain dead. She was disconnected from life support two days later. No charges were filed in her death, although the state of Florida introduced legislation to more tightly regulate nonsanctioned bouts.

What the fistic women of the 1990s needed (and in some instances continue to need) was access to a safe place to refine their skills. Amateur competition, still outlawed for women, was the ideal, as the rules of the ring, trained referees, an equitable judging system, and the overall governance of a national boxing authority would protect them. The first glimmer of opportunity for women in the amateurs was to come toward the end of 1993—but for women who'd already started fighting, the professional boxing ring remained the place where they were schooled in the sport.

THE COAL MINER'S DAUGHTER

It's what makes the victory sweeter. She knew I was a superior fighter, and the only chance she had was in the early rounds. Once I got my rhythm going, she knew it was just a matter of time.
—Christy Martin, June 1997[3]

Born Christy Renea Salters in Mullens, West Virginia, in 1968, the renowned world champion Christy "The Coal Miner's Daughter" Martin began boxing in a Toughwoman contest in 1986 on a dare. By the time Martin, a gifted college basketball player majoring in education, took up the gloves hoping for the chance to win a thousand dollars, Arthur Dore's Toughwoman franchise had begun sponsoring fights in West Virginia. Martin went on to win six Toughwoman fight nights over the next three years before she turned to professional boxing in 1989.

The sport at this time offered a few gimmicky avenues into boxing that ranged from the Toughwoman contests to foxy boxing nights (where bikini-clad women traded punches in a boxing ring) on through to legitimate boxing contests. Martin chose to begin contesting in the latter along with such fellow Toughwoman alumnae as Andrea DeShong, who was also beginning her career in the pros.

Coming out of the Toughwoman contests, Martin was a novelty and if she wanted to seriously pursue a professional career in boxing she knew she needed more experience. Her mother had been told of a boxing gym in Bristol, West Virginia, that was willing to train women. Martin's mother contacted the gym owner who told her to come by with her daughter. Shortly thereafter, Martin met a boxing trainer named Jim Martin (Christy's future husband). His initial reaction was to discourage Christy from boxing and planned "to have her ribs broke. A couple of ribs anyway," he told a reporter some years later.

"The boss shows up, the guy who invited her out to the gym, so I thought I'd put that off for a couple of days. How would it look if I had her ribs broke right away? See what I'm saying? But I'm sort of a macho guy, and I didn't think women belonged in the fight game. So there was no question I was going to have her ribs broke."[4]

What with the boss "hanging around and hanging around," Martin never had a chance to enact his plan. Somewhere along the way he changed his mind and became enamored with Christy's skills, toughness, and, important-ly, her willingness to listen and focus—an attribute missing in many of his male fighters. He was also aware of Christy's femininity, planting the seeds of her eventual trademark "pink" ring persona around the idea that a woman fighter could be also be an attractive woman.

Fairly soon after she began to train with Jim Martin, she turned professional with mixed results—amassing a record of two wins and one draw before her first loss on the night of November 4, 1989, in Bristol, Tennessee. Her opponent was the unbeaten Andrea DeShong who had amassed five wins in as many fights. DeShong had already been a two-time World Toughwoman champion before turning to professional boxing in the same year as Martin. Both fighters had met once before in a Toughwoman contest where DeShong gave Martin her only loss. (Martin left the Toughwoman circuit with a final 6-1 record.)

The scheduled five-round boxing bout held in Bristol, Tennessee, was the toughest to date for Martin and in characterizing it years later Christy said, "When I lost in 1989 to Andrea DeShong, I got hit so hard in the first round I didn't remember the rest of the fight."[5] Through sheer willpower and tenacity, Martin managed to box through the rest of the five-round slugfest without getting dropped once and only lost the fight by five points—even surviving a purported bite on the cheek from DeShong (which DeShong rigorously denied).

Martin clamored for another go at DeShong and headed back to the gym. Once there, she worked even harder to perfect her skills and improve her defensive ring strategies in preparation for a rematch the following April. The bout was scheduled as a repeat of their first professional fight—a five-round bruiser at the same venue as their previous battle.

Feeling ready to avenge her loss to DeShong, Martin came on so strong in the first round that DeShong was given a standing eight-count by the referee after being on the receiving end of a barrage of Martin's left-right combinations. In the second round, DeShong rallied and managed to back Martin onto the ropes, but that onslaught was not enough.

Listening to her coach, Jim Martin, say, "You've gotta' be brave," as he attended to her between rounds, Martin resumed her constant barrage from the third round on. It made for an exciting fight, as DeShong gave back just as hard and answered plenty. In the end, though, Martin won by a unanimous decision with a five-point advantage.

The win dropped DeShong's previously unbeaten record to 8-1, and led her to retire from the ring for the next six years. The DeShong camp argued that Martin had been held back by the referee more than once to give her time to recover between blows. Though unsubstantiated in the official record— nor on viewing the fight, which has resurfaced on YouTube—the loss certainly colored DeShong's feelings for Martin who insists DeShong "dogged" her around for years after their 1990 bout.

Martin and DeShong did fight a "rubber" match years later. In their third and final meeting in 1997, DeShong suffered a TKO loss at 1:43 of the seventh round in an eight-round battle. DeShong took the fight on short notice, and both Martin and DeShong, borrowing a page from the men's side of the game, trash-talked each other in the run-up to the fight.

In one exchange, Martin was quoted as saying, "This is the first time I've seen you dressed respectable, like a woman," while DeShong retorted that she would be a "dead canary," making reference to Christy's ring alias, "The Coal Miner's Daughter."[6]

Christy's comments were in keeping with her promotional gambit to develop a fan base—a gambit following precisely on her appeal as a "feminine" woman who happened to box with all the ferocity of a man. It was a strategy both Christy and Jim felt had paid off.

If DeShong came to the fight on short notice in their last (1997) contest, so did Martin, who had been on an eight-month layoff over a contract dispute with Don King. This was not an uncommon occurrence with King's fighters, although it was a first for Martin. Reflecting on it after the fight, Martin said, "But I wanted to work things out with Don. In the end I learned that being a nice person doesn't necessarily help you out. You have to focus on the bottom line."[7]

Once in the ring, DeShong fought energetically in the opening of the fight, giving Martin a bloody nose in the second round. Martin was also effective against DeShong, showing her different looks with body shots and straight rights. After a close second round, Martin's constant barrage from the third round on—including more body shots and straight rights—made for an exciting fight. DeShong gamely stayed in the battle, showing strong skills and a good chin, but nonetheless she was noticeably tiring in the fourth round. By the fifth round, Martin slowed the pace a bit, but fought crisply and was in control of the ring, showing even stronger control in the sixth with a series of solid left hooks. Martin proved to be too much for DeShong in the seventh round, with the fight stopped after Martin delivered four quick devastating unanswered jabs. It gave Martin the TKO win and effectively ended their rivalry.

Martin's other early fights were carefully managed. She perfected her straight-right knockout punching power on novice boxers who were intent on making their own professional debuts. This strategy of mismatches gave Martin a rapid string of victories in the early 1990s and a growing reputation as a female fighter who could actually *fight*. Her parallel strategy of appearing in pink created a buzz among her growing fans who, like Jim Martin, were impressed with Christy's feminine attributes.

Martin's growing prowess and string of KO wins came to the attention of the famous boxing impresario Don King. She went to see him when he made a swing through Florida in the hopes of putting a deal for her in place. King had been entertaining the idea of women's boxing since writing an editorial for the World Boxing Union (WBU) in 1980, stating in part, "Being a member of a minority it would be very difficult for me to go against any minority trying to do anything they support and advocate, so whatever the women want to do I think it's a personal decision and I certainly do support the women."[8]

In truth, he had done nothing but murmur platitudes, and when Lady Tyger attempted to confront him during her month-long hunger strike to bring publicity to the lack of opportunities for women in the fight game, he had brushed her off completely.

No stranger to controversy and with an uncanny knack for making a buck, King's instincts for promotion kicked in over any trepidations he might have had about women's boxing. He was, in truth, immediately hooked and signed Martin in October of 1993 after her big win by way of a third-round knockout against a future IWBF champion, "Battling" Beverly Szymanski, a denizen of Detroit's famed Kronk Gym, who'd also fought competitively as a kickboxer.

In watching Martin, King saw what boxing fans in places like Bristol, Tennessee; Daytona Beach, Florida; and Auburn Hills, Michigan, were seeing: a fierce competitor with actual boxing skills winning her bouts by TKO and all wrapped up in a pretty pink package. As a reporter for the *Spokesman-Review* newspaper put it later, "Boxing has long used sex appeal to sell its product, but scantily-clad women holding round cards are not as involved as a pink-clad boxer who can knock out opponents in the ring and be a miniskirted knockout at the post fight news conference."[9] It also left no doubt as to who was a woman—leaving the issue of gender stereotypes somewhat intact. As long as the "she" was in pink, having a great left hook was somehow less threatening.

Love him or hate him, Don King was a visionary in the world of boxing from the "Rumble in the Jungle" to the inspiration to bring women's boxing to pay-per-view. Pushing King toward his decision were the other big news grabbers in women's boxing, one of which was the reemergence of one of women's boxing's truly bright lights—the renowned Barbara "The Mighty Atom of the Ring" Buttrick of 1940s and 1950s fame. Buttrick stepped out of the shadows of her earlier behind-the-scenes work to found the WIBF, her own scheme for promoting female participation in the sport while elevating its status and improving the overall opportunities for female boxers.

Another important event in the world of women's boxing that grabbed the attention of the media in the year that King signed Christy was the story of a sixteen-year-old teenager from Bellingham, Washington, with boxing dreams in her heart. Jennifer McCleery, fighting under the name "Dallas Malloy," had become enamored with boxing after seeing Marlon Brando's performance in *On the Waterfront*. Taking the last name of Brando's character, Terry Malloy, as her nom de guerre, she added Dallas because it had an appealing sound—and even changed her named legally.

Malloy filed suit, along with her parents, in Washington State's King County Superior Court for the right to box in the amateurs against other women. She challenged the rules that barred women from amateur competition—even against other women—based on sex discrimination. Almost immediately after the suit was filed, U.S. district court judge Barbara Rothstein issued an injunction against the United States Amateur Boxing Association, the International Amateur Boxing Association, and Malloy's local Pacific Northwest Amateur Boxing Association. The ruling meant that she was free to pursue her dreams of fighting, and she proved successful in October of 1993 when she defeated twenty-one-year-old Heather Poyner by unanimous decision after boxing three two-minute rounds. Her win also showed that much had happened since Jill Lafler, the first woman to sue for the right to fight in the amateurs, failed in her lawsuit eleven years earlier.

Thanks to Dallas Malloy's lawsuit along with Gail Grandchamp's unrelenting pursuit of the right to box in the amateurs in the state of Massachusetts and Dee Hamaguchi in New York, the amateurs began to provide women opportunities to compete—legally.

In New York City, Dee Hamaguchi set the whole thing in motion in 1994 when she applied for a slot in the Golden Gloves under the name "D. Hamaguchi." She was turned down, in part because her application was late, but she eventually opened up the New York Daily News Golden Gloves tournament in New York City to female participants beginning the following year, 1995, when sixty-five women competed in the tournament.

Canadian by birth, Hamaguchi began studying judo as an eight-year-old, eventually earning her black belt in 1987. She had also earned her BA degree in architecture at Yale University—but falling deeper in love with martial arts, she never practiced as an architect. Hamaguchi competed in and won Canadian judo competitions, and she also won her division at New York's Empire Games in 1990—eventually becoming the U.S. national champion at forty-five kilograms in 1998 after becoming a United States citizen in 1997.

Aside from judo, Hamaguchi tried karate and then, finding her way to Gleason's Gym, began training with Yoel Judah (boxer Zab Judah's father), a martial artist who had competed as a kickboxer and boxer.

Hamaguchi learned to box alongside a growing group of women who trained for the amateurs including writer Kate Sekules, who chronicled her brief boxing career in her memoir *The Boxer's Heart: A Woman Fighting.* Other members of this group included filmmakers Katya Bankowsky (*Shadowboxers*) and Karen Kusama (*Girlfight*). Although the four did not share trainers or even train together, their shared experiences and occasional locker room banter aligned them with a loose community of female boxers.

With the 1995 Golden Gloves opened to women, Hamaguchi was finally able to compete and made it all the way to the 101-pound final against Jill "The Zion Lion" Matthews. A former gymnast, Matthews had been training at the Wall Street Boxing Club—a well-known white-collar boxing gym— for a short while before entering amateur contests.

Fighting at Madison Square Garden, the first woman to do so since Jackie Tonawanda's kickboxing bout, was a dream come true for both fighters. Unfortunately for Hamaguchi, Matthews's brawling style overpowered her early and Matthews went on to become the first woman to win the Golden Gloves—having defeated Hamaguchi by a knockout in the first round. As Hamaguchi told WBAN in an interview several years later:

> The toughest loss for me ever in any sport was losing to Jill Matthews at [Madison Square] Garden. Media from all over the world was there, so I felt like I embarrassed myself in front of everyone on planet earth. Ironically that was my first sparring session. . . . Imagine fighting at Madison Square Garden with zero rounds under your belt. . . . There weren't enough women to spar with at that time. [10]

In assessing the state of women's boxing, Don King had recognized something else—the dollar-sign potential of promoting the sport at a time when the novelty of female fighting was beginning to pique some interest again. What he saw in Christy Martin was a woman well on her way. All that was needed was to promote her to the next level by putting her on the fight cards of upcoming championship fights—while making certain that her opponents brought at least reasonably equivalent boxing skills into the ring against her.

THE "PINKING" OF THE RING

After recognizing the opportunity to propel women's boxing onto a larger stage, Don King astutely made his move to get into the game by signing Christy Martin to a contract for a minimum of four fights. Sending shockwaves through the boxing world was nothing new for King, and he immediately put his promotional acumen to the test by taking Martin's career in a different direction. She would no longer be fighting in small venues in Florida, the Virginias, or Michigan. King wanted more for her and immediately began slotting her onto fight cards he had running in one or another of the Las Vegas casinos.

King banked on Martin being able to capitalize on her strong record of achievement and she delivered—improving her winning streak and making a name for herself on the undercard of the huge championship bouts of King's stable of male boxing stars.

Originally thinking he would put Martin on his December 18 card, the details fell through because—as the press reported—King couldn't find her a suitable opponent. He certainly wasn't going to take any chance of failure as he wanted an opponent who would enhance Martin's record and get the crowd behind her as the bruiser who could win by KO or TKO almost every time. This meant finding fighters who would enter the ring without necessarily having the professional experience or a huge number of wins to otherwise counter Martin's ever-sharpening skills.

There was one other difference too: Christy came into the ring clad in pink satin shorts and a matching pink satin jacket and wearing a hint of lipstick, claiming, "That's just the way I go to the fights." This was something most fight fans had never seen—an attractive woman who could actually box well. The effect on the crowd was mesmerizing.

Martin's first fight after signing with Don King was a case in point. It was set for January 29, 1994, in Las Vegas at one of boxing's most prestigious venues, the MGM Grand Hotel. The press covering the event made note of Martin's appearance on the undercard of the Julio Cesar Chavez v. Frankie Randall fight, but what set Martin's fight apart was also a bit of luck. Christy's debut as a King fighter just happened to be on the night Chavez suffered his first loss in a career of ninety professional fights.

In the run up to the bout, King told reporters that the fight was "a giant step for womankind." For her part Martin said, "I don't consider myself a pioneer. I just want to be the one everybody remembers." She added, "We've been more or less taken to a new level now. You can't even say this is a dream come true. This is a fantasy."[11]

Even without the knowledge of what was about to happen in the main event, Martin's performance alone in the ring was stellar and played to the crowd. From the onset she circled her opponent, Susie "Sluggin'" Melton, and was quick to score with a series of punches. Melton had actually begun boxing professionally in 1982 and purportedly had a 16-1[12] record coming into the bout (though her current Boxrec list of fights shows her as 2-2). She had even fought against Andrea DeShong in 1989 (losing on points) and had been scheduled to fight Martin the year before at the Township Auditorium in Columbia, South Carolina—although the records ultimately list Martin's opponent as a woman named Susie Hughes who was making her debut fight.[13]

Martin's aggressiveness in the ring against Melton had the crowd roaring and firmly in her corner from those opening moments before Martin toppled Melton forty seconds into the first round of their scheduled six-round bout with a knockout punch. Standing in her corner, the pink-clad Martin basked in the sounds of a crowd going wild.

Her debut couldn't have been more promising. She showed boxing skills and aggression, and she gave the crowd a KO—and she did it all in pink. Even so, King stated later that he was so nervous that he couldn't watch.

Martin's big win no doubt disappointed any naysayers who might have questioned King's decision to put her on the card. King followed with a bout against the twenty-one-year-old Sonja Donlevy on March 4. That fight pitted Martin—fresh off her latest KO victory—against the novice professional from Richmond, Virginia, who was making her pro debut. As expected, Martin made quick work of Sonja and took the fight by TKO in the first round. It was to be Sonja's only fight as a professional.

Don King's ploy of pitting lesser-known fighters against a rising star was nothing new in the fight game. If anything, it gave credence to the idea that the seamy side of boxing—ringing up huge winning records for prospects—was the one place where men and women were actually equal. Promoters were out to make money on their fighters, even if it meant building up records with lots of quick KO wins in a series of mismatches with fighters who had no business being in the ring with such strong opponents.

Christy's next fight was on the undercard of *The Ring* magazine's 1994 event of the year—the storied "Revenge: The Rematches" fight card. The May 7, 1994, pay-per-view boxing extravaganza included the highly antici-pated rematch between light welterweight Julio Cesar Chavez and WBC titleholder Frankie Randall.

Due to the quirks of the pay-per-view telecast—where the first few fights were not broadcast—what no one quite remembers about that night is that Christy, hoping to continue her eighteen-fight winning streak, fought a six-round bout on the card. In the run-up to that bout, Don King, ever mindful of his new hot "property," had taken a promotional swing through Christy's hometown of Orlando, Florida, touting Christy as "not one of those fighters who people look at and say she's beat up and she's dumb. She's very articu-late and is a lady who could really find other means of earning a living without going into fisticuffs," adding that "organizations are commending us on giving women an opportunity," and how "very happy" he is "to be the recipient of a positive note, instead of an arrow or a dart."[14]

In the context of 1994, King's comments were high praise indeed and by placing Christy's next bout on the "Revenge: The Rematches" card, he was more than boasting about how he really felt when it came to the only female in his stable of boxers. Christy was a "keeper" and if King was going to put women's boxing on the map, she was a more than capable partner with a running patter that sought to play down anything that hinted of feminism. As Christy was to put it later, "I'm not trying to put women in the forefront, and I don't even think this fascination [with women in the ring] has much to do with that. This is about Christy Martin."[15]

For the fight, Don King had chosen the unknown Mexican boxer Laura Serrano, making her professional debut in the United States. The contest, though, was anything but the anticipated walkover he might have envisioned.

Laura Serrano was an accomplished soccer player who had taken up boxing ostensibly to lose weight while attending Mexico City's National Autonomous University. Her experiences in the gym ignited her burning desire to box competitively and she began training at the famed house of champions in Mexico City—the Nuevo Jordan gym. Her mother strenuously objected to her taking up boxing and Serrano had to overcome the skepticism of the crowd at Nuevo Jordan, who taunted and harassed her for daring to train. With perseverance and a dedication that rivaled the tenaciousness of the women who boxed in the 1970s, she won over her trainers who eventually gave her the same workouts and sparring opportunities as the professional male fighters at the gym—a story played out by many of the pioneer female boxers the world over.

Aside from her battles to gain entry into the world of boxing in Mexico City, her training had to be kept secret from the authorities because Mexican laws at that time made it illegal for her to fight (even as late as 1997). Serrano, who was also studying to be a lawyer, fought legal challenges on her route to eventually become a licensed fighter while clandestinely training.

Having sparred hard against male fighters and fought in a loose underground network of illegal fights, Serrano was more than ready to take on Martin for her debut fight in the United States. While a stranger to the professional ring in America, she was a fierce competitor with a will to win—and the boxing skills to back it up. In speaking of her years in the ring, the famous Mexican sports writer Ricardo Castillo has said she was "absolutely the finest woman boxer we've ever had."[16]

It wasn't often that two college-educated fighters would square off against each other—but such was the case with Martin and Serrano as they made their way into the ring to the barely audible applause of the early fight fans.

Famed boxing announcer Jimmy Lennon Jr. grabbed the microphone and introduced the challenger, Laura Serrano. Lennon informed the crowd of her record of five wins, one loss, and one draw, with one win by way of a knockout—although there was no mention of how she had obtained her win-loss record. He went on to announce Christy Martin, wearing her characteristic pink boxing shorts with white trim, and introduced her as a three-time Women's World Champion.

King had the clout to make certain there would be three seasoned Las Vegas fight judges ringside: Al Lefkowitz, Dick Hauck, and Al Siciliano. The equally experienced referee, Kenny Bayless (who had counted Susie

Melton out), was announced as the "third man" in the ring—aligning with King's strategy to heighten the legitimacy of Christy's appearances.

From the moment of the opening bell to the end of the fight, the Martin-Serrano bout was something different for Christy. She was facing a fighter who could go toe to toe with her, trading jabs and hooks, uppercuts and straight rights, while dancing defensively around the ring. Exchanging hard shots and fighting with evident skill, both fighters engaged the crowd early on. While Christy was the aggressor in the first round, Serrano fought back admirably off the ropes going to the head and the body to push back against Christy with a "game on" expression clearly discernable in her eyes.

For the second round, Serrano came out swinging, landing a series of jabs and left-right combinations that momentarily stunned Christy. Fighting with equal intensity, Christy threw bombs to the body and the head that eventually backed Serrano into the corner. Serrano pivoted out for more back-and-forth punching that went on relentlessly until the bell.

The third round found both fighters engaged in an out-and-out war with no letup in intensity throughout the entire two minutes of the round. The fourth round was more of the same, as was the fifth, with both fighters jabbing and switching up with right-hand leads. Both fighters were clearly tired, but their bravura performance thrilled the cheering audience, who if anything saw Serrano pull ahead of Christy with cleaner shots and even more intensity, factors that were accounted for on unofficial score cards in the fourth and fifth rounds.

In the sixth round, Christy and Serrano had the crowd shouting and screaming as the two boxers showed what they were made of with toughness, crisp skills, and the temerity to fight and fight hard. After six nonstop rounds of flat-out boxing, the bout was judged a unanimous draw with the score of 57-57—in some quarters a gift to Martin that was greeted by a mixture of cheers and boos, but nonetheless, a battle of which both fighters could be proud. The score, more than anything, was a testament to Laura Serrano's perseverance in the ring.

If ever two fighters were well matched in the burgeoning world of women's professional boxing, they were Christy Martin and Laura Serrano. In the context of their fight, however, the untested Serrano was a huge underdog in comparison to the well-known, savvy professional. Serrano's skills and heart made for an incredibly exciting match, certainly equal to the hype of the "Revenge: The Matches" fight card. Serrano solidified her appeal as one of the foremost fighters in women's boxing in both the United States and Mexico. Still, Serrano felt she was robbed of the win but was gratified by the experience.

Under King's promotional guidance finishing out 1994 and through 1995, Christy handily defeated her rivals by TKO or KO—continuing her trend of competing with women with much less ring experience. She was certainly open to fighting women with long records and real skills, but fighters were at times hard to come by especially on the kind of short notice typical of King promotions. Even so, by 1996, Christy had amassed a stunning 25-1-2 professional record. Clearly, Christy was on a roll as she prepared for her fight set for March 16, 1996. This fight would be different though. Don King had chosen to put her up against the highly experienced, hard-hitting Irish-born boxer Deirdre Gogarty, fighting out of Lafayette, Louisiana.

Deirdre "Dangerous" Goharty was not the most likely of boxing opponents. Born in Ireland, Gogarty's father was a renowned oral surgeon and her mother was a dentist—far from the typical family background of a professional fighter. They were none too happy about her desire to box either.

"They told me horror stories about what could happen to my teeth and my jaw," Gogarty told an interviewer, laughing at the recollection. "I kept it vague with them but after a while they had to accept it. They thought I was nuts. It's interesting that all my sisters came to my fights but none of my brothers or my parents."[17]

After working out in her hometown in Ireland, Gogarty moved to Dublin and began to train seriously—at first on her own because no one would coach her, but eventually with a former British light welterweight champion named Pat McCormack who'd fought in the late 1960s through the mid-1970s. It wasn't an easy process, and speaking of those experiences Gogarty said, "I kept asking so many questions they kind of tolerated me. After Pat trained me for a while I asked him why he was doing it. He told me if his daughter was in boxing he'd want someone to show her how to defend herself."[18]

In June of 1991, Gogarty had her professional debut against Anne-Marie Griffin in a six-round bout staged in Limerick, Ireland. Griffin was an experienced kickboxer who wanted to break into boxing, so Gogarty actually fought her first boxing match on a kickboxing fight card that was judged by kickboxing judges. While not sanctioned as a true boxing contest, it was "legal" for women to fight in Ireland under the rules of a kickboxing match—much as it was in the United States and other parts of Europe.

What seemed like an auspicious beginning—a win on points against her opponent—ended in a losing battle with the Irish Boxing Union (IBU) to gain approval to allow her to compete professionally as a true boxer. When asked why she thought the kickboxing-sanctioning bodies allowed women to compete and not the IBU, Gogarty replied:

> It was a younger sport having started in the 1970s and was a little more open-minded. The boxing was much more traditional with a lot of old-schoolers. They claimed there were no facilities for women and that there wasn't enough medical evidence to show that boxing wasn't harmful. To me it was a lot of excuses really. One other reason might have been the quality of how women could box. They were not necessarily skilled at that time. What I don't know is

if they didn't want to be embarrassed by it or if it was just too non-tradition-al.[19]

Not satisfied to sit and wait, nor to give up her dreams of being a great champion, Gogarty managed to get a match in England—part of the thriving underground women's boxing scene that included the future founder of the British Ladies Boxing Association, Sue Atkins, who had singlehandedly put British women's boxing back on the map in the 1980s. As in Ireland, Gogarty found that women either fought underground or as part of kickboxing cards.

Her first fight in Britain was held in a seedy old venue—literally underground—in a small gym in the basement of the Park Tavern pub on the afternoon of April 11, 1992. Gogarty fought and won her second fight by a TKO in the fourth round of a six-round bout against Jane Johnson who, in speaking of the sport some time later, said, "Boxing is simply pitting your skill against another fighter, knowing that if you hadn't trained properly you could get hurt—that's what gives you the edge."[20]

Of that time Gogarty remembers her trainer, Pat McCormack's, prescience when he told her, "You're opening doors ten or fifteen years down the line," but what Gogarty wanted was "to walk through the door now."[21]

After the fight and with the help of McCormack, she was able to meet with a British referee and former boxer named Paddy Sower. He'd helped her get fights in the U.K. and thought she had done very well. Learning of her frustrations, he told her about Beau Willford's gym in Lafayette, Louisiana, where she might be able to train and have the chance to box legally.

Of those early years, Gogarty has said, "I had written letters to people in the U. S. about boxing and got back things suggesting topless boxing or mud wrestling. It was so disgusting. Then Paddy suggested I write to Beau. I never heard a word. He finally called nine months later saying Paddy Sower had called him."[22]

Willford was not exactly enthused by the prospect of training a woman, but as he stated, "Paddy put the pressure on me. He reminded me that he'd done me a lot of favors. To be honest, she was forced on me. That goes to show you something."[23]

Except for one other fight in England—a rematch against Jane Johnson—Gogarty fought exclusively in the United States, making her home in Louisiana and honing her growing complement of skills with Beau Willford. Her first fight in the United States was in Kansas City, Missouri, in January 1993 against Stacey Prestage, ending in a technical draw due to a head butt. She was to go back to Kansas City again to face Prestage for a rematch the following August, having already racked up four quick wins. That rematch also resulted in a draw after six grueling rounds.

Gogarty, who was becoming known for her stinging jabs and hard left hooks, was invited to fight for the new Women's International Boxing Association (WIBA) lightweight title shortly after her second Prestage fight. The contest was to be set for October or November of 1993, and according to Gogarty, her originally scheduled opponent was none other than Christy Martin—although that pairing for the championship came to naught. Instead, Gogarty was tapped to fight Prestage for a third time. As Gogarty said, "I was lucky to get matched, mostly because Prestage was my weight and size,"[24] and with that in mind, she made her way back to Kansas City to fight in a ten-rounder on November 23, 1993, where she eventually lost her first bout on points after another hard-fought bruiser.

Although Gogarty lost her championship bid, she was able to continue to get quality fights, including her next shot at a championship against none other than Laura Serrano for the WIBF lightweight title. The fight was part of the first all-female boxing card and was set for the Aladdin Hotel in Los Vegas on April 20, 1995.

The card, put together by Barbara Buttrick, was videotaped for later distribution and featured five ten-round world championship title matches and one five-round exhibition bout between the soon-to-be world champion and former kickboxing champion Bonnie Canino and Carol Stinson. The boxers were a veritable United Nations, representing the United States, Belgium, Holland, Ireland, Mexico, Northern Ireland, and Norway, proving that the rise of interest in the sport was truly international.

Gogarty and Serrano's bout was set for the main event and they delivered, fighting a fierce, unrelenting battle from the moment the bell rang in the first round. While Gogarty threw her patented hooks and jabs, Serrano gradually overwhelmed her with an onslaught to the body that pushed Gogarty's stamina to the limit. After taking huge punishment through the fifth and sixth rounds—but never backing down—Gogarty's manager tossed in the towel to stop the fight at 1:23 into the seventh round. Both fighters fought their hearts out and were repaid by a crowd that was wildly enthusiastic. What had made the bout even more remarkable was that it was only Laura Serrano's second sanctioned fight as a professional and the caliber of the fighting was truly equal to anything male professionals at that level had to offer.

Unfortunately for the fighters and Barbara Buttrick in particular, the fights occurred the day after the April 19, 1995, Oklahoma City bombing. All of Buttrick's careful planning and cultivation of the press to ensure their coverage went for naught as every television outlet had pulled their schedule to cover the bombing in Oklahoma City.

This proved to be catastrophic for Buttrick who had expended a good portion of her personal savings in order to secure the venue and the television rights, and to bring the fighters to Las Vegas, an expense from which she barely recovered. It also was a big setback for women's boxing as the display of such skilled and talented fighters could have otherwise helped advance the sport as well as the careers of the individual fighters.

THE FIGHT OF THE NIGHT

I like to come in there and brawl. So it was more difficult than I expected. We knew she was tough but not this tough.
—Christy Martin, March 17, 1996[25]

As with many events that take on a life of their own, Christy Martin's appearance against Deirdre Gogarty on the night of March 16, 1996, seemed to be in keeping with all of her other fights. It was a good matchup, but no one quite expected the meteoric aftermath and media frenzy that accompanied Christy's win. Still, what made Christy a luminary among boxing fans was her appearance against Gogarty on the undercard of heavyweight Mike Tyson's decidedly uninspired world championship bout against Great Britain's reigning champion, Frank Bruno.

For Deirdre Gogarty, the fight was equally unanticipated. Speaking of it in an interview several years ago she said, "Most people expected me to get knocked out in a couple of rounds. I got ten days notice, and arrived in Las Vegas a few days before the fight. I was left out of the hoopla, but got my share later on. It was a good thing for women's boxing. For the first time people talked about it as a legitimate sport."[26]

The matchup, as on other Don King fight cards where he added Martin to his all-male lineup, was third on the list. When it came to the crowd, generally a placement on the early part of the card meant that many of the spectators wouldn't have yet been seated. For the Martin-Gogarty fight, however, the arena was already full with a near-capacity crowd of boxing fans. The fight was also being televised on pay-per-view, widening the exposure of the bout to millions of households around the world—who also were able to watch the undercard.

For the fight, Deirdre Gogarty wore a white satin robe, white shirt, and white shorts with a green stripe—clearly aligning herself with her Irish roots—while Martin wore her customary pink satin trunks and a pink satin jacket with white fringe on the sleeves. With the ringing of the bell to start off the first round, Martin came out ready to battle. She was aggressive and fast, and she worked her combinations hard against her equally hard-hitting competitor with the round running even toward the end after a terrific series of combinations from Gogarty that backed Martin up.

In the second round, Martin dropped Gogarty with a stunning straight right thirty seconds in and was looking to end the fight there and then, even cornering Gogarty with a huge barrage toward the end of the round. Gogarty continued to fight tough though, showing off excellent boxing skills that impressed the on-air announcers as much as the fans—even as Martin continued to show her ring mastery with a series of bombs. By the fourth round, Gogarty had given Martin a bloody nose, but Martin continued to unload with huge combinations even as Gogarty fought off the onslaught—continuing to impress the on-air announcers with the caliber of her fighting.

The fifth round saw Gogarty landing a straight right that had Martin on the ropes, but Martin used her ring savvy to fight her off and pushed herself back to the center of the ring, gaining the momentum to take the round. The sixth and final round saw more of the same with Martin continuing to throw lefts and rights up until the bell—gaining accolades for both Martin and Gogarty from the on-air announcer, who said they'd showed "brilliant" heart.

Both women had fought bravely and with courage—two important attributes for fighters of any gender. They'd also showed tremendous boxing skills of the "science" variety and the willingness to take and give punishment.

Martin proved too much for Gogarty and earned a well-supported unanimous decision from the judges even though she was bleeding badly with what turned out to be a broken nose.

The boxing extravaganza had been beamed around the world from the MGM Grand in Las Vegas, Nevada, on Showtime's pay-per-view channel, with press from all over the world in attendance who were drawn by Mike Tyson's comeback fight. The battle that resonated with the worldwide audience, though, was the "girl fight," and it became a seminal moment pinpointing the entry of women's boxing onto the world stage.

For fight fans and commentators alike, the image of Martin's triumphant face, bloodied and flushed red with exertion, brought a new concept to the popular notion of the men's-only club of professional boxing. Women could box with all of the talent, strength, ring savvy, and fortitude of a man. Boxing legend Sugar Ray Leonard was quoted as remembering Martin's "combinations, poise," and "discipline" in the ring and that "she was perpetual motion."[27] Equally impressed was the esteemed trainer and HBO ring announcer (prior to his death in 2012) Emanuel Steward, who described Martin as "in a class by herself."[28]

Christy's achievement was immediately heralded as the "fight of the night" and by the end of the evening, boxing fans the world over began to see why the daughter of a coal miner from the little town of Mullens, West Virginia, was a force to be reckoned with. She was a woman who could fight like a man and wasn't afraid to take a punch.

Her efforts even won her recognition from one of the more prestigious boxing sanctions bodies, the WBC. They awarded Martin the title of WBC Women's Lightweight Champion—although this was an informal nod, as they did not offer actual title belts for female competitors until 2005.

Martin has been quoted as saying she was "not out to change boxing,"[29] but change it she did by proving that a woman could fight harder than a heavyweight prizefighter of the caliber of a Mike Tyson, whom it is said had asked to see videos of Christy's past fights at the conclusion of the night.

In speaking of the fight in an interview for ESPN in 2011, Christy said, "I remember leaving the arena and some reporters coming up to me and saying, 'Do you realize what you just did? You basically just rocked the world.'"[30]

Her accomplishment also made Christy Martin a household name beyond the legions of followers of the sport. Within a month of her entry into the high-stakes world of elite professional boxing, she earned a coveted position on the cover of *Sports Illustrated* magazine and was reported on in *Time* magazine. With the promotion machine in full swing Christy lined up media appearances on *The Today Show, Prime Time Live*, and *Inside Edition*.

With her win against Deirdre Gogarty, Martin had built up an impressive record of twenty-nine wins, two draws, and only one loss. It was also her seventh year as a pro and she was a long way from the Toughwoman contests that had heralded her start in the fight game. What was to come, though, was a veritable *pink rush* into the ring—something of which Christy was a huge part as she continued to ply her trade as the most recognized woman in boxing.

THE PINK RUSH

A few months after Lady Tyger Trimiar's month-long hunger strike in the spring of 1987, Top Rank's Bob Arum had famously stated he'd "never promote another women's bout."[31] Arum had not softened his position much by 1994 when he stated that women "make good doctors, lawyers and engineers" in addition to staying at "home making babies."

The Christy Martin v. Deirdre Gogarty fight changed all of that. Don King had scored a huge success—a success that translated into financial gain and the chance for a lot more. It was also certainly compelling enough to cause Arum to "evolve" his thinking when it came to promoting female fighters in the ring. The question was what boxer would he sign to a contract and what sort of promotion would he bring to bear as the scramble to sign up female boxers began to have the feel of a "pink" rush.

There was certainly a pool of talented boxers to choose from. By 1996 fighters who'd been big draws in the late 1970s and 1980s were resurfacing to include Cora and Dora Webber, Del Pettis, Toni Lear Rodriguez, and Britt Van Buskirk. It was a new fighter on the boxing scene, however, who was beginning to generate a lot of interest: former kickboxer Lucia "The Dutch Destroyer" Rijker.

Originally from the Netherlands, Rijker had achieved world renown not only with her perfect 37-0 kickboxing record—including twenty-five KO wins—but also for her fierce fighting style and competitive spirit. She won four kickboxing world championships during her career in the sport and competed widely throughout Europe and Japan.

Rijker began martial arts as a six-year-old judo student. A gifted athlete, she excelled at softball, began studying karate at nine, and became the Netherland's national junior fencing champion at thirteen. Following her brother to the gym where he was studying kickboxing, she took a class and never looked back, beginning to compete shortly thereafter.

As Rijker's notoriety in the kickboxing world widened, she grew tired of the constant grind. Feeling overly bound by the terms of her contract she decided to travel to Los Angeles in late 1994 to possibly pursue an acting career and to otherwise retire from kickboxing. She managed to earn a living working in health clubs, eventually working at Bodies In Motion. Over time, she grew intrigued by the growth of women's boxing and began training at the Ten Goose Boxing Club in 1995 with its owner, Joe Goosen—well-known in boxing circles for turning out great fighters.

Even before the Martin-Gogarty fight, Don King's entry into women's boxing promotion (coupled with the legalization of women's amateur boxing) pushed smaller promoters to add women's bouts to their fight cards. The WIBF was also in full swing, ranking fighters and beginning to sanction women's boxing titles. Matchmakers and promoters were on the lookout for possible talent and thus combed the gyms, club fight nights, and amateur matches.

Lucia Rijker certainly had the talent and experience, having begun to box in local amateur shows. With the support of a great trainer, she was given the nod to fight her debut professional boxing bout on the regular Thursday night fight card at the Olympic Theater in L.A.—a good venue to begin a professional boxing career. Her first fight was also a mere five days after women's boxing had been thrust into "prime time" by the Martin-Gogarty matchup.

Rijker cut an impressive figure walking into the ring: five-feet, six-and-a-half-inches tall, her dark curly hair pulled back. Her unmarred features chiseled from a lifetime of sports and an athletic body with perfect musculature gave her the look of a true warrior. She also possessed boxing skills, ones that wowed the crowd as she made quick work of her opponent, Melinda Robinson, dropping her with a stunning knockout in the first round.

The fact that Robinson was a seasoned professional with an official 3-3 record coming into the fight (she had fought Martin two months before, taking a loss on points after six rounds of boxing at Miami's Jai Alai Fronton) also played in Rijker's favor. As did Robinson's comment after the fight that Martin's hardest punch didn't compare to Rijker's lightest.

Rijker's next step, however, would prove to be the crucial one. Still working at Bodies In Motion, a gym client of hers, Sam Simon (who co-developed and produced the hit television show *The Simpsons)* was also a boxing enthusiast who worked out at L.A.'s Wild Card Gym, competed in amateur fights, and eventually took on a sideline job as a boxing manager. Simon introduced Rijker to the Wild Card's owner, an ex-fighter named Freddie Roach. At thirty-four years of age, Roach—who'd had an explosive boxing career of his own under the tutelage of famed trainer Eddie Futch— was beginning to make a name for himself training fighters alongside the actors and stunt doubles he trained for the movies.

At the time Sam Simon approached him, Freddie Roach was not interested in training women fighters. Those that he'd seen were wholly unimpressive to him, presumably including Christy Martin, but as a favor to Simon, he agreed to meet with Rijker. All it took, however, was one round of pad work in the ring to convince Roach that Rijker was not only a great boxer but also pound-for-pound better than most of the men in the gym possessing the kind of KO power that would be a promoter's dream.

A few years later he said, "She will impress you. I heard so much about her and thought she can fight for a girl. I got to realize that she can fight anybody."[32]

Rijker also liked Freddie Roach, and while her experiences with Joe Goosen had been great, she decided to switch over to the Wild Card Gym figuring there were things Roach could teach her that would expand abilities as a fighter in the ring. Roach also became invested in seeing Rijker not only grow as a fighter but become a leading figure in the women's side of the game. He introduced her to Stan Hoffman who became her co-manager with Roach, and he also helped engineer meetings with Don King and Bob Arum to assist her getting signed up for big fights.

Meeting with King first—who'd flown her and Roach to Las Vegas— Rijker did not like the terms he offered and turned him down. She and Roach next met with Bob Arum, telling a reporter a year later, "Bob shook my hand, gave me a look, then started talking about women's boxing, how he didn't like it, blah, blah, blah."[33]

Rijker insisted that he view her highlight tape and, when he refused, said they wouldn't leave until he watched it. Arum obliged and decided that she was "the one." Having signed a promotional agreement with Arum, there were still a few months before Rijker could climb back into the ring for her first fight under the new Arum management.

During the wait for her first Top Rank fight Rijker was not alone. Filmmaker Katya Bankowsky and her crew had earlier begun filming a documentary on the topic of women's boxing entitled *Shadow Boxers*. Rijker gave the okay to be a subject of the documentary and was filmed sporadically as she trained in the gym and behind the scenes at several of her fights in the winter and spring of 1997.

Her first fight for Top Rank was on December 6, 1996, in Reno, Nevada, at the Lawlor Events Center—almost nine months after her triumph over Robinson. She was slated to fight against Kelly Jacobs on the undercard of fellow Wild Card Gym fighter James Toney's World Boxing Union (WBO) light heavyweight title defense against Montell Griffen.

With the Toney-Griffen championship contest scheduled to be aired on HBO, the pressure was on Rijker to perform well and to impress not only the fight crowd but also the sportswriters and fight commentators who sat at ringside. From the opening bell, Rijker clearly outclassed Kelly Jacobs (with a 3-2 win-loss record), defeating Jacobs by TKO at 1:43 into the first round. In the process, Rijker wowed both the boxing crowd and the group sitting in judgment on press row. What they saw was a woman who was so obviously skilled it was hard to diminish her by calling her "merely" a "woman" boxer.

Within two weeks, Rijker was back in the Netherlands fighting there for the first time in three years and working out at Gleason's Gym in Rotterdam to prepare for the bout. (She also became the first licensed female boxer in her native country in the process.) Fighting a Hungarian boxer named Zsuzsanna Szuknai, Rijker dispatched her opponent in the first round by TKO after Szuknai's corner threw in the towel. Rijker remained in the Netherlands as she prepared for her next bout—a WIBF European Light Welterweight title fight against another Dutch fighter named Irma Verhoef (also an early MMA fighter). Impressive again with her mixture of strong skills, strength, and growing ring savvy, Rijker won the title by TKO after the fight was stopped in the fourth round.

Rijker's next three fights demonstrated her growing abilities and added to the fame she was beginning to gain for herself. Back in the United States, she fought a relative newcomer, Chevelle Hallback, handing her a TKO loss in the fifth round after knocking her through the ropes. The fight commentators considered it a "closely contested match" of two skilled fighters at a time when there was a perception was that there were not a lot of competitive fights between women.

Against Dora Webber—the seasoned pro from the late 1970s who had taken a break from the game in the 1980s and then returned as opportunities opened up in the 1990s—the six-round fight went the distance. Webber was a tough, savvy fighter—and likely Rijker's most competitive opponent up to that point. Rijker clearly dominated. The judges agreed, giving her a unanimous decision on all six rounds. The ringside crowd was also clearly in Rijker's corner and referee Steve Smoger said in response to a query from the press, "I thought Rijker could fight. She was technically sound. She threw good combinations. I was very, very impressed."[34]

By the end of the summer of 1997, having knocked out Gwen Smith (a fighter out of Charlotte, North Carolina) with another fourth-round TKO in June, Rijker was poised to fight one of the better names in women's boxing, Andrea DeShong, whose long history of fights with Christy Martin clearly placed her in Rijker's league.

Given how fast and how far Rijker was coming up in the sport, the question of a Martin-Rijker fight was becoming the topic du jour among sportswriters whenever the two were interviewed.

Ahead of her upcoming fight against Andrea DeShong, Rijker told a reporter, "I don't need Christy Martin to make a name for myself. It's just that people keep asking me about her. . . . I've been asked the question 1,000 times, 'When are you going to fight the girl?' I don't know."

Martin's perspective was "there's no reason why those fights can't be made. Personally, though, I'm willing to fight anybody." Along with her seeming willingness to fight Rijker, however, were the questions she raised about Rijker's gender, insisting that she'd only fight her if she took a chromosome test to prove she was a woman.[35] This last was in keeping with Martin's "pink" boxing motif—where "real" boxers were "girly" women, not muscle-bound specimens of indeterminate gender or sexual orientation. To the boxing world, however, the question was more a matter of who had skills—and who didn't—as Rijker began to supplant Martin as the "best" woman boxer on the scene.

In the ring against DeShong in Las Vegas, Rijker spoke with her fists and was fierce. She outboxed and outclassed DeShong, taking the fight with a third-round TKO and leaving no doubt that she would be a formidable opponent against Martin.

With her win against DeShong, Rijker was now set to fight for the WIBF World Super Lightweight Championship in November against a German fighter named Jeanette Witte back at the Olympic Theater in Los Angeles. Within the first few seconds of the fight, it was clear that Rijker was in control, although she'd been hit on the ear and lost her hearing from the first round. Rijker was able to win the title easily with a third-round TKO at 1:25 and displayed masterful boxing technique—devastating her opponent with body shots, a developing signature of her recent fights.

Rijker had established herself as a strong force for the sport. Here was a fighter with undisputed skills on par with male fighters and a fighter who was elevating the level of the game and garnering respect along the way. Even Bob Arum, who continued to denigrate all women's boxing except for Rijker's matches, was firmly in her corner, along with trainer Emanuel Steward, who was also fast becoming a fierce advocate for her.

Along with Martin and Rijker, other female fighters were making a mark. Boxer Deirdre Gogarty (after losing to Martin) went on to win the WIBF Super Featherweight Championship over former kickboxer Bonnie Canino (with a kickboxing record of 28-4-1). Canino, since making the jump to boxing in 1996, was fighting some of Rijker's old opponents such as Beverly Szymanski and Cora Webber. Against Szymanski in particular, she had won a unanimous decision after ten rounds of superb boxing, thus netting Canino the IFBA World Featherweight Championship and the chance to fight on lucrative televised cards.

Based out of Dania, Florida, Bonnie Canino had gone the route of kickboxing in part because boxing had been closed to her. She had always wanted to box and watching Muhammad Ali's fights had inspired her to pursue it. She walked into a gym in 1979 hoping to make a go of it, but she said, "I wasn't one of the guys [and] was a little bit discouraged." She sought out a karate gym next, and said, "Within a week I had gloves on and was fighting. I didn't really care at the time if it was boxing or karate or what. . . . My dream was to pack an arena like Muhammad Ali."

Having studied karate, she took a job as an instructor and in 1984 partnered with trainer Burt Rodriguez. Canino credits him with teaching her how to be a fighter and with inculcating into her the three things he was looking for, "heart, conditioning and skills." Later she said, "That's what [he] liked about me, when the going got tough, I got going."

Rodriguez pushed Canino, showing her the intricacies of the game, and in the process she said, "I got into his heart because I wouldn't stop. . . . I used to train for six hours." The partnership between Canino and Rodriguez was to last throughout Canino's career as both a kickboxer and as a boxer when she made the transition in 1996, as opportunities for women began to open up.[36]

With the scramble for fighters and the slots open for women to try their luck at professional boxing, the results were mixed and problematic. Women like Rijker and Canino were in their late twenties and early thirties when they entered boxing—both with a long pedigree of kickboxing behind them. The women who'd reentered the game, having boxed in the late 1970s and 1980s, were older. Dora Webster was boxing at forty. But these were the women who had developed superb skills in the ring, having been boxing for a long time, and having put in the time in the gym in between the earlier fights and the matches opening to them in the Martin and Rijker era.

Fighters who were coming into boxing from the Toughwoman contests were less skilled. That didn't seem to matter though. Promoters were eager to put women on fight cards, and if their skills weren't as crisp as the elites, it didn't seem to matter much as long as there were crowds in the stands and television audiences that kept tuning in.

Floridians Chevelle Hallback and Melissa Del Valle (Salamone) and the former Argentinean kickboxing champion, Marcela Eliana Acuna, were among the younger fighters entering the sport who found themselves on fairly important fight cards and who did bring skills.

In the case of Acuna, her visibility was huge in just her first two contests as a boxer. In her debut bout she fought Christy Martin, losing a unanimous decision after ten rounds, but acquitting herself very well—so well that the questions continued to swirl around Martin's standing as being at the "top" of the heap in women's boxing. As a debut fighter, it was obvious she'd been brought in as a walkover, but Acuna was anything but that, fighting in the mold of Canino and Rijker.

In Acuna's second match she lost to Lucia Rijker by KO in the fifth round of the Women's International Boxing Organization's light welterweight title fight, but only after having impressed the ESPN commentators (including Al Bernstein) with her strong boxing skills. Another mismatch—given that Acuna was only fighting in her second boxing match—her background as a kickboxer had certainly given her the skills to acquit herself well and impress the commentators at ringside. Acuna went back to Argentina and later became an important figure in the growth and popularity of the sport there, which continues unabated into the 2010s with many well-known figures and champions.

Other boxers who were considered "real" fighters by 1998 included Kathy Collins, a former shot-putter from Long Island, New York, who began boxing as a form of exercise at a gym and participated in the finals of the Golden Gloves in New York City in 1995—fighting alongside Dee Hamaguchi. (One of Collins's opponents in her fight leading up to the finals was filmmaker and director of *Shadow Boxers*, Katya Bankowsky, whom she defeated.) Collins's trainer was Frankie "G" Globuschutz, who had founded the IWBF in 1992—and had helped Collins steer her career as her manager before the pair eventually married.

Boxing as a pro, Collins continued to train and became a better and better fighter, defeating Andrea DeShong in Collins's third fight as a pro in August 1996 at Madison Square Garden (a month before DeShong met Rijker in the ring), and again in 1998 when she defeated DeShong at the Tropicana. That fight proved to be momentous for Collins. She won the ten-rounder by unanimous decision and captured the IWBF light welterweight title in the process.

Sumya "The Island Girl" Anani was another fighter with excellent skills, who turned professional in 1996 and was considered in the same league with Martin, Rijker, and Collins. Anani came to boxing having started as a competitive weightlifter with a background in yoga. She quickly amassed an 11-0 record (with seven KOs) when she faced Christy Martin.

The women's pound-for-pound championship fight was originally scheduled for November 13, 1998, but due to Martin's ongoing contract dispute with Don King, it was finally held on December 18 at the Memorial Auditorium in Fort Lauderdale on a card that also featured Melissa Del Valle fighting Tawayna Broxton in an eight-rounder. The fight card was broadcast on the U.S. Satellite Broadcasting network.

Commentators forecast that the fight would be a war—a tribute to Anani's fighting capabilities. From the beginning, both fighters came out swinging, with Anani bloodying Martin's nose and giving her a small "mouse" under her left eye. While not the most elegant of fights, both fighters threw bombs. Anani backed Martin into the ropes in the third round to galvanize the crowd, and the two fighters went toe to toe in the fourth. In the fifth, both fighters switched back and forth to southpaw stances and continued to throw bombs. Although Anani didn't show the same level of skills as Martin, she was game, and later commended for the heart she was showing by the commentators. The fight was dead even after six rounds.

By the tenth round, Anani had taken control of the fight, having battered both of Christy's eyes until they puffed up. The judges gave the win to Anani by split decision.

Asked about her keys to victory, Anani said, she'd been told to "stay on her and don't get off."

Martin said, "She was just the stronger fighter, she hit me with her head a lot and it wore on my face so bad, I just couldn't keep taking the punishment so I couldn't stand in there and exchange punches."

Martin had also been asked if she wanted a rematch. Her response was anything but positive after pushing back tears. "If we can't fight Rijker and we can't fight Kathy Collins, I'm done. . . . You know what, I've made over a million dollars and no other woman is going to come close to that, and I would have had to taught school for forty years to make that much money so I'm way ahead of the game."[37]

Her career was far from over and she had just suffered the second loss in her career to an up-and-coming fighter who had out swarmed her in the ring. She eventually went on to fight Collins in Madison Square Garden, winning the ten-round bout by decision on an HBO pay-per-view fight card that featured title fights with the likes of Felix Trinidad, Chris Byrd, and Vernon Forrest.

Anani continued to fight professionally for another ten years before retiring. Earlier in her career (in her fourth fight) she had defeated boxer Katherine (Katie) Dallam—a boxer making her pro debut, who outweighed Anani by about thirty-five pounds—for a $300 payday. Dallam, a recovering alcoholic who made a living as a counselor for people suffering from substance abuse, had only recently turned to boxing. (Prior to boxing she had been a marathoner and a kickboxer.) Within a few weeks after beginning her training, she decided to try her luck in a pro fight with a newly minted license she received the day before the fight.

Dallam had been in a minor car accident prior to the bout, but seemingly had not suffered any ill effects after spending a night at a hospital for observation. On fight night, however, neither Dallam nor Gallegos—a seasoned denizen of the sport who had trained world champion boxer Stacey Prestage—reported the car accident to the officials at ringside.

During the four-rounder—with both boxers wearing fourteen-ounce gloves due to the weight discrepancy—Anani continuously battered Dallam. In total, Anani scored between 120 and 140 direct hits to Dallam's head before the referee waved Anani off, giving her the win by TKO in the fourth and final round. Dallam was profusely bleeding from the nose, a condition neither the referee nor the ring doctor attended to.

After the fight, Dallam collapsed in her dressing room and was taken by ambulance to a hospital where she immediately underwent surgery to alleviate the bleeding in her brain. According to Dallam's sister, "What [the doctor] found after opening Katie's head was not a 'slow brain bleed,'" which might have indicated an effect from the car accident, but a "complete and utter shredding of the main blood vessel in her brain." She had further been told that this was "caused from repeated battering of the brain from blows hitting her from both sides of her head."[38]

Dallam never fully recovered from the severe injury, suffering from memory loss and other problems. She spent years in rehabilitation attempting to gain back even a modicum of functionality including relearning how to walk. No one blamed Anani for the tragic circumstances of the aftermath, but the incident brought to the fore the extreme consequence of allowing novice fighters with no appreciable experience to fight as professionals.

The incident was seemingly forgotten, save for Anani's prayers for Dallam before her fights. Forgotten, that is, until the release of the film *Million Dollar Baby*, which told the story of a fighter who was paralyzed during a very rough fight—a storyline purportedly inspired in part by Dallam's story.

By the late 1990s, Lucia Rijker had seemingly solidified her place at the top of the pound-for-pound list with two championship belts to her credit, and was now on the cusp of dethroning Martin from her position. However, such success did not necessarily mean that Rijker was now the "darling" of boxing.

Mia "The Knockout" St. John, born the same year as Lucia Rijker, 1967, was a Tae Kwon Do black belt who began competing in amateur tournaments at the age of eighteen. She'd gone to college and earned a BA in psychology, but decided somewhere along the way to try boxing and went directly into the pros. She was also a beauty with long flowing black hair and a voluptuous body.

Her debut was in February 1997, fighting another novice, Angelica Villian, whom she defeated by a first-round knockout after swarming Villian with wide windmill punches. She came to the attention of Don King, who immediately signed her to a contract.

St. John was equally successful in her next series of fights—four-rounders with other fledgling boxers whom she readily dispatched in the ring. While she was winning, her skills showed no apparent improvement, but that didn't seem to bother Don King or the audiences who watched her fight.

After about a year and a half with Don King, St. John switched to Bob Arum at Top Rank on a contract that would have her opening for all future Oscar De La Hoya fights, De La Hoya being one of Arum's hot boxing properties at the time. Arum also had something in mind for St. John, something very different than his management style with Lucia Rijker, whom he dropped after signing Mia St. John.

She and Arum came up with the idea of promoting her as a truly "feminine boxer"—in essence "out-pinking" Christy Martin—by having her appear "feminine and soft and sweet" and wearing hot pink instead of baby pink. As St. John put it, "[Martin] came out on the cover of *Sports Illustrated*, and so I came out on the cover of *Playboy*." They had also cooked up countering Martin's boxing on the undercard of Tyson fights, with St. John opening for the reigning ring king, Oscar De La Hoya.

"The marketing worked," St. John said, "And so basically, Bob Arum and I were geniuses."[39]

For Rijker, the switch from Arum's support of her as a solid boxer to Mia St. John's silly froth was a harsh blow. Rijker was by all accounts the pound-for-pound best female fighter in the business and the antidote to every negative comment about the skills female boxers showed in the ring.

The fact was simply that she was being passed over to sell sex in the ring. And whereas Martin had used femininity as a means of making men more comfortable with the idea of women fighting, Mia St. John's brand of femininity was sexual in nature.

The selling of female boxers as sex objects was also indicative of the changes women's boxing was undergoing as promoters looked to find more ways to capitalize on putting female fights on pay-per-view cards, and even though selling sex was one of the strategies, more and more women were spurred on to enter into the fight game despite the hype.

Chapter Ten

Women's Boxing and the Fame Game

I wouldn't compare myself to my father because we're two different people, but I know that because I am his daughter that I naturally have boxing skills that most people probably don't have when they start. At the level that I'm at, I would rate myself as excellent.
—Laila Ali, September 1999 [1]

With the clamoring for more and more "product" came gimmicky female boxing matches that bordered on "cheesecake." Bob Arum's decision to sign Mia St. John—who looked more like a ring card girl than a professional athlete despite her years as a martial artist—was a case in point. The question was would Arum's apparent success push other promoters to do the same.

It was the sudden appearance on the scene of famous boxing daughters, however, that really began to change the sport. Beginning with Muhammad Ali's daughter, Laila Ali—who combined marketing savvy, beautiful looks, and a star quality—the sport underwent yet another metamorphosis. Promoters—eager to cash in on the latest craze—put together the "famous daughter" matches in the hopes of capitalizing on a viewer interest peaked by a somewhat tangential stardom, especially after Muhammad Ali began showing up at his daughter's fights.

Meanwhile, female boxers began to feel whipsawed between the pressures to "feminize" boxing and the new attention (and major paydays) now given to the famous, if questionably skilled, daughters. A sanctioned female-male bout in Seattle, Washington, also did little to promote the sport, as the backlash was decidedly negative from most boxing quarters including from some women.

Professional fighters who weren't boxing in pink or famous daughters continued to box, but felt as if they were now being left with the scraps. This meant—except for a small minority—that there were fewer opportunities for

219

matches, continued low payments for fights—even championship bouts—and the reality of having to work a "day" job just to make ends meet.

WOMEN'S BOXING AS CARNIVAL SIDESHOW

It's a circus, it's a sideshow. It's an old carnival act, updated for the 1990s.
—Burt Sugar, October 1999 [2]

October 1999 proved to be a banner month for women's boxing. In the span of a few weeks, three events rocketed women's boxing onto the news around the country.

Laila "She Bee Stingin'" Ali, the twenty-one-year-old (and youngest) daughter of boxing legend Muhammad Ali and his third wife, Veronica Porsche Ali, stepped into the ring for her professional debut against April Fowler, a novice boxer and waitress from Indiana with an 0-1 record and no apparent boxing skills. The contest, a four-round co-feature promoted by Mike Acri—and not associated with "Big" promotion—was held on October 8, 1999, at the Turning Stone Resort and Casino in Verona, New York.

Ali made short work of her opponent, winning by knockout thirty-one seconds into the fight. Given the quality of the bout, it was an inauspicious beginning; however, it proved that Ali might have inherited some of her father's abilities.

At the beginning of January 1999, Laila Ali, a community college graduate and owner of a nail salon in Los Angeles, had made the decision to box professionally. She'd been taking boxing lessons as part of a weight-loss exercise program. Her exercise program morphed into Layla Ali training in earnest with her boyfriend, cruiserweight champion Johnny McClain, at the L.A. Boxing Gym, also home to boxer "Sugar" Shane Mosely.

She was making an impression. As gym owner Richard Allen put it, "She works really hard. She wants to learn. And she's not a prima donna."

Visiting her father, who was staying at the Beverly Hills Hotel, she said, "Well, Daddy. I want to tell you I'm going into professional boxing." After the elder Ali expressed his concern, she said, "I'm going to be fighting women, not men. And I have your genetics." This brought on a laugh followed by the two of them mock sparring and practicing the stare down—a ring staple between two fighters as the bout is ready to get underway. [3]

The press first got wind of the story in mid-January at Muhammad Ali's fifty-seventh birthday bash in Las Vegas. A guest at her father's party, Laila Ali told the press, "It's in my blood. . . . What can I say."

She also admitted she'd just seen her first female fight the night before at the MGM Grand—a four-round bout between two novice fighters. [4]

By late February, the *New York Times* ran a feature piece about Laila Ali. While she'd found a promoter, her pro debut wasn't planned until the summer.

Her possible entry into the ring, however, became news with much speculation about the ramifications for the sport.

Christy Martin, when asked for a comment for the *New York Times* piece, said:

> She is Muhammad Ali's daughter and that's fine. . . . But at some point, she's got to prove that she can fight. People are really going to be waiting to see that. It won't last long if she can't fight. It won't take many fights, maybe two or three, before people turn away.

The *New York Times* also approached Jackie Kallen, a former commissioner for the IFBA, who had started out as a boxing journalist before becoming a boxing manager for fighter James Toney. Kallen was quoted as saying, "Everybody is well-aware of Laila, and everybody is waiting to see what she is going to do. She has the looks, the background, and if she has the skills, she will be the whole package."

Kallen also felt that due to Ali's name she'd have a higher "earning potential" as "the marketing factor alone [would] . . . set her apart." Her words proved to be prophetic and were a source of contention among elite female fighters such as Lucia Rijker who earned considerably less per fight despite her exceptional ring skills and her own star power.[5]

The next round of press coverage began in September when Laila Ali's first fight was announced. Much of the coverage centered on whether her father would be in attendance, and the truth was, the prospect that he might be there certainly sold seats. By fight night on October 8, the frenzy of publicity included camera crews and photographers with press from as far away as Great Britain and Germany in attendance.

As the *Boston Globe*'s boxing reporter, Ron Borges, put it at the presser before the fight, the excitement was palpable. The assembled members of the fourth estate ignored all of the other proceedings as they waited for the five-foot, ten-inch statuesque young woman who "sauntered through the door with the regal carriage of Xena the Warrior Princess." Borges further wrote:

> When the 21-year-old daughter of Muhammad Ali began to speak, it was clear no one else was in the room. Though it was jammed with bodies, no one else mattered now that she had arrived.
> Same as it was for her father.[6]

As frenzied as was the press coverage for Laila Ali's fight and the possibility of getting a glimpse of Muhammad Ali, publicity for her debut bout was in competition on the sports pages with an explosive women's boxing event: a mixed-gender bout set for October 9, 1999, at the Mercer Arena in Seattle, Washington—a day after Laila Ali's pro debut.

Margaret "The Tiger" MacGregor, a thirty-six-year-old female boxer from Bremerton, Washington, sporting a 3-0 record had been having trouble finding an opponent. In talking to her fight promoter, Bob Jarvis of O'Malley Promotions, she had casually said since they couldn't find a female opponent, why not match her against a man.

Fighting as a lightweight and usually weighing in at around 130 pounds, MacGregor had a black belt in karate and moved on to a kickboxing career amassing an 8-0-1 record with several wins by KO. She felt certain that both she could hold her own against a male opponent and it would be a highly competitive fight.

Her promoter, Jarvis, game to the idea and thinking of the promotional opportunities, put out feelers. He found some interest in Vancouver and offered the fight to a part-time jockey and former kickboxer originally from Hong Kong named Loi Chow, who had a 0-1 boxing record. After Chow turned him down, he signed one of Chow's sparring partners, Hector Morales, a lightweight fighter looking to make his pro debut.

What made the fight feasible were the gender-equality laws of the state of Washington. While boxing itself was regulated, there was nothing in those regulations that gave the state authority to segregate fights by gender. Fights were solely approved based upon "weight, skill level, a physical-health test, vision exam, and blood and urinary tests." The only gender-specific requirements had to do with protective gear: breast protectors for women and cups for men. This effectively meant that male and female boxers could compete against each other in sanctioned matches.

The announcement to the press in early September was the next step, with both fighters available for comment. At the presser MacGregor was clear on why she wanted to fight a male opponent. "I'm looking to improve. But it's not going to happen if I'm restricted to fighting only women. I'm not saying I want to fight men all the time, but I don't see why my options should be limited."

As for Morales, he admitted that the prospect of fighting a woman was "embarrassing," especially when he told his mother, but he still offered that he would "knock [MacGregor] out in the second round."[7]

Within a few days of the press event, Morales pulled out. Promoter Bob Jarvis said, "I think the publicity got to him. . . . And when I heard he was embarrassed to tell his mother . . . that really scared me. . . . We didn't expect all of this attention." Jarvis also quickly announced that Loi Chow, his original choice, would be fighting MacGregor.

Jarvis, MacGregor, and her trainer, Vern Miller, had all been assailed with questions and opinions. It was also beginning to take on the atmosphere of the famed Billie Jean King v. Bobby Riggs tennis match of 1973—with much pandering to women and verbiage on the superiority of the male sex. Chow, however, seemed ready for the onslaught.

Miller, in his statement to the press, said, "All the chauvinists are saying 'There's no way a woman could beat a man.' That may be, but look who has the courage to go through with it." To those who were saying it was denigrating the sport—including negative remarks from some members of the team backing Martin O'Malley—the only answer seemed to be the brisk ticket sales, which were ahead of expectations.[8]

By the third week of September, the issue of the mixed-gender fight was being pushed to the desk of Washington's governor, Gary Locke—mostly spearheaded by former boxing commissioner Dale Ashley. In a statement to the press, Ashley called the bout "ridiculous . . . this is just a gimmick to sell tickets." He went on to state, "Someone is going to get killed and then what is the Department of Licensing going to say?"

Ashley, who had been the commissioner in place when Dallas Malloy won her lawsuit in 1993 (eventually authorizing her bout), had seen his share of controversy. When it came to the issue of mixed-gender boxing he was adamantly opposed and not only spoke out to the press but bombarded officials with a letter-writing campaign. The state's position, however, was clear. The fight would go on as long as the two fighters met the basic criteria, which included tests seventy-two hours before the bout. The state attorney's office was also being dragged into the fray, but Marty Brown, the deputy chief of staff for the governor, definitively said, "If the gender question is the only issue, they'll most likely go ahead and approve the fight . . . otherwise you're looking at a lawsuit."[9]

By early October one other bombshell hit the press—with the pun intended by a lot of reports. Mia "The Knockout" St. John, Bob Arum's female boxing sensation—whose presence in the ring had already elicited a string of negative press based on her hyperfemininity and mismatched bouts—appeared on the cover of the November issue of *Playboy* magazine with an accompanying twelve-page spread.

Shown wearing red boxing gloves that barely covered her breasts and short red shorts with a *Playboy* logo belt and white side stripes with blue stars, the "bunny boxer," as she came to be known, shared the cover with the headlines for *Playboy*'s interview with former professional wrestler and newly elected governor of Minnesota Jessie Ventura.

To be sure, St. John was neither the first nor the last female athlete to appear nude for a *Playboy* spread. Given the precarious place of women's boxing and its struggles for legitimacy, however, her appearance only added to the controversies afflicting the sport.

With this last piece of the puzzle—the entry of Laila Ali into the ring— Mia St. John's *Playboy* cover and the MacGregor/Chow fight were conflated into a general condemnation of women's boxing, with the MacGregor/Chow fight leading the pack.

Top Rank matchmaker Bruce Tampler told reporters, "It's a freak show. . . . If he beats the crap out of her to teach her a lesson, I'm all for it. But if she wins . . . they should put him in a dress and buy him a ticket out of town, never to show his face again. This is ridiculous, and I would never set something like this up."

Some female boxers even objected on the basis that there were indeed quality fighters willing to take on MacGregor. Tracy Byrd, ranked number two in the lightweight division, who had recently lost a title bout to Laura Serrano, was particularly incensed and told the press, "Nobody called me . . . and I could name 10 more looking for a fight."

Lou DiBella, a senior vice president at HBO Sports responsible for boxing (who went on to become a boxing promoter, and in the late 2000s began putting women on his fight cards), said, "It's pure exploitation." He went on to articulate HBO's position on broadcasting the sport, saying, "Televising women's boxing isn't in our immediate plans. It has such a long way to go before it's considered a world-class sport, we're not looking at it even though it would boost ratings one time."[10]

With the actual fight night came more controversy.

MacGregor, with a three-inch height advantage, seemed to tower over Chow who stood five-feet, two-inches tall. From the outset, MacGregor peppered Chow with an unrelenting assault whilst her opponent covered up, ducked, backpedalled out of the way, and complained to the referee.

The fight fans in attendance, 2,768 cheering spectators—including many women who had come out to cheer on MacGregor—were becoming antsy at the obvious mismatch, thus it was no surprise when MacGregor swept all three judges' cards. Afterward Chow said that he'd had an episode of high blood pressure in the hours before the match, which was treated with medication. He went on to claim he "didn't feel right" and that he didn't believe he "got whipped."

The crowd, however, "roared with delight at the decision in her favor" having already "booed Chow for his defensive, lackluster effort."

Regardless, MacGregor showed excellent boxing skills. The female fans in attendance were ecstatic with her win, telling reporters the fight broke "a lot of barriers" and that being in the arena was like "taking part in this big event in history." Still another woman said, "We've come a long way."[11]

The next day, Laila Ali proved victorious in her battle, defeating her opponent, April Fowler, by knockout at thirty-one seconds into the first round.

Ali's dominating and reasonably skilled performance, however, seemed to sum up many of the concerns being raised about women's boxing. From the moment her opponent started fighting, she swung wildly with no ring skills whatsoever. Asked later about the KO she said simply, "I got knocked down and I stayed down. I wasn't getting any more [money] for getting up."

Sportswriter Ron Borges, pushing on the theme, wrote:

> For every skillful fighter like Ryker [*sic*], there are 100 women like Fowler. Out of shape and unskilled, they fight with their head down, arms windmilling, looking like a barroom brawler after a long night tapping a keg. For women's boxing to ever approach acceptance, it must lose that sideshow flavor and develop real fighters. Ali at least is trying to do that, but there are so few like her that it's a struggle to find worthy opponents.[12]

It had been MacGregor's contention that there weren't any skilled fighters willing to take a fight. That Chow wasn't particularly skilled didn't help MacGregor's argument. Regardless, the bout touched a raw nerve in the sport: While women's boxing was barely tolerated, there was an almost visceral response to women being in the ring at the same time as men.

This was reminiscent of how Belle Martell was once hounded from the ring more than a half century before when she had dared to enter it as a referee at men's fights. While women were now able to legally officiate, entering the ring with gloves to encounter a male opponent still seemed to be a taboo that was not to be crossed.

The theme of sexualizing women's boxing was also at play with the press vilifying Mia St. John for posing in the nude and otherwise making a mockery of the ring with mismatched fights and sexualized antics. Ron Borges voiced even more frustration when he wrote, "[Lucia] Ryker [*sic*] was recently dropped by promoter Bob Arum not because she lost a fight, because she never has; he dropped her because he believes he has a better shot at making money promoting a Playboy model."[13]

Borges's conclusion, however, was to state that while the issues might be different, professional women's boxing was proving to be the equal of men's boxing after all—corrupted by mismatched fights, poor paydays, poor promotion, and exploitation of the boxers.

HBO's Lou DiBella, in considering the triumvirate of issues that had propelled women's boxing into the news, didn't have much to say about Mia St. John. He also continued to contend that the MacGregor fight was nothing more than "exploitation." He did, however, say that HBO's position on airing women's bouts "may change with the emergence of Laila Ali, who is clearly a box-office fighter."[14]

The fact that her debut fight had been a mismatch seemed less important to DiBella, a boxing insider who was well aware of how the game was played. Laila Ali not only possessed real boxing skills (these would only develop further with the right handlers), but more importantly she had a charisma that seemed to embody what Jackie Kallen had called the "full package."

As Muhammad Ali's daughter, she was also boxing royalty at a time when there was nostalgia for the Muhammad Ali boxing era. The hope was that she might recapture some of the magic of boxing not only for women's boxing but for the sport as a whole. Whether she would deliver was a question to be answered over time—but whatever the case, she had certainly made an impression on the boxing public and her presence was soon to become a factor in the further development of women's boxing.

BOXING DAUGHTERS

> Laila Ali, you wanted to know if I was a professional fighter, now you see. I'll kick your butt, Laila Ali. I'm challenging you. Don't make me come and get you.
> —Jacqui Frazier-Lyde, February 6, 2000 [15]

To sit in a boxing gym in 1999 was to observe females aged from seven to seventy learning the old one-two. The growing popularity of the sport also extended to a unique group of women led by Laila Ali who captured the imagination of the sporting world both negatively and positively: daughters of famous boxers. With the coming of this second generation of boxers also came all of the championship hype most artfully expressed in that bombastic era when Muhammad Ali was the king of boxing.

An improbable daughter moving into the spotlight was Jacqui "Sister Smoke" Frazier-Lyde whose father was the legendary heavyweight champion "Smokin' Joe" Frazier. Growing up in Philadelphia, Frazier-Lyde had been a gifted high school athlete in basketball, hockey, softball, and lacrosse—and a scholar. Her prowess on the field won her a sports scholarship to American University where she was captain of the women's basketball team. From there, she went on to get a law degree at Villanova University and, after a stint as a public defender, opened her own law practice. She also married Peter Lyde, an official of the Laborer's International Union in Philadelphia, with whom she raised three children.

At the time of Laila Ali's debut in the ring, Jacqui Frazier-Lyde was an overly committed workaholic well on her way to her thirty-eighth birthday. A couple weeks after Ali's debut, *Philadelphia Daily News* reporter Bernard Fernandez had contacted Frazier-Lyde because he thought an interview might be newsworthy—and he was right. Frazier-Lyde recalled he had sought her out to talk about Laila Ali:

> [He] asked me how I thought I would measure up to Laila.
>   Well, sometimes I can say things off the top of my head, but I am very competitive. And I just said—it just came out: 'Oh, I could whip her butt.'

Well, since that day I've been training two hours a day, every day, at my dad's gym.

By December things had heated up. The Muhammad Ali–Joe Frazier rivalry had always been an intense side story in boxing. Their last fight in 1975, the "Thrilla' in Manila," or "Ali-Frazier III" had been a total war—with both boxers having fought beyond their endurance until Frazier's trainer, Eddie Futch, threw in the towel just before the fifteenth round, a call that Futch recalls as having devastated him. With a 2-1 advantage to Ali in the Ali-Frazier series, Jacqui Frazier-Lyde figured that if she defeated Laila Ali, she would even the score. "It's about history, competition, family and legacy," she said.[16]

Her father wasn't exactly thrilled with the idea, but thought her progress in the ring was great. Speaking to reporters at an open workout, he smiled and turned to remark on her progress after she finished her rounds on the speed bag, saying, "This is after two months, can you believe it?"

Laila Ali's camp was prosaic, vowing not "to address it" for the time being. Laila Ali's trainer summed it up when he said, "Let [Frazier-Lyde] get in the ring and become a professional. Then we'll deal with it."[17]

Frazier-Lyde's debut bout was held in early February 2000 at the Cultural Center in Scranton, Pennsylvania. Her opponent was a novice boxer named Teela Reese who had lost her only other professional contest by KO in the first round. Reese was reportedly a substitute for Frazier-Lyde's original opponent who was rumored to have had real boxing skills.

Not unlike Laila Ali's debut, the crowd of thirty-five hundred fans was sorely disappointed by a poorly fought match that lasted all of 1:23 into the first round. Frazier-Lyde dominated Reese, with a barrage of "wild punching and mauling" before backing her into the ropes and raining another onslaught of punches onto her. After absorbing the battering, Reese turned her back and referee Gary Rosatto stopped the contest, giving Frazier-Lyde the TKO win.[18]

To taunting chants from the fight fans, it was clear that Frazier-Lyde had "a long way to go before she could make a compelling match with Ali, who is polished and much more skillful than her counterpart."

Regardless of how the fight went, with a win in hand, Frazier-Lyde told the press she had a message for Ali. "Laila Ali, you wanted to know if I was a professional fighter, now you see. I'll kick your butt, Laila Ali. I'm challenging you. Don't make me come and get you."[19]

Unbelievably, Frazier-Lyde was reported to have earned $25,000 for her night's work, an unheard-of payday for a debut fight and exponentially higher than the typical payout for female fighters, who were often only making $200 to $300 a round. A case in point was Reese, who only earned $800. Frazier-Lyde had also lined up a fight for the following month against another novice fighter in Chester, West Virginia—part of a three-fight deal with promoter Don Elbaum.

A few days after Frazier-Lyde's debut bout, Laila Ali—who was also starting to earn $25,000 a contest—was asked whether she'd consider fighting her. In response, Ali told reporters she wasn't interested in a match because it wouldn't be "competitive." She went on to say, "She (stinks). The only comparison with her dad is her looks. . . . She fights that bad, she should keep her mouth shut."[20]

Another boxing daughter who "bit the bug" was twenty-three-year-old Freeda "Big" George Foreman, third eldest of champion heavyweight boxer George Foreman's children. She had been watching—first Laila Ali and then Jacqui Frazier-Lyde—from the sidelines. Feeling inspired by both fighters, Foreman intended to box professionally as well, timing her announcement for just after Frazier-Lyde's debut.

Asked why she wanted to box, Foreman, the single mother of a four-year-old daughter, said, "My goal is to change history and knock Laila [Ali] out." Later, making reference to the infamous 1974 matchup in Kinshasa, Zaire, between Muhammad Ali and George Foreman, nicknamed the "Rumble in the Jungle," she said, "It's not revenge, but the opportunity is there for me."[21] That was taken to mean not only the prospect of an avenging rematch but also the chance to earn considerable paydays alongside the other daughters in the ring.

Foreman, five feet, eleven inches and weighing in at 180 pounds, had been working in customer relations for United Parcel Service near her family home in Greenville, South Carolina. She quit her job in February to begin training in Colorado Springs for a projected debut fight in April. Asked how her famous father felt about her entering the ring she said, "It's an opportunity that my father does not exactly embrace. He flat-out doesn't like it. But I do have his love and support. That's what counts."[22]

Foreman eventually had her debut bout on Father's Day, June 18, 2000, in a fight promoted by Don Goossen at the Regent Hotel and Casino in Las Vegas. The Father's Day card featured not only Foreman in her debut fight, but also thirty-four-year-old Maria Johansson, daughter of the Swedish boxer and world heavyweight champion Ingemar Johansson, who had defeated Floyd Patterson by TKO in the third round of their 1959 title bout. To round out the card, Goossen had a famous boxing son, Hector Camacho Jr., as the main event, fighting Manard Reed in a twelve-round light welterweight championship fight which Camacho Jr. won by KO in the fourth round.

In the days leading up to her debut, Foreman's father had reportedly given her a $15,000 check to walk away from the fight—matching her fee. But she refused it and went ahead with the bout as scheduled. Foreman's opponent was Laquanda Landers, a hairdresser from Milwaukee with a background in Tae Kwon Do making her debut as a pro fighter. Landers came in weighing

168 pounds—twelve pounds lighter than Foreman. She was also six inches shorter, putting her at a decided disadvantage.

Foreman sent Landers to the canvas with her first punch. In the second round, Landers managed to survive until she was dropped again at 1:44 into the round, but this time, she was unable to get up. Foreman took the fight—however inelegantly—by KO.[23]

The debut bout of the other boxing daughter on the card, Maria Johansson, was less successful. She'd managed to draw an actual boxer from Indiana named Karrie Frye who was eight years younger and sported a 4-1 record including a first-round KO win in a fight promoted as the Midwest female light heavyweight championship. A four-round slugfest, Johansson was badly bruised and lost the bout by a unanimous decision. She fought one more bout and, losing by KO, retired from boxing shortly thereafter.

Two more daughters of boxing legends also boxed professionally: Irichelle Duran, the twenty-three-year-old daughter of the renowned Panamanian world champion Roberto Duran, and J'Marie Moore, daughter of the famed heavyweight boxer Archie Moore. In addition, two sisters of professional boxers began boxing professionally. Tracy Byrd, whose brother Chris Byrd had been an Olympian in 1992 and was now angling for his chance at heavyweight title, was one. Tracy Byrd had begun to box in August 1996 and by 2000 had amassed an 11-2 record, including one title. She was considered a legitimate boxer and retired in 2006 with a 13-10-1 record.

Melissa "Honey Girl" Del Valle (Salamone), in winning the New York Daily News Golden Gloves in 1996, became the first sister of a Golden Gloves champion to win the award. Her brother, Lou "Honey Boy" Del Valle, had become a champion four years earlier. Melissa Del Valle (Salamone) went on to an illustrious career in women's boxing (30-6-1), winning major titles plus the reputation as a "real" boxer. She was also the subject of a feature-length documentary film released in 2000 by filmmaker Joe Cardona. Entitled *Honey Girl*, it appeared in film festivals and on the Miami-based PBS affiliate. Despite critical acclaim it did not gain much traction or notice due to the release of filmmaker Karen Kusama's feature *Girlfight* in the same year, which was garnering a lot of press attention.

In the case of Irichelle Duran, her father reportedly didn't speak to her for a week after she made her announcement. She went on to a difficult loss on points in her first fight against another novice fighter named Geraldine Iglesias at the Hard Rock Hotel and Casino in Las Vegas and had two more bouts before retiring from the ring with a 1-2 record.

J'Marie Moore had entered the ring in 1997—two years before Laila Ali's 1999 entrance. This would make her the actual "first" boxing daughter, but she never garnered much attention before Ali began fighting. Moore's second—and last—fight was in 2000. She won by TKO in the third round against Anita Wells, who was making her debut.

In the pecking order of notoriety and publicity, Laila Ali and Frazier-Lyde rose to the top—both in terms of money earned and fighting potential. Ali in particular also managed to carve out a spot for herself among the "elite" women boxers and was spoken of in the same league as Christy Martin and Lucia Rijker. By 2003 even the Internet site Women Boxing Archive Network (WBAN) began making mention of her boxing abilities.

The preponderance of famous daughters in the sport, however, seemed to change the entire calculus of women's boxing. The national conversation about the sport was increasingly focused on boxing daughters as a "side-show" and "circus." What was absent was mention of the increasing number of skilled women who were serious contenders. These fighters filled out the undercards of boxing events every weekend at venues large and small across the United States—and increasingly in Europe and South America—but often did so with little notice except on the website WBAN, an increasingly important resource for news about the sport started by former boxer Sue TL Fox in 1998. (A magazine called *Lady Boxer* had also begun publication in 1997. It provided news about fights, articles about fighters, and photographs—many of them taken by Mary Ann Owen, who was starting to make a name for herself as a women's boxing photographer. *Boxing Illustrated* magazine also published articles about the state of women's boxing, rankings, and other stories, and even the venerable *The Ring* magazine published pieces about women fighters.)

The growing ranks of professional women boxers were also still appearing on television in local markets and occasionally on cable or pay-per-view, although the latter were typically "name" fighters that included Christy Martin and Mia St. John, who continued to appear on every Oscar De La Hoya fight card. In St. John's case, however, press reports continued to castigate her appearances as a "sideshow."

An opening salvo about the state of women's boxing in the United States came from Tim Graham, writing for ESPN, the day after Frazier-Lyde's debut fight. In his estimation female boxers "had laid a foundation of legitimacy," particularly "talented ladies like Christy Martin, Lucia Rijker, Sumya Anani and Kathy Collins." He went on to write, "It wasn't implausible the sport one day might be mentioned in the same breath as basketball or tennis."

With the likes of Frazier-Lyde in the sport—women boxers who "showed skill comparable to a preschooler in a playground scuffle"—the sport was "turning into a joke, even by boxing's comical standards."[24]

The day before Frazier-Lyde's debut fight on February 5, of the six fight cards contested around the United States fully five of them had female bouts on the cards (while on a similar weekend five years earlier there had been none). One fight card even featured women as the main event—a six-round competitive fight (contested in Warren, Ohio) between Sabrina Hall and Vickie Woods. In addition, two WIBF women's title fights in Germany were also featured prominently with one of the contenders, Eva Jones Young, hailing from Indiana.

While Hall and Woods had some local coverage in Ohio, there seems to have been none for Young. There was also no acknowledgment that female boxing had reached the point where women were featured on multiple cards across the United States—an incredible accomplishment in a brief span of time. But the growing popularity of the sport did, with some justification, open it to criticism due to some of the unevenness of the fighters.

The following Friday, on February 11, 2000, ESPN2 broadcast an all-female card from Kenner, Louisiana, featuring three IFBA ten-round title-fight bouts and three six-round bouts on the undercard.

The women fighting for a title may not have had the marquee names of Martin or Rijker, but they were serious about the sport and had worked hard to perfect skills that were improving over time. The bouts included such fighters as Jolene Blackshear and Margaret Sidoroff in a much anticipated matchup—among those who followed the sport—that ended up with Sidoroff, a highly skilled pressure fighter, getting the nod by unanimous decision after ten rounds of truly competitive boxing.

Both women had garnered their share of notices in the press since they turned pro, but their work that night and those of the other fighters on the card including newcomer Ann Wolfe, a powerful super middleweight who was a definite comer, were barely noticed by the press.

Boxer Jolene Blackshear, interviewed for a newspaper article a month later, voiced concerns similar to those raised by Graham. She was fearful that these hard-won gains would be lost due to the focus on the hype surrounding those boxing daughters who'd yet to show any real skills. As she put it, "Boxing takes athletic prowess, skill, coordination, hard training and profound dedication."

She went on to say, "It's not street fighting or mud wrestling . . . and it's not something you just step into the ring and do. You have to be really dedicated to succeed."[25]

As the year wore on, much of the press attention about women's boxing continued to center on the boxing daughters—even outside of sports pages. An article published in *Bloomberg Businessweek* in July 2000 was a case in a point. Entitled "Daddy's Little Girls Come Out Swinging," the article posed the question, "Can the daughters of famous boxers turn female boxing into a marquee sport?"

It, too, argued that the boxing daughters would have to deliver real fighting ability in order to aid the sport—while balancing the fact that according to an unnamed executive at Don King Productions, Inc., "We don't have enough serious women boxers around to meet demand." He went on to say, "I don't think the whole daughter syndrome is viable because they're not all serious athletes. I don't want to see girls closing their eyes in the ring."[26]

The flipside of the argument was the reality that more women were entering the sport each day, with some fifteen hundred women in the amateurs and pros in the United States alone, plus the growing number of women who were entering the ranks of women boxers in the rest of the world.

What many fighters and advocates for the sport feared was that all the hard work and improvement in the performance of female boxers was being undermined by the continued focus on boxing daughters.

MILLION DOLLAR BABIES . . . NOT

With the advent of the boxing daughters, the clamor for a Martin-Rijker showdown had somewhat lessened in the press, which had muted its enthusiasm for their possible matchup in favor of an Ali-Frazier IV. That's not to say the possibility of a Martin-Rijker toe-to-toe battle went away, as the rivalry between the pair had, if anything, become even more intense over time. The two even had a couple of very public face-offs that rivaled the confrontations between male marquee fighters.

The prize money for the fight was reported to be the largest purse ever offered for a women's boxing contest—$750,000 a piece. There were stipulations however. Martin insisted that Rijker take a chromosome test before she'd even consider fighting her, which the Rijker camp rejected as insulting.

In 1998 Rijker had publically challenged Martin in the middle of a press conference at the Olympic Theater in Los Angeles—one that provoked a shrill response from Martin who was infuriated at Rijker's effrontery.

The enmity between the pair only increased when Rijker later showed up at a public workout being held to promote a Don King card in 2000. On it, Felix Trinidad was set to challenge David Reid in a WBA title fight with Martin only appearing in an eight-rounder on the undercard against Belinda "Brown Sugar" Laracuente, a slick boxer with impressive skills, who'd won a WIBF light welterweight title. (Martin won the fight by split decision—one that was widely disputed by boxing experts at ringside, the boxing press, and the fans who watched the fight. They all gave Laracuente at least five out of the eight rounds.)

At the presser held at the L.A. Boxing Gym, as Reid worked out in the ring, Rijker and Martin got into a confrontation that spilled onto the floor, subsided, and then rose up again on the other side of the ring.

The question never answered was whether the confrontation was part of an elaborate script to hype a possible bout then under negotiation between Rijker's manager, Stan Hoffman, and Don King, or whether the years of "trash talk" had led to real enmity.

Rijker's most recent fight had been in August 1999 against Diane Dutra. Although Rijker had defeated Dutra by TKO in the third round, Rijker had burst an eardrum. Rijker was scheduled to fight again in November on a Tyson undercard but the bout was canceled, along with a second one and a December fight that she canceled due to a stomach ulcer. She was still in the "game," but the Dutra fight proved to be her last until she returned to the ring in February 2002.

In the interim, Rijker did publicity for *Shadow Boxers* (which was receiving rave reviews), and she was in the beginning stages of carving out a television and film career. Questions about Rijker continued, however, especially since she wasn't facing women considered at the top of the division such as Sumaya Anani and Kathy Collins, who were both pushing ahead despite any negative publicity the boxing daughters had generated.

By the end of 2000 women's boxing seemed to be in two worlds: female fighters who'd achieved hype such as Martin, Rijker, St. John, and Laila Ali; and the nonmarquee fighters who while skilled were not able to garner the attention of the top tier.

In the hyped camp, Ali was gaining real celebrity and a crossover appeal with a string of wins (against less than stellar opponents). Her fighting ability still had much room to grow, and in her eighth fight—against boxer Kendra Lenhart—Ali was definitely "rocked" a few times, in what could be characterized as an "ugly" bout with lots of wide shots as they both fought toe to toe through many of the rounds. It was also the first time Ali had gone the distance—a full six rounds—winning the fight by unanimous decision.

Jacqui Frazier-Lyde was also busy winning a total of five four-rounders and one six-rounder, all ending in either TKOs or KOs. Her fights were mismatches, but they hadn't stopped her from touting her wins nor from clamoring for a showdown with Laila Ali. Press reports alluded to negotiations that would commence in October 2000 about a fight to occur sometime in March 2001, the thirtieth anniversary of the first meeting between Muhammad Ali and Joe Frazier at Madison Square Garden on March 8, 1971.

"The fight is on. We just need to make it official," said Peter Lyde, Jacqui Frazier-Lyde's husband and manager.[27]

The boxing daughters aside, women who'd begun boxing professionally in the late 1990s were a new class of professional female boxers. Fighters such as Ann Wolfe, Belinda Laracuente, Layla McCarter, Ada Velez, Chevelle Hallback, Yvonne Reis, and former kickboxers Alicia Ashley and Melissa Del Valle were all crisp, technically proficient boxers who were elevating the game, joining the likes of Collins, Anani, and Byrd, who were already garnering attention and respect. Alicia Ashley had also appeared as a boxer in the film *Girlfight*, displaying her consummate ring abilities in the fight scenes with Michelle Rodriguez.

The skills exhibited by Laracuente in her bout with Christy Martin were a case in point: Laracuente, twenty-one, moved with the grace and ease of a boxer who'd grown up in the ring. She had slick moves that saw her using her defensive prowess to stymie Martin through much of the bout, while peppering her almost at will with stiff jabs and hard-hitting combinations that mottled Martin's face. As if to further crystallize the difference in style and boxing pedigree, Laracuente was quoted as saying she "beat up the old lady," despite losing by majority decision.[28]

If Lucia Rijker was the first "visible" female boxer with "real" boxing skills, then the fighters who were competing for WIBA, WIBF and IFBA titles were in her wheelhouse and beyond in terms of skills, determination, and courage. The nonmarquee fighters, however, were primarily boxing for "house" money, meaning virtually nothing. And while Rijker may have complained that she hadn't earned $25,000 for a title fight whereas Laila Ali earned that amount right out of the gate, fighters such as Laracuente, Hallback, and McCarter, by comparison, barely earned tip money.

Dan Cucich, a past president of the Women's International Kick Boxing Association (now defunct), raised the issue of a two-tiered boxing system on a WBAN fight review site after the Martin-Laracuente fight. He opined that "big money" was perpetuating a system where the technically sound fighters were being pushed out of matches in favor of "the famous daughters" fighting as one-fight wonders. The perpetuation of Christy Martin and Mia St. John as marquee fighters was also to the detriment of the excellent boxers who were hard at work perfecting their craft for peanuts and with limited financial opportunities—despite their consistent displays of good ring skills and exciting matches.[29]

Still, these boxers were undaunted and pushed themselves each day for the love of the sport and any little recognition they might garner on occasional television appearances and in the press.

WOMEN'S BOXING AND THE WORLD

With the advent of the 2000s, women's boxing was no longer confined to the United States and was proving very popular throughout Europe, Japan, and Latin America. The organization that Barbara Buttrick had started in 1989, WIBF, was particularly active in Europe, conferring its first title there two months after introduction of the WIBF championships in April of 1995.

The first European WIBF titleholder was Regina Halmich,[30] who won the WIBF European Super Flyweight Championship in June 1995.

Halmich was rapidly becoming Europe's best-known (and best-paid) female boxer with a career that began back in 1994. A pretty five-foot, three-inch blonde, she had been a kickboxer and had won championships three years running from 1992 to 1994, before switching over to boxing. She also faced a global boxing "Who's Who" over the span of her career, although she fought almost exclusively in Germany. She eventually amassed an impressive 54-1 record, having boxed for thirteen years. As the face of women's boxing in Europe, Halmich helped popularize the sport and had a legion of fans who supported her.

Another European champion was the British fighter Jane "The Fleetwood Assassin" Couch. A native of Fleetwood, England, Couch had been on the fast track to a life of drugs, alcohol, and street brawls when she happened to see a documentary about women boxing in the United States. Intrigued, she took to the gym and, shortly thereafter, entered her first fight—a Muay Thai bout.

She proved successful in the ring, amassing a 4-0 record (one that was unsanctioned in the United Kingdom) before heading to Demark in 1996 to fight in a WIBF light welterweight title fight against French boxer Sandra Geiger (1-0). Couch won the title, and went on to defend it in New Orleans, Louisiana, the following year, when she won a seventh-round TKO decision over veteran boxer Andrea DeShong. She continued to successfully defend her title, winning a unanimous decision over boxer Leah Mellinger (who went on to defeat Kathy Collins in an IWBF and IFBA title bout).

After losing two bouts to the 1970s boxing great Dora Webber (in 1997 and 1998), Jane Couch began her fight against the British Boxing Board of Control (BBBC—the same group that had prevented Barbara Buttrick from fighting nearly fifty years before) to be licensed to box. The BBBC denied the license on the premise that women were too emotionally unstable to box due to "premenstrual tension." The battle was taken before the British Industrial Board where Couch argued that she was being discriminated against. She had previously won the backing of Britain's Equal Opportunities Commission. The board ruled in her favor and "ridiculed" the BBBC "for their defence." Couch was issued her license shortly thereafter with her first licensed bout set for November 1998 against a Yugoslavian fighter, Simona Lukic (1-4-1).

Couch's fight garnered a lot of controversy in the United Kingdom. Some was predictable, given the public's lack of exposure to the sport. The then current heavyweight champion Lennox Lewis's manager, Frank Maloney, was among the more vocal critics who maligned the fight as a "freak show"—one of the more common pejoratives hurled at female boxing.[31]

The "usual suspects" railing against the entry of women's boxing into the sporting world were not the only critics. Even before Couch's win against the much less experienced Lukic, Barbara Buttrick had expressed her dismay at the obvious mismatch—one that in her mind would only serve to leave the sport open to more criticism and controversy.

Speaking with a reporter from the British newspaper the *Independent*, Buttrick said:

To be honest I'm surprised they let this girl box Jane, because we certainly know very little about her. We [WIBF] offered them a good opponent but the promoter turned us down. This has made a mockery of women's boxing, and it's no good saying there are no good women boxers, because there are plenty out there.

It's not fair to Jane. She's worked so hard. She won the fight [to box] but she's going to lose her credibility. [32]

Boxer Laura Serrano had a similar role to Couch in opening up women's boxing in Mexico in 1998. An established fighter in the United States with her tough debut bout against Christy Martin behind her, Serrano, an attorney, waged a battle against Mexican authorities and eventually won the right for women to contest in boxing matches there—especially in Mexico City, which had long disallowed women to fight in the ring. The authorities had argued that boxing could injure female reproductive organs. Serrano, citing changes to the Mexican Constitution in 1992 that established equal pay for equal work, won the right for women to box in Mexico.

Argentine Marcella Eliana Acuna had famously fought her first two professional fights against Christy Martin and Lucia Rijker. Back in Argentina she helped establish women's boxing as a legitimate sport when she fought in the first legal boxing match there against an American, Jamilla Lawrence, in 2001. Acuna won the four-round fight by split decision. She also fought in the first women's world championship bout to be contested in Argentina, in 2002, when she fought and lost to the Brooklyn-based Jamaican fighter Alicia Ashley in the WIBF super bantamweight title fight. Acuna went on to lose a rematch to Ashley, staged in Argentina the following year.

In Australia female boxing was legal in some parts of the country and illegal in others. Queensland legalized it in 2000, but inexplicably the sport was banned in New South Wales from 1986 to 2008 (the ban was dropped in part to allow women to eventually compete in the Olympics). Nonetheless, women boxed, and a burgeoning amateur program began in the late 1990s.

Author Mischa Merz began her amateur career in 1998, eventually winning gold in 2001 at the Australian National Championships. On the professional side, boxer Sharon Anyos began her career in 1998 as well, becoming one of the most successful boxers from Australia in that period.

Anyos (originally from Geelong, Victoria, near Melbourne) had studied karate as a child and won an Australian karate women's title when she was sixteen years of age. From there she launched into kickboxing and Muay Thai, taking an Australian kickboxing title at age nineteen in 1989. She continued to compete as a kickboxer for the next several years, winning additional championships.

Anyos made her boxing debut in July 1998 fighting in Australia's first sanctioned women's world championship fight under the auspices of the Australian National Boxing Federation (ANBF). Her career soared from there as she fought a series of tough opponents—including losses to Jane Couch and Japanese fighter Fujin Raika—that helped to solidify her reputation as an excellent boxer. In 2005, Anyos handed Marcela Eliana Acuna one of her few losses when she defeated her in a ten-round WBC championship fight for the vacant title. Defeating Acuna established Anyos as one of the top female professional boxers in the sport.

Japan's Fujin Raika had begun her career in 2000 in Tokyo, losing her first fight to Layla McCarter who'd come to Japan to fight her in April 2002. Raika went on to become the WIBA featherweight champion in December 2002, defeating Australia's Sharon Anyos. Amassing a 25-8 record as of August 2013, Raika boxed such elite fighters as Chevelle Hallback, Jelena Mrdjenovich, Olivia Gerula, Ann Saccurato, and Belinda Laracuente.

With the international character of women's boxing beginning to take hold, the sport met a mixed reception. In some countries, such as Germany and Denmark, the boxing establishment, the public, and the broadcast industry were providing their fighters marquee status and helping women to advance their careers. Great Britain and Australia, along with others, were much slower to embrace the sport giving very few women real chances to build their careers in their home country.

As the decade of the 2000s wore on, women's boxing in most of Europe, Latin America, and Asia continued to grow, with many of the fighters from those regions consistently winning championships and appearing high up on the list of top female boxing talent.

THE DISAPPEARANCE OF THE SPORT

What began as a far-fetched salvo lobbed by Jacqui Frazier-Lyde became a veritable industry as Laila Ali and Frazier-Lyde negotiated their Ali-Frazier IV battle in 2001.

The first major promotion held between the two was on March 2, 2001—marking nearly thirty years to the day since their fathers' epic first battle.

With Laila Ali and Jacqui Frazier-Lyde's joint appearance in separate fights on a card billed as the "March to Destiny" at the Turning Stone Resort & Casino in Verona, New York, the plan was to announce their impeding Ali-Frazier IV battle after both fighters finished contesting their bouts.

The proceedings began with both women winning their bouts in a pair of mismatches. Ali had to actually work for hers—five "vicious" rounds worth until she got the TKO—whereas Frazier-Lyde won hers in the first round.

Ali-Frazier IV was set to be an eight-round pay-per-view extravaganza with the viewing fee set at $29.95 (although also reported at $24.95). It would be fought in a tent erected in the parking lot at the Turning Stone with seating for eight thousand. It also coincided with the International Boxing

Hall of Fame (IBHOF) weekend held in nearby Canastota, New York, which guaranteed press attention and the presence of some number of the boxing elite at ringside. The fight was listed among the festivities of the weekend.

By fight night, the press was in a frenzy of condemnation for the hyped-up battle. Writer Jack Newfield, invoking Mohammad Ali and Joe Frazier's legendary third battle in Manila, wrote, "Friday's event between their daughters will be a burlesque, a P.T. Barnum hustle to exploit two sacred names, and the hatred between the fathers that has become Shakespearean over the years."

He went on to quote Mark Kram, author of the newly published *Ghosts of Manila* about the famous battle and its aftermath. Kram had said, "It's a non-event. What's the purpose, except to trade on the bitterness between the fathers?"[33]

Not all of the prefight publicity was negative. A photograph of Laila Ali and Jacqui Frazier-Lyde appeared on the cover of the May 28, 2001, edition of *TV Guide* magazine and an article ran in *People* magazine. Laila Ali also appeared on *The Today Show*, proving her crossover appeal as a celebrity and the kind of interest the fight had piqued among the general public.

In response to all the criticism, both fighters were clear in stating that it was about them and not their fathers and also pointed to the hypocrisy of some of the arguments. Jacqui Frazier-Lyde was particularly incensed:

> They should be ashamed. The investment that Joe Frazier and Muhammad Ali made in boxing 30 years ago, a lot of people are still trading off that. People are still writing books and making TV shows and movies. I don't see a problem with their children benefiting. Besides, we've sweated and worked to get here.[34]

Joe Frazier, who was asked to comment, also took the fight out of the realm of a blood feud and said, "I think it's all showbiz."[35]

Laila Ali noted, "It's about worldwide exposure. It's going to be on television and it's going to be shown all over the world."

With a purse rumored to be anywhere from hundreds of thousands of dollars to "between $1.7 and $2.4 million, mostly from sales of television pay-per-view," the fight—whatever the motivations—was likely to be the highest payday on record for a female boxing match.[36]

On the night of the fight, sixty-five hundred fans came to Verona, New York—including Joe Frazier who sat proudly at ringside for the eight-fight card. Muhammad Ali, however, was not in attendance, reportedly due to a prior commitment at an auto show. There were also three hundred reporters, photographers, and film crews credentialed for the event from all over the world.

If the audience in the tent and those watching on pay-per-view had thought they were showing up at the "Groaner in Verona" they were wrong.[37] Both women had come to fight.

At the weigh-in, the five-foot, ten-inch, twenty-three-year-old Ali came in at 160¾ pounds while Frazier-Lyde, who was thirty-nine, was five-feet, nine inches and weighed 164 pounds. Both were in peak condition having truly worked diligently.

Ali, sixteen years younger and the more skilled of the two, was the odds-on favorite coming into the bout and managed to edge her way to a majority win. Frazier-Lyde, however, was no pushover as the pair shocked the crowd with a tough, hard-fought battle that could easily have been called a draw.

Both fighters showed grit and heart in what was clearly the most difficult ring outing either of them had ever fought. And while their skill level could not be called a refined ring science, their sustained output of punches and determination more than made up for it. Frazier-Lyde, in particular, rose to the challenge in the later rounds, even managing to jab, something the brawl-er had found hard to do in the early going.

After all the hype and controversy, the fight was competitive and enter-taining. It also went the distance with such a continued high level of intensity that the pundits were forced to give the pair their admiration for their efforts. The crowd, too, was totally invested in the fight and was on their feet cheer-ing as the two women faced off even before the festivities began.

Of the two fighters, Ali was probably the most surprised at the outcome, telling reporters, "I know she had feeling behind this fight. I didn't think she was going to get me tangled up like that."

Frazier-Lyde said, "I feel fantastic. My family is here with me and I feel like a winner." She added, "The Ali camp did not want a rematch called, but maybe public demand will change that."[38]

In the aftermath of the fight, boxer Mia St. John perhaps best summed up all of the hoopla when she remarked, "Nothing can hurt the reputation of boxing. It has such a bad reputation already. It's what people love about it. It's kind of dark, kind of crooked. People love that."

St. John was also purportedly about to embark on the next "big thing" in women's boxing—a possible fight date with Christy Martin. "It's a fight that has to happen," St. John said. "I've taken a lot of criticism for my boxing and the way I look, but my goal has always been to fight her, beat her [Martin], and get out. Her biggest mistake will be she'll underestimate me."[39] While the opening salvo in the discussions would have put the fight on a card in September 2001, the pair actually met in the ring a year later, in 2002, at the Silverdome in Pontiac, Michigan, as the main event of the evening. The pay-per-view show was touted as the WBC Pound-for-Pound Women's Cham-pionship bout.

The fact that Mia St. John was willing to fight Christy Martin—for a reported $100,000, her largest payday—garnered a lot of respect for St. John. She'd begun training with Robert Garcia, a former fighter with a good reputation as a trainer, and St. John even had woman boxer Fredia Gibbs, who was well regarded in the sport, in her corner for the fight.

St. John was also making a conscious decision to walk away from "pitty-pat" fighting into the realm of real boxing. Although she lost the unanimous decision to Martin, no one had expected her to last ten rounds (having previously only ever gone four), least of all against Christy. St. John also showed, in some instances, better skills than Martin, boxing her on the angles and getting in a fair number of clean shots, which served to increase her stock as a fighter.

What people forgot watching the pair was that they were also only one year apart in age. And if Martin had ushered in the era of "pink" in the early 1990s, St. John had brought "hot pink" into the lexicon of women's boxing in the latter part of that decade. The name of the game, however, was not so much their promotional gimmicks, but the contesting of a highly competitive boxing match—with St. John seemingly the younger and hungrier fighter as they boxed toe to toe in the ring.

Martin was to later explain away some of that by stating she'd not had adequate sparring hours to prepare for the fight due to money constraints. She hadn't received the promised $200,000 advance, but she'd also clearly underestimated just how much St. John wanted to prove that she was a skilled boxer. The ringside audience had been only a meager five hundred or so "live fans," which put a damper on what was otherwise a good night of boxing.

Lucia Rijker, who'd watched from the audience, also created fireworks of her own by "jumping into the ring" and challenging Martin. [40]

Christy, with her mind on her legacy, still wanted to fight Lucia Rijker, although nothing much had come of it so far. In the interim Martin had added Laila Ali to her short list, now that she had joined her as a marquee fighter.

Martin had already fought two other highly acclaimed female boxers in her weight class (her second career loss was to Sumya Anani in 1998, and she won a squeaker against Kathy Collins in 2001 at Madison Square Garden). With those contests out of the way she did not have a plethora of options unless she was willing to go against the up-and-coming fighters, who were now stronger and more ring savvy (as Belinda Laracuente had proven). Laila Ali—who was rapidly displacing Martin as the most bankable female boxing star—was in many ways her only option in terms of "star power." Given that Ali was younger, taller, and outweighed her by at least twenty pounds, she was not all that viable as a beatable opponent.

Ali was also still clearly in the ascendant part of her career even though she'd taken a year off after her bout with Frazier-Lyde, electing to have shoulder surgery. She spent some of that year recuperating and after rehabilitation developed and taught an aerobics class she called "The Ali Way."

Returning to the ring in June 2002, Ali easily won a tune-up fight before fighting for the vacant IFBA female super middleweight title two months later in front of a capacity crowd on pay-per-view. Ali made quick work of her opponent, Suzanne Taylor, by gaining a TKO in the second round. (Taylor had previously fought Jacqui Frazier-Lyde in December 2001 for the vacant WIBA light heavyweight title, and lost by TKO in the fourth round.)

Ali's win set her up for a super middleweight "alphabet soup" unification battle for the WIBA, IWBF and IBA championships. Her opponent was Valerie Mahfood (sporting purple short-cropped hair), considered one of women's boxing's stronger fighters and the holder of the WIBA title. The fight was shown on ESPN2, with Ali receiving an eighth-round win by TKO. Throughout the bout, Ali had used a stinging left jab, combinations, angles, and strong punching, proving that her skills were increasing. The win also further established her among the elite in the sport.

Having claimed two more championship belts, Ali enhanced her name recognition both inside and outside of the ring—pushing Martin back a notch to "pioneer" status. It also set up the pair for a confrontation, but not before Ali defeated Mahfood for a second time by TKO in a nontitle rematch on the undercard of the Lennox Lewis–Vitali Klitschko heavyweight megabattle. Ali's showing garnered positive press and helped to further solidify her position in women's boxing.

At the end of June, it was announced that Christy Martin and Laila Ali would fight on August 23, 2003, at the Mississippi Coast Coliseum in Biloxi. The fight card also featured two other female bouts. One pitted the hard-fighting Ann Wolfe—whom many thought should be Ali's real opponent—versus Valerie Mahfood in a ten-rounder, plus a pair of local fighters making their pro debut.

In order to fight Ali, Martin had to move up in a weight class but still gave Ali close to a twenty-pound advantage, not to mention a height advantage of six inches. It was also to be Martin's first fight since defeating Mia St. John—nine months before—so questions of ring "rust" were inevitable, given that she'd also been underprepared for the St. John fight.

Giving up that much in weight and height was a questionable move, especially since Martin never really brought her weight up to 160 and was even allowed to weigh-in fully clothed in heavy combat fatigues. The $250,000 payday would be the first she'd had in nine months and had to be one of the factors in signing on to the "Superfight."

As it happened the bout was more than a lopsided affair with the much younger Ali towering over Martin and beating her to the punch, although Martin worked tirelessly to slug it out in the center of the ring. Ali also utilized her longer reach, testing Martin who tried hard to adjust by fighting

from all angles. Still, Martin was in big trouble—even in the first round—
due to Ali's slugging power.

Martin showed tremendous heart as she fought back hard at a blistering
pace. Ali's constant onslaught, however, proved too much for Martin who
took a knee for the first time in her career in the third round, and went down
taking a knee in the fourth round before she was counted out. The win gave
Ali the moniker of the "reigning" champion of women's boxing.

Lucia Rijker, the other big name in women's boxing, returned to the ring
in 2002 in a tune-up against Carla Witherspoon and garnered a win by TKO
in the fourth round. Rijker next fought British boxing pioneer Jane Couch at
the Staples Center in Los Angeles in an eight-round bout—taking all eight
rounds by unanimous decision of all the judges at ringside.

Despite the promise of fighters like Belinda Laracuente, Layla McCarter,
Chevelle Hallback, and Ann Wolfe, no one had attracted the notice of the big
promoters—which meant that, aside from Ali, there was really no one waiting in the wings to step up into the "center ring," despite there being a raft of
skilled fighters.

MILLION DOLLAR BABY

Rijker's appearance as the character Billie "The Blue Bear" in Clint Eastwood's 2004 film about women's boxing, *Million Dollar Baby*, brought a
brief renewal of interest in the sport—and placed Rijker alongside Ali as a
boxing star. (Rijker was also a technical advisor during the filming of the
fight sequences.)

The storyline was a simple one. Maggie Fitzgerald had a singular desire
to be a boxer. Through hard work and determination, Maggie begins her
professional career and steadily improves. She eventually faces Blue Bear, a
"take-no-prisoners" boxer, who paralyzes Maggie by hitting her with a chair
after the bell as Maggie walks back to her corner. The film ends with Maggie
lying paralyzed in a hospital. After several twists and turns involving her
estranged family, she asks Frankie, her trainer, to end her life—which he
does out of love for her.

Aside from the controversy that was generated by critics claiming *Million
Dollar Baby* endorsed euthanasia, the film was criticized for its unrealistic
portrayal of the world of women's boxing—something that certainly could
also be said of films about male boxing—especially to those who don't know
much about the sport.

Bob Arum—ever the showman—took the title of the film literally and
came up with the idea to promote the "Million Dollar Lady" boxing match.
The match would finally pit Christy Martin against Lucia Rijker for a
$1,000,000 winner-take-all purse. The problem was, no one much cared any

more—ticket sales went at a slow clip and not much interest was generated by the press.

Both fighters did take it seriously enough, and Rijker—now back in the gym—began preparing for it. Unfortunately, she tore her Achilles tendon, necessitating surgery, which ended the chance for the once-heralded "dream" fight.

Tragedy of another sort struck and left the boxing world reeling.

Becky Zerlentes was a thirty-four-year-old amateur boxer and geography professor at Front Range Community College in Larimer County, Colorado, not far from her home in Fort Collins. An avid sports woman, Zerlentes had been a synchronized swimmer, a triathlete, and earned both a black belt in Goshin Jitsu and a brown belt in Tae Kwon Do. As a boxer, she eventually amassed a 6-4 amateur record in her native Illinois before stepping out of the ring in 2002 after having won a regional Golden Gloves title. In early 2005 Zerlentes began her boxing training again and entered the Colorado Golden Gloves scheduled to be held at the National Western Complex in Denver.

On the night of April 2, 2005, Zerlentes stepped into the ring to compete against Heather Schmitz, thirty-two—the only other woman in her weight class. The two had met a few days before at the weigh-in and had become friendly, having found that they shared a love for geography and boxing. Both women entered the ring with regulation gloves and helmets and both felt comfortable as they began their match.

In the third and final round of their bout, Zerlentes was ahead on points when Schmitz threw a straight right to Zerlentes's left temple.

The blow sent Zerlentes lurching forward to the canvas and she lost consciousness after the knockout punch. Ringside physicians, alert to her fall, attended to her immediately, giving her oxygen. But seeing no response when they flashed a light into her eyes, they screamed out for an ambulance.

Zerlentes never woke up and she was pronounced dead the following day after having undergone emergency surgery during which doctors had discovered a subdural hematoma on her brain. The cause of death was initially listed as blunt-force trauma. An autopsy reached the same conclusion.

Becky Zerlentes's death on April 3, 2005, was the first boxing-related death of a female boxer ever recorded.

Speaking to a reporter, Dr. Russ Simpson, who had attended her ringside, said:

> I was thinking, "What did I miss?" The punch was not that hard. I thought she had just lost her balance. She was wearing headgear. The amateur mats are thicker and softer than pro mats. The velocity of the punches aren't that hard.

A review of the fight footage by Dr. Armando Sanchez, USA Boxing's medical director, revealed that she had been attended to promptly and properly, and that during "the last 15 or 20 seconds, [she didn't] look hurt." He also stated, "At the moment of impact, she [was] defending herself."[41]

Following so close on the film *Million Dollar Baby*, the comparisons to Maggie's fate were inevitable—as were the calls to make boxing illegal. At the end of the day, however, the death just seemed terribly sad, especially knowing that everything had been done "right" when it came to ensuring that both fighters were safe in the ring.

Boxing promotion for women seemed to fall precipitously from there, although in regional pockets, female fighters still enjoyed a strong following and even some pay-per-view shows. Layla McCarter, fighting out of Las Vegas, became wildly popular there garnering respect in the sport as a true "boxer's boxer."

In November 2006 McCarter faced Belinda Laracuente for the vacant Global Boxing Union (GBU) lightweight title, contested at the Orleans Hotel and Casino and promoted by CSI Sports. Both boxers were considered among the best in the sport and the matchup excited followers of women's boxing. While the contest was not going to be aired live, a tape of it was broadcast on cable a week after the fight with a worldwide distribution.

What distinguished this fight was the decision to allow three-minute-round durations in the ten-round bout—the first since a few had managed to slip through in the 1970s. The issue of round duration had been a contentious one since women's boxing became popularized as far back as the 1950s. Detractors of the sport had used the shortened rounds as fodder for their condemnation of women's boxing, claiming women didn't have the stamina for "real" fighting—an issue that continues to vex the sport.

Excited by the prospect of fighting with the three-minute rounds ubiquitous in male boxing, McCarter said, "It's a matter of principle. We train as hard as men and our fights are sometimes better than men's so we should be allowed to fight the same amount of rounds and minutes."

Her trainer, Luis Tapia, who routinely sparred ten or twelve rounds with her on a three-minute-round clock, added, "Layla is very strong mentally. She's not afraid of anyone. She's the best."

The fight had originally been scheduled to be contested as a twelve-round bout—the standard number of rounds for male championship prizefights—but the Nevada Athletic Commission determined that since Belinda Laracuente had six losses in a row coming into the fight, they would only sanction it for ten rounds.

Addressing Laracuente's record, McCarter said, "This is going to be a tough fight. Most of her losses have come to good fighters in their home-towns."[42]

Indeed, Laracuente's 2006 bouts had included two highly competitive back-to-back WBA female light welterweight championship battles against the acclaimed French fighter Myriam Lamare. Both contests were fought in

France and went the distance with Laracuente losing on points. (Laracuente went on to win the GBU Light Welterweight Championship at the Orleans Hotel and Casino against Melissa Del Valle by unanimous decision. For her fight against Del Valle, the Nevada Athletic Commission authorized a twelve-round contest, but the rounds were limited to two minutes each. Still, the twenty-four minutes of boxing time was more than the standard twenty minutes for women's title bouts.)

The McCarter-Laracuente battle was an exciting one and the commentators made sure the audience knew the historic significance of the fight. Both women were excellent technical boxers, in great condition, with superb defensive and offensive skills. They fought ten electrifying rounds that represented boxing at its best, regardless of whether men or women were fighting.

McCarter, who sustained a cut under her right eye from an accidental head butt, was given the GBU female lightweight title by unanimous decision. She was also the beneficiary of some overly generous scoring. Nonetheless, she pursued Laracuente with a sustained effort and clearly won the fight.

Another important aspect of the matchup between two such skilled boxers was that it showed that the sport—outside of the glare of the marquee fighters—had significantly evolved in the ten years since Martin faced Gogarty. Both McCarter and Laracuente had clearly inculcated ring science with a pure commitment to the art of boxing. It spoke to hours and hours of gym time day in and day out, and to the willingness to risk losing a fight in order to box at the highest level of the sport—something that was illusive in large swathes of the careers of Martin, St. John, Rijker, and Ali.

For McCarter's first title defense in January 2007, she pushed to gain the approval of the Nevada Athletic Commission to contest an historic twelve-round fight with three-minute rounds. Her opponent was another seasoned veteran, Donna Biggers, who came into the fight having lost only one fight in her last five. Overcoming the objections that had been raised in her fight with Laracuente, the commission sanctioned the contest at twelve rounds.

McCarter won the historic bout by TKO in the second round, making the twelve-round breakthrough somewhat moot. Speaking about it after the fight, McCarter said, "I wanted it to go 12 rounds to prove women can do it, but I have a cold and didn't want to risk looking bad."

Clearly outgunning Biggers, McCarter had dropped her in the first round with "a six-punch combination."[43]

Her next title defense was also a twelve-rounder with three-minute rounds against an up-and-coming New York City-based boxer named Melissa Hernandez who trained at Gleason's Gym with Belinda Laracuente. Hernandez lost the contest by TKO in the eighth round, but not before impressing everyone with her obvious skills—skills that were so strong she actually defeated McCarter by split decision in an eight-round rematch two months later.

Other strong fighters on everyone's pound-for-pound lists winning titles in the period from 2005 to 2012 are American fighters Chevelle Hallback (with her enviable "abs" of steel), Ann Wolfe (who retired in 2006 with a 24-1 record and went on to become a highly successful trainer), Melissa Hernandez, Cindy Serrano, Ann Saccurato, Holly "The Preacher's Daughter" Holm (who defeated Christy Martin and Mia St. John by decisions in back-to-back wins in 2005), Ada Velez, Alicia Ashley, Kaliesha West, Ana Julaton, Melinda Cooper, Olivia Gerula, Victoria Cisneros, and Mary Jo Sanders. With these America-based fighters are Canada's Jelena Mrdjenovich, French fighters Myriam Lamare and Anne Sophie Mathis, Argentina's Yesica Bopp and Marcela Eliana Acuna, Mexico's Mariana "Barbie" Juarez, Jackie Nava, and Ana Maria Torres, Germany's Susi Kentikian and Rola El-Halabi, Norway's Cecilia Braekhus, Sweden's Frida Wallberg, Australia's Sharon Anyos and Susie Ramadan, and the Japanese fighter Fujin Raika.

Retiring from the scene was Lucia Rijker, who hung up her gloves in 2004. She returned to boxing as a trainer, most recently working with Australian fighter and WBC champion Diana Prazak.

Laila Ali left boxing in 2007 and, as a nod to her growing celebrity, appeared on the hit ABC television series *Dancing with the Stars*. She remains synonymous with women's boxing in the public's perception of the sport, and during the run-up to the 2012 London Olympics was identified as an important pioneer.

Christy Martin took a nearly two-year layoff after her fight with Ali in 2003. Returning to the ring in 2005, she attempted some competitive fights, but was hampered by the lessening of her earlier star power. In the decline of her career, she had mixed results in her ring battles, but eventually went on to defeat another old warrior of the ring, Dakota Stone, in a split decision—taking the WBC middleweight title in 2009.

Approximately fifteen months later, personal tragedy struck Martin when her husband Jim brutally stabbed and shot her. In overcoming her misfortune, Martin reunited with her onetime promotional foe Bob Arum, who helped put her back in the ring with the hope that she could win her fiftieth fight before retiring from the ring for good. The bout was scheduled for March 2011, although it had to be postponed due to a rib injury Martin had sustained in training.

Setting up a new date for June 2011, that fight was set for the Staples Center in Los Angeles on the undercard of the Julio Cesar Chavez Jr. fight on HBO.

Martin's fight was a six-round rematch against Dakota Stone at the Staples Center in Los Angeles, but it ended in controversy. Showing some of her old style, Martin had thrown a lot of bombs and managed to drop Stone in the fourth round before injuring her hand. Martin was clearly favoring her left in the fifth and six rounds, but in the sixth she let loose her trademark overhand right. The shock caused her to wince and dance away in pain, momentarily turning her back on Stone. As Martin began to turn back to face Stone, referee David Mendoza, having observed her turning away, stopped the fight. The ringside physician examining Martin's hand ruled she could not continue, giving Stone the TKO win. Later it was determined that Martin had broken her hand in several places.

Martin was clearly disappointed with the decision and asked her attorney, Gloria Allred, to contest the decision to the California Athletic Commission. In the lead-up to the hearing, Martin said, "In my 22 years of experience as a professional boxer, I have never seen a fight stopped by a referee or a fight doctor because of a broken hand or because a boxer winced."

Allred for her part echoed the position, saying that "Christy had a right to be treated as a fighter, not a female fighter who needed more protection from risk of harm than a male fighter needs."

Charging the absence of discrimination, the commission chairman "took issue with the accusations," and said he was "disappointed it's come to this."[44]

As expected the five-person panel unanimously upheld the referee's decision.

Martin's second attempt at achieving her fiftieth win came a year later in August of 2012 against another boxing veteran: her old foe Mia St. John.

St. John had also continued to box and had even had some competitive— but unsuccessful—fights against the likes of Jelena Mrdjenovich (losing a ten-round unanimous decision in 2006) and the up-and-coming German fighter Rola El-Halabi (losing by TKO in the fifth round of a ten-rounder). Those fights increased St. John's stock in women's boxing, bringing her a lot of respect and admiration.

Although St. John hadn't had a bout since 2010 she was still game to have a rematch with Martin. In the end St. John proved that she had more stamina in the ring than Martin when she defeated her with a multitude of clean shots that were enough to win a unanimous decision.

Martin retired after that loss with an official record of 49-7-3, while St. John went on to wage two more fights, finally retiring in 2013 with a 47-13-2 record.

The Martin-St. John fight—while lackluster at best—was a bookend to the history of the sport that had first unfolded during Martin's career in the squared circle. When Martin first fought, the only outlets for female boxers—aside from sports like competitive karate and kickboxing—were the Toughwoman contests or the nearly vacant professional prizefighting ring. And when it came to pure boxing, there were virtually no opportunities to contest in amateur competition. If a woman wanted to box she had to try her luck as a professional.

As Martin left the ring for the very last time, the first female Olympic champions were basking in the glory of their victories and medals, having fought as competitors in the 2012 London Games.

It can truly be said that in the end boxers Christy Martin, Lucia Rijker, Mia St. John, Laila Ali, and Jacqui Frazier-Lyde had helped to establish the sport in a way that was inspiring to other women, enabling thousands to take up the gloves. Both Rijker and Ali have credited Martin for inspiring them to enter the ring, much as Barbara Buttrick credited Polly Fairclough Burns for awakening in her a desire to box.

Chapter Eleven

The Amateurs

Dee Hamaguchi . . . is the reason why women were here at the Daily News
Golden Gloves in the first place.
—Wayne Coffey, New York *Daily News*, April 7, 1995 [1]

In parallel with the expansive growth in women's professional boxing was
the rise of American and international women's amateur boxing. The momentum and growth of amateur boxing worldwide—including such unlikely
locales as Afghanistan—eventually led to the decision in 2009 by the International Olympic Committee to include women's boxing as an Olympic
sport in the London Games of 2012—bringing the sport full circle from its
first exhibition at the 1904 St. Louis Games. It also fueled a huge boom in the
number of women joining gyms to box. While some of the women were
interested in recreational boxing and boxercise/kickboxing classes, others
had their sights set on entering amateur tournaments with the hopes of becoming Olympians or professionals.

Nowhere has the spirit of the amateur movement shown its value more
than in the squeals of delight emanating from the Afghan Women's Boxing
Club in Kabul, Afghanistan. Set in the very stadium where the Taliban once
stoned women, the young ladies of the club have braved threats and taunts to
practice the sweet science, all the while dreaming of one day boxing in the
Olympics.

FROM AMATEURS TO OLYMPIANS

Since the time of the Ancient Greeks, the pinnacle of amateur sports has been
the Olympic Games. While the games were eventually abandoned in Greece,

periodically throughout Western history, gatherings of athletes—some even under the banner of an Olympic competition—have been held.

Boxing—a sacred sport in the Greco-Roman tradition—was contested at the original Olympic Games, and after the modern Olympics were restarted in 1896, it was finally added to the roster of sports at the 1904 St. Louis Olympic Games.

In the United States the amateur movement had been an important component of boxing beginning with the advent of amateur sports in the 1880s. The bouts were fought under the strict rules promulgated by the American Amateur Union (AAU)—and although female boxers were excluded from participating, women's boxing grew in popularity across all strata of society.

At the 1904 Olympics Games in St. Louis (part of the larger St. Louis Exposition) male and female demonstration boxing events were held. The men's boxing events became part of the official program with the results recorded for posterity, whereas the women's exhibition boxing did not.

After the 1904 Olympics, women's boxing remained outside of the auspices of the amateur boxing movement nationally and internationally. Nonetheless, women fought matches at amateur boxing clubs using rules promulgated by the AAU and other national bodies over the years.

With the advent in 1946 of the International Amateur Boxing Association, which takes its acronym, AIBA, from the original French name of the organization (Association Internationale de Boxe Amateur), the sport created an umbrella organization governing boxing, with all participants adhering to a global set of rules and regulations. It also became closely associated with the IOC and promulgated rules for the Olympic Games.

The AIBA opened its ranks to women's boxing in 1993—following the lead of the Swedish Amateur Boxing Association's sanctioning of the sport for women five years earlier. The inclusion of female contests under the AIBA umbrella was always with a view that the sport would eventually be included in the Olympic Games.

Individual countries continued to sanction female amateur boxing throughout the 1990s and into the early 21st century, with a current roster of more than 120 countries having organized amateur boxing programs for girls and women. Although a few countries have still not sanctioned such programs—including Cuba—the momentum and excitement generated by the 2012 Olympic Games is currently helping to overcome any lingering doubts surrounding the legitimization of the sport.

From Kabul to Bejing, Ankara to Scranton, Pennsylvania, Buenos Aires to Kampala, and New Dehli to Mexico City, women have embraced the international amateur boxing movement to become fierce competitors—often while overcoming deep prejudices and stereotypes. In the United States alone, some three thousand girls and women currently register each year to compete under the auspices of USA Boxing.

With the introduction of the first AIBA-sponsored Women's World Championships in 2001, held in Scranton, Pennsylvania, 125 fighters from thirty countries took their first steps into international competition, steps that culminated with women's participation in the 2012 London Games.

It was not until women began fighting in AIBA-sponsored international events that the possibility of competing in the Games began to take shape. With the success of this first women's international competition, planning began for the second Women's World Championships in Antalya, Turkey. That tournament eventually included twelve divisions, with gold medals won by athletes from Russia, Sweden, Canada, China, Hungary, Italy, Turkey, and the United States. India sent Mary Kom (Mangte Chungneijang Merykom), who won a silver medal and became the only one of the contestants to go on to the 2012 Olympics.

Held in October 2002, the second tournament drew 185 boxers from thirty-five countries. Several of the women who had medaled at the 2001 championships also won medals in the second international competition, including a returning Mary Kom, who improved her standing by winning a gold medal.

The third AIBA Women's World Boxing Championship was held some three years later in Poldosk, Russia, between September 26 and October 3, 2005. While participation fell somewhat to a total of 139 boxers from thirty countries, women competed in a total of thirteen divisions. India's Mary Kom proved her superiority again by winning gold, and future Olympian Mary Spencer of Canada, elected the best boxer in the tournament, dazzled the other contestants and audiences alike with her skills in taking the gold. It was also Ireland's future Olympian Katie Taylor's first tournament, although she was eliminated after the second round.

Russia continued its place as a powerhouse in women's boxing by sweeping seven of the gold medals—and set an AIBA record by capturing twelve of the fifty-two medals won. They were followed by the People's Republic of Korea (PRK) and Turkey, both of whom won six medals. The success of these first three championships set the stage for the AIBA to submit a proposal in early October 2005 to the IOC to include women's boxing in the 2008 Olympic Games to be held in Beijing, China. The IOC agreed to vote on the proposal at its executive meeting to be held in Lausanne, Switzerland, in late October.

In reviewing the merits of the proposal, however, the IOC determined to reject the request for inclusion in the 2008 Games. Kelly Fairweather, the IOC sports director, in discussing the committee's determination on female boxing, said, "The IOC did not feel it has reached the stage where it merits inclusion. We will watch the progress of women's boxing in the next few years."

In part, the reasoning was based on what the IOC felt were the limited number of nations that would be represented at the 2008 Games, along with concerns that the skill levels of the athletes might not be remarkable enough to warrant inclusion. Mention was made of Laila Ali's visibility in the sport, which had served to widen its popularity, but not to the point where the IOC might add the sport to the roster of events for 2008.

Female boxers were deeply disappointed by the rebuff. Amateur boxer Tika Hemingway, a former USA National Champion, said, "I've fought in a couple of different countries. Why not the Olympics? Why not China?"[2] Others who had been boxing since the first AIBA tournament in 2001 felt bitterly disappointed, having worked for years for the chance to become Olympians.

The AIBA had, however, been offered a lifeline in the form of an invitation to resubmit a proposal for inclusion in the 2012 London Games. Under the new leadership of Dr. Ching-Kuo Wu, following his election to the presidency of the AIBA on November 6, 2006, the organization made the commitment to try again.

To coincide with the change in management of the organization, the fourth AIBA championships were held in New Delhi, India, beginning on November 18, 2006, along with the decision to hold the international championships every two years.

Some 174 boxers from thirty-three nations competed in New Dehli. Mary Kom was able to achieve her third consecutive gold medal, and Katie Taylor, returning for her second tournament, took the gold. Future Olympian Marlen Esparza from the United States competed for her first time and brought home a bronze medal. Canada's Mary Spencer won a bronze. In all, a total of four future Olympians medaled at the tournament.

While participation in women's international competition had gone barely noticed in some participating countries, the twenty-year-old Katie Taylor, who had also won gold medals at the European championship and world championships that year, was well on her way to becoming a heroine in her home city of Bray and throughout Ireland. She was even shortlisted for the coveted RTÉ Sports Person of the Year Award for her accomplishments in 2006. (RTÉ is the Irish national broadcasting network, akin to Great Britain's BBC.)

Taylor, the daughter of former Irish champion Peter Taylor, had grown up in the boxing gym alongside her two brothers, watching her father train. By the age of ten she was in gloves. Though she was forbidden from competing, she trained and started boxing in exhibition fights. Her father would put her down as "K. Taylor" with no one the wiser until her headgear was removed at the end of the bout. At the age of eleven, she even wrote a letter to boxer Deirdre Gogarty about her aspirations.

With approval by the Irish Amateur Boxing Union to allow women's boxing in 2001, Taylor made history when she fought in Ireland's first sanctioned boxing match against Alanna Audley, defeating her by the score of 23-12. Taylor was also making a name for herself in soccer and played on Ireland's national team, although her true love was boxing.

In 2007, true to their word to fight for women's boxing to be included in the 2012 London Games, the AIBA scheduled two special exhibition bouts at the World Boxing Championships in Chicago, Illinois, for an audience of invited IOC officials.

The boxers selected for the bouts were all highly motivated, with exemplary skills, determination, and Olympic-style boxing expertise. The first pairing was between Russian fighter Olesya Gladkova, a twenty-seven-year-old former kickboxer who won both the European and world championships two years running, and Marlen Esparza, who'd just turned eighteen but had already won a silver at the Pan American Games and a bronze at the world championships. Ironically, even though she was the youngest, she was one of the most experienced, having boxed competitively in the amateurs since first taking to the sport at the age of eleven.

Katie Taylor, who'd added another European championship title to her growing list of accomplishments, was chosen to fight Canadian Pan American champion and world bronze medalist Katie Dunn in the second exhibition bout.

One thing was clear: All four fighters were acutely aware that this was their chance to show the IOC that women's boxing deserved to be added to the roster of sports at the 2012 Games—and all four performed to the best of their abilities at the special contests held just before the men's finals.

Other AIBA women's boxing initiatives in 2007 included the establishment of a women's commission, the announcement of a new junior female boxing competition series, and closer alignment of the rules governing men's and women's boxing.

The following year, in November 2008, the fifth AIBA Women's World Championships were held in Ningbo City, China. It was the most successful to date with 237 boxers representing forty-two countries—a huge jump from 2006. Held over a seven-day period, such future Olympians as China's Ren Cancan and Dong Chen, the U.K.'s Nicola Adams and Natasha Jonas, and American Quanitta "Queen" Underwood joined the likes of Katie Taylor (who won the competition's best boxer award), Mary Kom, Mary Spencer, and Marlen Esparza. Taylor went on to be named the 2008 best fighter of the year by AIBA.

With the unanimous decision on February 19, 2009, by the AIBA executive committee to send the IOC a proposal to include women's boxing in the 2012 London Games, the AIBA went into high gear to promote the sport in anticipation of the IOC's decision. (The IOC had originally anticipated rendering a decision in October 2009, but in April announced the decision would be made in August.)

In a statement announcing the actions taken, AIBA's president, Dr. Ching-Kuo Wu, said, "The IOC understands the importance of women's boxing and knows the current developments and its popularity. We are the only sport without women in the Olympics. We are the only sport where women's rights are not fully respected. We have to work with the IOC to gain their understanding and support."[3]

In making their pitch, AIBA determined to improve their chances by maintaining the same number of competitors that had competed in the 2008 Beijing Games. This meant limiting the number to 286 boxers. In their proposal to the IOC, they reduced the proposed number of male boxers to 246 to allow for a total of forty female fighters contesting in five weight categories—eight women for each.

Support for AIBA's efforts was also requested from other quarters. Great Britain's Olympics minister, Tessa Jowell, made a strong pitch for allowing women to "take part in more masculine sports" including boxing, while conversely advocating for men to also appear in traditional women's sports such as synchronized swimming. She also called on amateur sports organizations to heed her call by contacting the IOC.[4]

In June 2009 the AIBA proposal was revised to add three female Olympic weight categories with twelve boxers in each for a total of thirty-six competitors. The AIBA further proposed ten weight categories for men's boxing, allowing for 250 competitors—one less weight category than had contested in 2008. The net effect was only four fewer female competitors than the AIBA had proposed in their initial submission; however, the limitation on the weight categories meant that with the exception of women who normally contested in one of the three weight categories (flyweight, lightweight, and middleweight) all others would need to gain or lose a substantial amount of weight (and in some cases muscle mass) in order to compete.

With the IOC's announcement that women's boxing would be included in the 2012 London Games, the women's boxing world erupted. IOC president Jacques Rogge said, "I can only rejoice about the decision of inclusion of women's boxing. The sport of women's boxing has progressed . . . a tremendous amount in the last five years and it was about time to include them in the Games."[5]

Now that women's boxing was going to be an Olympic sport, the sixth AIBA Women's World Championships in Barbados, held in September 2010, was bigger than ever with seventy-five countries represented and 306 women vying for medals. AIBA also sponsored a "Road to Barbados" training camp that offered forty women from less affluent nations an all-expenses-paid trip to Barbados for two weeks of training prior to the start of competition.

Previous champions Mary Kom, Ren Cancan, Katie Taylor, and Mary Spencer competed, with Kom winning an unprecedented sixth medal. The highlight fight of the competition was the semifinal battle between Katie Taylor and Queen Underwood. While Taylor easily took the first round, in the second and third Underwood pulled up to within five points going into the fourth and final round. From the moment the bell rang, Underwood relentlessly pursued Taylor—who actually had a point deducted for hold-ing—but in the end Underwood fell two points short to give Taylor the win and the chance to box for the gold. Underwood won a bronze for her efforts.

Prior to the Barbados event, the question of issuing new uniforms specifically for women had been raised, mostly because the male tops were ill fitting. During the championship there was an announcement that a new uniform would be forthcoming. What no one knew until just before the semifinals got underway was that the uniform consisted of a skirt and a tight-fitting sleeveless shirt (called a vest). Teams were encouraged to have their fighters contest the semifinals and finals in the skirts. According to an e-mail received by boxing columnist Michael Rivest and published in his article about the skirts issue, many of the teams encouraged their fighters to wear the skirts for fear that the fighters would not be judged correctly. However, of the forty competing athletes who'd been told to wear the skirts only fourteen complied.[6]

Rivest also spoke with AIBA's Dr. Wu, asking why skirts were added:

> I have heard many times people say, "We can't tell the difference between the men and the women," especially on TV, since they're in the same uniforms and wearing headgear. We have a Women's Commission that evaluated every-thing and they met and gave their recommendations. The uniform was present-ed [in Barbados] as optional.[7]

Backpedaling somewhat, the question of requiring skirts as part of the Olym-pic boxing uniform was deferred for further study and remained optional. Still, women felt betrayed by the controversy, with Katie Taylor stating, "I don't even wear miniskirts on a night out, so I definitely won't be wearing miniskirts in the ring."

With the issue still undecided, petitions were circulated worldwide in late 2011, with more than fifty thousand signatures collected within two months. One of the women who started the petition on the website Change.org, boxer Elizabeth Plank, said, "It is all very demeaning. Our petition is not about a piece of fabric, it's about athletes. It's about their credibility."[8]

It was not until March 2012, however, that the AIBA finally ruled that skirts were optional. With the official change, technical rule 8.1.3 now read: "For all AIBA Approved Events, Women Boxers must wear a red or blue form fitting vest and either shorts or the option of a skirt as per the Boxer's respective corner allocation, which shall be their own responsibility."

The decision on whether to require skirts was pushed out to the national organizations and most did not require their athletes to wear skirts in competition.[9]

During the time that the skirts issue was still looming, national entities began their national championships in 2011 in anticipation of the only Olympic female qualifying event: the seventh AIBA Women's World Boxing Championships to be held in Qinhuangadao, China, in May 2012.

In the United States, USA Boxing organized its first-ever U.S. Olympic team women's boxing trials and scheduled them to be held at the Northern Quest Resort & Casino in Airway Heights, Washington, near the city of Spokane. Set to run from February 13 to 19, 2012, twenty-four women were qualified to compete at the boxing trials—limited to the three Olympic weight classes. Additionally, as a double-elimination bout, each woman had two chances to advance.

The women invited to the trials had won a berth by successfully completing the qualifying tests as top competitors in the 2011 Pan American Games, USA Boxing National Championships, the National Golden Gloves Championships, or the National PAL Championships. Among the competitors was a then sixteen-year-old boxing machine from Flint, Michigan, named Claressa Shields, who had won the PAL championships—her first competition in the women's open division. (She had previously won two USA Boxing Junior Olympic gold medals.)

Shields had begun boxing as an eleven-year-old, having listened to her father talk about Laila Ali. A former boxer on an underground boxing circuit and ex-con, he didn't really want her to go into boxing, but he eventually relented. By then, Shields was living with her grandmother, having endured horrific abuse as a young child while her father was in prison.

In the gym at the Berston Field House, Shields worked harder than everyone else, with trainer Jason Crutchfield who not only helped mold her as a fighter but provided her with a level of stability she didn't have bouncing from home to home in Flint—especially after her grandmother died of cancer in 2010. She was also an A student, wrestling with Advanced Placement classes in between her competitions.

Along with Shields, the women who competed had fought hard-won contests to appear at the Olympic trials and also defied the long odds of battling through the lingering doubts about the sport and whether women should fight at all. Queen Underwood, twenty-seven, from Seattle, Washington, who entered the trials as the Pan American Games representative, was also a five-time national champion who had been boxing competitively since 2006.

Underwood was receiving a lot of press coverage, and there were those who thought her explosive boxing style meant that she would be a sure winner all the way to the Olympic podium. She'd seen the sport evolve since her first championship and had a lot of experience with international competition, but as a competitor she too wrestled with appalling childhood experiences, in her case at the hands of her abusive father.

Marlen Esparza, twenty-three, had been boxing over half her life—and had the medals to prove it. Boxing out of Houston, Texas, she'd actually taken a year off to build up her body from her normal weight at 106 pounds to compete as a flyweight at 112 pounds. In terms of confidence, she had it in abundance, crediting a strong family, great home life, and the support of an extended network in and around the sport.

As the Olympic trials proceeded, Esparza, Underwood, and Shields gave dominating performances. Shields, who would be turning seventeen in March, shocked the assembled crowds, press, and fans at home watching the fights via the Internet, with her hard shots and laser focus. She also shocked her opponents, champions all, who went down in defeat by wide margins.

By then end of the competition, Esparza, Underwood, and Shields were crowned as the three Olympic trials champions—an historic first in the history of boxing—and as winners each of them would represent the United States at the qualifying event in China scheduled for May.

The next test for the three women was for each to successfully win one of the coveted twelve slots in each of their weight classes. However, contesting for a spot was not only a matter of qualifying in China. A quota system had been set up by the AIBA, which designated the number of spots to be allotted from five separate regions: Africa, America (northern and southern hemispheres), Asia, Europe, and Oceania.

Furthermore, points were allotted for each weight class and assigned on a region-by-region basis. The rationale for this was to balance out the participants so that no one country or region could dominate at the expense of others. Additionally, a tripartite commission was set up that would allow the national Olympic committees to petition for additional spots based on the points allotted by region.

In all, twenty-four spots were available to fighters who met the quota allotments, and the tripartite commission would award the additional eleven places, based on the merits of the member petitions. The last remaining spot would be offered to the United Kingdom as host nation.

Based on the quota for the Americas, there were a total of five spots available: two for flyweight, two for middleweight, and one for lightweight. For the flyweight and middleweight divisions, this meant that boxers had to be ranked first or second relative to the other fighters in their weight class fighting for countries in the American region. Boxers in the lightweight division had to come in ahead of everyone in their region.

By the end of the tournament, although neither Esparza nor Shields had medaled—with Shields suffering her first loss to England's Savannah Marshall—both won a coveted place as Olympians because they ranked within the top two for the America region. As for Queen Underwood, while she placed second for the Americas, it was not enough to gain her a berth, which meant she had to wait on the petition to the tripartite commission. Canadian middleweight fighter Mary Spencer had also failed to qualify.

At the conclusion of the qualifying competitions, countries scrambled to submit petitions to the tripartite commission on behalf of their fighters. While it took some time, the announcement of the remaining eleven Olympians was made in mid-June, based in part on who AIBA deemed worthy of inclusion as a result of their record of achievement. Among the women awarded spots were Queen Underwood, Canada's Mary Spencer, China's Cheng Dong, and Sweden's Anna Laurell. All were previous medalists in AIBA competitions.

With the Olympics set to begin at the end of July, in the United States Esparza, Underwood, and Shields became the darlings of the media—although that did not necessarily translate into additional sponsorship opportunities. Marlen Esparza was the exception and was the recipient of rather generous sponsorship from the likes of Cover Girl, Nike, and Coca-Cola, including her appearance in national advertising campaigns. Her image even appeared on Coca-Cola cans as part of a series of images that advertised different Olympic sports.

Other issues also surfaced. USA Boxing did not hire a head coach until a month before the Games. The coach they hired, Basheer Abdullah, was well respected in the sport, but he had worked a corner in a professional bout in March, breaking an AIBA rule that stated coaches had to have at least a six-month interval between a professional and an amateur fight. This meant that he was disqualified from actually being in the ring with any of the Olympic fighters. In USA Boxing as a whole, there were also a number of individual fighters' coaches who did not have the credentials needed to assist during the matches.

Regardless, the excitement generated by the debut of female boxers in the Games seemed to trump any of these problems. Esparza, Underwood, and Shields—along with the thirty-three other first-time Olympic women's boxers—were never prouder than when they first walked through the Olympic stadium during the opening ceremonies.

As the Games got underway, the women's preliminary bouts were set to begin on August 5, 2012, with the quarterfinals on the following day. For the first day of competition in the flyweight division, top seed Ren Cancan from China, number two seed Nicola Adams from the United Kingdom, and Marlen Esparza each had byes, meaning they automatically advanced to the quarterfinals.

In the quarterfinals Ren and Esparza both advanced easily, setting themselves up to meet in the semifinals. Nicola Adams handily defeated her opponent to meet the intrepid Mary Kom who had come up in weight in order to qualify as a flyweight. She'd also easily won her preliminary and quarterfinal bouts.

In the lightweight division, top seed Katie Taylor and Russia's Sofya Ochivava, who was considered a real contender for a medal and the number two seed, also advanced on a bye. Queen Underwood, however, fought in a preliminary contest against Great Britain's Natasha Jonas. It was the first time the fighters had met in the ring, and Natasha Jonas won the day by the score of 21-13, despite Underwood's valiant efforts.

Speaking to a reporter about her loss, Underwood fought back tears at having put so much of her life into obtaining the goal of being an Olympian and said of her historic role, "I don't think it's enough."[10]

Jonas fell to Katie Taylor in Taylor's dominating performance in the quarterfinals, while Ochigava had won her match to get into the semifinal rounds.

In the middleweight division, top seed Savannah Marshall, number two seed Nadezda Torlopova from Russia, Claressa Shields, and Mary Spencer all advanced with byes. In the quarterfinals, both Marshall and Spencer lost, leaving Shields to face Kazakhstani boxer Marina Volnova in the semifinals, and Torlopova to face China's fearsome Li Jinzi.

On August 8, in the semifinals, Marlen Esparza fell in a closely contested bout against Ren Cancan by the score of 10-8. Esparza had previously lost to Cancan in the quarterfinals of the qualifying competition in May. Regardless, she won the first Olympic boxing medal by any American woman—a bronze. Speaking shortly after the bout she said, "I can't be anger [*sic*] about getting any medal at all but [bronze] wasn't my goal."[11]

In another low-scoring historic battle, Nicola Adams defeated the venerable Mary Kom by the score of 11-6. Kom—who'd actually contested in the first AIBA international women's championships—said afterwards, "Adams was very clever, a counter-puncher but, although she carried power, she wasn't very tactical."[12] Kom brought home a bronze medal.

As expected, Katie Taylor put on a dominating performance, defeating Mavzuna Chorieva from Tajikistan—which gave Chorieva the bronze. Also as expected, Ochigava handily defeated Brazilian fighter Adriana Araujo, giving Brazil a coveted medal for women's boxing.

Middleweight Claressa Shields dominated again, defeating Volnova soundly by the score of 29-15, while Russian fighter Torlopova squeaked through 12-10 win over her opponent, Li.

By the finals the next day on August 9, the sold-out crowd of ten thousand at the ExCel Arena, where all of the boxing matches were held, was in a frenzy. The noise level at the venue had already surpassed anything on record as British boxing-mad fans waited for Nicola Adams to take to the ring in her battle against Ren Cancan, which would decide the historic first gold and silver medals to be awarded to female boxers in the history of the Games. Adams, who made her home in Liverpool, had previously lost to Cancan in the finals at the qualifying championship, but was buoyed by the crowds chanting her name as she entered the arena.

From the moment the bout started, Adams was unrelenting in her attack and even managed to send Cancan to the canvas in the second round after tagging her with a left hook. After a dominating third round, Adams finished the job with a flurry of punches, winning the gold. Of her win she said, "I can't believe I've actually done it. I've been dreaming about this moment since I was 12 years old. It's a fairytale ending for me."[13]

In the next bout, Katie Taylor went to work on Sofya Ochigava to the roar of the crowd who was already wild with anticipation of a Taylor win. It was a somewhat messy, low-scoring fight, but after two rounds, Taylor was down on the scorecards: 4-3. In the third round, Taylor worked hard and caught her opponent with some hard shots—pulling up on the scorecard by the end of the round. Both women hung tough in the fourth round with the crowd willing Taylor to win as they shouted her name. Just at the end of the round Taylor got caught and went down, but bounded back and let loose just enough to pull out the win and the gold by the score of 10-8. Winning the gold medal was an amazing triumph for her, and after the win was announced she ran laps around the ring with the Irish flag draped around her shoulders.

For the third and final match, Claressa Shields, still in shock at winning her semifinal bout, was nothing less than a poised professional as she came into the ring to fight her thirty-three-year-old opponent, Nadezda Torlopova. The match was pure Shields as she used her power punches and high-spirited antics to dominate the bout—despite a 3-3 score in the first round—winning the gold by a score of 12-10. With her victory, she raised her arms and leapt in triumph with a smile that radiated with the energy of the sun.

In the final medal count for men's and women's USA boxing at the Olympics, Shields won the only gold medal and, along with Marlen Esparza's bronze medal performance, won the only two medals for the team.

With the outstanding performances and incredible support of the crowds at the ExCel arena, a new era in boxing had been born. Perhaps most fitting of all was the appearance of Barbara Buttrick at the arena who said of the Games, "When I was around, I would never have dreamed women boxers would ever get into the Olympics. But now they've got that credibility and that will bring a lot more girls into it because they'll feel more comfortable going into a gym."[14]

Buttrick's words proved prophetic, as girls all over the world, inspired by the Olympics, have entered the gym at record numbers to pick up the gloves.

Conclusion

The State of Things — 1722 to 2012 and Beyond

In women's boxing things have changed massively. . . . But there is still a lot
of work to be done.
—Nicola Adams, Olympic gold medalist [1]

From the first forays in the ring in the 1720s to the triumphs of the 2012
London Games, women have continuously labored at the sport in one manner
or another.

In the recent past, the sport underwent tremendous growth in the years
that coincided with Christy Martin's career as a professional boxer (roughly
1989 to 2012). That is not to say that many of the problems facing women in
this period disappeared. Quite to the contrary, issues of poor promotional
opportunities, minimal media exposure, and low pay were (and are) perva-
sive in the sport, as are continued mismatches, a plethora of competing
boxing organizations, and the same "big promotion" controls over the sport
that existed before the 1990s.

Still, with the success of the thirty-six female boxers who competed in the
2012 London Olympic Games (including three Americans), there is a hopeful sense that the sport will continue to grow, having garnered more than a
modicum of respect for the level of prowess exhibited in the ring.

The tremendous excitement generated by the Olympics has resulted in
thousands of girls and women hitting the gyms to learn to box all over the
world. That was reflected in the 30 percent jump in participation in the 2013
Women's Junior/Youth World Boxing Championships. In Great Britain and
Ireland, gold medal winners Nicola Adams and Katie Taylor have obtained
rock-star status. Adams was awarded an MBE (Member of the Order of the

British Empire), an honor previously bestowed upon only one other female boxer—Jane Couch. Taylor also finally won the highly coveted RTÉ Sports Person of the Year Award in 2012, the first woman to do so. India, too, has seen a huge rise in interest among girls after Mary Kom returned home with a bronze medal, where she is now the subject of a Bollywood biopic.

In the United States, boxer Marlen Esparza has continued to enjoy promotional opportunities with the Coca-Cola Company and Cover Girl; however, Queen Underwood and Claressa Shields have been less successful despite multiple appearances on national television talk shows and continued press coverage. And as distinct from Adams, Taylor, and Kom, the American medalists have not achieved national stature as role models for young women—although Esparza has become a particularly potent symbol for the Latin American community.

In Shields's case, her gold medal notwithstanding, she faced the disappointment of being knocked down to youth-level competition (ages seventeen and eighteen) because of changes in the age limits for elite women (ages nineteen to forty). (When Shields competed in the Olympics the minimum age for elite women was seventeen.) She became eligible for status as an elite woman boxer only in 2014, but she will have lost well over a year of competitive fighting on the road to Rio in 2016. She has otherwise turned down offers to turn pro and has begun her freshman year in college. Shields did, however, win the American Boxing Confederation 2012 Woman Athlete of the Year and also received AIBA's 2013 Female Youth Boxer of the Year award.

In women's professional boxing outside of the United States, the growth of the sport has led to greater pay equity, media recognition, and fandom, along with more opportunities to fight and to earn a decent living. It has also meant that women holding championship belts hail from countries as far-flung as Japan, Australia, South Africa, and Argentina. This has led top-tier American fighters to travel to Europe and Latin America (especially to Mexico) to find quality fights.

For American female professional boxers, on the other hand, the struggle is still day to day, with many of the same problems that have plagued women's boxing for years. The fighters themselves, while not ready to go on the hunger strikes of the past, have a new militancy at work and are taking advantage of social media tools to popularize their case to the boxing world and to demand their place in the sport. The recent crescendo of voices applauding women's mixed martial arts (MMA) is also causing the decision makers to rethink their conceptions of female boxing. But only the future will tell whether the sport's landscape is ready for a push of women's boxing onto a reluctant American broadcast media again.

Boxing in general has a decreased viewership in the United States, and has been supplanted in many instances by televised MMA and other extreme fighting contests, which have shown a huge surge in popularity. In terms of viewership, women's MMA has perhaps shown the greatest rise, with more bouts and more fighters than ever.

Women's MMA stars Ronda Rousey, Mischa Tate, and Cristiane "Cyborg" Justino are replacing the likes of Christy Martin, Mia St. John, Laila Ali, and Lucia Rijker as the superstars of women's martial arts—to the point where Holly Holm, who has consistently led or been in the top ten of the pound-for-pound best female boxers lists for years, retired from boxing in 2013 to become an MMA competitor. Holm has garnered a 5-0 record in her new sport and may well be signed by the UFC soon. She is also beginning to capture a wider press exposure, something that had previously been limited to the boxing world.

While women's MMA fighters have begun to gain a lot of publicity beyond the sports pages, female boxers such as Alicia Ashley—who at forty-six is still winning highly competitive title belts over women half her age—are not. Kaliesha West—a twenty-five-year-old from California—is another boxing champion who, despite winning the IFBA super bantamweight title in October 2012, has yet to defend her title as of October 2013.

Despite a boxing press that has become more inclined to write positively of female achievements, the stresses on professional female boxers have remained. They must work full-time jobs and often seek sponsorship, management, training, promotional opportunities, and fight matchups with little or no assistance. While this is not so dissimilar from the travails of male boxers at the lower end of the chain, the struggles for female boxers are all the harder because they are effectively closed out of opportunities to appear on television and must overcome continuing negative stereotyping of their efforts. Issues such as finally sanctioning three-minute rounds and twelve-round championships are also becoming an important part of that conversation.

At Gleason's Gym alone, professional boxers Alicia Ashley, Heather Hardy, Melissa Hernandez, Sonya Lamonakis, Belinda Laracuente, and Keisher McLeod-Wells all augment their boxing careers with income derived from working as trainers or helping manage the day-to-day operations at the gym. McLeod-Wells supplants her income with modeling jobs and also appeared on a reality television show about female boxers filmed in Mexico, while Lamonakis earns her regular living as a New York City school teacher in addition to the hours she puts in at the gym.

Whatever the challenges, women continue to practice the sweet science with dedication and fortitude. Hundreds of thousands of amateur, professional, and recreational boxers the world over labor at their craft from the early hours of the morning until late at night. Each one of them is imbued with the courage and resilience necessary to find personal transformation and triumph in the ring.

Boxing has persevered as a sport since the 1720s, with women among the first to embrace the wonders of the prize ring. That spirit of adventure continues to this day—and while the sport will inevitably twist and turn, the women of the squared circle will be there every step of the way.

Notes

INTRODUCTION

1. Malissa Smith. "Exclusive Interview with Sonya Lamonakis Set to Fight on June 14th @ Roseland Ballroom." *Girlboxing*, June 10, 2012.
2. "Bout Time: Claressa Shields." *New York Times*, January 25, 2012. [NYTimes.com]
3. Sandra Johnson. "2012 Olympians: Marlen Esparza Becomes First American Female to Qualify for the Olympic Games." Yahoo Sports. May 22, 2012. [Yahoosports.com]
4. Pierce Egan. *Boxiana.*
5. Herodotus. *The Histories.* A. D. Godley, ed. Cambridge: Harvard University Press. 1920. Section 4.110–117. [Faculty.fairfield.edu]
6. Mischa Merz. *The Sweetest Thing*, p. 5.
7. "Nonsensical Exhibition at Henry Hill's." *New York Times*, March 17, 1876. [NYTimes.com]
8. Nellie Bly. "A Visit with John L. Sullivan." *New York World,* July 28, 1889. [Bareknuckleboxinghalloffame.com]
9. "Kaliesha West Interview." Transworld Sports. June 7, 2012. [Youtube.com]

1. SHE-DEVILS AND AMAZONIAN TIGRESSES

1. James Bramston. *The Art of Politicks*, p. 41.
2. *London Journal*, June 23, 1722. Quoted in Christopher Johnson and Henry Fielding. "'British Championism:' Early Pugilism and the Works of Fielding." *The Review of English Studies, New Series.* 47:187, August 1996. Pp. 333–357, n. 33, p. 343. [JSTOR]
3. Zacharias Conrad von Uffenback. *London, in 1710*, p. 90.
4. Martin Nogue. *Voyages et Aventures*, p. 364.
5. *London Journal*, August 31, 1723. Quoted in Christopher Johnson and Henry Fielding. "'British Championism': Early Pugilism and the Works of Fielding." *Review of English Studies, New Series.* 47:187, August 1996. Pp. 333–357, n. 33, p. 343. [JSTOR]
6. *Weekly Journal*, October 1, 1726. [Georgianlondon.com]
7. James Peller Malcolm. *Anecdotes of the Manners and Customs of London during the Eighteenth Century*, 2nd ed. Vol. 2. London: Longman, Hurst, Rees, and Orme, 1810, p.176. [Google Books]

8. *Daily Post*, July 17, 1728. Georgianlondon.com; See also William Shepard Walsh. *Handbook of Literary Curiosities*. Philadelphia: J. P. Lippincott, 1893, p. 22. [Google Books]

9. Eliza Haywood. "A Wife to Be Let," p. 159.

10. Samuel Pepys. *Diary*, 4: 168.

11. Allen Guttman. "English Sports Spectators," p. 114. Quoted in Maria Kloeren, *Sport und Rekord*. Leipzig: Tauchnitz, 1935, pp. 42–43.

12. William Hickey. *Memoirs*, p. 82.

13. Ibid.

14. Ibid., p. 83.

15. Ibid., p. 85.

16. *Daily Advertiser*, June 22, 1768. Quoted in John James Sexby. *Municipal Parks, Gardens and Open Spaces of London*. Cheap ed. London: Elliot Stock, p. 535. [Google Books]

17. *Pancratia, or, A History of Pugilism: Containing a Full Account of Every Battle of Noted from the Time of Broughton and Slack down to the Present Day*. London: W. Hildyard, Poppin's Court, 1812, p. 120. [Google Books]

18. Ibid., p. 113.

19. Ibid.

20. Ibid.

21. Pierce Egan. *Boxiana*, p. 9.

2. VICTORIAN LADIES BOXING

1. Jack London. *A Daughter of the Snows*. Quoted in Kasia Boddy. *Boxing*, p. 165.

2. *Sporting Magazine*, vol. 39., no. 231. December 1811, p. 139. [Google Books]

3. "Female Pugilism." *Stamford Mercury*, October 15, 1824. [British Library Board]

4. *Chester Chronicle*, June 18, 1819 [British Library Board]

5. "Female Pugilism." *Stamford Mercury*, October 15, 1824. [British Library Board]

6. "Female Pugilism." *Westmorland Gazette*, October 16, 1824. [British Library Board]

7. "Female Pugilists." *Hampshire Chronicle and Courier*, October 27, 1817. [British Library Board]

8. *London Times*, March 24, 1807. Quoted in Allen Guttmann. *Women's Sports*, p. 76. Guttmann's work is a definitive resource for historical accounts of women's participation in sports.

9. "Pugilism: White-Head Bob (Baldwin), and O'Neal." *Westmorland Gazette*, October 30, 1824, p. 2. [British Library Board]

10. Frederick Douglass. *Narrative of Life*, p. 63.

11. *The American Fistiana*. New York: H. Johnson, 1849, p. 29. [Google Books]

12. *New York Daily Tribune*, March 25, 1843, p. 2. [Library of Congress]

13. *Brooklyn Eagle*, September 24, 1852, p. 2. [Brooklyn Public Library]

14. *Brooklyn Eagle*, March 26, 1847, p. 2. [Brooklyn Public Library]

15. *Fayetteville Observer*, October 16, 1856, p. 1. [Library of Congress]

16. *Holmes County Farmer*, May 31, 1860, p. 1. [Library of Congress]

17. "A Female Boxing Match. A Novel and Nonsensical Exhibition at Harry Hill's." *New York Times*, March 17, 1876.

18. *New York Herald*, June 8, 1876, p. 3. [Fultonhistory.com]

19. *New York Herald*, March 14, 1876, p. 6. [Fultonhistory.com]

20. *New York Herald*, June 8, 1876, p. 8. [Fultonhistory.com]

21. "A Female Prize Fight." *Hudson Evening Register*, March 14, 1872, p. 2. [Fultonhistory.com]

22. *Staunton Spectator*, October 21, 1877, p. 3. [Library of Congress]

23. Hattie Stewart. *Boxrec Encyclopedia*. [Boxrec.com]

24. *National Police Gazette*, May 17, 1884. [Fultonhistory.com]

25. "Loves to Fight." *Buffalo Express*, December 22, 1887, p. 8. [Fultonhistory.com]

26. *New York Herald*, April 4, 1884, p. 8. [Fultonhistory.com]

27. *National Police Gazette*, January 24, 1885, p. 10. [Fultonhistory.com]
28. *National Police Gazette*, December 27, 1884, p. 10. [Fultonhistory.com]
29. *National Police Gazette*, February 21, 1885, Page 10. [Fultonhistory.com]
30. *Buffalo Express*, December 22, 1887, p. 8. [Fultonhistory.com]
31. *St. Paul Daily Glove*, October 4, 1886, p. 3 [Library of Congress]
32. *St. Paul Daily Glove*, October 5, 1886, p. 3. [Library of Congress]
33. *St. Paul Daily Glove*, October 11, 1886, p. 3. [Library of Congress]
34. *St. Paul Daily Glove*, November 28, 1886, p. 2. [Library of Congress]
35. *St. Paul Daily Glove*, November 29, 1886, p. 2. [Library of Congress]
36. *St. Paul Daily Glove*, December 1, 1886, p. 3. [Library of Congress]
37. *St. Paul Daily Glove*, March 8, 1887, p. 3. [Library of Congress]
38. *St. Paul Daily Glove*, February 21, 1888, p. 2. [Library of Congress]
39. "Loves to Fight." *Buffalo Express*, December 22, 1887, p. 8. [Fultonhistory.com]
40. *Daily Morning Astorian*, September 24, 1890, p. 1. [Fultonhistory.com]
41. *Oswego Daily Times*, July 13, 1888, p. 1. [Fultonhistory.com]
42. *New York World*, September 17, 1888. [Boxinggyms.com]
43. "Women in the Prize Ring." *New York Herald*, September 17, 1888, p. 8. [Fultonhistory.com]
44. *World*, September 17, 1888. [Boxinggyms.com]
45. "Two Girls in the Prize Ring." *Sun*, September 17, 1888, p. 1. [Fultonhistory.com]
46. "Women in the Prize Ring." *New York Herald*, September 17, 1888, p. 8. [Fultonhistory.com]
47. Ibid.
48. *Alexandria Gazette*, September 17, 1888, p. 2. [Library of Congress]
49. "Women in the Prize Ring." *New York Herald*, September 17, 1888, p. 8. [Fultonhistory.com]
50. *New York World*, September 17, 1888. [Boxinggyms.com]
51. *Troy Daily Times*, September 17, 1888, p. 2. [Fultonhistory.com]
52. *Evening Star* (Washington, D.C.), September 17, 1888, p. 4. [Library of Congress]
53. *New York Herald*, September 18, 1888, p. 8. [Fultonhistory.com]
54. *Daily Leader*, September 21, 1888, p. 1. [Fultonhistory.com]
55. *Wichita Daily Eagle*, October 5, 1888, p. 2. [Library of Congress]
56. *The Brooklyn Eagle*, September 29, 1888, p. 1.
57. *New York World*, October 23, 1888, p. 1. [Library of Congress]
58. *National Police Gazette*, September 24, 1892, p. 11. [Fultonhistory.com]
59. Ibid.
60. *National Police Gazette*, February 7, 1885, p. 11. [Fultonhistory.com]
61. *New York Clipper*, April 17, 1880, p. 31. [Fultonhistory.com]
62. *Dallas Herald*, November 20, 1880, p. 8. [Library of Congress]
63. *National Police Gazette*, November 24, 1880, p. 14. [Fultonhistory.com]
64. *National Police Gazette*, January 12, 1884, p. 10. [Fultonhistory.com]
65. *New York Herald*, October 4, 1874, p. 4. [Fultonhistory.com]
66. *New York Clipper*, October 17, 1874, p. 230. [Fultonhistory.com]
67. *Brooklyn Eagle*, April 5, 1875, p. 1. [Fultonhistory.com]
68. *New York Spirit of the Times*, December 1875, p. 553. [Fultonhistory.com]
69. *New York Sun*, February 6, 1876, p. 1. [Fultonhistory.com]
70. *New York Clipper*, April 17, 1880, p. 31. [Fultonhistory.com]
71. *New York Herald*, November 29, 1878, p. 2. [Fultonhistory.com]
72. *National Police Gazette*, April 8, 1882, p. 14. [Fultonhistory.com]
73. *National Police Gazette*, May 12, 1883, p. 12. [Fultonhistory.com]
74. *National Police Gazette*, August 16, 1884, p. 14. [Fulton History.com]
75. *Syracuse Daily Standard*, January 29, 1885, p. 5. [Fultonhistory.com]
76. *St. Paul Daily Glove*, January 11, 1885, p. 6. [Library of Congress]
77. *Sun*, April 24, 1890, p. 4. [Fultonhistory.com]
78. *National Police Gazette*, February 7, 1885, p. 11. [Fultonhistory.com]
79. *Atchison Daily Champion*, August 30, 1888, p. 1. [Library of Congress]

80. *St. Paul Daily Globe*, March 8, 1887, p. 4. [Library of Congress]

81. Allen Guttman. *Women's Sports*, p. 99.

82. John L. Sullivan is alleged to have brought a husband-and-wife team, Hessie Converse (Donahue) and George Converse, along on his "Honest Hands and Willing Hearts" tour around the United States in the late winter/spring of 1892. The story goes that in a mock sparring match with Hessie, he punched her hard in the face by accident, and pivoting around, Hessie let loose with a right that landed Sullivan on the floor of the stage, knocking him out cold. *Milwaukee Journal*, August 17, 1989, p. G1. [Google News Archive]

83. T. R. Coombs. Quoted in Allen Guttman. *Women's Sports*, p. 101, n. 49.

84. *New York Herald*, January 31, 1888, p.12. [Fultonhistory.com]

85. *St. Paul Daily Globe*, April 25, 1886, p. 12. [Library of Congress]

86. *Derby Mercury*, May 25, 1887, p. 6. [British Newspaper Archive]

87. *Semi-Weekly Interior Journal*, April 28, 1887. [Library of Congress]

88. *Albany Times*, December 8, 1887. [Fultonhistory.com]

89. Nellie Bly. "A Visit with John L. Sullivan." *New York World*, Sunday ed., July 28, 1889. [Bareknuckleboxinghalloffame.com]

90. Mike Sowell. "A Woman in a Man's World: 'Annie Laurie,' One of American's First Sportswriters." In Linda K. Fuller, ed. *Sport, Rhetoric, and Gender*, p. 65 (65–70).

91. Ibid., p. 66.

92. Ibid.

93. Kasia Boddy. *Boxing*, p. 159.

94. Ibid., p. 158.

95. *St. Paul Daily Globe*, January 16, 1891, p. 4. [Library of Congress]

96. "Mr. Corbett through a Women's Eyes." *San Francisco Call*, February 25, 1897, p. 4. [Library of Congress]

97. *Salt Lake Herald*, March 14, 1897, p. 1. [Library of Congress]

98. *Hartford Herald*, March 24, 1897, p. 1. [Library of Congress]

99. *Sacramento Daily Record-Union*, March 23, 1897, p. 2. [Library of Congress]

100. *St. Paul Daily Globe*, August 17, 1897, p. 4. [Library of Congress]

101. *Evening Times*, September 8, 1897, p. 6. [Library of Congress]

102. Gordon Sisters Boxing/Thomas A. Edison, Inc. *The American Variety Stage: Vaudeville and Popular Entertainment, 1870–1920*. Edison Manufacturing Co., 1901. [Library of Congress] [Memory.loc.gov]

3. BOXING, WOMEN, AND THE MORES OF CHANGE

1. *Seattle Star*, July 21, 1914, p. 7. [Library of Congress]

2. "Brooklyn Correspondence." *Daily Argus News*, June 11, 1895. [Fultonhistory.com]

3. "Fights to a Finish." *Daily Argus News*, June 11, 1895, p. 6. [Google News]

4. "Laugh! I Thought I'd Die, the Night Hattie Boxed Gussie Freeman." *Brooklyn Eagle*, p. 12E. [Fultonhistory.com]

5. "Female Fighters." *Sunday Herald*, November 22, 1891, p. 1. [Library of Congress]

6. "Never Was Kissed." *St. Paul Daily Glove*, June 4, 1895, p. 3. [Library of Congress]

7. "She Is a Longshoreman." *World*, March 2, 1899, p. 14. [Fultonhistory.com]

8. "She's the City's Terror." *Brooklyn Daily Eagle*, November 22, 1891, p. 20. [Fultonhistory.com]

9. Donald K. Burleson. *Polly Burns (Polly Fairclough)—World Champion Lady Boxer, 1900.* [Travel-golf.org/genealogy/burns_Polly.htm]

10. William Fulton. "Boxing Queen, 77, Dies in Slum." *Chicago Daily Tribune*, January 3, 1959. [Chicago Tribune]

11. 1901 England Census. London. Lancashire. Liverpool. Islington. 24. P. 28 of 47. [Ancestry.com]

12. "A Good Looking Colleen." *Milwaukee Sentinel*, July 22, 1945, p. 23. [Google News]

13. *Montana Butte Standard*, February 16, 1935, p. 6. [Newspapers.com]

14. William Fulton. "Boxing Queen, 77, Dies in Slum." *Chicago Daily Tribune*, January 3, 1959. [Chicago Tribune]

15. *Times*, September 9, 1900, p. 5. [Library of Congress]

16. "'Shorty Kuhn' Put to Sleep." *Omaha Daily Bee*, April 24, 1909, p. 12. [Library of Congress]

17. *Morning Telegraph*, November 18, 1905, p. 4.

18. Some press accounts note her last name as Donavan, while others note her as Dunaman.

19. *National Police Gazette*, 1906, p. 11. [Fultonhistory.com]

20. "Women Pugilists Engage in a Fast Bout." *San Francisco Call*, August 21, 1906, p. 7. [Library of Congress]

21. "Amazons Fight Six Hot Rounds." *Evening Star*, August 20, 1906, p. 2. [Library of Congress]

22. "The Shame of 'Texas Mamie' and Another Female Pug." *Spokane Press*, August 26, 1906, p. 10. [Library of Congress]

23. "Amazons Battle in Prize Ring." *Minneapolis Journal*, August 21, 1906, p. 8. [Library of Congress]

24. The press account in the Brooklyn Standard Union notes that the fight occurred in Jersey City; however, the Corinthian Athletic Association was actually located in Staten Island, New York.

25. *Dawson Daily News*, October 6, 1906, p. 6. [Google]

26. "Women Battle in Ring; Texas Mamie a Wonder." *Brooklyn Standard Union*, 1906. [Fultonhistory.com]

27. "Texas Mamie Arrives." *Utica Herald-Dispatch*, October 24, 1906, p. 8. [Library of Congress]

28. "Texas Mamie to Open School." *Syracuse Daily Journal*, November 11, 1906. [Library of Congress]

29. "Texas Mamie Knocks Out Goldie O'Rouke in 13." *Los Angeles Herald*, November 5, 1907, p. 8. [Library of Congress]

30. "Texas Mamie Wins." *Victoria Daily Colonist*, November 1, 1917, p. 9. [Britishcolonist.ca]

31. "Texas Mamie Knocks Out Goldie O'Rouke in 13." *Los Angeles Herald*, November 5, 1907, p. 8. [Library of Congress]

32. Tippy Fay. "Miss Kid Broad Defeated by Miss Flora Ryan in Ten Rounds, Writes Tippy Fay." *Albany Evening Journal*, April 7, 1909, p. 3. [Fultonhistory.com]

33. T. S. Andrews. "Prize Fighting Becoming a Favorite Pastime for Women." *El Paso Herald*, July 28, 1914, p. 6. [Library of Congress]

34. "This Woman Boxer Weighs 105 Pounds and She Has Met Two Champions." *Tacoma Times*, November 27, 1917, p. 6. [Library of Congress]

35. *Evening Telegraph and Post*, June 29, 1914, p. 9. [British Newspaper Archive]

36. T. S. Andrews. "Prize Fighting Becoming a Favorite Pastime for Women." *El Paso Herald*, July 28, 1914, p. 6. [Library of Congress]

37. Elizabeth Tucker. "Woman Manager Says Boxing Is Best Training." *Tacoma Times*, October 16, 1917, p. 6. [Library of Congress]

38. "Trains Her Brother to Be a Fighter." *Binghamton Press*, September 26, 1916. [Fultonhistory.com]

39. "Girl Fight Manager Is Success with Brothers." *Tacoma Times*, December 11, 1916, p. 6. [Library of Congress]

40. *Milwaukee Journal*, July 22, 1921, p. 11. [Google News]

41. "France Has New Champion." *Washington Herald*, March 6, 1914, p. 4. [Library of Congress]

42. "Women's Boxing Championship." *Manchester Evening News*, March 6, 1914, p. 6. [British Newspaper Archive]

43. *University Missourian*, March 11, 1914, p. 4. [Library of Congress]

44. "Mlle. Carpentier Is Female Champ." *Ogden Standard*, April 18, 1914, p. 5. [Library of Congress]

45. *Newcastle Daily Journal*, July 4, 1914, p. 4. [British Newspaper Archive]

46. *Manchester Courier*, September 7, 1014, p. 2. [British Newspaper Archive]

47. "Nostalgia Letter: Tale of Lady Boxer." *This Is Strattfordshire*, February 5, 2011. [Thisisstratffordshire.com]

48. *Newcastle Daily Journal*, June 11, 1915, p. 9. [British Newspaper Archive]

49. *Hull Daily Mail*, June 22, 1915, p. 3. [British Newspaper Archive]

50. *Aberdeen Evening Express*, June 2, 1915, p. 2. [British Newspaper Archive]

51. *Aberdeen Evening Express*, November 26, 1918, p. 1. [British Newspaper Archive]

52. "Uppercut from the Fair Righter's Fist." *Hartford Herald*, May 1, 1912, p. 8. [Library of Congress]

53. "Clean Knockout in Girls' Bout." *Buffalo Courier*, April 27, 1912. [Fultonhistory.com]

54. "Girls in a Prizefight." *Chronicle*, July 6, 1912, p. 2. [National Library of Australia]

55. "This Woman Boxer Weighs 105 Pounds and She Has Met Two Champions." *Tacoma Times*, November 27, 1917, p. 6. [Library of Congress]

56. *Saratogian*, January 5, 1918, p. 8. [Fultonhistory.com]

57. "Woman Boxes One Round and Then." *New York Press*, March 1, 1916, p. 1. [Fultonhistory.com]

58. Robert George Rodriguez. *The Regulation of Boxing*.

59. "Woman Boxes One Round and Then." *New York Press*, March 1, 1916, p. 1. [Fultonhistory.com]

60. "This Woman Boxer Weighs 105 Pounds and She Has Met Two Champions." *Tacoma Times*, November 27, 1917, p. 6. [Library of Congress]

61. "Once Nerve Goes Fighter Is Gone, Says Woman Boxer." *Brooklyn Daily Eagle*, September 9, 1917, p. 3. [Fultonhistory.com]

62. *Sun*, May 24, 1919, p. 17. [Fultonhistory.com]

63. 1920 United States Census. New York, New York. Enumeration District. 834. Ward 11 AD. January 16, 1920. Line 86. [Ancestry.com]

4. ENCOUNTERING THE MODERN: FLAPPERS, MAE WEST, AND THE WAR YEARS

1. Djuna Barnes and Alyce Barry. "Jess Willard."

2. Djuna Barnes and Alyce Barry. "My Sisters and I," p. 169.

3. Ibid., p. 170.

4. Ibid., p. 173.

5. Edith E. Moriarity. "As a Woman Thinks." *Tulsa Daily World*, July 31, 1920, p. 6. [Library of Congress]. The author further wrote that Dempsey believed women in the future would go to the gym a few times a week to work out. In the opinion of the author, while women might take up "golf, swimming, tennis, basketball, bowling or skating," they would never "go in strong for boxing."

6. Djuna Barnes and Alyce Barry. "Dempsey Welcomes."

7. "Girl Athlete Says Boxing is Valuable for Protection." *Toronto World*, February 18, 1918, p. 5. [Google News]

8. Margaret I. MacDonald. "The Womanly Art of Self-Defense." *Moving Picture World*, December 22, 1917, p. 1773. [Learnaboutmovieposters.com]

9. Jack Dempsey. "The Life of a Champion." *Rochester Evening Journal and the Post Express*, February 2, 1925, p. 2. [Google News]

10. Erik N. Jensen. *Body by Weimar*, pp. 83–84.

11. "Female Announcer Boosts Boxing Game for Women." *Reading Eagle*, September 5, 1939, p. 30. [Google News]

12. Cecilia Rasmussen. "L.A. Then and Now: First Women Boxing Referee Rolled with Punches." *Los Angeles Times*, May 21, 2006, p. B2. [ProQuest]

13. "First Woman Referee Puts Pulchritude in Pugilism." *Utica Observer Dispatch*, May 19, 1940, p. 2-D.I [Fultonhistory.com]

14. Eddie Brietz. "Sports Roundup," p. 9. [Fultonhistory.com]

15. "Pasadena Books Woman Referee." *Spokane Daily Chronicle*, May 9, 1940, p. 24. [Google News]

16. Cecilia Rasmussen. "L.A. Then and Now: First Women Boxing Referee Rolled with Punches." *Los Angeles Times*, May 21, 2006, p. B2. [ProQuest]

17. Jeff Moshier. "Playing Square." *Evening Independent*, June 6, 1940, p. 10. [Google News]

18. Cecilia Rasmussen. "L.A. Then and Now: First Women Boxing Referee Rolled with Punches." *Los Angeles Times*, May 21, 2006, p. B2. [ProQuest]

19. "Woman Referee Retires." *New York Times*, June 1, 1940, p. 16. [ProQuest]

20. *Milwaukee Journal*, January 30, 1943, p. 16. [Google News]

21. Josephine Lewman. "'Boxing for Women Too.'" *Youngstown Vindicator*, November 8, 1944, p. 8. [Google News]

5. BOXING IN THE AGE OF THE "MIGHTY ATOM"

1. Alvin Steinkopf. "Girl Boxer Baffles Boxer." *Telegraph*, April 7, 1949, p. 22. [Google News]

2. Victoria Murphy. "Barbara Buttrick: World Pays Tribute to Brit Champ Boxer." *Mirror*, October 30, 2010, n.p. [Mirror.co.uk)

3. "Boxing for the Ladies." *Townsville Daily Bulletin*, October 12, 1948, p. 2. [British Newspaper Archive]

4. "Girl Boxer Banned from Public Ring." *Gloucestershire Echo*, January 11, 1949, p. 3. [British Newspaper Archive]

5. *Daily Mail*, November 11, 1948, p. 4. [British Newspaper Archive]

6. "They Train on Underdone Beefsteaks." *Northern Times*, November 11, 1948. [National Library of Australia]

7. "Challengers." *Daily Derby Telegraph*, November 17, 1948, p. 8. [British Newspaper Archive]

8. "Girl Boxer Banned from Public Ring." *Gloucestershire Echo*, January 11, 1949, p. 3. [British Newspaper Archive]

9. "Women Boxers, Bouts Officially Frowned On." *Northern Miner*, December 13, 1948, p. 2. [National Library of Australia]

10. "Weaker Sex!" *Central Queensland Herald*, March 3, 1949, p. 18. [National Library of Australia]

11. "Girl Boxer." British Pathe. 1949. [Britishpathe.com]

12. "Woman Boxer Waits." *Evening Telegraph*, February 9, 1949, p. 9. [British National Archives]

13. "Girl Boxer Show Goes On." *Dundee Courier*, February 10, 1949, p. 3. [British National Archives]; *Winnipeg Free Press*, February 15, 1949, p. 5. [Ancestry.com]

14. "Girl Boxing Act Defies Opposition." *Hull Daily Mail*, February 10, 1949, p. 3. [British Newspaper Archive]

15. "Barbara: Can Box or Can She?" *Milwaukee Journal*, February 12, 1949, p. 16. [Google News]

16. "Battling Barbara Not to Fight." *The Argus*, February 14, 1949, p. 16. [British National Archives]

17. "Barbara Will Not Fight Bert after All." *Aberdeen Journal*, February 17, 1949, p. 4. [British National Archives]

18. Kilburn Empire Theater. Advertisement. March 1949. [Malissa Smith Collection]

19. "Barbara Packs 700lb. Punch" *Evening Standard*, March 8, 1949. [Malissa Smith Collection]

20. "Girl Boxer Gives Stage Exhibition." *Yorkshire Post*, March 8, 1949, n.p. [Malissa Smith Collection]

21. "Cottingham Girl Will Box at Secret Rendezvous." *Hull Daily Mail*, March 26, 1949, p. 1. [British Newspaper Archive]

22. "Girl Boxer's Challenge." *Sunday Herald*, April 10, 1949, p. 24. [British National Archives]

23. A copy of a publicity handout from the early 1990s entitled "Barbara Buttrick: Sensational English Girl Flyweight Boxer" lists a total of twenty-six fights, with the proviso that "She had more wins which are not recorded here." [Malissa Smith Collection]

24. Alvin Steinkopf. "Girl Boxer Baffles Britons: She Wants Board to Approve Sport for Women." *Telegraph*, April 7, 1940, p. 22. [Google News]

25. "The Fair Sex in a Tough Sport." *An Illustrated Chronicle of West County Boxing*. Vol. 2, no. 9, September 1949, p. 9. [Google Books]

26. "Sports Gossip: Girls' Fight Off." *Hull Daily Mail*, July 26, 1949, p. 6. [British Newspaper Archive]

27. Tom Archdeacon. "Barbara Beacon Has Renewed Love Affair with Boxing." *Miami News*, June 7, 1980, p. B1. [Google News]

28. "'Keep Chin Down, Guard Up' ex-Boxer Advises Daughters." *Free Lance-Star*, March 21, 1972, p. 11. [Google News]

29. *Berkley-Post Herald*, June 20, 1950, p. 6. [Ancestry.com]

30. "'Powder Puff' Boxing Match." *Traverse City Record Eagle*, June 20, 1950, p. 13. [Ancestry.com]

31. "Girl Boxers Are Banned." *Palm Beach Post*, September 13, 1950, p. 11. [Google News]

32. Bill Moor. "In '50s, She Landed Blow for Women." *South Bend Tribune*, January 29, 1994, n.p. [NL.newsbank.com]

33. "JoAnn Hagen Fails to Last . . ." *Council Bluffs Nonpareil*, November 23, 1949, n.p. [Ancestry.com]

34. "'Keep Chin Down, Guard Up' ex-Boxer Advises Daughters." *Free Lance-Star*, March 21, 1972, p. 11. [Google News]

35. Women Boxing Archive Network's Sue TL Fox had a correspondence in 2010 with one of Emerick's daughters, who reiterated that the fight took place in Council Bluffs, Iowa, and that due to a fire all of Emerick's boxing memorabilia was destroyed except for the trophy.

36. "Girl Gladiators Settle Nothing." *Council Bluffs Nonpareil*, December 1, 1949, p. 17. [Ancestry.com]

37. "Girlboxers to Appear on Bill." *Council Bluffs Nonpareil*, December 28, 1949, n.p. [Ancestry.com]

38. "Women Athletes Make Southwest Iowa Headlines." *Council Bluffs Nonpareil*, December 25, 1949, n.p. [Ancestry.com]

39. Jeanne Hoffman. "West Coast Gal Seeks Featherweight Boxing Title." *Pittsburgh Press*, September 2, 1951, p. 39.

40. "Mat Matches Here Tuesday." *Miami Daily News-Record*, November 22, 1953, p. 5. [Newspapers.com]

41. "Mix Tag Match!" *Sheboygan Press*, February 1, 1954, p. 21. [Ancestry.com]

42. "Mixed Team Bout on Playdium Card Wrestling Match." *Sheboygan Press*, February 1, 1954, n.p. [Ancestry.com]

43. "Australian Tag Match." *Sheboygan Press*, February 1, 1954, p. 3. [Ancestry.com]

44. "British Bantam—Lass with Good Left Looking for Fights." *Corpus Christi Caller*, May 29, 1955, p. 5B. [Ancestry.com]

45. "Pretty Puglilists." *Bismarck Tribune*, July 3, 1954, n.p. [Ancestry.com]

46. "Briton Wins." *Billings Gazette*, July 12, 1954, p. 8. [Ancestry.com]

47. "Battling Barbara Is the Winner." *Dickinson Press*, July 10, 1954, n.p. [Malissa Smith Collection]

48. *The Prize Fighter.* Calgary, Canada. September 1954, n.p. [Malissa Smith Collection]

49. "Calgary's Great Fight Attraction." *Calgary Herald*, September 10, 1954, n.p. [Malissa Smith Collection]

50. "British Bantam—Lass with Good Left Looking for Fights." *Corpus Christi Caller*, May 29, 1955, p. 5B. [Ancestry.com]

51. Cary O'Dell. *June Cleaver*, p. 136.

52. Jim Meenan. "At 69, a Boxer at Heart." *South Bend Tribune*, October 14, 2005. [NL.newsbank.com]

53. Jim Meenan. "Way Ahead of Her Time." *South Bend Tribune*, September 19, 2005. [NL.Newsbank.com]

54. "Niles Girl Wins Title." *New-Palladium* (Benton Harbor, MI), December 15, 1956, sec 2, p. 2. [Newspapers.com]

55. Jim Meenan. "Way Ahead of Her Time." *South Bend Tribune*, September 19, 2005. [NL.Newsbank.com]

56. Jim Meenan. "At 69, a Boxer at Heart." *South Bend Tribune*, October 14, 2005. [NL.Newsbank.com]

57. "So These Gals Took Up Boxing." *Miami Herald*, August 15, 1957, n.p. [Malissa Smith Collection]

58. "So These Gals Took Up Boxing." *Miami Herald*, August 15, 1957, n.p. [Malissa Smith Collection]

59. Letter, Glenn "Shep" Sheppard to Johnny Nate. [Women Boxing Archive Network]

60. Advertisement Handbill: Kugler vs. Buttrick. October 8, 1957. [Malissa Smith Collection]

61. "English Girl Boxer in Classy Ring Drill." *San Antonio Express*, October 7, 1957, n.p. [Malissa Smith Collection]

62. *San Antonio Light*, October 9, 1957, p. 39. [Ancestry.com]

63. "Barbara a Lady, but What a Right!" *Milwaukee Journal*, October 9, 1957, p. E17. [Google News]; and "Female Fury in Texas Boxing Ring." *Milwaukee Journal*, October 17, 1957, p. B3. [Google News]

64. "British Girl Wins World Boxing Title." *San Antonio Express*, n.p. [Malissa Smith Collection]

65. "State Nixes Gal Boxers' Fistic Tour." *San Antonio Light*, October 10, 1957, p. 22. [Ancestry.com]

66. Robert Philip. "Robert Philip on Monday: Memoirs of a Happy Left-Hook." *Daily Telegraph*, March 1993, sport 7. [Malissa Smith Collection]

6. BURNING BRAS, TAKING ON THE "SHERIFF," AND WINNING THE RIGHT TO FIGHT

1. "Teen-age Miss Set to Stage Florida Fights." *Los Angeles Times*, January 2, 1960, n.p. [Folder: Miscellaneous. Box 45, Series 13. Fistic Arcana. Hank Kaplan Archive, Brooklyn College Archives and Special Collections, Brooklyn College Library.]

2. "Brunette Boosts Boxing." *St. Petersburg Times*, December 31, 1959, p. 20. [Google News]

3. Jack Cuddy. UPI. "Giant Gate Expect." *Pampa Daily News* (Texas), September 4, 1958, p. 12. [Newspapers.com]

4. Jack Hawn. "Aileen Eaton, Dynamic Boxing Promoter, Dies at 78 after Long Illness." *Los Angeles Times*, November 9, 1987, n.p. [LAtimes.com]

5. Sidney Fields. "Only Human: A Knockout in Fight Game." *Daily News*, July 1, 1969, n.p. [Folder: Miscellaneous. Box 45, Series 13. Fistic Arcana. Hank Kaplan Archive, Brooklyn College Archives and Special Collections, Brooklyn College Library.]

6. "Fight Fans to See Lady Announcer." AP. *Indiana Gazette* (Pennsylvania), March 15, 1967, p. 53. [Newspapers.com]

7. Al Goldberg. "Femininity Climbs into Ring." *News Journal* (Mansfield, Ohio), March 16, 1967, p. 37. [Newspapers.com]

8. "Gals' Boxing Decision Is: Stay at Home." AP. *Prescott Evening Courier* (Arizona), June 2, 1959, p. 3. [Google News]

9. "'Boxing' Fem Rasslers Shine." *Abilene Reporter-News*, October 5, 1965, p. 11. [Newspapers.com]

10. *Amarillo Globe-Times*, October 8, 1965, p. 16. [Newspapers.com]

11. "Noble falls to Antone." *Abilene Reporter-News*, June 21, 1966, p. 7. [Newspapers.com]

12. "Okay—Er, Ladies, Come out Fighting." *Independent* (Long Beach, California), June 30, 1966, p. C2. [Newspapers.com]

13. Ray Fitzgerald. "12-Year-Old Manomet Girl—A Real Knockout." *Boston Globe*, January 18, 1969, pp. 17–18. [ProQuest]

14. Bob Townsend. "Laura's Punch Shakes up Boxing Commission." *Brockton Daily Enterprise*, January 18, 1969, p. 21. [Folder: Miscellaneous. Box 45, Series 13. Fistic Arcana. Hank Kaplan Archive, Brooklyn College Archives and Special Collections, Brooklyn College Library.]

15. "Battling Little Laura Ends Boxing Career." *Boston Globe*, January 25, 1969, p. 16. [ProQuest]

16. "Boxing Club Shocked on Discovering Truth." *Lebanon Daily News* (Pennsylvania), March 25, 1972, p. 2. [Newspapers.com]

17. "Girls Welcome at Boys Club." *Daily Herald*, April 30, 1969, sec 2, p. 8. [Newspapers.com]

18. Bill Gilbert and Nancy Williamson. "Are You Being Two-Face?" *Sports Illustrated*, June 4, 2013, n.p. [Sportsillustrated.com]

19. "Female Boxing." *Pittsburgh Courier*, January 23, 1965, p. 12.

20. Abigail Van Duran. "Dear Abby: Female Boxing Blow-by-Blow." *Independent* (Long Beach, California), November 30, 1969, p. 73. [Newspapers.com]

21. *Seattle Times*, July 14, 1970, n.p. [Folder: Miscellaneous. Box 45, Series 13. Fistic Arcana. Hank Kaplan Archive, Brooklyn College Archives and Special Collections, Brooklyn College Library.]

22. "Pennsylvania Woman Lands Blow on Males." *Pocono Record* (Stroudsburg, Pennsylvania), February 2, 1975, p. 15. [Newspapers.com]

23. Ray Parrillo. "Carol Polis Recalls Her Days as the First Woman to Judge a Pro Boxing Match." *Philadephia Inquirer*, July 15, 2011, n.p. [Philly.com].

24. "Pennsylvania Woman Lands Blow on Males." *Pocono Record* (Stroudsburg, Pennsylvania), February 2, 1975, p. 15. [Newspapers.com]

25. "Boxing." *Lowell Sun*, January 2, 1973, p. 6740. [Newspapers.com]

26. Lennox Blackmoore interview with Malissa Smith, July 10, 2013.

27. Jay Searcy. "'Lady Tyger,' 135 Pounds, Launches a Ring Career: Women in Sport." *New York Times*, May 5, 1974, p. S6. [ProQuest]

28. Peter Coutros. "Missticuffs on Mulberry St." *Daily News*, September 3, 1974. n.p. [Folder: Fighters / Lady Tyger Trimiar. Box 45, Series 13. Fistic Arcana. Hank Kaplan Archive, Brooklyn College Archives and Special Collections, Brooklyn College Library.]

29. Bill Verigan. "Fem Boxing May Bloom in Garden." *Daily News*, October 6, 1974, p. 4C. [Folder: Fighters / Lady Tyger Trimiar. Box 45, Series 13. Fistic Arcana. Hank Kaplan Archive, Brooklyn College Archives and Special Collections, Brooklyn College Library.]

30. "The Ladies Want to Fight." *Morning Herald*, October 8, 1974, p.16. [Newspapers.com]

31. "Woman Sues New York for Boxing License." *Tampa Times*, December 26, 1974. [Folder: Fighters / Jackie Tonawanda. Box 45, Series 13. Fistic Arcana. Hank Kaplan Archive, Brooklyn College Archives and Special Collections, Brooklyn College Library.]

32. Garrett v. New York State Athletic Commission. Supreme Court, New York County, New York, Special Term, Part I. June 16, 1975. 82 MISC.2d 524 370 N.Y.S.2d 795 [WestLawNext]

33. "Girl Boxer Loses Round." *Raleigh Register*, January 22, 1975, p. 19. [Newspapers.com]

34. Garrett v. New York State Athletic Commission. Supreme Court, New York County, New York, Special Term, Part I. June 16, 1975. 82 MISC.2d 524 370 N.Y.S.2d 795 [WestLaw-Next]

35. Lena Williams. "Woman Boxer Set to Meet Male Foe." *New York Times*, June 1, 1975, p. S20. [ProQuest]

36. Jane Perlez. "Jackie Finally Gets a Fight." *New York Post*, June 6, 1975, p. 64. [Folder: Fighters / Jackie Tonawanda. Box 45, Series 13. Fistic Arcana. Hank Kaplan Archive, Brooklyn College Archives and Special Collections, Brooklyn College Library.]

37. Lena Williams. "Equal Status May Spur Interest in Women's Sports Injuries." *New York Times*, June 15, 1975, p. S4. [ProQuest]

38. "Woman Boxer Waits for License." *Reno Evening Gazette*, July 4, 1975, p. 19. [Newspapers.com]

39. Sue TL Fox. "Archived Exclusive Interview with Bill Dickson." Women Boxing Archive Network. May 20, 1999. [WBAN.com]

40. "People in Sports: 500 Hitter Decides Game's Not for Him." *New York Times*, July 12, 1975, p. 18. [ProQuest]

41. "Lady Boxer Needs a Foe." *Buck's County Courier*, September 6, 1975, p. 9. [Newspapers.com]

42. Steve Sneddon. "Caroline Svendsen Scared?" *Reno Evening Gazette*, September 17, 1975, p. 22.

43. "The Ladies Take to the Ring in Four-Round Bout Night." *Joseph Gazette*, September 19, 1975, p. 14. [Google News]

44. Steve Sneddon. "Strategy Is Simple for Svendsen's Debut." *Reno Evening Gazette*, September 18, 1975, p. 25 [Newspapers.com]

45. "Boxing Match between Women Ends Quickly." *Beaver County Times*, September 19, 1975, p. 29. [Google News]

46. Steve Sneddon. "Svendsen No Longer a Curiosity." *Reno Evening Gazette*, September 20, 1975, p. 8 [Newspapers.com]

47. "Ladies' Match Tentatively Set." *Eugene Register-Guard*, October 3, 1975. [Google News]

48. "Sock It to Her!" *Journal* (Meridan, Connecticut), October 9, 1975, p. 7. [Google News]

49. "Uppercuts, Not Powderpuffs Selection of Distaff Pugilists." *Daily Chronicle* (Centralia, Washington), October 23, 1975, p. 9. [Newspapers.com]

50. "Caroline Svendsen Wins Second Professional Fight." *Reno Evening Gazette*, October 24, 1975, p.14 [Newspapers.com]

51. "It's Caroline Svendsen by Unanimous Decision." *Times Standard* (Eurika, California), October 24, 1975, p. 4. [Google News]

52. "Women Win the Right to Box." *Gallup Independent*, November 15, 1975, p. 7. [Newspapers.com]

53. "A.A.U. Acts on Woman Boxer." *New York Times*, March 28, 1975, p. 45. [ProQuest]

54. Michael G. Lacey. "Okay, All the Boys in One Corner and This Girl in the Other." *Tucson Daily Citizen*, June 14, 1975, p. 32. [Newspapers.com]

55. "ASU Coed Boxer Willing to Fight." *Yuma Daily*, March 30, 1975, p. 18. [Newspapers.com]

56. Michael G. Lacey. "Okay, All the Boys in One Corner and This Girl in the Other." *Tucson Daily Citizen*, June 14, 1975, p. 33. [Newspapers.com]

57. Time O'Mara. "'Not My Idea' Her Boxing Career Technically at End." *Tucson Daily Citizen*, December 13, 1974, p. 12. [Newspapers.com]

58. Greg Oliver. "Remembering the Full Life of Princess Tona Tomha." Slam! Wrestling. [Slam.canoe.ca]

59. "Female Boxing Bout Called Off." *Milwaukee Journal*, November 1, 1975, p. 15 [Google News]

60. "Girls Match Off." *Bryan Times*, November 8, 1975, p. 5. [Google News]

61. Kevin Lane. "Controversy Reigns: Girls' Fight Dropped." *Anderson Herald*, November 8, 1975, p. 8. [Newspapers.com]

62. "Fight Her First, Last: Crumes Scores KO." *Anderson Herald*, November 10, 1975, p. 17. [Newspapers.com]

63. "Boxing Issue Skirted?" *Milwaukee Journal*, November 18, 1975, p. 13. [Google News]

64. Tracy Dodds. "Substitute Opponent No Test for Finch." *Milwaukee Journal*, December 9, 1975, p. 19. [Google News]

65. Phil Cash. "Women Boxers No Hit with Fans." *Milwaukee Sentinel*, December 9, 1975, p. 9. [Google News]

7. A RING OF THEIR OWN

1. "San Pedro Slugger Fights at Forum." *Independent Press-Telegram*, April 25, 1976, p. S3. [Newspapers.com]

2. Sue TL Fox went on to found Women Boxing Archive Network, a website that has become an important resource for female fighters.

3. Malissa Smith interview with Sue TL Fox, September 27, 2013.

4. Sue TL Fox. "In Sue Fox's Own Words." Women Boxing Archive Network. [WBAN.com]

5. Don Terbush. "Sideline Slants: Stateline Fight May Change Rule." *Times Standard*, March 4, 1976, p. 9.

6. Sue TL Fox. "In Sue Fox's Own Words." Women Boxing Archive Network. [WBAN.com]

7. Don Terbush. "Sideline Slants: Pro Boxing Is Family Affair." *Times Standard*, February 19, 1976, p. 9.

8. William C. Rempel. "Girls Invade Male Domain of Boxing Ring." *Los Angeles Times*, June 1, 1975, p. D1. [ProQuest]

9. Ed Meagher. "In This Corner . . . a Woman." *Los Angeles Times*, January 14, 1975, p. D1. [ProQuest]

10. Steve Sneddon. "From My Corner: Quiet Killer." *Nevada State Journal*, March 20, 1976, p. 2.

11. Don Terbush. "Sideline Slants: 'Princess' Convinced Them." *Times Standard*, March 25, 1976, p. 13.

12. Don Terbush. "Sideline Slants: Girls Impress SAC Onlookers." *Times Standard*, April 8, 1976, p. 11.

13. Jack Stevenson. "Kim Maybee Has Sports Future Mapped Out." *Independent Press-Telegram*, May 2, 1976, p. S7. [Newspapers.com]

14. Don Terbush. "Sideline Slants: Cheri Thought She Lost Her First Fight." *Times Standard*, April 21, 1976, p. 15. [Newspapers.com]

15. Bud Tucker. "Only 'Ring' Women Need Is on Finger." *Independent Press-Telegram*, April 18, 1976, p. S3. [Newspapers.com]

16. Jim Murray. "And May the Best Boxing Person Win." *Los Angeles Times*, April 27, 1976, p. 3C. [Google News]

17. Rich Roberts. "San Pedro Slugger Fights at Forum." *Independent Press-Telegram*, April 25, 197, p. S3. [Newspapers.com]

18. Cheryl Bentsen. "California Has Its First Ms.-Match." *Los Angeles Times*, April 27, 1976, p. D1. [ProQuest]

19. "Future No Concern of the Lady Boxer." *The Bee*, April 28, 1976, p. 44. [Newspapers.com]

20. Robert Lindsey. "Women Try Boxing on the Coast." *New York Times*, May 1, 1976, p. 42. [ProQuest]

21. Jack Stevenson. "The Lady Has a Punch." *Bakersfield Californian*, April 29, 1976, p. 24. [Newspapers.com]

22. Robert Lindsey. "Women Try Boxing on the Coast." *New York Times*, May 1, 1976, p. 42. [ProQuest]

23. Jack Stevenson. "The Lady Has a Punch." *Bakersfield Californian*, April 29, 1976, p. 24. [Newspapers.com]

24. "Death Threat to Aileen Eaton." *Independent Press-Telegram*, May 25, 1976, p. C2. [Newspapers.com]

25. "Death Threat Sent to Eaton, Chargin." *Los Angeles Times*, May 25, 1976.[ProQuest]

26. "Death Threat to Aileen Eaton." *Independent Press-Telegram*, May 25, 1976, p. C2. [Newspapers.com]

27. Don Terbush. "Death Vow Won't Stop Kibby Gal." *Times Standard*, May 26, 1976, p. 16. [Newspapers.com]

28. John Hall. "Around Town." *Los Angeles Times*, May 31, 1976, p. C3. [ProQuest]

29. John Hall. "Around Town." *Los Angeles Times*, June 4, 1976, p. D3. [ProQuest]

30. Don Terbush. "Death Threat Bout Went off Smoothly." *Times Standard*, May 30, 1976, p. 13. [Newspapers.com]

31. Sue TL Fox. "In Sue Fox's Own Words." Women Boxing Archive Network. [WBAN.com]

32. Gary Smith. "It's Ladies Day and the . . ." *Philadelphia Daily News*, p. 54. [Folder: Fighters / Lady Tyger Trimiar. Box 45, Series 13. Fistic Arcana. Hank Kaplan Archive, Brooklyn College Archives and Special Collections, Brooklyn College Library.]

33. Bob Wright. "Bald Woman Boxer Just Being Herself." *Philadelphia Evening Bulletin*, January 1976, n.p. [Folder: Fighters / Lady Tyger Trimiar. Box 45, Series 13. Fistic Arcana. Hank Kaplan Archive, Brooklyn College Archives and Special Collections, Brooklyn College Library.]

34. Robert Lindsey. "Women Try Boxing on the Coast." *New York Times*, May 1, 1976, p. 42. [ProQuest]

35. Don Riley. "Women Boxers a Smash in Vegas." *Salt Lake Tribune*, March 20, 1977, p. 151.

36. "Female Invades Male Territory." *Journal News* (Hamilton, Ohio), May 8, 1974, p. 26. [Newspapers.com]

37. *Boxing Illustrated*, October 1973, p. 62. [WBAN.com]

38. One of those fights may have been on January 27, 1977, at the Olympic Theater in Los Angeles. A newspaper article lists her as scheduled to fight against Lilly Rodriguez, black belt in karate, in a four-rounder. Takatsuki was listed under the name Fumiki Takasuki. See "Perfect fighter." *Valley News*, January 27, 1977, sec. 4, p. 3. [Newspapers.com]; "Sandoval Tops Olympic Card." *Independent*, January 27, 1977, p. C7. [Newspapers.com]

39. Don Riley. "Women Boxers a Smash in Vegas." *Salt Lake Tribune*, March 20, 1977, p. 151.

40. "Gal Boxers Go to Draw." *Daily Herald* (Provo, Utah), March 20, 1977, p. 13. [Newspapers.com]

41. "Women Boxers Stir Emotions in Even Bout." *Redlands Daily Facts*, March 10, 1977, p. 12. [Newspapers.com]

42. "'Princess' to Seek Work Welter Crown." *Times Standard*, March 17, 1977, p. 15. [Newspapers.com]

43. Sue TL Fox. "The Father of Women's Boxing: Bill Dickson." Women Boxing Archive Network. May 20, 1999. [WBAN.com]

44. Sue TL Fox has a partial copy of the letter sent to Theresa Kibby on the Women Boxing Archive Network website. [WBAN.com]

45. "Big Money for Lavonne." *Nevada Evening Gazette*, May 15, 1977, p.17. [Newspapers.com]

46. Don Terbush. "'Princess' Hit Jackpot." *Times Standard*, April 24, 1977, p. 17. [Newspapers.com]

47. *Independent Press-Telegram*, April 17, 1977, p. S6. [Newspapers.com]

48. Sue TL Fox. "In Sue Fox's Own Words." Women Boxing Archive Network. [WBAN.com]

49. Pedro Abigantus. "The Sweet Science, A Woman's Place Is in the Ring." *Chicago Sun-Times*, February 7, 1994, p. 94. [Newslibrary.com]

50. Lacy J. Banks. "Women's Matches Stir Furor." *Chicago Sun-Times*, July 27, 1987, p. 118. [Newslibrary.com]

51. "Women Boxer Banned in Cincinnati Rings." *Hays Daily News*, January 2, 1977, p. 18. [Newspapers.com]

52. Malissa Smith interview with Sue TL Fox, September 27, 2013.

53. Sue TL Fox. "Women's Boxing World Ratings 1977–1986." Women Boxing Archive Network. [WBAN.com]

54. "Shades of Muhammad Ali!" *Silina Journal*, December 20, 1976, p. 1. [Newspapers.com]

55. "Gilmore Repaid Thoughtful Young Girl's Help." *Corpus Christi Times*, January 24, 1977, p. 38. [Newspapers.com]

56. "Amber Hunt Loses 1st Bout to Bobby Banks in Salt Lake." *Ogden Standard-Examiner*, February 19, 1977, p. 7. [Newspapers.com]

57. "Amber Jim Files Suit." *Ogden Standard-Examiner*, November 22, 1977, p. 16. [Newspapers.com]

58. Kelly McBride. "Young Girl Aspires to Greatness in Era Filled with Possibilities." *Spokesman-Review*, March 23, 1997, p. B13. [Newslibrary.com]

59. "Women Practice Boxing." *Reading Eagle*, p. 63. [Googlenews.com]

60. "Female Boxers Bitter." *Rapid City Journal*, April 8, 1978, p. 11. [WBAN.com]

61. "Judge KOs Lady Boxer." *Ludington Daily News*, February 9, 1982.

62. "Woman Boxer Not Afraid of Men." *Daily Leader*, January 21, 1982.

63. "Battles Sex Bias in Ring." *Argus-Press*, January 21, 1982.

64. Ibid.

65. Lafler v. Athletic Bd. of Control. No. G82-45 CA1. United States District Court, W.D. Michigan, S. D.

66. "Female Barred from Competition: Boxer Disappointed at Ruling." *Times Daily*, February 12, 1982.

8. THESE LADIES LOVE THE RING

1. Tom Archdeacon. "Women Boxers: These Ladies Love the Ring." *Miami News*, June 6, 1980, p. 1C. [Google News]

2. Brian Kates. "Prettier Than Men: Cat Davis vs. Floyd Patterson." *Daily News*, June 24, 2003, p. 27. [Malissa Smith Collection]

3. A 1973 yearbook from Louisiana State University identifies a junior named Cat A. Davis, along with an accompanying unlabeled photograph that bears a striking resemblance to her. [Ancestry.com]

4. "Seeks Women for Boxing." *Evening News*, January 16, 1976, p. 12. [Google News]

5. "Gal Boxer's a Knockout." *New York Post*, June 8, 1977, p. 7. [Folder: Fighters/Davis, Cathy "Cat." Box 45. Series 13. Fistic Arcana. Hank Kaplan Boxing Archive, Brooklyn College Archives and Special Collections, Brooklyn College Library]

6. The P.O. box on the letterhead was one and the same as Algieri's when the organization first started. By 1980 the letterhead reflected an address in New Rochelle, New York, where Gallello maintained his home.

7. "World Fight Sanctioned as World Title Battle." Press release. Global Productions Ltd., June 24, 1977. [Folder: Fighters/Davis, Cathy "Cat." Box 45. Series 13. Fistic Arcana. Hank Kaplan Boxing Archive, Brooklyn College Archives and Special Collections, Brooklyn College Library]

8. "Cat Davis Deeps Women's Mitt Title." *Cumberland Evening Times*, June 30, 1976, p. 40.

9. "Davis Wins Women's Bout." *Delta Democrat-Times*, June 17, 1976, p. 27. [Newspapers.com]

10. Margo Nash. "Jersey Footlights." *New York Times*, March 13, 2005, n.p. [NYTimes.com]

11. Joan Ryan. "Female Boxing Match Draws 2,400 Suckers." *Atlanta Journal*, August 25, 1976, p. 4B. [Folder: Fighters/Davis, Cathy "Cat." Box 45. Series 13. Fistic Arcana. Hank Kaplan Boxing Archive, Brooklyn College Archives and Special Collections, Brooklyn College Library]

12. Margo Nash. "Jersey Footlights." *New York Times*, March 13, 2005, n.p. [NYTimes.com]

13. Hank Narrow. "Cathy Davis Shows Ring Saavy in KO'ing Margie Dunson in Two." [Folder: Fighters/Davis, Cathy "Cat." Box 45. Series 13. Fistic Arcana. Hank Kaplan Boxing Archive, Brooklyn College Archives and Special Collections, Brooklyn College Library]

14. "Copy of typewritten note describing the Cathy Cat Davis v. Margie Dunson Fight at the Wagner Ballroom in Phila, Pa. Hand written date, 3/2/77." [Folder: Fighters/Davis, Cathy "Cat." Box 45. Series 13. Fistic Arcana. Hank Kaplan Boxing Archive, Brooklyn College Archives and Special Collections, Brooklyn College Library]

15. John Feinstein. "As Sport Returns to N. Carolina." *Washington Post*, February 5, 1978, p. E5. [Folder: Fighters/Davis, Cathy "Cat." Box 45. Series 13. Fistic Arcana. Hank Kaplan Boxing Archive, Brooklyn College Archives and Special Collections, Brooklyn College Library]

16. Jack Newfield. *Village Voice*, October 9, 1978, pp. 1, 15–16. [Google News]

17. *Davis v. New York State Athletic Commission*. December 22, 1977. [WestlawNext]

18. "Women May Take Ring." *The Eagle* (Bryan, Texas), May 20, 1978, p. 14. [Newspapers.com]

19. Will Grimsley. "'Cat' Hears Sad Tale of the Tyger." September 20, 1978. [Folder: Fighters/Davis, Cathy "Cat." Box 45. Series 13. Fistic Arcana. Hank Kaplan Boxing Archive, Brooklyn College Archives and Special Collections, Brooklyn College Library]

20. Jeff Meyers. "Champ Woman Boxer Hopes She Never Looks the Part." *St. Louis Post-Dispatch*, February 23, 1978, p. 2D. [Folder: Fighters/Davis, Cathy "Cat." Box 45. Series 13. Fistic Arcana. Hank Kaplan Boxing Archive, Brooklyn College Archives and Special Collections, Brooklyn College Library]

21. Judy Kessler. "With Boxer Cat Davis, Cauliflower Doesn't Come to Mind—Tomato, Maybe?" *People*, May 15, 1978, 9:19. [People.com]

22. "Remember Sal Algieri?" *Sydney Morning Herald*, June 25, 1978, p. 43. [Google News]

23. Don Pierson. "Woman Boxer Makes Name, but Whose?" *Chicago Tribune*, June 18, 1978, p. B1. [ProQuest.]

24. Randall V. Beriage. "They Know the Ropes—In and Out of the Ring." August 21, 1978. [Folder: Fighters/Davis, Cathy "Cat." Box 45. Series 13. Fistic Arcana. Hank Kaplan Boxing Archive, Brooklyn College Archives and Special Collections, Brooklyn College Library]

25. "New York Gives In, Grants Ring Permits to Women." *Lawrence Journal-World*, September 20, 1978, p. 19 [Google News]

26. Sal Algieri. "'Cat' Davis, Woman Boxer, Could Be Start of a New Breed." *The Ring*, August 1978, pp. 6–7, 42. [Malissa Smith Collection]

27. Jack Newfield. *Village Voice*, October 9, 1978, pp. 1, 15–16. [Google News]

28. "Cat Davis Stops German for Women's Boxing 'Title.'" *Los Angeles Times*, July 3, 1979, p. D2. [ProQuest]

29. Jerry Kirshenbaum. "Scorecard." *Sports Illustrated*, July 23, 1979, n.p. [Sportsillustrated.com]

30. Jamie Lowe. "Cat Davis: Boxing Pioneer Now Throws Hash, Not Punches." *Sports Illustrated*, July 7, 2005. [Sportsillustrated.com]

31. Sue TL Fox. "Archived Exclusive Interview with Bill Dickson." Women Boxing Archive Network. May 20, 1999. [WBAN.org]

32. Alastair Segerdal. "The Acceptable Face of Women's Boxing: A Report from an All-Female Card in Hawthorne, California in 1979." [Womensboxing.com]

33. Jack Hawn. "Woman Boxer Is a Nurse, Too." *Los Angeles Times*, February 10, 1979, p. C9. [ProQuest]

34. "Baby Bear Roars Back into Town." *Tewkesbury Admag*, June 23, 2011, n.p. [Tewkesburyadmag.co.uk]

35. An article on the fight (cf. 34) notes the sanctioning body as the Women's Boxing Federation; however, Vern Stevenson, the promoter, was the head of the Women's World Boxing Association (WWBA), and it is possible that the bout was actually sanctioned by the latter organization.

36. "'Greatest Ladies Battle Ever' Ends in Loss of Bonnie's Title." February 1979. There is a handwritten note from Vern Stevenson to Hank Kaplan on a copy of the article. "Please read completely Hank when you have time." Certain passages of the article are also underlined. [Folder: Articles: Miscellaneous. Box 46. Series 13. Fistic Arcana. Hank Kaplan Boxing Archive, Brooklyn College Archives and Special Collections, Brooklyn College Library]

37. Tom Archdeacon. "Women Boxers: These Ladies Love the Ring." *Miami News*, June 6, 1980, pp. 1C–2C. [Google News]

38. Tom Archdeacon. "Barbara Buttrick Has Renewed Love Affair with Boxing." *Miami News*, June 7, 1980, pp. 1B, 6B. [Google News]

39. Gary Picknell. *Ottowa Journal*, September 14, 1979, p. 15. [Newspapers.com]

40. "Toughwoman Contest: Local Favorite Claims Her Secret Is Not to Get Hit." *Tyrone Daily Herald*, May 21, 1981, p. 3. [Newspapers.com]

41. Malissa Smith interview with Bruce Silverglade, July 10, 2013.

42. Paul Sullivan. "These Women Go Toe-to-Toe for Extra Dough." *Chicago Tribune*, August 17, 1987, n.p. [Chicagotribune.com]

43. Jim Jenkins. "Women Fight Discrimination in Battle for Bouts." *Sacramento Bee*, April 18, 1985, p. D11. [Newslibrary.com]

44. Sue Dillingham. "Maine Lady Boxing Champ Has Local Ties; Her Goal Is to Annex the World Title" *Lewiston Journal*, January 14, 1982, p. 6. [Google News]

45. Paul Sullivan. "These Women Go Toe-to-Toe for Extra Dough." *Chicago Tribune*, August 17, 1987, n.p. [Chicagotribune.com]

46. Lacy J. Banks. "Women Boxers Battle in 10-Round Title Fight." *Chicago Sun-Times*, August 15, 1987, p. 106 [Newslibrary.com]

47. "Laura Holt Collects World Boxing Crown." *Bangor Daily News*, March 26, 1986, p. 32. [Google News]

48. Lacy J. Banks. "Women Boxers Battle in 10-Round Title Fight." *Chicago Sun-Times*, August 15, 1987, p. 106 [Newslibrary.com]

49. Paul Sullivan. "These Women Go Toe-to-Toe for Extra Dough." *Chicago Tribune*, August 17, 1987, n.p. [Chicagotribune.com]

50. Friends of Lady Tyger. Hunger Strike Flyer. [Folder: Fighters: Trimiar, Marian "Lady Tyger." Box 45. Series 13. Fistic Arcana. Hank Kaplan Boxing Archive, Brooklyn College Archives and Special Collections, Brooklyn College Library]

51. Leigh Behrens. "Boxer Hungry for Recognition." April 19, 1987, p. 2. [Newslibrary.com]

52. "Woman Boxer on Hunger Strike, Demands Equality." *Atlanta Journal and the Atlanta Constitution*, April 28, 1987, p. D2. [Newslibrary.com]

53. Lacy J. Banks. "Lady Tyger's Fast Didn't Help Cause." *Chicago Sun-Times*, July 27, 1987, p. 114. [Newslibrary.com]

9. CHRISTY MARTIN AND THE PINKING OF THE VELVET ROPES

1. Thomas Hauser. "Christy and Laila." SecondsOut.com. 2003, n.p. [Secondsout.com]

2. "Sergeant, Welder, Clash in Women's Boxing Match." *Star-News*, August 28, 1986, n.p. [Google News]

3. Bob Raissman. "Martin Punishes Deshong." *Daily News*, June 29, 1997, n.p. [New York Daily News Archives]

4. Richard Hoffer. "Gritty Woman." *Sports Illustrated*, April 15, 1996, n.p. [Sportsillustrated.com]

5. "Bio File: Get to Know Christy Martin." BoxingInsider.com. n.p. [Boxinginsider.com]

6. Steve Buffery. "Tyson's Trainer Confident." *Toronto Sun*, June 26, 1997, n.p. [Google News]

7. Bob Raissman. "Christy Won't Pull Punches vs. Tough Foe." *Daily News*, June 29, 1997, n.p. [New York Daily News Archives]

8. Don King. "Is a Woman's Place in a Boxing Ring?" *WBB*, March 1980, n.p. [WBAN.com]

9. Bernard Fernandez. "This Lady's a Real Knockout." *Spokesman-Review*, September 8, 1996, n.p. [Google News]

10. Dee Williams. "Dee Hamaguchi." Women Boxing Archive Network. January 2, 2005. [WBAN.org]

11. George Diaz. "Boxer Wears Lipstick, and She Is a Winner." *Orlando Sentinel*, January 29, 1994, n.p. [Orlandosentinel.com]

12. "Martin Wins Women's Fight." *The Day*, January 30, 1994, p. 23. [Google News]

13. Christy Martin's official fight record notes that she defeated Susie Hughes by a first-round TKO on January 29, 1993. A newspaper article that came out two weeks before the fight, however, indicated that she would be fighting Susie "Sluggin" Melton. It is unclear if Susie Hughes was a substitute or if Melton's name was incorrectly listed on the records that are now listed on Martin's official record of fights. See: "Title Fight Slated for Township." *The State*, January 12, 1993, p. 4C [Newslibrary.com]

14. George Diaz. "No Ordinary Ring Girl." *Orlando Sentinel*, April 15, 1994, n.p. [Orlando-sentinel.com]

15. Richard Hoffer. "Gritty Woman." *Sports Illustrated*, April 15, 1996, n.p. [Sportsillus-trated.com]

16. "Laura Serrano." Women Boxing Archive Network. [WBAN.com]

17. Ron Borges. "Deirdre Gogarty Is Still Blazing Trails." The Sweet Science. May 10, 2008, n.p. [Thesweetscience.com]

18. Ibid.

19. Malissa Smith interview with Deirdre Gogarty, June 2, 2012.

20. Gamini Perera. "Women Invade the Boxing Ring." *Sunday Times*, January 31, 1999. [Google News]

21. Malissa Smith interview with Deirdre Gogarty, June 2, 2012.

22. Ron Borges. "Deirdre Gogarty Is Still Blazing Trails." The Sweet Science. May 10, 2008. [Thesweetscience.com]

23. Ibid.

24. Malissa Smith interview with Deirdre Gogarty, June 2, 2012.

25. Bob Raissman. "Holmes' Hook Stuns Taylor for KO in 9th." *Daily News*, March 17, 1996. [New York Daily News Archives]

26. Robert Mladinich. "Deirdre Gogarty, No Titillating Sideshow." The Sweet Science. January 15, 2007. [Thesweetscience.com]

27. Aimee Berg. "Boxing: This Fighter Is Making Fans of Her Skeptics." *New York Times*, March 17, 1996, n.p. [NYTimes.com]

28. Ibid.

29. Ibid.

30. Christy Martin on *E:60*, ESPN Sports, October 4, 2011.

31. Lacy J. Banks. "Women's Matches Stir Furor." *Chicago Sun-Times*, July 27, 1987, p. 114. [Google News]

32. Ken Hissner. "Lucia Rijker Interview—More Than the Greatest Women's Boxer of All Time!" Doghouse Boxing. [Doghouseboxing.com]

33. George Diaz. "Orlando's 'Queen of Boxing' Checks out the Competition." *Orlando Sentinel*, September 12, 1997, n.p. [Orlandosentinel.com]

34. Terry Price. "Rijker a Unanimous Women's Winner." *Hartford Courant*, May 15, 1997, n.p. [Courant.com]

35. George Diaz. "Orlando's 'Queen of Boxing' Checks out the Competition." *Orlando Sentinel*, September 12, 1997, n.p. [Orlandosentinel.com]

36. Malissa Smith interview with Bonnie Canino, September 7, 2013.

37. Christy Martin vs. Sumya Anani. U.S. Satellite Network. December 18, 1998. [You-Tube.com]

38. Stephanie Dallam. "Dallam: Setting the Record Straight." Women Boxing Archive Network. April 22, 2005. [WBAN.com]

39. Mia St. John. "Mia St. John—A Girl and Her Title." Videojug, n.p. [Videojug.com]

10. WOMEN'S BOXING AND THE FAME GAME

1. Beth Harris. "Ali's Daughter Follows in Her Father's Famous Footsteps." *Galveston Daily News*, September 29, 1999, p. 22. [Newspapers.com]

2. Sam Howe Verhovek. "When a Man Meets a Woman (in the Ring)." *New York Times*, October 3, 1999, n.p. [NYTimes.com]

3. Timothy W. Smith. "Boxing; Another Ali Enters the Ring: His Daughter." *New York Times*, January 23, 1999, n.p. [NYTimes.com]

4. "Ali's Daughter May Fight." *Miami Herald*, January 18, 1999, p. 3D. [Newslibrary.com]

5. Timothy W. Smith. "Boxing; Another Ali Enters the Ring: His Daughter." *New York Times*, January 23, 1999, n.p. [NYTimes.com]

6. Ron Borges. "The Champ's Daughter." *Boston Globe*, October 8, 1999, p. F1. [Boston Globe Archive]

7. Jayda Evans. "Woman vs. Man Bout Set for Boxing History." *Seattle Times*, September 11, 1999, p. C1. [Newslibrary.com]

8. Jayda Evans. "Woman Boxer's Foe Drops out of Bout." *Seattle Times*, September 16, 1999, p. C1. [Newslibrary.com]

9. Jayda Evans. "Boxing: Gender Issue Stirs up Headed Debate." *Seattle Times*, September 22, 1999, p. D1. [Newslibrary.com]

10. Jayda Evans. "Male-Female Fight? 'Freak Show'—Boxing Officials Universally Clobber Seattle Mixed Bout." *Seattle Times*, September 16, 1999, p. C1. [Newslibrary.com]

11. "Battle of the Sexes." CNN/SportsIllustrated.com. October 14, 1999, n.p. [Sportsillustrated.CNN.com]

12. Ron Borges. "Women Dealt Low Blows Mismatches Were Sideshows, Not Fights." *Boston Globe*, October 10, 1999, p. C18. [Bostonglove.com]

13. Ibid.

14. Associated Press. October 19, 1999, n.p. [WBAN.com]

15. Timothy W. Smith. "Boxing; Frazier's Daughter Has Fast Debut." *New York Times*, February 6, 2000, n.p. [NYTimes.com]

16. Steve Dunleavy. "Call It Frazier vs. Ali the Next Generation—Joe's Girl Says She Knows the Ropes & Is Ready for Laila." *New York Post*, December 21, 1999, n.p. [Newyorkpost.com]

17. "Ali-Frazier IV." *Victoria Advocate*, p.13. [Google News]

18. "Joe Frazier's Daughter Wins First Bout; Ali Next?" *Kingman Daily Miner*, February 4, 2000, p. 26. [Google News]

19. Timothy W. Smith. "Boxing; Frazier's Daughter Has Fast Debut." *New York Times*, n.p. [NYTimes.com]

20. Michael Katz. "Every Daughter of Ali Era Being Fitted for Ring." *Daily News*, p. 79. [Newslibrary.com]

21. "Foreman's Daughter Next to Throw Hat into Ring." *Herald-Journal*, February 11, 2000, p. 10. [Google News]

22. "Plus: Boxing; Foreman's Daughter Plans to Fights." *New York Times*, February 11, 2000, n.p. [NYTimes.com]

23. "Foreman's Daughter Wins Debut." *Star News*, June 19, 2000, p. 16. [Google News]

24. Tim Graham. "Women's Boxing Becomes a Real Joke." ESPN.com. February 8, 2000. [ESPN.com]

25. Penny Hastings. "Is Women's Boxing a Serious Sport?" *Ventura County Star*, p. C02. [Newslibrary.com]

26. Heather Timmons. "Daddy's Little Girls Come out Swinging." *Bloomberg Business-week*, July 9, 2007. [Businessweek.com]

27. Bernard Fernandez. "Ali-Frazier, the Second Generation, in the Works." *Philadelphia Daily News*, September 27, 2000, n.p. [Philly.com]

28. Michael Katz. "Flashes." *Daily News*, March 4, 2000, n.p. [Nydailynews.com]

29. "Women's Boxing Page Open Forum: Belinda Laracuente vs. Christy Martin." Women Boxing Archive Network. March 3, 2000, n.p. [WBAN.org]

30. Regina Halmich actually contested in Las Vegas on WIBF's card but lost the match for the flyweight title after four rounds of boxing with Yvonne Trevino. (A cut under Halmich's eye led the referee to stop the fight on the advice of the ring physician. Trevino, who had been ahead on the scorecards at that point, was given the win.)

31. Neil Bennett. "Sport: Round One for Women's Boxing." BBC News. November 24, 1998, n.p. [BBC.co.uk]

32. Nick Halling. "Boxing: First Night Jane Couch—Women Face an Even Bigger Fight." *Independent*, August 18, 1998, n.p. [Independent.co.uk]

33. Jack Newfield. "A Boxing Sham in the Name of the Fathers." *New York Post*, June 3, 2013, n.p. [Nypost.com]

34. Tim Smith. "For Daughters, Thrilla Goes on, Ali-Frazier IV Renews Family Feud." *Daily News*, June 4, 2001, n.p. [Nydailynews.com]

35. "Ali, Frazier Daughters Rekindling Old Rivalry." SportsIllustrated.com. June 8, 2001, n.p. [CNNSI.com]

36. James Langton. "Sting Like a Queen Bee." *Telegraph*, May 28, 2001, n.p. [Telegraph.co.uk]

37. Dee William. "Laila Ali vs. Jacqui Frazier-Lyde." Women Boxing Archive Network. June 8, 2001, n.p. [WBAN.com]

38. Edward Wong. "Boxing; Laila Ali Wins by Decision in Battle of Boxing Daughters." *New York Times*, June 9, 2001, n.p. [NYTimes.com]

39. Ron Borges. "Fight in Courtroom May Not Go Distance." *Boston Globe*, June 12, 2001, p. E3. [Boston Globe Archives]

40. Sue TL Fox. "Christy Martin." Women Boxing Archive Network. August 17, 2013, n.p. [WBAN.org]

41. Lem Satterfield. "Female Boxer's Death a Shattering Blow to Sport." *Sun*, April 17, 2005, p. 7F. [Newslibrary.com]

42. David A. Avila. "Layla McCarter Meets Belinda Laracuente for GBU title." The Sweet Science. November 12, 2006, n.p. [Thesweetscience.com]

43. "Most Popular Articles." The Sweet Science. n.d., n.p. [Thesweetscience.com]

44. "Christy Martin Loses Appeal." ESPN Boxing. August 15, 2011, n.p. [ESPN.com]

11. THE AMATEURS

1. Wayne Coffey. "Ladies Night with a Punch." *Daily News*, April 7, 1995, n.p. [Nydailynews.com]

2. Brian Gomez. "Exclusion from Olympic Games Frustrates Women Boxers." *The Gazette*, n.d., n.p. [www.actove.com]

3. "Women's Boxing Proposed for Games." ESPN Boxing. February 18, 2009, n.p. [ESPN.com]

4. Dan Newling. "Jowell's Fight to Bring Female Boxing to London Olympics." *Daily Mail*, February 15, 2009, n.p. [Dailymail.co.uk]

5. "Women's Boxing Included on 2012 Olympics List." CNN.com. August 13, 2009, n.p. [CNN.com]

6. Michael Rivest. "Disturbing News from the Women's World Championships: Warriors, but Still in Skirts." *Albany Times Union*, September 18, 2010, n.p. [Timesunion.com]

7. Michael Rivest. "A Conversation with Dr. C. K. Wu—More on Warriors in Skirts." *Albany Times Union*, September 23, 2010, n.p. [Timesunion.com]

8. David Smith. "'No Need to Sexualize Boxing,' says Katie Taylor." *Evening Standard* (London), January 18, 2012, n.p. [Standard.co.uk]

9. Tom Degun. "AIBA Confirm Decision to Allow Women Boxers Shorts or Skirt Choice." Inside the Games. [Insidethegames.biz]

10. Chris Mannix. "Underwood Drops Historic Match for Future of Olympic Women's Boxing." *Sports Illustrated*, August 5, 2013, n.p. [Sportsillustrated.cnn.com]

11. Ignacio Torres. "Marlen Esparza Gets Bronze and Makes Olympic History." NBCLatino.com. August 8, 201, n.p.[NBClatino.com]

12. Kevin Mitchell. "Nicola Adams Beats India's Mary Kom to Reach Olympic Flyweight Final." *The Guardian*, August 8, 2013, n.p. [Theguardian.com]

13. Jonathan Liew. "Nicola Adams Becomes First Ever Winner of an Olympic Women's Boxing Tournament." *Telegraph*, August 9, 2012, n.p. [Telegraph.co.uk]

14. Ben Dirs. "Nicola Adams Wins Historic Boxing Gold for Great Britain." BBC. August 9, 2013. [BBC.co.uk]

CONCLUSION

1. "Nicola Adams Wants More Coverage for Female Boxing." TheBoxingScene.com. December 18, 2013, n.p. [boxingscene.com]

Selected Bibliography

The American Fistiana: Containing a History of Prize Fighting in the United States, with All the Principal Battles for the Last Forty Years, and a Full and Precise Account of All the Particulars of the Great $10,000 Match between Sullivan and Hyer. New York: H. Johnson, 1849. Print.

Anasi, Robert. *The Gloves: A Boxing Chronicle.* New York: North Point Press, 2002. Print.

Arbena, Joseph, and David G. LaFrance. *Sport in Latin America and the Caribbean.* Wilmington, DE: Scholarly Resources, 2002. Print.

Asbury, Herbert. *The Gangs of New York: An Informal History of the Underworld.* New York: Thunder's Mouth Press, 1998. Print.

Baker, Aaron, and Todd Boyd. *Out of Bounds: Sports, Media, and the Politics of Identity.* Bloomington: Indiana University Press, 1997. Print.

Barker, Hannah, and Elaine Chalus. *Gender in Eighteenth-Century England: Roles, Representations, and Responsibilities.* London: Addison Wesley Longman, 1997. Print.

Barnes, Djuna. *New York.* Edited by Alyce Barry. Los Angeles: Sun & Moon Press, 1989. Print.

Barnes, Djuna, and Alyce Barry. "How It Feels to Be Forcibly Fed." *New York World Magazine*, September 6, 1914. [University of Maryland, Digital Collections]

———. "My Sisters and I at a New York Prize Fight." *New York World Magazine*, October 18, 1914. In Djuna Barnes, *New York*, edited by Alyce Barry, 168–173. Los Angeles: Sun & Moon Press, 1989. Print.

———. "Jess Willard Says Girls Will Be Boxing for a Living Soon." *Vanity Fair*, April 25, 1915. [University of Maryland Digital Collections]

———. "Dempsey Welcomes Women at Boxing Matches." *Niagara Falls Gazette*, May 3, 1921. [Fultonhistory.com]

———. *New York.* Los Angeles, CA: Sun & Moon Press, 1989. Print.

Bechdolt, Fred R. "Jeff Outboxed at Every Turn in One Sided Fight." *San Francisco Call*, July 5, 1910. [Library of Congress]

Beecher, Catharine Esther. *Physiology and Calisthenics for Schools and Families.* New York: Harper & Bros., 1856. [Google Books].

Berg, Aimee. "Boxing: This Fighter Is Making Fans of Her Skeptics." *New York Times*, March 17, 1996. [NYTimes.com]

Blackmoore, Lennox. Interview with Malissa Smith. July 10, 2013.

Boddy, Kasia. *Boxing: A Cultural History.* London: Reaktion, 2008. Print.

Bodner, Allen. *When Boxing Was a Jewish Sport.* Westport, CT: Praeger, 1997. Print.

Bourdieu, Pierre. *Masculine Domination.* Stanford, CA: Stanford University Press, 2001. Print.

Boyle, Ellexis. "Representing the Female Pugilist: Narratives of Race, Gender and Disability in *Million Dollar Baby.*" *Sociology of Sport Journal* 23 (2006): 99–116. Print.

Brailsford, Dennis. *A Taste for Diversions: Sport in Georgian England.* Cambridge, UK: Lutterworth Press, 1999. Print.

Bramston, James. *The Art of Politicks.* Quoted in Henry Benjamin Wheatley, *London, Past and Present: Its History, Associations and Traditions.* Vol. 2. London: John Murray, 1891. [Goggle Books]

Brietz, Eddie. Sports Roundup. *Kingston Daily Freeman,* June 3, 1940. [Fultonhistory.com]

Broughton, Jack. *Broughton's Rules to Be Observed in All Battles on the Stage.* (1743). [Scribd.com]

Brownell, Susan. *The 1904 Anthropology Days and Olympic Games: Sport, Race, and American Imperialism.* Lincoln, NE: University of Nebraska Press, 2008. Print.

Butler, Judith. *Gender Trouble: Feminism and the Subversion of Identity.* New York: Routledge, 1990. Print.

Cahn, Susan K. "From the 'Muscle Moll' to the 'Butch' Ballplayer: Mannishness, Lesbianism and Homophobia in U.S. Women's Sport." *Feminist Studies* 19, no. 2 (1993): 343–368. Print.

Caines, Michael, ed. *Major Voices: 18th Century Woman Playwrights.* New Milford, CT: Toby Press, 2004. Print.

Canino, Bonnie. Interview with Malissa Smith. September 7, 2013.

Caples, Yvonne T. "Public Perception, Attitudes and General Knowledge of Women's Boxing in Central Las Vegas." Thesis, United States Sports Academy, 2004. Print.

Chapman, David L., and Patricia Anne Vertinsky. *Venus with Biceps: A Pictorial History of Muscular Women.* Vancouver, Canada: Arsenal Press, 2010. Print.

Cobbett, William, and James Gillray. *Cobbett's England: A Selection from the Writings of William Cobbett.* London: Parkgate Books, 1997. Print.

———. *Defence of Pugilism.* Quoted in Scott J. Juengel, "Bare-Knuckle Boxing and the Pedagogy of National Manhood." *Studies in Popular Culture* 25, no. 3 (April, 2003). [ProQuest]

Cohen, Leah Hager. *Without Apology: Girls, Women, and the Desire to Fight.* New York: Random House, 2005. Print.

Cohen, Patricia Cline, Timothy J. Gilfoyle, and Helen Lefkowitz Horowitz. *The Flash Press Sporting Male Weeklies in 1840s New York.* Chicago, IL: University of Chicago Press, 2008. Print.

Cooper, Helen M., Adrienne Munich, and Susan Merrill Squier. *Arms and the Woman: War, Gender, and Literary Representation.* Chapel Hill: University of North Carolina Press, 1989. Print.

Costa, D. Margaret. *Women and Sport: Interdisciplinary Perspectives.* Champaign, IL: Human Kinetics, 1994. Print.

Cove, Leslie. "Negotiating the Ring: Reconciling Gender in Women's Boxing." Thesis, University of Calgary, 2006. Print.

Cove, Leslie, and Marisa Young. "Coaching and Athletic Career Investments: Using Organizational Theories to Explore Women's Boxing." *Annuals of Leisure Research* 10, nos. 3 and 4 (2007): 257–271. Print.

Craig, Maxine Leeds, and Rita Liberti. "'Cause That's What Girls Do': The Making of a Feminized Gym." *Gender and Society* 21, no. 5 (2007): 676–699. Print.

Crawley, Sara L. "Visible Bodies, Vicarious Masculinity, and 'The Gender Revolution': Comment on England." *Gender and Society* 25, no. 6 (2011): 108–112. [Sage]

Creswick, Paul. *Bruising Peg: Pages from the Journal of Margaret Molloy, 1768–9.* London: Downey, 1898. Print.

Daily Advertiser. June 22, 1768. Quoted in John James Sexby, *Municipal Parks, Gardens and Open Spaces of London.* Cheap edition. London: Elliot Stock, 1905. [Google Books]

"Defending Bare-Knuckle Boxing." September 4, 1842. Quoted in Patricia Cline Cohen, Timothy J. Gilfoyle, and Helen Lefkowitz Horowitz, in association with the American Antiquarian Society. *The Flash Press: Sporting Male Weeklies in 1840s New York.* Chicago, IL: University of Chicago Press, 2008. Print.

Dell, Cary. *June Cleaver Was a Feminist! Reconsidering the Female Characters of Early Television.* Jefferson, NC: McFarland, 2013. Print.

Di Falco, Philippe. *Fight.* San Francisco, CA: Fitway, 2007. Print.

Dillingham, Sue. "Maine Lady Boxing Champ Has Local Ties; Her Goal Is to Annex the World Title." *Lewiston Journal*, January 14, 1982. [Google News Archive]

Dizikes, John. *Sportsmen and Gamesmen.* Boston: Houghton Mifflin, 1981. Print.

Douglas, Mary. *Purity and Danger: An Analysis of Concepts of Pollution and Taboo.* London: Routledge, 2005. Print.

Douglass, Frederick. *Narrative of the Life of Frederick Douglass, an American Slave.* Boston, 1845. [Elegant Ebooks]

Dugaw, Dianne. *Warrior Women and Popular Balladry, 1650–1850.* Cambridge, UK: Cambridge University Press, 1989. Print.

Dunn, Katherine. *One Ring Circus Dispatches from the World of Boxing.* Tucson, AZ: Schaffner Press, 2009. Print.

———. "Lucia Rijker—War with Christy Martin—War Rumors and More Rumors." Cyber Boxing Zone News. [Cyberboxingzone.com]

———. "Stan Hoffman Says Lucia Rijker Will Fight a Man in the Year 2000." Cyber Boxing Zone News. [Cyberboxingzone.com]

Egan, Pierce. *Boxiana: Or, Sketches of Ancient and Modern Pugilism.* Vol. 1. 1830. Reprint. London: Elibron Classics, 2005. Print.

Farrell, Bill. *Cradle of Champions: 80 Years of the New York Daily News Golden Gloves.* Champaign, IL: Sports Publishers, 2006. Print.

Fielding, Henry. *The History of Tom Jones, a Foundling.* Vol. 1. New York: White, Stofle & Allen, 1885. [Google Books]

Fields, Sarah K. *Female Gladiators: Gender, Law, and Contact Sport in America.* Urbana, IL: University of Illinois Press, 2005. Print.

Fistiana; or, The Oracle of the Ring. Results of Prize Battles from 1700 to 1859 Alphabetically Arranged. London: Bell's Life in London, 1868. Print.

Fox, Sue TL. "About WBAN." Women Boxing Archive Network. May 9, 1999. [WBAN.org]

———. "Archived Exclusive Interview with Bill Dickson." Women Boxing Archive Network. May 20, 1999. [WBAN.com]

———. "The Father of Women's Boxing: Bill Dickson." Women Boxing Archive Network. May 20, 1999. [WBAN.com]

———. "Christy Martin." Women Boxing Archive Network. August 17, 2013. [WBAN.org]

———. Interview with Malissa Smith. September 27, 2013.

———. "In Sue Fox's Own Words." Women Boxing Archive Network. N.D. [WBAN.org]

Fuller, Linda K., ed. *Sport, Rhetoric, and Gender: Historical Perspectives and Media Representations.* New York: Palgrave Macmillan, 2006. Print.

Gaines, Charles, and George Butler. *Pumping Iron II: The Unprecedented Woman.* New York: Simon & Schuster, 1984. Print.

Gay, John. *Beggar's Opera.* Project Gutenberg, 1765. Print.

Gems, Gerald R., Linda J. Borish, and Gertrud Pfister. *Sports in American History: From Colonization to Globalization.* Champaign, IL: Human Kinetics, 2008. Print.

Gogarty, Deirdre. Interview with Malissa Smith. June 2, 2012.

Gogarty, Deirdre, and Saloom Darrelyn. *My Call to the Ring: A Memoir of a Girl Who Yearns to Box.* Dublin: Glasnevin, 2012. Print.

Gorn, Elliott J. *The Manly Art: Bare-Knuckle Prize Fighting in America.* Ithaca, NY: Cornell University Press, 1986. Print.

Green, Thomas A., and Joseph R. Svinth. *Martial Arts in the Modern World.* Westport, CT: Praeger, 2003. Print.

———. *Martial Arts of the World: An Encyclopedia of History and Innovation.* Santa Barbara, CA: ABC-CLIO, 2010. Print.

Griffin, Pat. *Strong Women, Deep Closets: Lesbians and Homophobia in Sport.* Champaign, IL: Human Kinetics, 1998. Print.

Grindon, Leger. *Knockout: The Boxer and Boxing in American Cinema.* Jackson: University Press of Mississippi, 2011. Print.

Grombach, John V. *The Saga of the Fist: The 9,000 Year Story of Boxing in Text and Pictures*. South Brunswick, NJ: Barnes, 1977. Print.

Guttman, Allen. "English Sports Spectators: The Restoration to the Early Nineteenth Century." *Journal of Sports History* 12, no. 2 (1985): 116. Print.

———. *Women's Sports: A History*. New York: Columbia University Press, 1991. Print.

Halberstam, Judith. *Female Masculinity*. Durham, NC: Duke University Press, 1998. Print.

Halbert, Christy Lynn. *The Ultimate Boxer: Understanding the Sport and Skills of Boxing*. Brentwood, TN: ISI, 2003. Print.

Hargreaves, Jennifer. *Sporting Females: Critical Issues in the History and Sociology of Women's Sports*. London: Routledge, 1994. Print.

———. "Bruising Peg to Boxerobics: Gendered Boxing—Images and Meanings." In *Boxer: An Anthology of Writings on Boxing and Visual Culture*, 121–131. London: Institute of International Visual Arts, 1996. Print.

———. "Women's Boxing and Related Activities." In *Martial Arts in the Modern World*, edited by Thomas A. Green and Joseph R. Svinth, 209–228. Westport, CT: Praeger, 2003. Print.

Hauser, Thomas. *A Beautiful Sickness: Reflections on the Sweet Science*. Fayetteville: University of Arkansas Press, 2001. Print.

———. "Christy and Laila." SecondsOut.com. 2003. N.P. [Secondsout.com]

———. *An Unforgiving Sport: An Inside Look at Another Year in Boxing*. Fayetteville: University of Arkansas Press, 2009. Print.

Haywood, Eliza. "A Wife to Be Let." 1724. In *Major Voices: 18th Century Woman Playwrights*, edited by Michael Caines. New Milford, CT: Toby Press, 2004. Print.

Heiskanen, Benita. *The Urban Geography of Boxing: Race, Class and Gender in the Ring*. Routledge Research in Sport, Culture and Society. New York: Routledge, 2012. Print.

Henning, Frederick W. J. *Fights for the Championship, the Men and Their Times*. London: Licensed Victuallers Gazette, 1903. Print.

Hickey, William . *Memoirs*. Vol. 1, *1749–1775*. London: Burst & Blackett, 1913. Print.

Hietala, Thomas R. *The Fight of the Century: Jack Johnson, Joe Louis, and the Struggle for Racial Equality*. Armonk, NY: M. E. Sharpe, 2002. Print.

Hitchcock, Tim. *English Sexualities, 1700–1800*. New York: St. Martin's Press, 1997. Print.

Hoffer, Richard. "Gritty Woman." *Sports Illustrated*, April 15, 1996. [Sportsillustrated.com]

Hole, Christina. *English Sports and Pastimes*. London: B. T. Batsford, 1949. Print.

Holmes, Oliver Wendell. *The Autocrat of the Breakfast-Table*. 1858. Champaign, IL: Project Gutenberg, 1999. Print.

Jensen, Erik Norman. *Body by Weimar: Athletes, Gender, and German Modernity*. Oxford, UK: Oxford University Press, 2010. Print.

Johnson, Christopher, and Henry Fielding. "'British Championism': Early Pugilism and the Works of Fielding." *Review of English Studies*, New Series 47, no. 187 (1996): 333–357. [JSTOR]

Kacirk, Jeffrey. *Forgotten English*. New York: William Morrow, 1997. Print.

Kimball, George, John Schulian, and Colum McCann. *At the Fights: American Writers on Boxing*. New York: Library of America, 2011. Print.

Klein, Binnie. *Blows to the Head: How Boxing Changed My Mind*. Albany, NY: Excelsior Editions/State University of New York Press, 2010. Print.

Kotz, Cappy. *Boxing for Everyone: How to Get Fit and Have Fun with Boxing*. Seattle, WA: AmandaLore, 1998. Print.

Lang, Arne K. *Prizefighting: An American History*. Jefferson, NC: McFarland, 2008. Print.

Laqueur, Thomas Walter. *Making Sex: Body and Gender from the Greeks to Freud*. Cambridge, MA: Harvard University Press, 1990. Print.

Leen, Jeff. *The Queen of the Ring: Sex, Muscles, Diamonds, and the Making of an American Legend*. New York: Atlantic Monthly Press, 2009. Print.

Lefkowitz, Mary R. *Women in Greek Myth*. 2nd ed. Baltimore, MD: Johns Hopkins University Press, 2007. Print.

Lefkowitz, Mary R., and Maureen B. Fant. *Women's Life in Greece and Rome: A Source Book in Translation*. 3rd ed. Baltimore, MD: Johns Hopkins University Press, 2005. Print.

London Times. March 24, 1807. Quoted in Allen Guttmann, *Women's Sports: A History*. New York: Columbia University Press. 1991.

LoPrete, Kimberly A. "Gendering Viragos: Medieval Perceptions of Powerful Women." In *Studies on Medieval and Early Modern Women: Pawns or Players*, edited by Christine Meek, 17–38. Dublin: Four Courts, 2005. Print.

MacLachlan, Bonnie. *Women in Ancient Greece: A Sourcebook*. London: Continuum, 2012. Print.

Martin, Debra L., David W. Frayer, and Phillip L. Walker. "Wife Beating, Boxing and Broken Noses." In *Troubled Times: Violence and Warfare in the Past*, edited by Debra Martin and David W. Frayer. Amsterdam: Gordon & Breach, 1997. Print.

Matthews, George R. *America's First Olympics: The St. Louis Games of 1904*. Columbia: University of Missouri Press, 2005. Print.

McClintock, Anne. *Imperial Leather: Race, Gender and Sexuality in the Colonial Contest*. New York: Routledge, 1995. Print.

McClintock, Anne, Aamir Mufti, and Ella Shohat. *Dangerous Liaisons: Gender, Nation, and Postcolonial Perspectives*. Minneapolis: University of Minnesota Press, 1997. Print.

McCracken, Peggy. *The Curse of Eve, the Wound of the Hero: Blood, Gender, and Medieval Literature*. Philadelphia: University of Pennsylvania Press, 2003. Print.

McCrone, Kathleen E. *Playing the Game: Sport and the Physical Emancipation of English Women, 1870–1914*. Lexington, KY: University Press of Kentucky, 1988. Print.

Mee, Bob. *Bare Fists: The History of Bare-Knuckle Prize-Fighting*. Woodstock, NY: Overlook Press, 2001. Print.

Meek, Christine, ed. *Studies on Medieval and Early Modern Women: Pawns or Players?* Dublin: Four Courts, 2003. Print.

Mennesson, Christine. "'Hard' Women and 'Soft' Women: The Social Construction of Identities Among Female Boxers." *International Review for the Sociology of Sport* 35, no. 1 (2000): 21–33. Print.

Merz, Mischa. *Bruising: A Journey through Gender*. Sydney: Picador/Pan Macmillan Australia, 2000. Print.

———. *The Sweetest Thing: A Boxer's Memoir*. 1st ed. New York: Seven Stories Press, 2011. Print.

Montrose, Louis. *The Subject of Elizabeth: Authority, Gender, and Representation*. Chicago: University of Chicago Press, 2006. Print.

Moreau de St. Mery, Robert. *Moreau de St. Mery's American Journey, 1793–1798*. Translated and edited by Kenneth Roberts and Anna Roberts. Quoted in Elliott J. Gorn, *The Manly Art: Bare-Knuckle Prize Fighting in America*. Updated ed. Ithaca, NY: Cornell University Press. 2010. Print.

Natta, Don. *Wonder Girl: The Magnificent Sporting Life of Babe Didrikson Zaharias*. New York: Little, Brown, 2011. Print.

Newfield, Jack. "The Great White Hype." *Village Voice*, October 9, 1978. [Google News Archive]

———. "A Boxing Sham in the Name of the Fathers." *New York Post*, June 3, 2013. [Nypost.com]

Nogue, Martin. *Voyages et Aventures de Martin Nogue en Europe*. Paris: A La Haye, Chez [original book published prior to 1923, reissued by Nabu Press in 2011].

"NP." *San Antonio Light*, October 9, 1957. Ancestry.com. July 31, 2013.

Oates, Joyce Carol. *On Boxing*. Expanded ed. Hopewell, NJ: Ecco Press, 1994. Print.

O'Dell, Cary. *June Cleaver Was a Feminist!: Reconsidering the Female Characters of Early Television*. Jefferson, NC: McFarland, 2013. Print.

Oden, John E. *White Collar Boxing: One Man's Journey from the Office to the Ring*. New York: Hatherleigh Press, 2005. Print.

Ortner, Sherry B. *Making Gender: The Politics and Erotics of Culture*. Boston: Beacon Press, 1996. Print.

Padilla, Adriana Sophia. "Girls against the Ropes." Thesis, University of Southern California, 2008. Print.

Palmer, Alan Warwick. *The East End: Four Centuries of London Life.* New Brunswick, NJ: Rutgers University Press, 2000. Print.

Pancratia, or, A History of Pugilism: Containing a Full Account of Every Battle of Note from the Time of Broughton and Slack Down to the Present Day. London: W. Hildyard, Poppin's Court, 1812. Print.

Pancratia, or, A History of Pugilism. London: W. Oxberry, 1813. Print.

Papadopoulos, Maria. "The Women in Ancient Sparta: The Dialogue between the Divine and the Human." *SPARTA* 6, no. 2 (2010): 5–10. Print.

Parei, Inka, and Katy Derbyshire. *The Shadow-Boxing Woman.* London: Seagull Books, 2011. Print.

Parker, Mrs. William B. "Exercise for Women." *San Francisco Call,* April 5, 1903. [Library of Congress]

Parrott, Catriona M. "Athletic 'Womanhood': Exploring Sources for Female Sport in Victorian and Edwardian England." *Journal of Sport History* 16, no. 2 (1989): 140–157. [Google Scholar]

Peiss, Kathy Lee. *Cheap Amusements: Working Women and Leisure in Turn-of-the-Century New York.* Philadelphia: Temple University Press, 1986. Print.

Pepys, Samuel. *The Diary of Samuel Pepys.* Online ed. London, 1670. www.pepysdiary.com.

Polis, Carol B., and Rich Herschlag. *The Lady Is a Champ.* Oak Park, CA: Velocity, 2012. Print.

Reilly, Jean, and Susan K. Cahn. *Women and Sports in the United States: A Documentary Reader.* Boston: Northeastern University Press, 2007. Print.

Remnick, David. *King of the World: Muhammad Ali and the Rise of an American Hero.* New York: Random House, 1998. Print.

Rivest, Michael. "Disturbing News from the Women's World Championships: Warriors, but Still in Skirts." *Albany Times Union,* September 18, 2010. [Timesunion.com]

———. "A Conversation with Dr. C. K. Wu—More on Warriors in Skirts." *Albany Times Union,* September 23, 2010. [Timesunion.com]

Rodriguez, Gregory. "Boxing and Masculinity: The History and (Her)story of Oscar de la Hoya." In *Latino/a Popular Culture,* edited by Michelle Habell-Pallan and Mary Romero. New York: New York University Press, 2002. Print.

Rodriguez, Robert George. *The Regulation of Boxing: A History and Comparative Analysis of Policies within American States.* Jefferson, NC: McFarland, 2009. [Google Books]

Rotella, Carlo. *Good with Their Hand: Boxers, Bluesmen, and Other Characters from the Rust Belt.* Berkeley: University of California Press, 2002. Print.

———. *Cut Time: An Education at the Fights.* Boston: Houghton Mifflin, 2003. Print.

Salmonson, Jessica Amanda. *The Encyclopedia of Amazons: Women Warriors from Antiquity to the Modern Era.* New York: Paragon House, 1991. Print.

Sammons, Jeffrey T. *Beyond the Ring: The Role of Boxing in American Society.* Urbana: University of Illinois Press, 1988. Print.

Sandburg, Carl, Dale Fetherling, and George Fetherling. *Carl Sandburg at the Movies: A Poet in the Silent Era, 1920–1927.* Metuchen, NJ: Scarecrow Press, 1985. Print.

Satterland, Travis Delmar. "Fighting for an Authentic Self: An Ethnographic Study of Recreational Boxers." PhD diss., North Carolina State University, 2006.

Schiebinger, Londa L. *Nature's Body: Gender in the Making of Modern Science.* New Brunswick, NJ: Rutgers University Press, 2004. Print.

Scraton, Sheila, and Anne Flintoff. *Gender and Sport: A Reader.* London: Routledge, 2002. Print.

Sekules, Kate. *The Boxer's Heart: How I Fell in Love with the Ring.* New York: Villard, 2000. Print.

Selections from the Fancy; or True Sportsman's Guide. Barre, MA: Imprint Society, 1972. Print.

Silverglade, Bruce. Interview with Malissa Smith. July 10, 2013.

Slave Narratives: A Folk History of Slavery in the United States from Interviews with Former Slaves. Vol. 16 of the Federal Writer's Project, 1936–1938.

Spencer, Alfred. *Memoirs of William Hickey.* Vol. 1, *1749–1775.* S.l., 1948. Print.

———. *History of Woman Suffrage*. New York: Arno Press/New York Times, 1969. Print.

Sugden, John Peter. *Boxing and Society: An International Analysis*. Manchester, UK: Manchester University Press, 1996. Print.

Sullivan, Paul. "These Women Go Toe-to-Toe for Extra Dough." *Chicago Tribune*, August 17, 1987. [Chicagotribune.com]

Swift, Owen. *The Hand-Book to Boxing with a Complete Chronology of the Ring*. London: Nicolson, 1849. [Google Books]

Todd, Jan. *Physical Culture and the Body Beautiful: Purposive Exercise in the Lives of American Women, 1800–1870*. Macon, GA: Mercer University Press, 1998. Print.

Toole, F. X. *Rope Burns*. London: Secker & Warburg, 2000. Print.

Toulmin, Vanessa. *A Fair Fight: An Illustrated Review of Boxing on British Fairgrounds*. Oldham, UK: World's Fair, 1999. Print.

Van Ingen, Cathy. "Seeing What Frames Our Seeing": Seeking Histories on Early Black Female Boxers." *Journal of Sport History* 40, no. 1 (Spring 2013): 93–110. [Courtesy of Author]

von Uffenback, Zacharias Conrad. *London, in 1710, from the Travels of Zacharias Conrad von Uffenback*, translated by Willam Henry Quarrell and Margaret Mare, p. 90. New York: Faber & Faber, 1934. [Google Books.]

Wacquant, Loîc J. D. "The Pugilist Point of View: How Boxers Think and Feel about Their Trade." *Theory and Society* 24, no. 4 (1995): 489–535. Print.

———. *Body and Soul: Notebooks of an Apprentice Boxer*. Oxford, UK: Oxford University Press, 2004. Print.

Walker, Phillip L. "Wife Beating, Boxing and Broken Noses." In *Troubled Times: Violence and Warfare in the Past*, edited by Debra L. Martin and David W. Frayer. Vol. 3 of *War and Society*. Amsterdam: Gordon & Breach, 1997.

Waterfield, Robin, and Carolyn Dewald. *The Histories*. Oxford, UK: Oxford University Press, 1998. Print.

Wheatley, Henry Benjamin. *London, Past and Present: Its History, Associations and Traditions*. Vol. 2. London: John Murray, 1891. Print.

Wheelwright, Julie. *Amazons and Military Maids: Women Who Dressed as Men in the Pursuit of Life, Liberty, and Happiness*. London: Pandora, 1989. Print.

Whitemead, Paul. "The Gymnasiad or the Boxing Match. A Very Short, but Very Curious Epic Poem." 1744. In *The Works of the English Poets from Chaucer to Cowper*, vol. 16, edited by Dr. Samuel Johnson. London: J. Johnson, 1810. [Google Books]

Woodward, Kath. *Boxing, Masculinity, and Identity: The "I" of the Tiger*. London: Routledge, 2007. Print.

Woolum, Janet. *Outstanding Women Athletes: Who They Are and How They Influenced Sports in America*. Phoenix, AZ: Oryx Press, 1992. Print.

Wyck, Frederick. *Recollections of an Old New Yorker*. New York: Liveright, 1932. Print.

Zirin, Dave. *A People's History of Sports in the United States: 250 Years of Politics, Protest, People, and Play*. New York: New Press. 2008. Print.

Index

About the Author

Malissa Smith first walked into the storied Gleason's Gym in Brooklyn, New York, in January 1997. She has been boxing on and off ever since and maintains a popular blog about the sport—Girlboxing. Smith was awarded her master's in liberal studies from SUNY Empire State College in March 2012. Her final thesis project, *Boundaries in Motion: Women's Boxing*, discussed the complex relationship between gender and women's boxing and was the genesis of *A History of Women's Boxing*. She lives and works in Brooklyn, New York, with her family and writes frequently on the topic of women's boxing.